Learning Curves
in Business

Learning Curves in Business

Hits, Misses and Home Runs

21 Stories of
Ann Arbor Area
Business Leaders

As told to Jeff Mortimer

Momentum Books, Ltd.
Troy, Michigan

To our teachers, our mentors, our families,
and to those who held out a hand when that made all
the difference. Without them, these stories could never
have been written.

Amster, Herb   1

Place and Date of Birth: January 2, 1935; Brooklyn, New York
Present Residence: Ann Arbor
Education: MIT 1956–57
Family: Married to Carol, three children
Civic Activities: United Way, University Musical Society, Washtenaw Jewish Community, United Jewish Appeal
Professional Activities: Industrial Technology Institute
Hobbies: Travel, reading, and music
Major Career Accomplishment: Irwin Magnetics CEO

Bradley, Jim   22

Place and Date of Birth: November 26, 1936; Detroit, Michigan
Present Residence: Ann Arbor
Education: Michigan State University 1957, University of Michigan 1960
Family: Married to Juanita, two children
Civic Activities: Washtenaw Community College, EDC, Big Brothers, Ann Arbor Community Center
Professional Activities: Minority Dealers Advisory Council, GM Dealers Association, NAACP
Hobbies: Golf, tennis, fishing, and music
Major Career Accomplishment: CEO Jim Bradley Pontiac, Buick & GMC

Butcko, Joe 40

Place and Date of Birth: January 10, 1925; Ypsilanti,
    Michigan
Present Residence: Ypsilanti
Education: Plymouth High School, Tool and Die
    Apprenticeship
Family: Married to Mae Alice, two children
Civic Activities: Ypsilanti City Council; Mayor pro tem,
    Ypsilanti; United Way, Chamber of Commerce
Professional Activities: Ypsilanti Building Authority,
    Industrial Development and Council
Hobbies: Golf, flying, and travel
Major Career Accomplishment: Founder and Chairman,
    Crescive Die & Tool, Inc.

Campbell, Brian 58

Place and Date of Birth: August 23, 1940; Oak Park,
    Illinois
Present Residence: Ann Arbor
Education: DePaul University 1963, Northwestern
    University 1966
Family: Married to Mary, one child
Civic Activities: Ann Arbor Area Community Foundation,
    Boys and Girls Clubs of Michigan
Hobbies: Running and woodworking
Major Career Accomplishment: Founder and President of
    Trimas

Carlson, Dwight 73

Place and Date of Birth: March 28, 1944; Standish,
    Michigan
Present Residence: Ann Arbor
Education: GMI 1967
Family: Married to Denise, one child
Civic Activities: Eating Disorders and Exercise Network
Professional Activities: Michigan Manufacturing
    Technology Center, Michigan Future, National
    Coalition for Advanced Manufacturing

Hobbies: Tennis, water sports, and auto racing
Major Career Accomplishment: Founder and CEO of
Xycon, Inc. and Perceptron, Inc.

Chisholm, Don   93

Place and Date of Birth: March 28, 1934; Hackensack,
New Jersey
Present Residence: Ann Arbor
Education: University of Michigan BA 1955, MBA 1956
Family: Married to Betty
Civic Activities: Ann Arbor Hospice Board; U-M Music
School Advisory Board; Michigan Theatre, past
President; Summer Festival Advisory Board
Professional Activities: Urban Land Institute
Hobbies: Music, golf, and boating
Major Career Accomplishment: Ann Arbor real estate
development

Deal, Herm   114

Place and Date of Birth: October 8, 1923; Bulloch
County, Georgia
Present Residence: Ann Arbor
Education: Georgia Southern University 1945
Family: Married to Helen, eight children
Civic Activities: United Way, Junior Achievement,
Church Elder
Professional Activities: Washtenaw Sales and Marketing
Association, Washtenaw Industrial Development
Board, International Car Wash Association
Hobbies: Fishing, gardening, and photography
Major Career Accomplishment: CEO of Huron Valley
Sales, Inc.

Dempsey, Jack   134

Place and Date of Birth: December 25, 1935; Corry,
Pennsylvania
Present Residence: Ann Arbor
Education: Cornell University 1957, American College

Life Underwriters 1962

Family: Married to Barbara, three children

Civic Activities: Ann Arbor Hospice, American Cancer Tournament, United Way, Chamber of Commerce

Professional Activities: Washtenaw Estate Planning Council, Washtenaw Life Underwriters, Million Dollar Round Table, Top of the Table Board

Hobbies: Golf, music, and reading

Major Career Accomplishment: Founder and CEO of Dempsey, Inc.

Dobson, Bill   154

Place and Date of Birth: April 8, 1920; Ann Arbor, Michigan

Present Residence: Ann Arbor

Education: University of Michigan BA 1942, MBA 1948

Family: Married to Molly, three children

Civic Activities: Ann Arbor Area Community Foundation, United Way, Republican Party, L.I.S.C. Affordable Housing

Hobbies: Golf and travel

Major Career Accomplishment: CEO of Dobson-McOmber Insurance Agency

Edwards, Marty   169

Place and Date of Birth: December 4, 1931; Ann Arbor, Michigan

Present Residence: Ann Arbor

Education: University of Michigan BA 1953, MBA 1954

Family: Married to Rosalie, four children

Civic Activities: United Way; Republican Party; St. Francis of Assisi, Chairman Capital Fund; Fr. Gabriel Richard High School, Co-Chair Capital Fund

Professional Activities: Printing Industries of America, Book Manufacturers Institute

Hobbies: Golf

Major Career Accomplishment: President and CEO of Edwards Brothers, Inc.

Gelman, Chuck 187

Place and Date of Birth: December 14, 1931; New York, New York

Present Residence: Ann Arbor

Education: Syracuse University 1953, University of Michigan MS 1958

Family: Married to Rita, four children

Civic Activities: Jewish Community Center, Ann Arbor YMCA, Hands-On Museum

Professional Activities: Science and Environmental Policy Project, World Presidents Organization

Major Career Accomplishment: Founder and CEO of Gelman Sciences, Inc.

Griffin, Dick 211

Place and Date of Birth: July 12, 1938; St. Louis, Missouri

Present Residence: Ann Arbor

Education: University of Notre Dame BS 1960, Northwestern University MS 1961

Family: Married to Lisa Marie, three children

Civic Activities: Knights of Columbus; Fr. Gabriel Richard High School Board

Professional Activities: Association for Corporate Growth

Hobbies: Golf and sports

Major Career Accomplishment: Real estate and business acquisitions

Jenkins, Phil 230

Place and Date of Birth: August 4, 1923; Detroit, Michigan

Present Residence: Ann Arbor

Education: Purdue University 1947

Family: Married to Lyn, one child

Civic Activities: Intergenerational Center, Hands-On Museum

Professional Activities: Equipment Manufacturing Institute

Hobbies: Travel
Major Career Accomplishment: President and CEO of
  Sweepster, Inc.

McClelland, Nina   248

Place and Date of Birth: August 21, 1929; Columbus,
  Ohio
Present Residence: Ann Arbor
Education: University of Toledo 1951, 1963; University
  of Michigan 1964, 1968
Civic Activities: Cleary College Board, St. Joseph Mercy
  Hospital Board, Work Skills Corporation, Chamber
  of Commerce, United Way
Hobbies: Boating and music
Major Career Accomplishment: Chair and CEO of NSF
  International

McPherson, Larry   264

Place and Date of Birth: June 5, 1945; Lisbon, Ohio
Present Residence: Ann Arbor
Education: Clemson University, 1963; Georgia State
  1971
Family: Married to Charlene, three children
Civic Activities: United Way, Washtenaw Development
  Council, Washtenaw Community College, Hands-On
  Museum
Hobbies: Golf
Major Career Accomplishment: President and CEO of
  NSK Corporation

Sarns, Dick   280

Place and Date of Birth: June 20, 1927; Mt. Clemens,
  Michigan
Present Residence: Ann Arbor
Education: University of Michigan 1955
Family: Married to Norma, two children
Civic Activities: United Way, Chamber of Commerce,
  Hands-On Museum, Washtenaw Education and

Work Consortium
Professional Activities: Michigan Technology Council,
American Management Association
Hobbies: Reading, music, boating, and travel
Major Career Accomplishment: Founder and CEO of
Sarns/3M

Serras, Dennis   301

Place and Date of Birth: November 27, 1946;
Schenectady, New York
Present Residence: Ann Arbor
Education: Cleary College
Family: Married to Ellie, two children
Civic Activities: Main Street Area Association, Director;
YMCA, Dawn Farms
Professional Activities: National Restaurant Association
Hobbies: Fishing, golf, skiing, and flying
Major Career Accomplishment: President of Mainstreet
Ventures

Thomson, Ned   317

Place and Date of Birth: September 8, 1931; Coshocton,
Ohio
Present Residence: Ann Arbor and Scottsdale, Arizona
Education: Denison University 1953
Family: Married to Mary Jane, three children
Civic Activities: National Institute of Burn Medicine,
Washtenaw Community College, Church Elder,
Church Choir
Hobbies: Furniture building, stock market, tennis and
reading
Major Career Accomplishment: Co-Founder and
President of Thomson-Shore

Turner, Nub   333

Place and Date of Birth: April 16, 1938; Ann Arbor,
Michigan
Present Residence: Ann Arbor

Education: University of Michigan 1959
Family: Married to Janeth, two children
Civic Activities: Chamber of Commerce
Hobbies: Skiing, auto racing, and tennis
Major Career Accomplishment: CEO of GT Products, Inc.

Vincent, Monty   348

Place and Date of Birth: July 21, 1936; Portland,
    Oregon
Present Residence: Ann Arbor
Education: Lewis and Clark College 1957, Dartmouth
    College 1969, Stanford University 1979
Family: Married to Julianne, three children
Civic Activities: Care Choices HMO, board member;
    Peace Neighborhood Center, board vice-chair
Professional Activities: Michigan Technology Council,
    Medical Marketing Association, Association for
    Advancement of Medical Instrumentation
Hobbies: Travel, fishing, stock market, and gardening
Major Career Accomplishment: Founder and President of
    Arbor Technologies, Inc.

Wilson, Iva   371

Place and Date of Birth: March 8, 1938; Zagreb, Croatia
Present Residence: Ann Arbor
Education: University of Zagreb 1961, University of
    Stuttgart 1967
Family: Married to Tom, one child
Civic Activities: Michigan Futures, ERIM
Professional Activities: Society for Organizational
    Learning
Hobbies: Reading, golf, and music
Major Career Accomplishment: President of Phillips
    Display Components

Acknowledgments

We gratefully acknowledge the contributions and participation of those people who gave their time and moral support as we embarked on our maiden voyage into the land
of book publishing. My next door neighbor of 30-plus
years, C. Merle Crawford, U-M business professor emeritus, shared his book experiences and encouragement. He
referred us to the popular business professor, Andy
Lawler, who also lent his enthusiasm for our project.

Fred Kissling, a peer in the life insurance industry,
also a publisher, referred us to *What Matters Most,* a book
about Nashville's business, civic and entertainment leaders that served as an initial prototype. We were also
inspired by Bill Earls' *Million Dollar Profiles,* a life insurance industry book that had a profound influence on
many of us through the trials of our early years. The
Million Dollar Roundtable and their Foundation leadership also were supportive as they continue to promote volunteerism and community involvement worldwide.

Jim Taylor, editor of Ann Arbor's *Independent Times*
and *Ann Abor Area Business-to-Business,* was instrumental in bringing our writer, Jeff Mortimer, into the fold. We
had admired the work Jeff did for the latter publication in
"person-to-person" interviews with businesses and civic
leaders. This book is really an expansion of that concept.

Subsequently, Ann Arbor's resident mystery writer,
Jerry Prescott, shared the realities of publishing and marketing, which was very enlightening. Ned Thomson, the

subject of one of our profiles, brought us his printing experience and also introduced us to our publisher, Bill Haney of Momentum Books, Ltd. Ned also worked with us in the critical editorial review process to make our two-year dream become a reality before the millennium.

Jim Beuche and Chris Vaughan kindly volunteered their legal and accounting expertise, a generosity which nicely matched the spirit of our entire project.

Others not named here also contributed significantly. We hope that, through this book, others may be guided by the light you all have shown us.

J.D.

Introduction

The title of this book tells much about its content and about the people profiled in its pages. The "learning curves" that define the careers and lives of these individuals differ greatly from each other. Virtually none of their paths was predictable and, in fact, their great variety makes an eloquent statement about the many roads to success.

These are men and women of achievement, so it is no surprise that each profile has its accounts of important "hits," even "home runs." But what may surprise some readers is the subjects' candor about their "misses," not to mention their gratitude for them and the lessons they taught.

Each story is unique, yet they also have much in common. Each person was driven to his or her success...by a desire to do something that hadn't been done before, or to do something better than anyone else had done it, or to create something new, or to build upon a foundation laid by others.

The lives of these people have other common threads. They all recognize and prize the contributions of others. They all speak about "giving back." And they all have done just that, sharing the fruits of accomplishment with their families, their peers, their colleagues, their employees, and their communities.

It is out of this spirit of sharing, of giving back, of passing along to those who come afterwards, that this book grew.

Another trait shared by these 21 people is a sense of wonder, a curiosity about how things worked, about how to do something that had never been done before, or how to put their personal stamp on a work already in progress. The reader whose interest is piqued by this book will find soulmates here, and perhaps even an insight or two to illuminate the way.

We had a quick and simple answer when our publisher asked how we would measure the success of this book—if someone's career choice or business direction is affected in a positive way as a result of reading these stories, that would be our measure.

Virtually every individual profiled found some part of the past uncomfortable or even painful to deal with. But there were important lessons in that material. It took a professional writer, skilled at the art of interviewing, to gain the confidence and respect of the men and women portrayed herein, and then to capture in their stories the same spontaneity, honesty and bluntness that characterize their daily activities.

This book is the product of thousands of hours in the interviewing, writing, developing, shaping, and producing. Even more important, it is the product of the lives and careers of 21 people. Everyone involved in this venture is grateful for your interest and shares the hope that you will find something in these pages that will stimulate, illuminate, or otherwise enrich your own life.

Jack Dempsey
Ann Arbor
November 1999

"It's always better to do better than you say you will."

Herb Amster

Herb Amster tried not to be an entrepreneur. He really did. He had seen what it was like for his father, Gershon Amster, a Russian immigrant who started his own millinery business in the garment district of Manhattan. The family lived in the Brighton/Manhattan Beach section of Brooklyn, where Herb was born on January 2, 1935. He was sure his parents' lifestyle was not for him.

The company, in business since 1930, was called Amrose Hat. His mother, Rose, did the office work. Both parents were often on the job from 7:30 in the morning to 7:30 at night, six days a week.

"My father was a manufacturer of better millinery—fur hats, felt hats, straw hats, and wool hats matching to suits," he says. "When the furs were in style, he did very well, and when furs weren't in style, he struggled. Each season is a new business. It's like you started over; it's very competitive. The matching hats, you had to know what you were doing. I think he even made WAVE hats for the Navy during World War II. I worked for my father summers, cleaning suede hats and writing production tickets and packing, this type of stuff. It was not a great business, but it got my sister and me through college, and we lived in a nice area in a semi-attached house. We had no complaints, but it was a tough business."

Not so tough was sharing a seat with Carol Puterman in fourth grade. They started dating when they were sophomores at Abraham Lincoln High School near Coney Island, and were married in September 1956, three months after getting their undergraduate degrees, Carol from Brooklyn College and Herb from the Massachusetts Institute of Technology. The first of their three children was born on their first anniversary.

"Our relationship has always been one that was supportive of each other," he says. "Carol did more than her share in raising our children and in moving away from her friends and family with me. She has always been my best supporter and closest friend."

Herb had had a clear picture of what he wanted to do at the Cambridge campus. "I was one of the few people that went to MIT for business as an undergraduate," he says. "A lot of engineers switched into the business program, but I had gone straight for the business program, and I figured I'd also learn as much as I could about science and engineering. I really thought that it was better, after having watched my father in the business, to be a manager in a larger business rather than to have your own business. I don't believe that anymore."

It took a while, however, and Amster often found himself swimming against the tide, either someone else's or what he had imagined to be his own. Perhaps it was reinforced by the six-week Encampment for Civilization program that he attended—on a scholarship—the summer before he started at MIT. He had been active in student government in high school, including service as school president, and had crossed paths with Algernon Black, the head of the Ethical Culture movement, one of whose activities was sponsorship of the encampment.

"The program took seniors in high school and freshmen and sophomores in college from all over the country, all different backgrounds," he says. "There were poor people and wealthy, from the daughter of a very famous Harvard professor to poor black people who were working 12 hours a day to eke out enough money so they could go to college, and white people from towns in the south who had never really interacted with blacks before. When I got this scholarship, it was the time of McCarthyism, and I said to myself, 'How can I go? I'm liable to be branded a Communist.' But prudence said that I should go, and it was a great experience because it woke me up to the fact that the world is big and there are different people with different backgrounds who all have a meaningful role to play, and my problems were completely different from most of theirs and my opportunities were different from most of theirs. That was a major influence in my thinking about what you do on earth and what you can do."

As he recalls, there were about a hundred campers, housed in Riverdale "in a beautiful school setting. Basically, New York was the campus for the school," he says. "We visited all kinds of places: Democratic and Republican party headquarters, union headquarters. We sat in the Security Council seats at the United Nations, visited Eleanor Roosevelt at Hyde Park, heard lectures from various professors."

One such talk, in particular, stood out. "It was by the judge who made the first civil rights decision in a small southern town and was ostracized thereafter by the rest of the town, never spoken to again," he says. "It shows you what can happen, but he had the courage to do the right thing. This was a great experience. I was very lucky."

His luck held in college. "MIT was a great place to go to school," he says. "I was trying to decide between RPI (Rensselaer Polytechnic Institute, in Troy, New York) and MIT, and the idea of being in the Boston area versus Troy made me decide that MIT was the winner, even though I knew some people at RPI who had taken a similar type of program."

That would be "engineering administration, which was their business program. It was a basic science and engineering curriculum with business courses instead of the design courses. I was very good in the sciences and business. Engineering, I struggled through. I still made Tau Beta Pi, the engineering honor society, because they used the total average."

He had taken most of the graduate courses in business as an undergraduate, so it wasn't much longer before he earned his MBA from the now-renowned MIT Sloan School, where he was also a research assistant in "something called Operations Research, the application of math and other sciences to solve business problems. It was an interesting addition to traditional management consulting."

MIT undergraduates in 1952 numbered roughly 4,000, about the same as the number of students at Lincoln High, and Amster again plunged into school government. He was chairman of Baker House, his dormitory, then chairman of the campus-wide Dormitory Council and a member of the campus-wide student government board.

It was in that capacity that he "got to know Jim Killian, the president, pretty well," as Amster led negotiations that preserved some of the student social advances that were made when World War II veterans, mostly subsidized by the GI Bill and unaccustomed to the traditional restrictions on college students, flooded campuses.

"It was a time of turmoil at schools because the veterans had just about graduated and the schools were trying to have different parameters for their students than they did when the older veterans were there," says Amster. "I was involved in trying to make sure that there weren't too many changes. As opposed to Harvard, we had the freedom to have whoever we wanted in our room up to a certain hour, with the doors open or closed. And other freedoms that were nice."

He still has the plaque memorializing his efforts to retain those freedoms. It's the Karl Taylor Compton Prize, awarded "to Herbert Sheldon Amster, May 15, 1956, in recognition of devoted, selfless, determined efforts throughout his undergraduate years to the development of an MIT house system based on belief in the highest ideals of community living and in the capacity of free young men to handle their own affairs responsibly."

"They canceled classes and held an assembly and gave these awards," Amster remembers. "It was amazing."

He also found some comments by Alfred Sloan amazing, and they no doubt challenged his thinking that being a cog was preferable to running the machine.

"When Sloan visited the school and talked to the student society that invited him, someone asked him if he had it to do all over again, would he pursue the same career?" Amster recalls. "And he said, after thinking about it for a minute or two, 'Probably not. What I'd do is own a Chevrolet dealership in a small city and live a much better life.' That was interesting. He did think about it, though."

Instead of a Chevy dealership—although eventually he did work for Ford—Amster got a job with Grace Lines. "At that time the largest division of W.R. Grace and Company was the chemical division," he says, "but the steamship company was the part of the company that made the most money. Grace Lines had steamship operations between the U.S. and the west coast of South America, and 12-day cruises/refrigerated cargo trips to the Caribbean."

Amster's boss was a man named Jack Gilbreth, the youngest son in the family made famous in *Cheaper by the Dozen*. He was the manager of operations research. "It was a good group of people," Amster says. And, for a time, the logistical challenges of his work kept him interested.

"It was a time when people were talking about container ships, so freight could go from a ship and over land without packing and unpacking," he says. "One of the things I worked on was determining the number of containers necessary to service a route, how long these things would go inland, what type of schedule the boats would have. It was interesting. I also did the pricing for the cruises."

After Amster had been with Grace Lines for two and a half years his father fell ill, so the young man joined Amrose Hat on a full-time basis, meanwhile taking courses at New York University toward a PhD in business. "The millinery business was so far from what I had been interested in, but I thought it was worth a try," he says. "The business was mine if I wanted it, but after two years I decided 'no.'"

Instead, he said "yes" to a job offer that resulted from, of all things, answering a blind ad in *The New York Times*, and found himself back in the Boston area, with Raytheon in Lexington, Massachusetts. "I joined a corporate group to do financial analysis and to work with their non-military businesses," he says, "all of which were a relative disaster."

Raytheon was a major manufacturer of military equipment, having developed the radar tube during World War II, and its biggest business was the Sparrow and Hawk missiles. Despite its creative fecundity, though, the company couldn't seem to get it right when it came to civilian enterprises.

"They were the first company in the microwave cooking business," he says. "They had the original patents. They were in the computer business way back when, and were pioneers in semiconductors. They got out of all of these businesses at the wrong time."

His Raytheon experience went on to provide even more negative lessons, although he made invaluable personal contacts there. "I was the person assigned to the semiconductor division, which was losing money at the rate of 50 cents for every dollar of sales," he says. "They decided they really wanted me to work within the division, and I became budget manager of the division, and then controller of their largest manufacturing plant in Lewiston, Maine. There we were, leaving Boston, a great place to live, after New York, a great place to live, to Lewiston, a very strange place for us.

"But it was there I learned a major business lesson. Raytheon decided they needed to be in certain types of products, so they bought two losing companies, Rheem Semiconductors and CBS Semiconductors, and they put the three companies together. What happens when you put three sick businesses together is you end up with the plague. Management effectiveness just wasn't there. You have three times the problems and your ability to deal with three times the problems is probably one-ninth because you can't focus."

Eventually, the plant was closed. "It was the best plant Raytheon ever had, the best workforce, the best productivity," says Amster, "but it was manufacturing products that didn't have a very long-term future. And they felt that convincing the type of engineers necessary for future products to go to Lewiston, Maine, was beyond their ability. There were over 1,000 people in the plant. I stayed with one other person and helped close it."

That other person was the plant manager, Leo Leary, who became the connection that brought Amster to Michigan. "Raytheon offered to move me back to Lexington and then move me as controller of their next acquisition," he says, "but the idea of moving back to Massachusetts and then moving again to somewhere else didn't appeal to me."

Leary, too, was job-hunting, and an offer that he declined for himself seemed like it might be a good fit for Amster. "Why don't you talk to them?" he said.

He did, in part because "Ford had a reputation as a good place for smart, ambitious young people," he says, and was soon en route to Ypsilanti, Michigan, to become a senior product planning analyst for Ford's General Parts Division, which made shock absorbers, windshield wipers and, at that time, alternators and carburetors.

"I never had been to Michigan, except for an Institute of Management Sciences meeting in Detroit," Amster says. "I knew nothing except that people said Ann Arbor was a great place."

At first, though, he barely had time to find out. He might have thought he was back at Amrose Hat. "Ford was an interesting experience," he says. "It was a growing division that was bringing business in-house from out-sourcing. My boss, Ray Latimer, and I worked late into the night every night except Friday, and most Saturdays up until around noon or one o'clock.

"The biggest thing that our group did—and something in which I wasn't directly involved—was we went into the plastics business. The big Saline plant was built because of our group, and we went into the heating and air-conditioning business in a big plant at M-14 and Plymouth Road in Northville. It was an exciting place to work."

That excitement was seasoned by Amster's increasing corporate savvy. "One of the lessons I learned in that role was if you're good and you're working at a big company, you want to start out at corporate headquarters and not in one of the divisions," he says, because "the pay is less, even though the work is harder, and the ability to migrate up is much more difficult because you don't know people. The ability to migrate down from corporate headquarters to divisional leadership is much easier. Getting to meet some of the people at corporate, as I did at Raytheon, served me in very good stead. But at Ford, I had to threaten to quit to get moved into one of the car divisions, the Ford Division."

And did they have a job for him. "There I was," he says, "in charge of warranty administration at a time when the Ford Motor Company was having terrible warranty problems."

Amster, though, took advantage of the situation. "None of the higher-ups ever wanted to go to meetings with corporate staff on warranty, so I ended up at all these meetings, which was a great experience for me," he says. "You were with these executives, some of whom were very sharp, and you were able to influence their view of what was going on."

In his next job, he had a bit more influence, which was one of the principal reasons he took it. His old friend and boss from Raytheon, Jim Davidson, called to suggest Amster contact Nathan Rosenfeld, "who runs this specialty store group in Michigan."

That was Jacobson's. Amster first became its chief financial officer, then its chief technical officer when the company computerized its systems and "it was easier to find a financial officer." He stayed with the company for seven years.

"Even though I made a little bit less money, and the prospects for making money like I could have at Ford were nowhere near as good, the plus of this decision was that I would be an officer of a small company and involved in the decision-making for the company," he says. "At Ford, I was in one small area and had very limited influence on the running of this 250,000-person company."

It was also a place where he felt at home because of his background in the millinery business. "And Jacobson's was a fine store and would use the type of quality product that I was used to," he adds. "I felt comfortable even though it was a completely different business than I had ever been in, certainly different from Ford."

Also different was the fact that he came in as a director of the company. "The business, even though it was private, was always run as if it were a public company," he says. "That taught me another lesson—if you're going to build a business, it's very wise to have a board of directors, even if you're not public."

There are two particularly clear strands in Amster's career. One is that he was learning how to build and run a business almost in spite of himself, and probably before he explicitly formulated any such plans. The other is phone calls from former colleagues at Raytheon.

The next call was from Joe Budris at a new Ann Arbor high-tech company called Sycor, which had invented—and was the first to make—intelligent computer terminals, the forerunner of today's personal computers. "He said he couldn't take the pressure of the job any more, but he couldn't leave until he found a replacement," says Amster, chuckling, "and I was the replacement."

It was appealing. He wanted to get back into technology, and "I had gone about as far as I could at Jacobson's," he says, although he remains a company director to this day.

He joined Sycor in 1974 and took over as vice president, finance, shortly thereafter when Budris finally did leave. The nature of the business was as different from Jacobson's as Jacobson's had been from Ford: in addition to being technologically based, it was young and small, albeit rapidly growing.

"Jacobson's was a great company, but Sycor was great in a different way because it was a very creative company with very smart and creative people in it," says Amster. "Sam Irwin, Paul Lavoi, Ted Smith, Dieter Heidrich, and Ray Kavlick were the major officers at the time besides myself. And Sam was the best product planner in technology that ever lived, as far as I'm concerned. He could see a hole in a product offering way in advance of other people, and he really understood the technology."

Sycor was one of several companies founded by Irwin, an electrical engineer who had come to Ann Arbor as a University of Michigan student in 1946. Its terminal sold so well that for a time in the mid-1970s, it was Ann Arbor's biggest private employer.

"In fact, the company had the basic patent that allowed the PC to work," says Amster, "and one of the expensive things that we did was to sue IBM for infringement. That is a challenging event, when David sues Goliath. Eventually, the suit got settled after Sycor was sold to Northern Telecom."

That happened in 1978, launching a chain of events that eventually doomed Sycor but propelled Amster ever closer to being in charge of his own business. "Northern had promised to build on it, to build a great business," Amster says of the sale. "There's not a lot else I can say about that."

Actually, there's a little more. What brought down Sycor, in his view, was a subsequent acquisition by Northern that went awry. "Sycor's foreign products for many years were distributed by Olivetti, but they no longer had Olivetti as a distributor as they wanted to do their own thing with their own products," he says. "We were looking to build our sales force internationally, and we had put together our first presentation to Northern about buying a European distribution company. We put together a very conservative analysis, with a 12 percent return built in. It's always better to do better than you say you will than to do a little bit worse on a much harder plan."

Irwin and Amster went to Montreal to present the plan to the Northern brass. "I wasn't allowed in the meeting," Amster recalls. "Sam met with the CFO and the chairman and president of Northern Telecom, and they turned our proposal down."

And later that same day, literally, they approved a plan to acquire Data 100, a Sycor competitor located in Minneapolis. "We had looked at buying Data 100 when we were independent and turned it down at a third the cost," says Amster. "Although they had a good organization, their products were far behind. They were living off leases that were going to expire and the company's technology just wasn't there."

But a McDonnell-Douglas tender offer for the company, of which Northern already owned 25 percent, had caught management's attention. "They said Data 100 had tremendous capability in sales and marketing overseas, and the fit would be great. The Northern philosophy was if you take these two companies and eliminate the duplicate overhead, you can save a lot of money and be very profitable. They brought in one of their big cost-cutters, who had done this in one of their steel businesses, I believe. He knew nothing about high technology and it became a disaster, and they decided, because Northern Telecom had a beautiful new building in Minneapolis, they would move Sycor there. They convinced, I think, only one executive of Sycor to go. I wouldn't go."

Sycor succumbed soon after, and Amster left Northern Telecom. "It was sad because Sycor was a really good business, and well positioned for the future," he says. "Data 100 was not positioned for the future. When you mix two things like that together, and you don't have somebody running the business who knows the business, you're going to get in trouble, and they did."

Three or so years of assorted pursuits followed, including real estate development ("with one of the best developers in Michigan, Sam Frankel, and I concluded very quickly that that business was not for me") and a role with Joel Tauber, an exceptional entrepreneur, at his auto industry conglomerate, Key International, in Southfield.

"That job turned out to be the most difficult for me," he says, "because I was hired as the CFO and they wanted me to do mostly clerical work because their attorney, who was well thought of by Joel, wanted to act as the CFO. And I left."

Nonetheless, Joel is well thought of by Herb, too. "He's a great guy," he says. "I first met him through the United Jewish Appeal. He turned Key International around in leveraged buyouts three different times and made a ton of money." A good chunk of which, Amster notes, funded the formation of a manufacturing institute at the University of Michigan.

Amster was doing some consulting when Irwin called to ask if he would accompany him on a trip to California to sound out potential investors in a new company that would make small but powerful hard-disk drives for personal computers, vastly increasing the amount of data they could store.

"He and I were well on our way to raising the money for this business," says Amster. "On the plane trip back, Sam talked about three or four other businesses that he wanted to start at the same time. And I said to myself, this wasn't for me, one business was enough. So I did not go with Sam at that time."

But he did go with him by the time Irwin International was in the middle of its development program. "We were beginning to think we had the product," he says.

"Sam's idea was to make a very good disk that was high-performance and fast and had a built-in tape backup for reliability," Amster adds. "Putting both the tape and the drive together could also save money by utilizing some of the same parts. He tried to develop with his technical people a 10-megabyte capacity and a 10-millisecond speed, which was very fast for the time. And to do it at the time, you had to use plated media. The trouble was that the plated media were never consistent and the interface between the reading heads and the plated media never was developed correctly."

Meanwhile, out in California, a company called Seagate "took exactly the opposite view," he says, "and made a slow, 5-megabyte device using an interface that they gave to everybody...and it was a simple interface."

The strategy worked. "The interface on our device was relatively complex and would have taken some time to be integrated into a computer system," says Amster. "Once there, it would have been much better, but there was a great demand for simplicity and Seagate took off like a bat out of hell."

And, after four years of trying, Irwin International went into the tank, to the tune of about $25 million. There were now 70 other companies in the hard disk business. "We couldn't make our device," Amster confesses. "Eventually, the investors, which included Olivetti and Windcrest Partners, both of whom were vitally involved with Sycor, decided to close the company down."

But they also decided, he says, "that if it were possible to close it down on a clean basis, that's the way they wanted to do it." In other words, no bankruptcy. "We went about closing the company as smoothly as we could," he says. "We sold off all the equipment, sold off all of the inventory, and paid almost all of our debts."

The investors turned to Amster to do the job "because I was the CFO, among other things." And he extracted a price: "I told them I would be willing to do that if I could find some technology within Irwin International and they would finance me in a new startup. They agreed to put in a million dollars if I could raise a million dollars from independent sources."

After Irwin International had lost so much money, raising yet another million wasn't that easy. On the other hand, largely due to Amster's reputation and relationships, it wasn't that hard, either.

Mike Gellert, the head of Windcrest Partners, a New York venture capital firm, had been an investor in Sycor and was the first major investor. Then Amster got $250,000 from the venture capital unit of the state's pension fund, and another $500,000 from Northern Telecom. "I got Paul LaVoie, who had been vice president of marketing at Sycor, out of retirement in Florida," he recalls. "He and I got on a plane and went to visit the v.p. of finance at Northern Telecom, who was controller when they bought Sycor and who I had a great interface with. We met for 15 minutes, he shook my hand and said you have $500,000. The venture capital people at Northern Telecom went ballistic. They hadn't done due diligence; they hadn't done anything. It just pays to be straight with people and don't surprise people.

"Another neat investor was Jack Daly, from Hoover Universal at the time. They didn't normally invest in these kinds of things but he had Hoover put $50,000 in because he liked the story that we were telling."

The story was the company's planned product, based on the technology Amster had sifted from the rubble: a backup tape drive to prevent accidental loss of data stored on PCs with hard disks. "We kept a number of engineers and decided if we were going to have a product, we were late for disk drives but not late for tape drives," says Amster. "We started with a clean sheet of paper to design a tape drive that we could sell as an independent product. We also had an exceptional board of directors, led by Gellert, Ted Doan from Doan Associates in Michigan, and Jim Daverman of Wind Point Partners in Chicago. Their support and advice really helped."

Amster and company then set up Irwin Magnetics, which initially had been within Irwin International as a separate corporation "so the investors were shielded from any unknown liabilities, although it turned out there were none." In addition to LaVoie, Amster had also lured Leo Leary, his old friend from Raytheon, out of retirement to become the new company's vice president for manufacturing.

In addition, "Olivetti lent us one of their good designers," Amster says, "and working with the people that we carried over from Irwin International, we designed a small, 5¼-inch tape drive. The biggest decision was whether we would make the drive floppy disk compatible. In layman's terms, that means somebody could buy the drive, plug it into their PC, and it would work. That's a great advantage. The disadvantage is that the floppy disk is very slow and the time to back up would increase. But we made the decision that ease of use was more important than speed at this time, and that was the right decision."

Perhaps the second biggest decision for Irwin Magnetic was the storage capacity of the tape. "Because of the problems Irwin International had in the disk, we decided we wouldn't go for a 10-megabyte tape but for five megabytes, which was much easier," he says. "But before we got too far, I hired an industry marketing expert, Ray Freeman, to review what we were doing and where we were going, so in case there was a flaw, he would be able to point it out."

Sure enough, Freeman spotted one. "He told us five megabytes wouldn't sell because the 10-megabyte disk was going to be around quicker than we would expect and we had better go for 10," Amster says, "so we changed in midstream and went for 10 megabytes for our first product. That was a wise decision. I spent two days with him; he was very helpful."

Some customers would also be helpful, and the company landed a big one in the summer of 1984, a little less than a year after it was incorporated: Compaq, the leading maker of IBM-compatible PCs, agreed to offer the Irwin drive as an option in its top model.

"We went to Compaq before we had the product finished and talked them into placing an order with us," says Amster. "They did it with the proviso that we would fill their needs first for the first year, whatever they needed, so the Irwin drive, which eliminated having to copy many floppy disks to back up the disk, was in their new product when they introduced it. That was a very successful relationship that lasted throughout the life of the company."

As the first deal of its kind between a major computer manufacturer and a backup-tape maker, it attracted attention to the fledgling operation. Sales and employment exploded. By mid-1985, the company was making money. Its sales in 1986 were $36 million. Amster was named the Michigan recipient of the Council of Great Lakes Governors Entrepreneur of the Year Award in 1986 and the Michigan Industrialist of the Year in 1987.

Herb Amster had come full circle from the sharp lad who craved a niche in a big corporation. He was not only unquestionably an entrepreneur, but also a highly successful one. And he is typically matter-of-fact about his motivation: "I was convinced that I could do a better job, and I wanted the opportunity to prove that, and that I could build a great company. I had a lot of experience in lots of companies and felt I was more than ready to do it."

One major component was assembling the management team, which looked a lot different, and certainly older, than those at most high-tech startup firms. But Amster knew what he wanted. "We built a team of people who could handle the company's growth, mature people who had done it before," he says.

That eventually included Ed Carlson, who took over as president when Amster was promoted to chairman in 1975. "We were looking for someone to be the chief operating officer who had a lot more experience in that role than I did," he says. "Luckily, the person that one of our investors started talking to on an airplane was Ed, who was a vice president at Burroughs and was interviewing for a job, and the investor passed his name on to me. Because Ann Arbor was such a great place to live, I was able to convince him to join Irwin Magnetics. In actuality, it was his wife who I convinced. I called her and said this is a great place to live, we really love it, come on out and look around. She did, and convinced him to join Irwin Magnetics."

Meanwhile, Amster had become afflicted with lupus, a chronic inflammatory disease in which the body's immune system forms antibodies that attack healthy tissues and organs. It is currently incurable, reasonably controllable, and a bit of an inconvenience when you're trying to start a company.

"When I got out of the hospital, we put together the business plan for Irwin Magnetics," he says; he remembers working on it in his pajamas in the living room. "The symptoms of lupus were such that I was very tired. I had to sit down and rest after taking a shower. But with the proper care, you're able to contain it and operate effectively most of the time, although occasionally you have relapses which cause you to miss work. To fight a disease that is really with you all the time, you have to have a positive attitude. I've managed to keep it that way for quite some time, and that helps me a lot, I think. It also pays to have a great doctor and I have a great doctor, Joe (W. Joseph) McCune, over at the University of Michigan."

Potential investors besieged Dr. McCune with calls, Amster says. "It was an interesting time. We hired a chief financial officer very early, given my physical situation," he adds. That was Francis Glorie, who was a great help and stayed with the company throughout its existence.

When Carlson joined Irwin Magnetics, it was "a difficult time," Amster says. "We had just laid off a few people; it wasn't an easy sell."

Selling the product was easier, and a second big deal was closed not long after Carlson's arrival. "We won IBM in a very competitive situation with a company in California called Archive," says Amster, "and we did it by working hard, listening to what they had to say, and doing the little extra to make sure that it happened. In fact, one day we had to hire an airplane to fly to Florida and deliver a part so that a test could be run that evening. And we did it. We actually won the business with our very proprietary format because (a) the product was the best and (b) they saw that we were willing to work very hard for them.

"That was a difficult situation because the other company was offering what they were indicating was a standard format rather than a proprietary one, and standard formats are much easier to sell than proprietary ones.

IBM endorsed our product and shipped our product with some of their machines, and bought the product as an aftermarket product for their machines. Eventually, we had every one of the major OEMs, and we also had a business selling through retail stores."

The upward spiral continued through the mid-'80s. "We had good people and a good organization, and the product was well tested," says Amster. "We believed in quality being built in. We had software that went with the product, and the software was tested to make sure that the product was working right. It slowed up our software a little bit and we got criticized for that, but someone who backs up wants to make sure that it's there."

Irwin Magnetics went public in 1987, and was sold for $77 million cash in 1989 to Cipher Data Products. "We sold because the peripheral business over the long term is a tough business," he says, "and at the time of the sale, everyone who invested turned out to be a winner, and the employees, who had a lot of stock because I believe in that, turned out to be winners. We thought if you could join up with a company that has a product that fits in with your product, it would make sense in the long run."

Alas, it didn't work out that way. "Cipher was doing very well at the time, but they had products that were aging and they didn't have the follow-on products ready, so when we merged, we continued to do well but they had a lot of problems," Amster says. "They didn't know what to do with me because my role as CEO was not nearly as important for a division as it was for a separate company. They had Ed Carlson running the operation, which made sense, but I stayed on to do whatever I could for them. After a while, Ed got responsibility for what was going on in their next product line in California and I was put on the board of directors. We were pretty excited about where we were going to be able to go; unfortunately, Cipher's other products were falling off rather rapidly in demand, and their earnings were significantly below expectation. The stock had been beaten down."

At the same time, Cipher filed a patent infringement

suit against Archive, who was also one of their competitors. The two companies negotiated a settlement, but it went awry at the last minute, resulting in an unfriendly tender offer by Archive for Cipher's stock.

"The CEO of Cipher and myself were designated by the board to negotiate with Archive," says Amster. "We were able to get them to up the price by a dollar a share, and Archive took control of the company. I was sort of the odd man out. When I asked the chairman of Archive for some things to do that were meaningful, he said, 'I can't give you anything meaningful because you were our enemy,' which is really a silly way to think about the world. So I left Archive. Later on, Ed left. Archive was our biggest competitor for our type of drive with IBM, and they couldn't believe that we won it legitimately. To this day, they don't believe it!

"Slowly but surely, the demand for the Irwin product disappeared because Archive stopped selling it," he adds. "They moved some of the technical people to southern California and eventually closed down the plant."

Ironically, Archive was subsequently bought by a hard-disk manufacturing company called Conner, Inc., which in turn was bought by Seagate. Thus, Irwin Magnetics, which started as a competitor to Seagate before either company had a product, ended up being part of Seagate.

Amster wound up on the boards of several more companies, notably Trimas, Mechanical Dynamics, First of America-Michigan, Allegiance, and XYCOM. He also served three years as president of the University Musical Society (UMS), was chair of the Industrial Technology Institute (ITI) for five years, and remained heavily involved, as he had been since the Lewiston days, with the United Jewish Appeal. He is currently on the community boards of St. Joseph Mercy Hospital and National City Bank and an advisor to two venture funds in Ann Arbor, Enterprise Development Fund and White Pines Partners.

"I think UMS asked me to join the board because of my finance background and business background, and I've really enjoyed that relationship," he says. "With the help of the other directors and the management, we were able to turn the Musical Society from a bad deficit position to a viable presenter that was awarded the Best Presenter Organization in the country the last two years I was involved as president. One of the most significant contributors was Norm Herbert. He and I worked hard together to help set the course for the music society with the management so it could be successful, and to convince the University that it could run successfully."

From the University of Michigan's point of view, that meant not losing money. "And we were able to turn it around," says Amster. "In fact, the University helped. One of the last acts of (former U-M President) Jim Duderstadt was to approve a $600,000 donation to the Musical Society, $200,000 per year, to provide a foundation in case they had a bad year. Believe me, to get them to do that was probably one of our biggest achievements. They're doing a really good job now."

Amster also pitched in at the Industrial Technology Institute. "I became chairman of ITI also, and ITI got into financial trouble almost immediately," he says. "I first hired Carlos Zorea, a management consultant, to initially help put ITI back on track. He did a good job, but wasn't interested in continuing to run it. I convinced the board that Ed Carlson was the right person to run the company. Together, we were able to turn it around, from where the governor flatly told us that after our contract was over they wouldn't give us another penny, to where it is now one of the state's favorite programs and is a very high performer nationally in a difficult marketplace."

Perhaps the closest to his heart is the United Jewish Appeal, which supports Jews in need throughout the world and funds the emigration and absorption of Jews, as he puts it, "from areas where they are not wanted to Israel and other places all over the world. I've always felt that it is necessary to help while you can, because when you think about what happened to the Jewish people during World War II and you read about boats of Jewish people being turned away, you realize that prejudice is something that is not predictable, and you have to take care of people when they're in trouble or when they believe they're in trouble."

The key is a sense of reciprocity, an obligation to repay the community that has provided the environment for financial success. "I've always been able to make a reasonable living," says Amster, "and Carol and I felt that it was our obligation to help people that were a lot less fortunate. Both of us believe you should give it while you're alive, rather than after you're dead."

A memento of mortality hangs on the Amsters' living room wall. It's a landscape painting by Herb's brother-in-law, David Lund. He survived Sally, Herb's younger sister, who died of cancer at the age of 50. Like her husband, she was an artist.

"Art is a marketing game, and if you're not willing to play the marketing game, it makes it very difficult," says Amster. "Neither of them would ever paint what people wanted; they painted what they wanted, mainly abstract expressionist landscapes. That was in style for a while, then pop art and op art came in and their sales slipped."

The painting in question hung at the White House during Lyndon Johnson's administration. "When Nixon got in, he said get rid of all this modern art," Amster says. "I ended up buying it. It's a great picture. Carol and I enjoy living with a great collection of Sally and David's works."

He shrugs and sighs. "We all have different tastes."

∞

"I started at the bottom of the curve."

Jim Bradley

When he bought his first car, Jim Bradley had no idea what a role they would play in his life.

He was just a student at Southeastern High School, living on Concord Street on the east side of Detroit, the oldest of James and Ethel Bradley's eight children, and thus the first to get a driver's license.

"It was a 1950 Mercury," he says. "I bought it from a neighbor who was going to trade it in, but she said if we gave her what the dealer offered, which was $250, we could buy it. It was a sharp car, a coupe with wide whitewalls and fender skirts. The rear end was shackled down and it had dual exhausts with glass pipes, so when you revved it up, it would purr and sputter and backfire and make a lot of noise. That's what we loved."

Americans do love their cars, but few of them get to parlay that love into as successful a career as Bradley's. He had other early experiences behind the wheel that played a role, but they were in his father's car, not his.

"My dad was a little bit of an entrepreneur himself," says Bradley. "He had a lot of small businesses. One was called the Home Accessories Company; he sold dry goods and small appliances door to door. He made me go along with him to keep me out of trouble and teach me a good work ethic. When I got my driver's license, he had me go around and collect the accounts. That was my introduction to accounting and accounts receivable. You also learn about people dodging you and not paying their bills, and what you have to do to collect from delinquent accounts."

There were plenty of other lessons from his father. When the senior Bradley was elected to the first of his 10 terms in the state House of Representatives, he was working for the post office and had a real estate license. "He always believed in having two jobs," says his son. During his 20 years as a legislator, he also owned a real estate company and a small construction business. It was not until he was elected City Clerk of Detroit, a post he also held for 20 years, that his principal job was sufficiently full-time to keep him occupied.

Young Jim Bradley had been a good enough basketball player at Southeastern to earn a scholarship from a small college in South Carolina, but his parents wanted him closer to home, so he enrolled at the Detroit Institute of Technology.

"When my counselor asked what I wanted to major in," he recalls, "I just said accounting. But I hadn't even thought about it."

It turned out to be a good fit. After two years, Bradley transferred to Michigan State, partly because it was stronger in accounting and partly because he wanted to play basketball for the Spartans. He was half right. "I was just on the junior varsity," he says. "It looked like I wasn't going to make the varsity, so I decided to stop playing ball."

When he got his degree, he found that Michigan State's reputation in his field could not neutralize his pigmentation. "That was a period of time when Afro-Americans couldn't get jobs in businesses," he says. "I think three

Afro-Americans graduated with degrees in accounting in 1959 and none of us received job offers. Everybody else with accounting degrees had four or five job offers."

He started applying for civil service jobs, still with no luck, until he got an employment offer...from the U.S. Army. "When I got drafted I was told there was a six-month program that you could take and be in the reserves for five years, or you could go for two years and be in the reserves for two years. I said I'll just take the six-monther."

He spent those six months at Fort Leonard Wood, Missouri, and when he returned, he found a job as a statistical clerk for Detroit Traffic Court. It wasn't a career path, but at least it was employment, and he was also attending Detroit College of Law at night.

After a year of that, "my applications started to bear some fruit," he says. "I got a call from the placement department for Michigan State saying that some companies were looking at my resume and had an interest in me. I received offers from General Motors, from General Electric, and from the IRS. It all came at once, so I had to make a decision, and I decided to go with General Motors. Having grown up in Michigan and close to the car business, GM had a certain mystique."

There was another appealing aspect. "I was the first Afro-American hired by the Central Foundry Division of General Motors in a salaried position," Bradley says. The division was located in Saginaw, so he had to drop out of law school and relocate. "But I thought if I got there and got started, maybe I could get back to Detroit and continue my education," he recalls.

He got there in July 1962. As it happened, his education continued in Saginaw, although not in classrooms.

"When I first went to Saginaw, it was a real segregated city," says Bradley. "I tried to get an apartment, and the landlady said, 'I can't rent to you because I've got other ladies living in these apartments. In fact, your people stay on the other side of town, so that's where you should go look.' I said, 'Okay, all right, that's the way that goes.' I had to learn how to persevere. But I found a place."

And not just to live. In six years, he moved from "basic training" to accounts payable, to cost analysis, to burden ("developing your indirect cost"), to operations analysis, to director of operations analysis.

Actually, the moves took place over a five-year period. After Bradley had been, for three years, at Central Foundry, which made castings for GM, he was still about where he had been when he started. One night, the division controller, Bob Waugh, noticed Bradley working late in his office and stopped by for a chat.

"How are things going?" Waugh asked.

"They're going fair," Bradley said, "but I'm not sure if this is the place for me."

"Why do you say that?"

"It just seems that other people are getting promoted and I'm not. I've got some aspirations and I can see where I'd like to be in five years. If I stay here in the same position, in five years I'm not going to be at my goal. Maybe it's best I look somewhere else."

After that conversation, says Bradley, "Things started happening. I started getting opportunities, and then as I made the most of them, other opportunities came."

Obviously, he knew who was behind it, and he still hasn't forgotten. "Bob was a Canadian guy who just took an interest in me and helped me," says Bradley. "I was somebody who came out of the east side of Detroit with some rough edges. Bob rounded off those edges and put me in a position to accomplish things at that division.

"I respect him because he did the kind of thing that was uncomfortable for a lot of people," he adds. "First, to hire an Afro-American on his staff, then to push me into certain positions that forced me to perform. It was uncomfortable for me because the people I was working with were uncomfortable with me, and I had to be a trailblazer to get them to accept me and appreciate my performance. And he had to take a risk and put me in that position. Bob Waugh was truly a mentor. When he asked me to become director of operations analysis, that forced me to sharpen my skills."

So much so, that new possibilities appeared on the horizon. As director of operations analysis, says Bradley, "You had to report to the general manager and his staff on what was happening in all these individual areas— accounts payable, cost analysis, burden, operations analysis—via a daily report coupled with a bimonthly operations review. To be able to make those kinds of presentations to such people caused them to begin to look at me differently, as one of them, or as part of that elite management group at Central Foundry.

"That was also my real education in running a business. I had to be able to prepare charts and material that would inform that general manager, so I had to put his hat on and think the way he would think and anticipate his questions and see what he was looking for. When I saw I could do that, I said I could run my own business."

At about the same time, General Electric beckoned, offering a job that was, to be sure, in relatively remote Evendale, Ohio, but that also entailed more responsibility and significantly more money. "I accepted the job because of the pay," he says, "but because of my respect for Bob Waugh and what he had done, I felt I had to talk to him about it."

Waugh was understanding. "At this division, I cannot match the kind of dollars they're talking about," he said. "But before you make your final decision, why don't you let me talk to some people at the corporation? They may have some other opportunities there that measure up."

The opportunity Bradley truly coveted was a dealership, so he arranged to meet with William Harvey III, the vice president of Motors Holding Division, GM's dealership financing arm.

"I told him of my interest," Bradley recalls, "and his comment was, 'That's nice, but in my experience, corporate people do not make good car dealers, so that's not a good investment for this division.' I wasn't happy with that remark, but I still felt he didn't completely shut the door. He was just telling me his feelings, and maybe testing me to see if I was sincerely interested and would continue pursuing it. If he could make that one statement and I would shut the door and quit my pursuit, I probably wasn't a good candidate anyway."

Then a corporate job came through, as an analyst on GM's financial staff. "They didn't match the kind of pay I was offered by General Electric," says Bradley, "but I liked the idea of becoming a dealer, so I said to GE, 'No, I'm going to stay close and take my chances.'"

He also stayed in touch with Harvey. "We would go to lunch and visit," he says. "One day, he said, 'Why don't you get some experience? You need to find out if you really like this.' I said, 'Why don't you help me?'"

Help came in the form of moonlighting jobs at various dealerships. "On Mondays and Thursdays, I'd work all day, get off at 5 p.m., then go to a dealership and work from 6 to 9 p.m., plus all day on Saturday," he says, "just to see if I'd still be interested and still liked it. I did that for about a year."

Harvey was implacable. "I went back to him and said, 'I still want to pursue this,'" says Bradley. "He said, 'Why don't you quit your job and go into it full-time?' I thought it was just another test, so I resigned from General Motors and took a job in the accounting department at Carter Chevrolet in Detroit."

Then there was a leadership void at a Chicago dealership. "Al Johnson, the first Afro-American General Motors dealer, had sold his Oldsmobile store to Rufus Dukes so he could move over to become the first Afro-American Cadillac dealer, which at the time were the most profitable dealerships," says Bradley. "Al took over the Cadillac store while they were still negotiating with Rufus. Somebody had to hold the Oldsmobile store together until the new owner came in, and that was my job. I got some experience out of that.

"I also saw Al Johnson's flavor, I saw Rufus Dukes' flavor. Al was more of an administrator type, while Rufus was a car-guy type who'd been in the business a long time. He was general manager of a Dodge store, and he'd been doing this 25 years. Probably you could find it only in your major markets like Chicago that an Afro-American had been in this business that long. So that was how I got my appetite whetted, working with those two. It really helped crystallize my thoughts that for sure this is what I want to do."

What he didn't want to do was continue commuting to Chicago. He had been married for almost eight years to the former Juanita Bass, who was teaching school in Detroit, and they had two small daughters.

"That's a strain on a marriage," says Bradley. "I would fly out on Mondays, work in Chicago, fly back for the weekend. It just got to be a grind, and I thought it best for me to come home. I asked Bill Harvey and company if they could get me a little closer to Detroit."

Indeed they could, back at Carter Chevrolet, where he performed a variety of tasks over the next two years. "I was just trying to get experience at a dealership, and get it in a short period of time," says Bradley. "A wise gentleman once said to me, 'If you're going to invest money in a business, you better know everything you can about it before you go and put your money down.' That was my thing, to make sure I understood everything about it."

He didn't miss many stops. "They needed somebody in the service department, so I went to work as a write-up person," he says. "Lo and behold, the service manager had a heart attack, so they said, 'You've got to run the service department,' so I did that for six months. I held it together and really learned how to run a department. Then the dealer came to me and said, 'I've got a more experienced service manager. I think he can do a better job for me, and I would like for you to go into car sales.' So I started selling cars, still trying to get more experience. I did that for about two months, and they caught the used car manager stealing, so they said go down and hold that together for us. So I ran that for eight months. Then they got another used car manager and said you have to go back to sales. So I went back to sales. Then they lost the new car manager, so I became the new car manager, and I did that until I opened up here in Ann Arbor."

Bradley had not neglected his relationship with Bill Harvey. "All while I was working, I was looking at opportunities," he says, "and I was saying, 'Hey, Bill, I've got enough experience now. How about showing me some dealership opportunities?' Finally, he called me in June or July of 1973 and said, 'There's a store out in Ann Arbor that looks like a good opportunity. You need to go take a look at it,' so I came out and drove the area with a friend of mine that worked for the Chevrolet dealer over in Ypsilanti. Then the branch manager of Motors Holding and I sat down with Mr. Harry Klinger, the owner, and hammered out a buy-sell. Klinger-Warner was the name, but Harry Klinger was the owner."

Bradley remembers Klinger as tough but fair. "He knew what he wanted and he got what he wanted, but he didn't try to gouge me," he says. "He got what it was worth, but he didn't get more than what it was worth. He wasn't going to let me steal it, and I don't think we came in with that in mind. He was a real respectful gentleman. I have a lot of respect for him, too. He gave me an opportunity. He didn't have to. There were some other people that were also bargaining for this store, some big dealers in Detroit, and he stepped up and gave me the opportunity."

Now Bradley needed a bank to do the same. "We got turned down by all the local banks," he says, "so while we had bought a store, I didn't know if we would ultimately be able to get it off the ground because it didn't look like we could get financing."

Bob Jarvis, the aforementioned branch manager, told Bradley to keep working on his operating plan and "we'll work something out. He probably had a game plan," says Bradley, "but he just didn't share it with me. The only thing I know is, in a couple of weeks, he called me and said, 'Why don't you go up and sit down with the people from First of America? They seem to have some interest in doing business with us.' So I sat down with those people and they agreed to finance the deal, and really financing was no more than a mortgage on the land and building. They gave that and General Motors was providing the startup capital, and that was all we needed to make this thing go. We continue to do business with the people at First of America, primarily because they were the first to step up and go with us."

Jim Bradley Pontiac finally opened its doors on October 5, 1973. "It was kind of scary," says Bradley. "It's one thing to work in a store and manage a store, but it's another thing to come in and manage it and the buck stops with you, and it has to rise and fall on your efforts. Employees are coming at you from all different angles, asking questions, trying to get direction, and you're trying to demonstrate to them your knowledge of the business, and they're wanting answers today, and you're trying not to make a bad decision."

The store also sold GMC trucks, Saabs, and Open Road mobile homes, but the latter two were off the menu by 1979. Bradley soon learned he was more like Al Johnson than Rufus Dukes. "Rufus was a car guy," says Bradley, "and he could take a rough building and renovate it and turn it into a dealership and make it look pretty good. When I was just getting into the business, I couldn't have done that. I was a little bit in awe of someone who could. Al Johnson was more of an administrator; he could get things done through people."

Thirty days after opening, Bradley had an even scarier day than the first one.

"I got a telegram from the Teamsters that my sales staff wanted to unionize," he recalls. "That was a shocker. There were no stores in Washtenaw County with a unionized sales staff. I thought, 'I'm going to have to grow this business with one arm tied behind my back. I'm going to have to compete with everybody else, carrying a greater load than my competition.'"

Why Bradley? "They were targeting me because I was a minority and because I was the weak kid on the block," he says. "I was vulnerable, so they could get a toehold with me and then start on the other dealerships."

Why his sales force? "They were working for an Afro-American and they were scared," he says. "The Teamsters painted a picture that I was going to fire all of them and bring people out from Detroit. That was scary for me; I had never gone through any negotiations."

Not to mention negotiating with an organization of the Teamsters' reputation. But the initial demand—for commissions equal to 5 percent of the manufacturer's suggested retail price—was clearly untenable, in Bradley's view. "I'm saying, wow, how am I going to stay in business doing this?" he recalls, "but because of it being the Teamsters, you wonder where is this going to lead?'"

But he didn't have much wiggle room. "This was my entire investment," he says, "and I just got to the point that I could not let somebody take that away from me. I was going to fight as hard as I needed to fight to not let that happen. I looked upon them as not coming in to help but coming in to destroy, and I wasn't going to let them destroy it before I even got a chance to swing the bat. I just wasn't going to roll over and let them take advantage of us. That's how I was going to deal with this union situation."

By then, the situation was that the union had been certified by a 6-0 vote. "Nobody voted for the company," says Bradley. "I went home like a whipped puppy and I woke up the next day and got my head together and said, 'Okay, the line has been drawn in the sand, you know what you've got to do.' I had to work toward them getting decertified, to get the employees turned around, to get confidence in me, to get this store on the same level as the rest of my competition, and that was a non-union store."

First, he had to stay in business. "It took almost a year to negotiate a contract," he recalls, "and what I had to do was get that behind us. After people started working with me, I think they found out I'm no different from anybody else, a guy trying to stay in business and make money. And they found out that we still have to sell cars, still have to treat people right, still have to service cars. All of that fits together, whether we've got a union contract or not. The sales consultant has to work with management and management has to work with the sales consultant.

We began to work together as a team and I had to focus on building a team."

And that necessarily meant some personnel changes. "I knew the people who voted and I knew they weren't part of this team and I had to come up with a plan to get rid of them or encourage them to work for somebody else," Bradley says. "Everything I did was legitimate. Gradually, we looked around, and the people that I hired were people who were not pro-union. I found out the union didn't do everything right, either. They weren't fair. It's amazing."

He remembers the day a union official came to him and said he wanted to buy a car. "I said, 'No problem, go out there and buy it from one of your union brothers.' He said, 'I want to buy it at less commission.' I thought to myself, 'And these guys are paying you dues; all right, now I really understand how this game works.'"

By 1976, the staff had been rebuilt, and when Bradley asked for a recertification vote, the Teamsters "found out they didn't have the votes and just let it go," he says, "and we got the union decertified."

That wasn't the only punch Bradley had to roll with in the first years of his dealership. Another was called the energy crisis, which hit with full force not long after the Teamsters' telegram arrived.

"When we bought this dealership, big engines were prevalent," he says. "A 350 V-8 was the smallest engine that we sold, and suddenly people wanted fuel-efficient engines. General Motors did not even make a four-cylinder engine at that time. They had to come up with one real quick and the first ones to get a four-cylinder car were the Chevrolet stores. So I'm stuck with buying Mr. Klinger's previously owned demos and previously owned cars and having an inventory with an excessive amount of fuel-inefficient engines. That led into a recession. I'm just getting into business, I'm hit with this Teamster thing, then hit with the energy crisis."

The business lost $27,000 in December 1973, and $57,000 in its first six months. Bradley put a full-page ad in *The Ann Arbor News,* offering cars for a penny over dealer's invoice. "We had the invoices out in a book so the customers could see them," he says. "I sold one car. I thought I was going to reduce my inventory, and I didn't make enough to pay for the ad. You talk about a scared soul."

He had come to another crossroads. "It looked like we weren't going to be in business," he says, "but I just said to myself, now we've got to sell. We'll meet people one at a time and convince them this is a good deal. Everybody doesn't want to be in a four-cylinder, small car. We had to get our heads right, too. Sometimes you get jolted like that and you kind of think nobody's going to buy these cars, but they've got some pluses. It may not be the most fuel-efficient but it's got the ride, it's got the comfort. You give people all the information they need to make a decision and hopefully those other attributes will override that fuel inefficiency. And we found that we still could sell them until GM got their house in order and started building a more fuel-efficient car."

He also got some good advice from another mentor, although his first arrival at the dealership only seemed like more bad news. Says Bradley: "I got a call from the switchboard operator that Mr. Robert Young, the regional manager of Motors Holding Division of General Motors, is here at the switchboard and asking to meet with you.

"My heart started beating fast. I had heard from other dealers that when this guy comes in, it's for the keys to the store, so it's all over with. I'm thinking, 'Aw, man, I'm in this business for six months, I've been bombarded by all these things outside of my control, and I'm not able to get a fair shot at operating this store.'"

When Young came into his office, Bradley threw the keys on his desk. "Godammit," he said. "I don't think it's fair. I'm here working 14, 15 hours a day trying to turn this store around, trying to operate it, I get hit with the energy crisis, I get hit with the Teamsters, and the only damn thing you guys do is come here and want to take the store away."

"What are you talking about?" Young asked.

"You're here to take the store," said Bradley. "Your reputation is that all you do is put guys out."

"No, Jim," Young answered. "I was just in the neighborhood and came in to see the store. Take the keys back, and take me around and show it to me."

When they returned to Bradley's office, Young asked how much money the store would make that month.

"Don't you know we're in a recession?" said Bradley. "Nobody makes money."

"Don't say that; people are making money," Young said. "What's your forecast?"

"My forecast is I'm going to lose $7,000 this month."

"You can't lose $7,000; you don't have $7,000 to lose. You keep going that way, and you are going to be out of business. Can you take a $400 a month cut in pay?"

"Damn!"

"It's hypothetical. Let's use $300."

After a painful brainstorming session, it was agreed Bradley would take a $300 a month cut, the staff of porters would be reduced to one, each manager would be asked to take a 10 percent pay cut. "And get hold of your purchase order book," said Young, "and don't allow anyone to buy anything over $5 without your approval."

"I closed the door, sweating bullets," Bradley recalls. "I had just come out here and asked these managers to stay with me and now, after six months, I have to ask them to take a 10 percent cut in pay. If I go cutting these managers' pay, everybody's going to walk out."

His opening, and perhaps smartest, move was to apply the knife to himself. "The first thing I did was call my office manager in and have her cut my pay $300 a month," he says. "Then I went and laid off the porters. Then I started with the managers, one by one, calling them in and talking to them. And they all agreed to a 10 percent cut in pay. I think the key to that was that I had taken my cut first, and mine was about 25 percent. The next month, we made $5,000. So I had stopped the bleeding."

By 1975, the store was profitable, and it stayed that

way until the recession of 1979. After losing "some significant money" in 1980, "we had to really tighten our ship back down," Bradley says. "I cut my pay, but I didn't cut my managers' pay. If I lost somebody, I didn't replace him. Those people who were not contributing and productive, we found a way to part company. Gradually, through attrition, we got our costs back in order."

Another external circumstance—interest rates in the 18-20 percent range—was complicating the picture. "So I learned another lesson," says Bradley.

"People were just starting to get cellular phones, and one of them was a dealer friend of mine named Bob Barnett. He called me one day and said, 'How are you doing?' I said, 'I'm all right.' He said, 'It looked like you were out of business. I'm on your lot and you don't have any cars. How the hell are you gonna stay in business without any cars?'

"I said, 'I'm trying to keep my floor plan expense [the cost to maintain the new car inventory on hand] down.' He said, 'Shit, that's the first store I've ever seen that's going to try to sell from an empty shelf; how do you stay in business if you don't have anything to sell?'"

That perspective made sense to Bradley. "I went about putting cars on the lot and getting my management team pumped up to sell," he says. "We started working, and I learned that you cannot cost-cut your way into profitability."

He was also learning that the motor vehicle business is truly cyclical, and that long-term success entails anticipatory management. In 1979, he joined a "20-group," a concept of the National Automobile Dealers Association, where dealers in similar situations (but not, of course, in geographic competition with each other) assemble three times a year to share information.

"I didn't have a father who was a dealer," says Bradley. "I didn't grow up in the business, so I needed help to get up to speed and compete with other dealers in Washtenaw County."

By 1981, interest rates had helped push the store back

into the red, and he was getting tired of putting out fires that he hadn't started. Says Bradley: "I said to Clay Blake, a member of my group, 'I've been a dealer now almost 10 years, and I've worked hard at it. What am I doing wrong? Where am I missing the boat? How should we react in this slump?' Blake said, 'You're not doing a lot wrong,' and took me through a scenario about how cyclical the car business is."

Blake also explained what to do about it. "When you get into these slumps, what you should do is prepare for the next increase in business," he said. "You trim the fat out of your operations, and you spend some additional dollars on training your people and making sure they are fine-tuned and ready to take advantage of this market when it swings up. You've got to know there's going to be an uptick in the market. And whenever that comes, make sure you're in a position to take advantage of that opportunity.

"You don't want the market to start moving and progressing and after it starts moving and progressing, you run in and try to find a way to take advantage of it. That's not pro-active, just reactive. The more pro-active you become, the more successful you become."

In other words, as Bradley phrases it, "Preparation takes place at the bottom of the curve. A lot of young business people don't start reacting until the market is at its highest point. By the time they get their game plan in effect, the market has started to go down again. If you are prepared at the right point, when it goes up, you will maximize all your opportunities.

"It's a whole mind-set that has to happen, too," he adds. "I had to become a little bit more mature. You couldn't have told me, back when I first got in business, about spending money on training and investing in the future when you're in a recession and business is slow. Someone can say it to you and it makes sense, but only after you've gone through a cycle or two."

In 1984, Bradley added Cadillac to his product line of Pontiac and GMC Truck, then bought out General Motors

Holding the following year. "It took a lot of cash out of the business to pay them off," he says, "so I had to build our reserves back. But 1 also realized that we needed to update our physical plant, just to make sure. If you look at the people at the malls, they're always updating them and keeping them fresh. I felt we needed to do that to our plant."

That happened in 1990. "It was tough," he says. "The most difficult thing was you had to try to operate a business, not let the dust and the dirt affect the customers, get the project done in a timely fashion, and still try to make a buck. And we did it.

"One of the tremendous things that happened from that, and one of the lessons I learned from it, was the impact it had on employee morale," says Bradley. "They were proud that we were remodeling the store. You would hear them take the customers around and describe what was being done as though they were doing it. The attitude of our customers improved significantly, probably as a result of the attitude of the employees. They took some ownership, and that had a tremendous effect on our sales, which picked up 15-20 percent."

About the same time, there was another downturn in the economy, but Bradley and company were ready for it. "Because of our past experience, we were able to weather that," he says. "It went real smooth. Because we had our people so well trained, we never really experienced the recession."

The Bradley domain expanded dramatically in 1993, opening a Saturn dealership just a little bit west of the original store on Jackson Road and renaming itself the Bradley Automotive Group. Although the company was far from "the bottom of the curve," it was not so robust that the taking of the plunge was routine.

"I was a little bit reluctant to go into it initially because of the investment it was going to take, in the $2 million category," says Bradley. "We had just gotten the Pontiac store paid for and were starting to get some meat on our bones, when we went back into debt with the remodeling of the store. How much more debt did I want to get into? But I was fortunate that Richard (Skip) LeFauve, the president and chairman of Saturn, lives in our town. He's a real dynamic individual, an impressive man. Just listening to him at the helm of Saturn caused me to decide to make the initial investment and go through with it."

It was not all charm, however. "You had to have some confidence in the concept," says Bradley. "Every General Motors dealer had an opportunity to go after that Saturn franchise, if you believed in it. When I saw the money that General Motors put in it, trying to establish that brand, I felt that no one would spend billions of dollars to come up with a car and not really market it and get a return on that investment."

Bradley had another strong card: Juanita, his wife. "A lot of my success has to do with this lady I've been living with for 35 years," he says. "She did a good job of holding the home front together and giving me the freedom to dedicate myself to making this business a success."

She had retired from the Washtenaw Intermediate School District in 1988, but it wasn't long before she was itching to be busier. She was now about to make her mark on the business front, too.

"We needed somebody to look at our customer satisfaction index (CSI) and help us understand and relate to our customers a little bit better," he says. "Juanita came in and became director of customer satisfaction for the Pontiac store."

The CSI skyrocketed, and that was one of Saturn's benchmarks. "They were looking for dealers who had a high customer satisfaction index and a high employee satisfaction index," Bradley says. "Her efforts helped Saturn single us out as the one to take over the new Saturn store that was coming to town. Because of her closeness to our CSI and what Saturn is all about in terms of trying to relate to the customer, I felt she would be the best person to help us get that up and running. She was real enthused about it and has done wonders with that division of the Bradley Automotive Group."

Juanita Bradley is now the vice president and general manager of Saturn of Ann Arbor, which is in negotiations with Scio Township to double the size of its physical plant.

Between its two stores, the Bradley Automotive Group now has more than 100 employees. Thanks in large part to the popularity of sport utility vehicles, sales rose more than 30 percent from 1997 to 1998, and Bradley figures he's smart enough now not to take all the credit.

"When we bought the store originally, one of the strong things about it was the GMC truck franchise," he says. "I wanted to have trucks, because I didn't want to have a single product line store. I wanted the flexibility. But I'm not saying that I knew in 1973 that truck sales would reach these levels."

But if you've learned to how to cope with the unanticipated problems in your business, then surely it's okay to profit from unanticipated successes. Besides, there's unfinished business.

"We've had two individuals who have come through our organization and subsequently become owners of car dealerships," says Bradley. "Tom Moorehead owns a store in Decatur, Illinois, called Moorehead Buick-GMC, and Carl Barnett has three dealerships in Houston."

And the beat goes on. "We've got some young people on our staff that we want to work with them and see them continue to grow and develop. I don't see myself retiring...right away."

∞

"It wasn't humdrum."

Joe Butcko

Joe Butcko says he was attracted to the tool and die trade early in life due to "the fact that it wasn't humdrum."

As a boy in Ypsilanti, Michigan, he says, "I lived close to two foundries. I used to look in the windows and see those guys pushing that stuff, the same thing every day."

He knew that wasn't for him. He also knew, which is the unusual part, what he wanted to do for a living, thanks largely to the fact that the Hatch family lived less than a block away from his.

"My brother, Frank, and I were very close friends with the Hatch family and I believe their father, Raymond Hatch, was most responsible for my determination to become a tool and die maker," says Butcko. "He was the tool room foreman at King-Seeley in Ann Arbor. He used to bring home prints and work and show me what tool and die making was. How do you make a fork? A spoon? An automobile? A sink? The creativity in tool and die always intrigued me.

"As Mr. Hatch pointed out, you really don't do the same thing twice. Every job is a challenge—every die, every jig or fixture or special machine that you have to create if you want to end up with a product. You have to figure out how to make it first, the best and most economical way. My brother Ed always told me I was the luckiest of the bunch because I always knew what I wanted to do for a living, even when I was 12 or 13 years old."

That bunch included Joe and his three older brothers. There had been a fourth, but he died in an auto accident at the age of 19 when Joe was 7. Their mother, Mary, had died three years earlier. Martin, their father, never remarried and chose to raise the boys himself, an uncommon path for a man in his situation in 1929.

That, says Butcko, with a customary twinkle in his eye, is why he spent three years in the first grade. "My father was given the job as custodian at Saint John the Baptist Catholic Church in Ypsilanti," he says. "He would drop me off at the convent first thing in the morning, then go tend to his duties, and the nuns took care of me."

In fact, Martin Butcko was what we would now call over-qualified for his custodian job, and had already had a colorful career by the time he found himself a single parent.

"My father was a wood turner by trade," says Joe. "He and my mother came to this country in 1913 from Austria-Hungary (now Slovakia). My oldest brother was born over there. My father foresaw World War I coming and that motivated him to get out of there. I've been to Czechoslovakia several times, and my cousins there only regret that their parents didn't do the same thing."

Martin Butcko spoke several languages, including Hungarian, German, Slovak, English, Russian and Italian. He was in the Austro-Hungarian navy at the time of the Russo-Japanese War. "He was well steeped in history and geography," says Joe, "and he used to talk about them quite a bit to us boys."

His skill with a lathe was equally impressive. "During the Depression, my dad had made a wood lathe, pumped by foot, not by electricity, and he made cigarette holders and cigar holders out of juniper wood, and lamps and candle holders out of black walnut, and we used to sell 'em," says Butcko. "The custodian job didn't pay a lot of money. Wood turner—that was really an art."

In addition to history, geography, and the joys of the manual arts, Joe also learned to pull his own weight, even though that didn't amount to much in those days.

"My dad became a pretty good cook, and he was also very, very clean," says Butcko. "I think it's some of the Slovak heritage or makeup or whatever you want to call it. We were always mopping floors or washing windows or doing the laundry. I recall when it became my turn, we still didn't have hot water. I had to heat the water in a double boiler on a gas stove, then pour the water into the old wringer Maytag. From the ages of about 10 to 15, I washed and ironed more shirts and pants than most housewives during the same period. There was no such thing as wash and wear. You can see why I chose tool and die as a business, rather than the laundry. We also had a large garden. We nicknamed it Dad's Garden of Weedin'."

There was time for recreation, too, and Joe's was boxing. Fighters are matched by weight, so his physical stature was irrelevant. Since Mr. Hatch was a boxing fan and followed the local Golden Gloves program, it was another way to connect with him.

Besides, says Butcko, "It was necessary for me to learn boxing because I'm only five-foot-five, and I was going with the prettiest girl in school. Incidentally, I married her."

He and Mae Alice Davis were wed when they were both 17. "My dad used to say that he raised my brothers but Mae Alice raised me," says Butcko. By then, he had already been apprenticed at several area shops... and won a trophy from the Golden Gloves as the outstanding boxer of 1940 in Washtenaw and Jackson counties. There is no official record of the role that competing for Mae Alice's attentions played in his success.

"I got started in my trade when I was apprenticed in

1940, while I was in the 10th grade at Ypsilanti High," he says. "This was not only allowed but it was encouraged by the industrial arts department. This was before all the bleeding hearts got involved. It wasn't a sin to work when you were less than 18. I'd work in a plant all week, then pick up my schoolwork from my shop teacher, which consisted of history and English. Math come along with the territory.

"I started at a place called Hamilton Rifle, in Plymouth, for 40 cents an hour, 16 dollars a week. I paid a dollar a week for my ride, and I had to buy a pair of micrometers at another dollar a week. They made .22s, but basically they were also in defense work at that time. The owner of the plant, John Holban, was also a boxing fan; I think that's why he gave me the job. It was a great system, where you could work and learn a trade and still go to school. Along with the bleeding hearts, I think the unions were instrumental in stopping the apprenticeships by closing the Ford Trade School and similar facilities, like the one Studebaker had in South Bend, Indiana, etc."

After more than a year at Hamilton, he moved on to Hoover Ball and Bearing in Ann Arbor. That's where he was working on December 7, 1941, when the Japanese attack on Pearl Harbor plunged the United States into World War II.

Whatever else it was, the war was a boon for those who were (as yet, in Butcko's case) ineligible for military service. "There was a tremendous demand for skilled labor, even for someone like me with only a year's experience," Butcko recalls. "We moved from shop to shop, more for the experience than for the money."

He remembers a day in 1942, when he was working at Motor State Products in Ypsilanti, making components for howitzers. "I was running a lathe, and our one-eyed shop steward came up from behind me and hit the stop button on my lathe," he says. "It broke the tool bit and damn near ruined the shaft I was turning. He said we were on strike. I told him I knew how to turn off my own machine without doing damage and if he ever did that again, I would close his other eye. We never got along well after that."

At the time of his contretemps with the steward, all three of his brothers were in service. "So much for my bout with the American Federation of Labor and their concern for the war effort," he says. "I left Motor State during their patriotic strike and went to work for Preston Tucker, the same Preston Tucker that built the Tucker automobile shortly after World War II."

Tucker's building was a wooden barn on Grove Street, a block west of Michigan Avenue in Ypsilanti. It was, as Butcko recalls, about 100 feet long and 50 feet wide, and filled with "every type of toolroom equipment imaginable—lathes, mills, shapers, grinders, etc."

Not to mention the 100 or so employees, including tool makers, draftsmen, engineers and auto mechanics. "We were building marine engines, working two 12-hour shifts, seven days a week," says Butcko. "The shop was so crowded, the mice were hunchbacked. This condition went on for about four months while a new plant was being built in New Orleans. When the plant was about 75 percent complete, we all moved, machinery and people, lock, stock and barrel. But not the mice. The roaches were too big down there for the mice."

Tucker had merged his operations with the Higgins Shipyard and Boat Company, whose founder, Andrew Jackson Higgins, styled himself as "the Henry Ford of the South." Higgins' company manufactured landing craft, and Tucker's made the marine engine they required.

The employees traveled in style. Tucker's brother, Bill, owned a moving company in Ypsilanti, and the government reimbursed the company for their expenses. "Everyone, families included, traveled first class and stayed in first-class hotels," says Butcko. "Our average cost was between $200 and $400 per employee that moved down with his family."

There was, however, one conspicuous exception. "I call him a Bible thumper," says Butcko. "Nothing personal, but he turned in a bill of less than $10 because his family lived in Arkansas and he was going there anyhow. Therefore, the Lord told him he should only charge gas (at 15 cents a gallon) and oil from Arkansas. After several hours of discussion with him, the personnel director ended up firing the guy, and I think they ate the $10 bill for his expenses. Trying to explain his expenses vs. ours to the government would have been a helluva job. Some things never change."

He found his time in New Orleans illuminating on many levels. "Along with the diversity of my work as a die maker, there were the diversity, incidences, and lives of the people I worked with," he says. "One of them was a tool and die maker about 65 years old in 1943, Mr. Art Chevrolet. He was the founder of Chevrolet Motor Car Company. His tool box was next to mine at Tucker's in New Orleans, but he was in charge of all engine testing. He told me he received $3 million from General Motors for his car company, but then lost everything on airplanes in the crash of 1929."

But his tenure on the bayou was short. As Butcko says, "Air conditioning wasn't ready to change the South for another 20 years." His wife and baby son, also named Joe, couldn't take the heat and humidity. The family returned to Ypsilanti after only a few months, and the senior Joe went to work for Woods Manufacturing at Stadium and Liberty in Ann Arbor, which was then in the country.

His boss was Hodd Woods, "a character unto himself," says Butcko. "There were 15 or 20 tool makers. The shop was engaged in about 90 percent defense work, making jigs, fixtures and mostly gauges. The other 10 percent was the bulk of Hodd's sales and profit."

That would be the stainless steel clothespins. Hod had invented them while working midnights as a tool and die maker at King-Seeley in downtown Ann Arbor. Hospitals, most of which at the time didn't have clothes dryers but rather huge drying rooms, bought them by the millions. Plastic hadn't been invented yet, and unlike conventional wooden clothespins, they wouldn't snag silk or nylon.

"They also could be sterilized," says Butcko. "It's the

damnedest thing you've ever seen. As I understand the story, the clothespin needed to be manufactured by a stamping die that ran in a punch press. Hodd didn't have the money to buy a die but he did work midnights, and he knew how to build one. How the die got built, you must use your own imagination. As far as the punch press was concerned, the job needed a very small press, 35-ton. They didn't come much smaller than that. King-Seeley had a warehouse full of 'em. The story was that Hodd bought an old junker from them, fixed it up, and started manufacturing clothespins in his mother's garage. That press was still running clothespins in a new building when I went to work for him in late '43."

The business also spun off a true cottage industry in the town. "Although the press ran automatically with one operator, about 2,000 pins an hour, the company had an average of 20 women assembling the little tension springs into each clothespin, in their homes. There was a driver delivering and picking up stainless steel clothespins all around Ann Arbor, all day, every day."

One of his colleagues at Woods Manufacturing was Walter Hatch, one of the four Hatch brothers he had grown up with, the eventual founders of Hatch Stamping Company. "Walter and I were working at Woods when we received our salutation letters from Uncle Sam," Butcko recalls. "We were inducted the same day; he went into the Marines and I went into the Navy. Ironically, we met on Guam."

He also met two of his brothers while serving on an LST (landing ship, tank; or, as Butcko remembers it, "large, slow target") in the Pacific, as well as a lot of servicemen who couldn't find where they belonged.

"The most incomprehensible thing to me was the amount of soldiers and Marines and sailors, primarily sailors, wandering around the Pacific, trying to find out where their ship was, or their company was," he says. "Because radio communication was verboten, when someone was assigned to a ship, they were apparently left on their own to go find that damn thing. Every time we tied up, these guys would go walking from LST to LST to ask if we had seen a certain number. They were all numbered; I was on 862. I just couldn't get over that. I would venture a guess there are still some guys out there looking for their ship."

Butcko describes the war as "97 percent boredom interrupted by about 3 percent of sheer terror." For him, much of the latter came in the Pacific front's last great land battle, on the island of Okinawa. Gen. Simon B. Buckner, Jr., who had led the successful invasion of the Ryukyu Islands, was killed in action only about 100 yards from where Butcko landed the small boat he was piloting, a boat made by Higgins and Tucker.

After the war, Butcko worked in several tool and die shops. Then, in 1949, a series of events nurtured the seeds of entrepreneurship within him. Jack Starwas, his former boxing coach and himself a one-time state light heavyweight champion, came to him with an idea for making snap-on golf cleats for shoes. "He had located a small garage shop on Jarvis Street in Ypsilanti," says Butcko, "and he would pay the owner, John Smith, to allow us to try to develop these snap-ons."

As it turned out, "Jack and I could not develop a marketable snap-on—it's a long story—but John and I became very good friends," says Butcko. "John wanted me to be his partner in his little tool shop and I worked with him on several jobs he had, but I wasn't interested in going into partners with anyone. I was working full-time afternoons at United Stove, about a block from John's shop in Ypsilanti, and helping John during the day."

On one of those days, Smith was backing out of his garage to go to National Guard camp in Grayling for three weeks. "He asked if I would handle his shop and he would just take a commission on whatever I did for his customers, mostly die repair," Butcko recalls. "I believe that's when I got the bug to go into business for myself."

He began assembling equipment for what would become his first shop. "Whenever possible, I would buy an old piece of equipment and rework it in my dad's old garage on Forest Avenue," he says. "I bought an old lathe, a surface grinder, and a milling machine. The lathe was an old line-shaft type so I had to put a motor on it and I used an old Chevy stick shift transmission to change speeds, three forward and one reverse. One stamping plant owner wanted me to put my equipment in his shop and be in for myself, but a friend of mine, a CPA named Harold Gregg, advised me not to do that because I would be obligated to do his work ahead of any other customer. I'm very happy I followed his advice."

By 1952, he was ready to rock, and perhaps even roll. "I rented an empty garage, 16 foot by 20 foot, that was attached to Clow's Welding Shop at 830 North River Street," Butcko says. Thus was Crescive Die and Tool born.

"It did have a toilet, uncovered, and a sink," he says. "Mr. Clow, the landlord, and myself took an old outhouse and put it over the toilet, but we had to cut a four-inch slot in the door to be able to open it because of the sink. Clow's Welding Shop was a great advantage to me because he had several machines that I was able to use such as a very large lathe, a drill press and a shaper. But the biggest advantage was all of his welding equipment, and his great welding ability. When I first started, about 70 percent of my business was die repair, which required a lot of welding."

Butcko named his company after a former employer, but with a twist and a tweak. "I worked at a place called Crescent Tool and Die in Lincoln Park, and that was probably the most efficiently run shop I ever worked in," he says. "I wanted to be very close to it, partly so people might mistake us for them, and I think 'crescive' was the next word in the dictionary. I liked the meaning, 'growing from within,' and that's where I got the name. I also named it 'die and tool' instead of 'tool and die' for two reasons. One reason is our primary function is dies, and the other reason is it causes people to ask."

In its June 1985 issue, *Success* magazine chose "crescive" as its "boardroom buzzword of the month."

"They were 38 years late," Butcko chuckles.

Within a year of its founding, Crescive was employing three die makers and getting orders directly from the Ford plant in Ypsilanti. "I'm wondering what would happen if the present-day plant evaluation engineer or vendor evaluation engineer, the ones that require vendors to have certain equipment even though they have no idea what it's for or why it's required, could have seen my shop back then, and I was doing Ford work direct, sometimes without a purchase order until the job was complete. Some things do change."

Luckily for Butcko, his first large-scale customer had no such inspectors. "A big break came at the beginning my second year when I was told there was a large semi-skilled production job at Bridgeport Brass in Adrian," he says. "They were making airplane wing struts, and they had one of the largest presses in the world at that time. Coming down, it exerted 15,000 tons. They took an aluminum cast strut about five inches wide, three feet high and five foot long, heated it, and then hit it in a die in that press to make it very dense and the strongest aluminum possible, but they needed to stress-relieve it by milling a slot in a certain area. There were to be thousands of these struts and they were to be run for several years."

The brass at Bridgeport Brass asked Butcko two questions: Did he have a boring mill? And could he do the job?

"I answered yes on both counts," he says, even though the correct answer to the first question was no. "Frankly, the smallest boring mill made wouldn't have fit in my shop even if I removed all the equipment I had," he says. "But I knew I could do the job, and I didn't think it would require a boring mill. I cut the required slot on a $500 milling machine. After submitting a couple of samples that they had given me to bring back, I was awarded the job."

He was now about to deal with the challenge of rapid growth. In 10 days, he built a 16-by-20-foot addition to his shop. "That was all the land that was available," he says. He now had all of 640 square feet, but that wasn't nearly enough to solve his next problem.

"When I brought the samples from Adrian to my shop, they were a couple of loose pieces," he says. "What I hadn't planned on was they shipped the struts to me by semi in crates, about 15 pieces per crate and a semi full of crates. When the first shipment arrived by common carrier, I not only had no place to put them but no facility to unload them, so I got the AAA wrecker to come and unload the semi."

And the crates were left in the alley until Butcko went to see an old friend, Preston Tucker, who was back in town after his ill-starred automaking venture in Chicago.

"Tucker owned a large brick building that was in front of the big wooden barn we had all worked in, and he was renting it out for storage," says Butcko. "Fork lifts were included, and thereafter I had the parts delivered to the warehouse. We would also ship from there. I received several letters of commendation from Bridgeport Brass for the fine job we were doing, and I was constantly concerned that the buyer might come down and see my setup. I think we both would have died...me first."

Butcko cites two motives for going into business for himself. One of them is droll: "An old Eskimo sled driver once told me that unless you're the lead dog, the view never changes."

The other is quite serious. "A lot of the shops I worked for lacked perseverance and stamina," he says. "They'd get a few thousand bucks, and the first damn thing they'd do is go out and buy a boat and put it on the Detroit River. But I went 75,000 miles at six knots—I checked the log— and I didn't need any boats. As soon as they got a few bucks, they thought they had to spend it. When I got a few bucks, I got more equipment or a building."

Across the street from Tucker's brick building was the Tucker Machine Tool building, which Tucker told Butcko he was vacating. "He said I was welcome to pick out as much of the equipment as I wanted, and pay him what I thought it was worth whenever I got the money," says Butcko. "Unfortunately, all the equipment he had was production equipment and was of no use to me."

But the two did spend some time together in the warehouse office. "He had terminal cancer and told me he had been going to South America for some treatments that were not allowed here in the states," Butcko says. "Close to Christmas, I went to his house and gave him a couple of bottles of White Horse scotch—that's what he always drank in New Orleans—for doing me a favor. He was pale, weak, sentimental and somewhat bitter. He said of all the SOBs he had given jobs to and paid them money they weren't worth, they didn't even send him a Christmas card, and I was thanking him for a favor he didn't remember."

About the time Butcko's company was busy filling orders for Bridgeport Brass, his old pal, John Smith, went into the building business. "He knew I had a couple of industrial lots on Ann Street in Ypsi and asked me why I didn't build," Butcko recalls. "I told him I didn't have the money for a building. He said he did, so I sketched up a building that was 2,400 square feet, 40 by 60 and 16 feet high. Being in the city, it required an architect, so John went to an architect with my sketch, gave him $100, and said he would pick up the plans the next day. On my way home, I had to pass the lots, and John had the necessary trees down and a bulldozer starting to move dirt. That was the way he did things."

Two months later, the building was finished, and Smith and Butcko asked the former's attorney, Robert Fink, to draw up the land contract whereby Smith would sell it to Butcko.

"During some of the whereases, either John or I pointed out that those building conditions were not necessary because the building was done and I had moved in," Butcko remembers. "Fink, in disbelief, said to John, 'You mean you built a building on Joe's land and you had nothing signed? He could tell you to just shove off.' And John said, 'Fink, you don't understand. Joe and I shook hands.'"

The new plant was practically palatial by Butcko's former standards. "I finally had a decent-sized drawing board," he says. "Just as important, maybe more so, Mae had her own office."

Prior to that, Mae had done all her work on the kitchen table. "As we grew, she spent as much time or more on the books as I did designing and selling and working in the shop," Butcko says. "Her tasks included insurance, accounts payable, receivables, payroll...I believe we had at least 15 or 20 employees before Mae had any help with the books. She also would accompany me, regardless of the time, whether I was delivering dies to Grand Rapids or heat treat to Detroit at 2 a.m. Sometimes she would drive; sometimes she would just keep me awake."

Butcko had one of his most memorable adventures shortly after the company moved. "I went up to Owosso to solicit some die business," he says. "When I submitted my equipment list to the buyer, he said I had enough tool room equipment, but not enough tryout presses. I told him I was half-owner of a stamping plant in Ann Arbor and we had several presses available.

"Then I told my friend Bob Diebold, who was the sole owner of the plant, Jebco Manufacturing on Gleaner Hall Road, of my conversation with the buyer in Owosso. Bob said okay. Unexpectedly, the buyer sent a tool follow-up man down to check our facilities. After showing him Crescive in Ypsilanti, he asked to see my other plant in Ann Arbor. I suggested that, inasmuch as it was in the general direction of Owosso, he follow me in his car. After about 15 miles of wandering around dirt roads, I had to stop and tell him I couldn't find the damn place. He was a good-natured guy, and was laughing hysterically. And Crescive became their largest supplier."

They had, as Butcko puts it, "twenty-three great years in Ypsilanti," during which the shop expanded from 2,400 square feet to 20,000 square feet. That physical growth came to a halt in 1960. "Eastern Michigan University was expanding very rapidly also and had acquired every inch of land around me," he says. "However, I had an option on one half-acre site to the south of me. Eastern offered their limit of $2 per square foot and I had to better their offer. I did, but that ended my expansion in the city of Ypsilanti."

During those years, 1952 to 1975, he served on the board, and as president, of the Ypsilanti Area Chamber of Commerce, as well as on the Ypsilanti City Council, including a stint as mayor pro tem.

"I will always remember an incident that happened while on the Chamber board," he says. "The vice president was Vanzetti Hamilton. He and I were in Ypsi High together, and now he was an attorney. We went to a chamber conference in Toledo, and as the afternoon wore on, the speeches became more boring. I whispered to Van, 'Let's sneak out of here and no one will ever notice.' He said, 'They won't notice you, but they sure as hell will notice me.' There were three or four hundred men there, and he was the only black."

His political "career" lasted from 1970 to 1972. "I missed only one session in two years," he says, "and I figured that it cost me about $18,000 a year, less the $350 I received for being on council. Two years was enough. The one bit of advice I have for all elected city officials would be to start each session with the prayer that says, 'God grant me the courage to change what should be changed, the serenity to accept what cannot be changed, and the wisdom to know the difference.' We spent so many hours trying to make city ordinances against what the Supreme Court had already said was legal."

His long run in Ypsilanti ended for one simple reason: His company had run out of room, due in large part to a burgeoning manufacturing business.

"We were almost forced into production," he says. "One of our customers was Motor State Products, the original mechanical convertible top manufacturer, where you didn't have to get out and have someone on each side to manually push the top up or pull it down. I was building dies for the metal portion, which are all link arms to actuate the convertible top. When the Mustang came out, Motor State was up to their capacity in convertible tops for Chrysler. The production projection for the Mustang was 1,000 a month, so they asked me, inasmuch as I had built the dies, if I would run the dies of that thousand a month. I didn't have any presses, but they had some old presses that they sold to me relatively cheap, so they could get out of the obligation of making that paltry 1,000 a month."

But the Mustang caught fire; the projections were off by a factor of, oh, 30 or so. Soon, says Butcko, "It became 1,000 a day, and I was in the production business thereafter."

Luckily, his older son, Joe D. (dad is Joe A.), who had worked in the shop since the eighth grade, had just graduated from Ferris State with an engineering degree. "He ran it 24 hours a day, seven days a week," says his father. At the time of the move to Saline, Joe D. Butcko became president of Crescive. Jim, five years younger than Joe D., also graduated from Ferris, in business administration, and is now CFO of the company.

"We were young with our boys," says Butcko. "We kind of grew up with them. Joe was 21 when he got married, 22 when they had their first son, Joe III, who has worked in the shop since he was in high school—in all phases, from production to maintenance to toolroom—and is now in sales. He also had two other children, Jacqueline and Tim, who both worked at the plant during their high school years. Jackie is now a teacher and Tim has elected to go back to Eastern Michigan. Jim was married 15 years before he had a family, then he had two daughters, the youngest is now 13. Our grandson also has two children, giving us the great-grandchildren. We've always had youngsters around; we've been very fortunate."

In 1975, Butcko bought a 50-acre farm within the city limits of Saline from Bob Merchant, and began developing the Saline Industrial Park. "The city had a very astute mayor named George Anderson," says Butcko, "and he and the city council wanted to assist in the development of the industrial park. The city floated a municipal bond for me for some $225,000. My civil engineer, Ken West, laid out the park, drew up all the plans for the sewer, water, curb, gutter, etc., presented the plans to the city, and the city sublet all the work of the above-mentioned utilities and submitted the bill to me, to be paid back to the city in 10 annual installments at 6 percent interest. I was in my new plant within six months after buying the land, and I paid the city back in less than four years."

By that time, in addition to two Crescive plants, the park housed the book printers McNaughton & Gunn, Inc.; two R&B Machine Tool Company plants...and a bowling center.

"When I was negotiating with city hall in Saline, the mayor mentioned that what they really needed was a bowling center," Butcko recalls. "I told him that if he would get me a liquor license, I would get him a bowling alley. That wasn't the biggest mistake in my life, but it was damn close. I did build a bowling alley; it's probably the nicest in the state. But I have never spent a moment managing it, I never got involved, and we also never made the first dime."

Late in 1998, "We sold it to one of the partners for a dollar to get us out of it," he says. "At the time we built it, a liquor license was worth $50-60,000. Today, people are trying to sell them or give them away because of the liability."

In addition to Joe D.'s elevation to the presidency, the move to Saline, and a backwoods adventure, the year 1975 was memorable for Joe A.'s debut in the banking field.

"There was a small bank, called Citizens Bank, here in Saline, and they asked me to be on their board of directors," says the latter. "At my very first board meeting, one of the requests was for a loan of a few hundred dollars, and the farmer wanted to put up two cows as collateral. That was true banking, to be able to lend him that money, because those cows meant a lot to that farmer, and we did give him the money."

Despite his nascent expertise in the field, Butcko felt that Crescive's rapid expansion required "a wiser head than mine in the financial end. Even though I was on a bank board, I soon found out that I was a neophyte in high finance."

The combined Saline facility grew from 25,000 square feet to 150,000. The company bought a plant in Milan with more than 120,000 square feet. Crescive's payroll grew to more than 500.

"Now enters my closest friend and associate in other adventures, Bill Bryan," says Butcko. Bryan was a former neighbor in Ypsilanti and a World War II veteran who had survived three years as a Japanese prisoner of war. He had retired from the Army as a lieutenant colonel after 27 years of service and became a professor of banking and finance at Eastern Michigan.

Bryan was captured on May 10, 1942, shortly after the infamous Bataan death march, and survived the sinking of two of the equally infamous Japanese death ships by swimming out of the hold when the ships broke apart. In both cases, the ships were hit by American pilots who didn't know that POWs were locked in below decks. When the second ship went down, only 19 of the 250 men in his hold survived. He was liberated by the Russians in 1945; by then, all but 200 of the 2,400 prisoners he had boarded the ships with were dead.

"Bill was most responsible for our acquiring the monies we needed for our various expansions," says Butcko. "And, on a personal basis, he was also able to get the financing necessary for some of our side ventures, such as buying land and selling it. He and I also bought and sold airplanes together."

That started sometime in the '60s. "He said, 'When we sell this farm, let's buy an airplane,' so we bought an airplane. We had several together. We flew airplanes from Halifax to the Caribbean. I still have a company plane and he's still the company pilot, although I can't fly anymore because I had a stroke."

The most conspicuous change he's seen in his customers' corporate cultures is that "it's much more bureaucratized," he says. "It's damn near impossible to find someone in our business—I'm not going to isolate it—who can make a decision and won't deny making it if something goes wrong."

Today, Butcko describes himself as "semi-retired. I still stay involved in the financial end."

His other major activity, he says, is "telling my life story and finding somebody dumb enough to listen."

"Never take yourself seriously; take what you do seriously."

Brian Campbell

Brian Campbell is nothing if not playful. He will, for example, show up for an interview wearing the fright wig that was also part of his costume for his company's annual "Founder's Day" celebration, he being the founder, of course. And he says he used to "encourage all our people to take vacations on Saturday and Sunday. Initially, it was also national and religious holidays, until I saw some of the damnedest holidays. I had to put the kibosh on National Tire Repair Day."

His company was TriMas Corporation, originally dubbed Campbell Industries—"a catchy name, I thought"—when he founded it in 1986, but two years later, after acquiring nine divisions from Masco Corporation, Campbell's former employer and a heavy investor in Campbell Industries, the name was changed.

"I'd lived my whole life with the goal of having a company named after me," he says. "After that name change, I seriously considered petitioning the circuit court here to change my name to Brian TriMas, so I could strut around town and have people say that's Brian TriMas of TriMas Corp., but somebody talked me out of it."

In case it isn't clear already, Campbell's theory is "You've gotta have fun. To spend 12 or 13 hours a day on your job, you damn well better enjoy it. Never take yourself seriously; take what you do seriously."

Campbell and his colleagues took what they did so seriously, and did it so well, that TriMas set earnings records in every year of its existence, from the time it took the name and went public on February 14, 1989, until MascoTech, Inc., another former chunk of Masco Corp., bought the 63 percent of TriMas stock that it didn't already own on January 22, 1998.

He was more than a little mischievous in his high school days, too. One of his pranks led to an unforgettable lesson from his electrician father, Andrew, whom Campbell calls "a great man. I got so much strength from him." It took an unexpected form one January day in 1958, which Campbell thought would be his last year at Lyons Township High School in LaGrange, Illinois, about 15 miles southwest of Chicago's Loop.

"I was a senior twice," he says. "It was easy, in retrospect. I started out strong my freshman year, then decided I was going to have some fun. When I was a senior, I said it's my last year here—little did I know it wasn't—so I did various things."

He got away with many, if not most, of them, before tempting fate once too often. "One day, near the end of English class," he says, "it struck me that if I just stopped at the front of the room on my way out and chatted with Miss Wallace, the teacher, and put my notebook and my books down on top of her grade book, which was so conspicuously on display there, that I could gently scoop up her grade book and go on to my next class. And along the way I disposed of it in one of the garbage cans.

"About two weeks later, another grade book appeared on her desk, and I thought it would be nice to do this shtick again. And I did it. This time I was foolish enough not to get rid of the evidence; I stuck it in my notebook and then proceeded on to trigonometry. About 10 minutes later, a picture of authority appears in the window of the door to the classroom, and it is Carl Workow, the dean of boys, who was familiar with me from other encounters. He caught my eye and pointed, thumbed, and I'm there with a 'who, me?' look. I knew this could be a tenuous situation. I had most of my stuff underneath my chair, so I got up, bent down, got the rest of my stuff and slipped the notebook to the guy behind me, who was the star quarterback of the football team. I can't think of his first name, his last name was Myers. He was, you know, Joe Quarterback, and I said, 'Get rid of this for me, will ya?' and he said, 'Oh, okay.'

"So Carl Workow and I then walked briskly to the dean of boys' office, where he interrogated me. He said, 'All right, what did you do with it?' I said, 'Do with what?' 'Miss Wallace's grade book.' 'Grade book?' 'I've had the janitors check every wastebasket between her classroom and Mr. Montgomery's classroom.' 'You won't find anything, as far as I know.' I did a Bill Clinton. I was trying to Clintonize Carl Workow."

Campbell was on the brink of succeeding when the class bell rang. "Into Carl Workow's office walks Mr. Quarterback," says Campbell. "He has tears in his eyes. 'Oh, Mr. Workow, Brian gave me this to get rid of. I don't want to get in trouble.' Now what do you do in a situation like that? Do you turn to the quarterback and ask who are you? Do you say to the dean, oh, is that the grade book you were quizzing me about? There's not much you can say."

Workow phoned Campbell's dad, who was at work in the Loop. He took the train out to LaGrange for a conference. "Carl Workow was suggesting that I perhaps take a sabbatical," Campbell recalls. "Unfortunately for me, all of this happened before the semester ended, which meant no credit, and I remember the ride home with my father."

Campbell's father, Andrew, too, didn't have much to say. It was, in fact, "like a deafening silence," says Campbell. "We walked into the house, got to the kitchen, and my peripheral vision spotted his left hand coming quickly at me. It alighted upon my neck. Direct vision then spotted his right clenched fist traveling at a high rate of speed toward my face. In a nanosecond, I determined I was in deep shit. I was not mistaken."

Andrew Campbell had spent a hardscrabble youth in the coal country of Pennsylvania. When he was 10, his father was killed in a mining accident. "The death benefit was they delivered the body home in a sheet and put it in the living room," says Brian Campbell. "And then promptly the next day, the manager of the company store showed up and asked my grandmother how she intended to settle up her account."

So Andrew and two of his brothers quit school, never to return, and went to work underground. At 15, he got into a scuffle with a foreman, decked him, and fled the company cops by hopping a freight for Cleveland, eventually making his way to Chicago and learning to be an electrician. It was no surprise that years later he always stressed the importance of education to his two sons. "Get all the education you can," he would say, "because they can take everything else away from you in life but they can never take away your education or your pride." He was disappointed, and angry.

"He pummeled me," says Campbell, "and as I crumpled to the floor, he said, 'You've got two choices. You get a job and go back to school, or I'm taking you down tomorrow morning to the Army recruiter.' I said, 'I think I'll get a job.' He said, 'I told you about education; you're going to screw it up big-time.' So I got a job in the Loop running an elevator, a job that did have its ups and downs."

He went back to school in September, had a good senior year (practice makes perfect) and finally graduated in June 1959. "After that, my father said, 'If you want any more education, you pay for it yourself,'" he recalls, "so I enrolled at the University of Illinois, which was then the Navy Pier campus, and I got a job at the Burlington Railroad, which was great because you got a free employee pass, so I could schlep out to LaGrange on the last train at night, which made every single stop."

His somewhat deviant ways notwithstanding, he had already settled on business as his career, and finance as his area of expertise because "it's a common thread that runs through just about every area of business. It always gets down to a finance issue." He transferred to DePaul University in the Loop, to finish his undergraduate degree therein, then attacked the job market. "It finally dawned on me that my father was right," he says. "Damn, education is important."

His first job out of college was as an analyst researching companies for a brokerage firm in the Loop, "the late, great Walston & Co., Inc.," he says. "I spent about two years doing that, then went to work for another investment banking firm, the late, great Glore Forgan, Inc."

He spent eight years with Glore Forgan; more precisely, he spent eight years under the influence and aegis of Kingman Douglass Jr., the man who ran the firm's Chicago office. "He was a real blueblood," says Campbell. "He was Lake Forest, he was Yale, he had movie star looks and a lineage that went back to the founding of Dun and Bradstreet in the 1830s or whenever. Dun and Bradstreet used to be called Dun, Douglass and Company. He was very patrician, real smart and a nice guy, and he gave me a big break.

"He also allowed me all the freedom to fail. I owe the guy a lot and still talk to him occasionally. He had a real big influence on my life. He just gave me all the freedom and encouragement that a real young person needs."

He also gave him a private name for his alma mater. "About a year and a half after I'm on the payroll, he walks into my office one morning with this puzzled look on his face," Campbell recalls. "He says, 'Brian, what college did you graduate from?' and I said, 'DePaul,' and he looks at me and says, 'DePauw?' And I said, 'No, DePaul.' He looks quizzical. 'DePauw University, Greencastle, Indiana?' I said, 'No, DePaul University, 25 East Jackson Boulevard.' And he looks at me and says, 'DePaul? Oh,' and turns around and walks out. Since then, I forever have referred to my alma mater as 'DePaul-Oh.'"

While at Glore Forgan, he added an MBA from Northwestern University and a master's in taxation from "DePaul-Oh" to his degree portfolio. "Having a full-time job with travel and going to night school is a great character builder," says Campbell. His character was already under construction from two years of evening law school at DePaul. "Four nights a week," he recalls. "There were no classes on Wednesday night, but they encouraged you to be in the library. I struggled with that and a travel schedule and I just said, I can't do it, and do I really want to be a lawyer that much, for two years more of that. So I dropped that. I approached the MBA program at Northwestern initially as a great credential to have, and nothing more than that. As I got into it, though, I was impressed with some of the other students. They were all working, all experienced, and we traded a lot of war stories and so forth. The learning experience from associating with my fellow students was equal to the learning experience from the classroom."

In the spring of 1973, a broker at Glore Forgan's Detroit office connected Campbell with Masco, which was looking for "an acquisition guy," he says. Seven months of talks produced an agreement on the day after Thanksgiving. He would join Masco as vice president of business development in January 1974.

"The same day that I started at Masco, the firm I left announced they were liquidating," Campbell recalls. "Timing again."

He left Chicago at 4:30 that Monday morning. "It was one of these real crisp, cold nights, but clear as a bell," he says. "I was heading south on the TriState Tollway and I looked over my left shoulder and I saw the lighted skyline of Chicago. And my heart sort of went, ah, jeez, you're going to Detroit. And, of course, I get off I-94 in Taylor and get on Van Born Road and I look down the road and see the utility poles on either side, the party store, the collision shop, the dinky hardware store, and I'm saying, 'Campbell, is this the right decision?'

"Well, as it turns out, it was a great decision." An important factor was finding a place to live that was decidedly unlike Van Born Road. After failing to be seduced by the charms of fancier suburbs, "the land of four- and five-car garages," Campbell found Ann Arbor.

"I said, 'This ambience reminds me of where I was living in Chicago. You know, this could be an interesting town. There's a lot of stuff going on, all kinds of people.' And it dawned on me that you could be as visible or as invisible as you might want to be in Ann Arbor. And I said, 'This is it,' so that's how I got to Ann Arbor. Which is a great town. It is a dynamite town. I still love Chicago, but this is home. It's the old story—you can never go home again; home is where you are."

In addition to acquisitions, "I subsequently picked up some operating responsibilities," he says. "One of the reasons I wanted operations experience was because, in the back of my mind, I said I'm broadening my horizons."

He improved his chances during his 12 years at Masco, which he describes as "a series of small successes; nothing like hitting the power ball, just a series of small successes and a series of small disappointments."

To a certain extent, it was in the nature of the job. "I've always maintained that in a large organization, the most entrepreneurially oriented person is the person that does acquisitions," says Campbell. "You've gotta go out and start something. You don't just sit there and process. It doesn't come from the right side of your desk and move across to the left. You've got to start something, you've got to go out and visit, you've got to have a little fire in your belly and want to do something. It's a very creative kind of activity, in my opinion, and I think it attracts a lot of creative people who have some smarts and are not happy with the status quo."

By the mid-1980s, a status quo making Campbell particularly unhappy was the one called "working for somebody else." "The old entrepreneurial juices started flowing," he says, "and I said I think I'm going to do it myself."

Not literally, of course. That would have contradicted

what he calls "the most important thing" to come out of his tenure at Masco. "I came to appreciate the value of people," he says. "You can't do a thing without people. No matter what you think of yourself and how great you are, try doing it alone."

But he wanted to do it with smaller crowds than Masco did. "The reason I left there was that I wanted to be in a small company environment, at least from a people standpoint," he says. "I dislike bureaucracy. I dislike crowded employee parking lots. I like to stay in touch with what's going on, and the old sticking-to-the-nuts-and-bolts approach to doing business."

He also felt pretty confident that he had learned a thing or three about acquisitions. "You have to have a strategy," he says. "You can't buy just anything. You look for good companies, well run—which means grrrreat people—that have great margins and great cash flow and very good growth. But you have to fit them into a strategy. Where do you want to go? Do you buy your first company and build other companies around it, the buy-and-build strategy, or do you just buy a bunch of disconnected companies?

"Our companies all have something in common. You don't want to get too far afield on your acquisition trips. I'm a manufacturing guy, an industrial products guy. I'm not going to buy an internet company. Number one, I don't understand the internet like somebody that's been in it for 10 years does, and I don't have time to get up to speed. Second, and even more important, all of their assets walk out the door at five o'clock. And if somebody offers them a thousand dollars a month more, they won't come back in the morning. Human capital is very important, but I don't like a business that is 95 percent dependent on human capital alone. I like an installed base of physical assets that are doing something proprietary. A factory floor cannot walk out every night."

In 1986, there weren't too many internet companies to invest in, but the principles were nonetheless valid. "The idea behind Campbell Industries was to get some financing and then go out and start buying manufacturing companies and create a diversified industrial company," he says.

Because the offering documents for the new company said that "on July 1, 1986, Campbell resigned from Masco Corp.," that was the date when he "dutifully went in and talked to the chairman of Masco and informed him that I was going to be history," he says.

But he made a discovery. "It seems nobody leaves Masco voluntarily," Campbell says. "The chairman didn't quite know what to make of it. He said, 'Don't do anything until we talk some more.' So a week or 10 days later, he came back and said, 'Why don't we put the money into Campbell Industries that you were going to go out and raise?' So they did. Short-cut the whole process."

Thus, Campbell Industries, Inc., was born on May 30, 1986. Why such apparent largess from a company he was leaving? "I don't want this to sound egomaniacal," says Campbell, "but they love to make money, and their investment in the original Campbell Industries and subsequently TriMas paid off big-time for them."

So Campbell Industries was off and running. Its first acquisition, at the end of December 1986, was a company in Cleveland called Lake Erie Screw Corp. "Not a bordello," says Campbell, "but a fastener manufacturer. Great company, great people." The Specialty Fasteners segment of TriMas, with Lake Erie as its flagship company, eventually represented almost a quarter of the company's sales.

Two years after its birth, Campbell Industries acquired nine divisions from what was then known as Masco Industries, Inc., which is where Masco Corp. had put all of its industrial operations in order to "keep Masco Corp. pristine as a building products company," says Campbell. "We paid for that acquisition by issuing common stock, preferred stock, and some high-yield bonds, and then changed the name of Campbell Industries, regrettably, to TriMas Corp."

He's kidding, of course. What else is new? But the real deal is that TriMas eventually comprised 16 companies in four segments: towing systems, specialty fasteners, specialty container products, and what was called "corporate companies," a group of businesses in related fields. Its earnings grew more than 15 percent annually for the final five years of its life, and it quickly, in the words of one analyst, "transformed a highly leveraged balance sheet into an excellent one with exceptional cash generation."

It was also too ripe a fruit to hang on the tree for long; thus the acquisition by MascoTech. At the time of the transaction, "We had $670 million in sales, big profit margins, and 10 years of record performance," says Campbell. "That deal, thank goodness, was a cash deal rather than a stock deal. After it closed, I became one of two presidents and co-chief operating officers of MascoTech. They didn't want to offend me, and they didn't want to offend the MascoTech chief."

Yeah, well. "The minute that deal surfaced, in late summer of 1997, I said to myself, 'I'm out of here,'" Campbell says. "That was just simply the old feeling that I'd come too far and I ain't co-anything. This is not an unusual phenomenon in American industry. The whole history of stuff is co-this and co-that, and it never works."

There was one major piece of unfinished business, however. "I was determined to do everything I could to protect the TriMas people who were in this office," says Campbell. The company had been based in Ann Arbor since its inception.

"We had a wonderful group of people, absolutely wonderful, like family," he says, "and we really cranked it out, 10 record years in a row. I insisted on getting employment agreements for them and, over the objection of the buyer, we got them. On May 27, 1998, a Wednesday, they all moved out of here over to the MascoTech office in Taylor. I had lunch the next day with the chairman—I had set this up a couple of weeks before—and informed him that I was going to become history."

His plan, as he told the chairman, was to go into private equity, IPOs and the like. "I said I would stick around for a reasonable period of time for whatever transition work was required," he says, "and also to allow them time to do whatever cosmetics were necessary to explain my departure to 'the street.' Well, it turned into June, it turned into July, and they were dragging their feet."

And that turned into a break. In early August, Campbell attended a board meeting of Kaydon Corp., of which he had been a director since 1995, in Clearwater, Florida. Kaydon was wrapping up its search for a new president and CEO, having reached a parting of the ways with the incumbent in June.

"The chairman was giving us a review of the candidates who had been presented," says Campbell, "and the bugger then goes into this thing of 'I don't like any of them, but I know Mr. X. How about Mr. X? He's been the CEO of a public company, knows acquisitions, knows operations, has good relations with Wall Street.' It's late morning and I'm sitting there with a 1:10 flight and saying to myself, 'Judas priest, just tell us who it is.' Then he turns to me and says, 'Brian, would you be interested?'

"I had never thought about this. It's the only company I would switch gears for, from the private equity route I was intending to go. So I resigned from MascoTech on September 22, was elected president and CEO of Kaydon on the 23rd, and the announcement went out on the 24th. And I'm trucking along."

And then there was the office space, the frosting on the cake. Campbell was still occupying the suite vacated by TriMas. "Had I gone the private equity route, I'd probably be down the hall in an office with my number-one assistant," he says. "But MascoTech dragged this thing out through the summer, Kaydon came along, and it was going to move its office somewhere north, out of Florida, anyway. I said, 'I just happen to know of some great vacant office space with furniture and a phone number and a fax number.' So I haven't left. It worked out just fine."

By the end of May 1999, Campbell had to give up the splendid isolation of having 11,000 square feet of office all to himself and his assistant. Which was fine with him.

"Kaydon was originally headquartered in Muskegon, Michigan, where it was founded, and we still have a good-sized plant there," he says. "In 1990, a decision was made to move somewhere warm, so Clearwater was chosen. But the company belongs here, headquartered in the North. Most of our facilities are above the Mason-Dixon line, the investment and financial community is in the North and East Coast, and most of our customers are here."

Campbell is generous in crediting luck and other people for the success of his ventures, and diffident about his own role. "I'm often amazed how all these so-called hotshots, these guys that really hit it big, believe their own bullshit that goes out in press releases," he says. "You never hear 'em say, 'Damn, I was lucky in life, I had some great breaks.' It goes to their head, obviously. The secret of success is being just smart enough to know when an opportunity is looking at you in the face. You don't have to be an Einstein or a rocket scientist, but you have to be smart enough to recognize an opportunity and, obviously, act on it.

"Never let your ego run away with you, no matter where you are in the socio-economic scale. Does he pump his own gas? Does he schlep out his trash on Wednesday morning? Just little tests. Are they basically human? And no matter where they came from, have they ever forgotten it? People move up and tend to forget their roots. All of a sudden, they believe everything they've done in life is only because of their genius, and luck or good timing had nothing to do with it. Go down to the homeless shelter and ask the people there what happened, and I bet they'll tell you it's bad luck. But how many successful people have said to you, 'I had a lot of lucky breaks, the timing was good, and I was just smart enough to see my opportunities?'"

The other big piece is the recruitment and cultivation of human capital, and that entails more than merely repeating the mantra. "The secret is hiring real smart people; you have to be just smart enough to understand that," he says. "It's based on the assumption that I'm the dumbest sonofabitch in the world, so feed me information. And you've got to treat 'em right. Sometimes it's tough love: You beat 'em up a little bit when they screw up, then hug 'em and tell 'em you love 'em. The most important thing is giving them the freedom to make mistakes, the freedom to grow. You don't learn from your successes, you learn from your mistakes. If you don't trip, it means you're not moving forward."

Once he's got these smart people on board, Campbell says, he tells them, "I'm going to give you enough rope; you can either hang yourself with it or build a rope ladder into the vault. You're here because you have certain competencies and skill levels and nobody is going to tell you how to do your job. If we have to tell you how to do your job, we've hired the wrong person, or we've kept the wrong person for too long. We want to know what's going on, we want you to have a sense of empowerment, and we don't want any surprises. If you make a mistake, tell us about it, and tell us about it when it's a small one, not when it's a real big one."

"Learn from your mistakes and go on—people respond very well to that. People who have controlling personalities want to micromanage. They can't understand how you would let people make those kind of decisions. 'You're actually letting adult people make a lot of these decisions? How radical.' You have to give people challenges and you have to provide an exciting environment, and you have to be with an organization that's growing. It's like a tree; if it isn't growing, it's dead."

Change is implicit in growth, and Campbell applies the same principles to his philosophy of management. "You don't want the five top guys to all be 60-65," he says. "You want them spread out to the early 40s or late 30s, and you always want to have the occasional newcomer entering the inner circle because he brings new viewpoints, a different experience base, hopefully a different common sense base, and he can start asking questions: 'Why are you doing this? Why haven't you done that?' That's what

I'm doing at Kaydon. We got three new senior level guys here, including myself. You need new people to come in to challenge the old order, to say, 'Yeah, we're really hot stuff, but can we be hotter, or are we about to cool off?' You need people who don't have territory to defend because they weren't part of building territory; irreverent people, so to speak, who have no ties to the past, no baggage. You need one or two people a year from the outside at the right age to come in and challenge you. I love to be challenged."

Sometimes that means addition by subtraction. "I've told people throughout my career, if you don't think you can do it, just resign and we'll bring in someone who's as full of piss and vinegar as you were 20 years ago, and they can do it," Campbell says. "You have to fight complacency and affluence. You have to fight that all the time. You earn your tenure every day and restructure the company every day. You make small changes in course day to day, so you don't have to do the $100 million write-off when you're restructuring finally. Vision and mission are not something coming down from the top of the mountain: 'Here are the tablets; at the peak above the clouds, where you cannot see, we have decided.' Bullshit. Vision and mission are what you do every day, all day.

"They say the truly ambitious person is never satisfied. Think about that. And the human dynamic is that people reach a certain level of affluence or comfort and they lose a lot in the belly. They become more concerned with preserving the status quo. They forget that when they were 25, they were filled with urine and vinegar and sulfuric acid and they wanted to go out and kill something. That's the human dynamic, so you have to keep challenging people."

He doesn't take anything for granted on the home front, either. "I am currently married," he says. "At least, my clothes were not in the back yard this morning."

Mary, his wife since 1977, is a partner in Enterprise Development Fund, an Ann Arbor venture capital firm. "I met her in Chicago," he says. "At that time, she was a workout specialist for a commercial mortgage lender. She ran their intensive care unit, so to speak. She's originally from Marshall, so she has a long Michigan history. She's a great gal, really cranks out the horsepower. Someone has to take care of me."

Their daughter, Elizabeth, graduated from high school in June 1999 and found that her dad's philosophy of "giving people the freedom to fail" also had domestic applications.

"This college choice process is a time of great angst for kids, and it's a decision that parents can 'interfere with' only so far," he says, "because the decision has to be the kid's decision. You can't force a kid to go somewhere they don't want to go. They'll resent you for it for the rest of their life, especially if it doesn't work out. You just have to have this counselor kind of attitude. You can talk to them about the strengths and weaknesses of each of their choices, you can ask if they've thought about this or thought about that, but you really can't interfere with that process. It has to be their process. For these kids, it's the first really big decision that they will make in their lives."

Here, as elsewhere, his approach is consistent with his fundamental philosophy: "Honor the past, but always be fearful of what's coming at you down the road. It's a fine balancing act, I'll tell you."

"I didn't know what I couldn't do."

Dwight Carlson

W hen I first started," says Dwight Carlson, "I had no background for running a business. I had no family in business, no friends in business. I had no business being in business."

In retrospect, that may have been an advantage. For one thing, like the bumblebee whose flight is scientifically impossible, he didn't know what he couldn't do. For another, the results—founding and running XYCOM and Perceptron, two wildly successful technology-based companies—certainly suggest that it wasn't an insuperable handicap.

But at the time, which was 1968, it seemed especially incongruous for the 24-year-old Carlson, not only because of his inexperience but also because, in terms of his culture's expectations, he already was where he was supposed to be.

And so was Frederick Trudo, the co-worker he had persuaded to join him in forming XYCOM, Inc. "Both of us were married and had children," says Carlson, "and we

73

had good jobs at Buick Motor Division in Flint, and we had gone through an engineering educational program, General Motors Institute, that was very tough. Parents, friends, family, neighbors—the whole infrastructure— defined that as success. Having completed your education and working at General Motors, you were a success.

"And what we were doing was departing from that success to take a path which said you had no salary and no job and you were going to create a company. The negative reinforcement was very significant. I cannot recall one person who thought that was a good idea."

As he points out, there was no Bill Gates, or even Bill Hewlett, around as a role model. There hadn't been role models like that in Michigan since Billy Durant and Dallas Dort.

Like many other entrepreneurs, however, Carlson was inspired as much by a perception of what he didn't want as a conception of what he did. "When you got out of GMI, you didn't know exactly what you wanted to be," he says, "but you knew a lot of things that you didn't want to be. One of those, I realized, was I didn't want to work in a big company."

He hadn't even particularly been a "car guy." He grew up in Pinconning, Michigan, 80 miles north of Flint, the youngest of Clarence and Caroline Carlson's three children. Clarence worked in "shipping, receiving, logistics, things like that" for several manufacturing companies in the Bay City and Midland areas, and Dwight enrolled at GMI not so much because of his passion for the auto industry but because "it was a way to go to school that I could afford; it was a cooperative program and you got paid when you were working."

He did have work experience, having stocked shelves and worked behind the meat counter in a local grocery store all through high school. His first job, he recalls, "was trapping muskrats, when I was about 9 or 10. That season, my friends and I got up at 4 o'clock every morning, tended to our traps, and at the end of the season, we split nine dollars three ways."

Fifteen years later, he had his sights set on bigger game...and rewards. The Clean Air Act of 1965 had mandated emissions testing of samples of all vehicles before they could be sold, first in California, then later in the entire United States.

"I had written my fifth-year thesis at GMI on vehicle emissions testing," says Carlson, "so I talked Fred Trudo into going down in the basement and starting a company, which is now called XYCOM, located in Saline, Michigan."

In addition to resembling Carlson in that he was a GMI alumnus and willing to start a company, Trudo was also from a small town, Cheboygan, Michigan. After GMI, he had earned a master's in engineering from the University of Michigan. He stayed on as XYCOM's CEO for five years after Carlson left to start Perceptron, "then he decided that he'd try his hand at retirement," says Carlson, "so he bought his father's farm up in Cheboygan and farmed for a couple of years. But that wasn't intellectually stimulating enough, so he came back and became a stockbroker here in Ann Arbor. And he's my broker, a wonderful guy."

Starting down in that basement, "We designed and made the computer system that took the output from the gas analyzers and the dynamometer to input into the mini-computer," Carlson recalls. "In other words, we designed the interface. We also provided the operator with an instruction panel on how to drive this federally defined vehicle emission test pattern. We developed that breakthrough technology with two entrepreneurs in Ann Arbor who'd founded Ann Arbor Terminals, Ed Zimmer and Mike Levine. That was a unique invention, which provided an electronic signal to the vehicle test driver."

It was a time of ferment, the cusp of a new era, the dawn of the computer age in manufacturing. This was better understood in some places than in others.

"We were in Michigan and we understood applications," says Carlson. "There were people in Silicon Valley and they understood the basic semiconductor technology. They had two significant advantages over us. They understood marketing. And they had the availability of risk capital."

The latter was scarce in the state, even scarcer in Flint, cushioned for decades by GM's seemingly endless prosperity.

"We went down into the basement with no money and got a purchase order, then we went to the bank to borrow the money," says Carlson. The bank was Michigan National and, he says, "I literally got thrown out. He asked me what my net worth was. I asked him, 'What is a net worth? Maybe I've got one.'

"But in Flint, Michigan, there are only two banks, and I had to get the money, so I went across the street to Genesee Merchants Bank and fortunately met a gentleman named Fenton Davison."

Those are also the names of two Flint suburbs, and Davison was a scion of both families so honored. "He just essentially gave me an unbankable loan," says Carlson. "He called up the people at Buick, he called up my neighbors. It was a character loan."

He might also have called Jack Nally, the district manager for a budding computer company called Hewlett-Packard. "We convinced him to deliver $35,000 worth of H-P equipment to our basement when we had a zero net worth," says Carlson. "He was a very courageous man, who saw the opportunity to get Hewlett-Packard minicomputers into the auto industry."

Carlson, Trudo and company used the Hewlett-Packard computers in their emission test systems, which they then, in 1971, began licensing Hewlett-Packard to sell in Europe and Asia. "Through that licensing, we implemented vehicle emissions test systems with Hewlett-Packard computers throughout this little unknown company in Japan called Toyota," says Carlson. "Little did we know. We benefited, but Hewlett-Packard benefited in a big way. Probably a billion dollars a year now of Hewlett-Packard computers are going to the auto industry. But we did very well also."

It would be tempting to say that XYCOM managed to beat the odds against entrepreneurial success in Michigan by surmounting the marketing hurdle as well as the financial one. Carlson is modest on that point.

"It turned out to be a very good marketing decision if marketing is matching a niche in the market with a company's capabilities," he says. "That niche was about an $8 million-a-year niche, or we developed it into that size, and we were able to pretty much dominate it. H-P came out with a brochure in '72 or early '73 that showed, I think, 19 installations with H-P mini-computers in the auto industry, and we had installed 18 of the 19 around the world."

"Developed" is the key concept, and it didn't stop with that first batch of installations. "We also got to know the people in the federal government who were coming up with the regulations for how vehicles would be tested," says Carlson. "Through our suggestions, they came up with a procedure that could only be realistically performed utilizing some type of computerized approach."

XYCOM nonetheless remained a shoestring operation for its first four years. "Essentially, we built the company with sweat equity until 1972, when we met Herbert D. (Ted) Doan," says Carlson. "Ted's grandfather had started Dow Chemical, and then his father had been CEO at Dow, and then Ted was CEO at Dow. He had recently retired and opened up Doan Associates, a venture capital operation in Midland. Ted was learning the venture capital business and I was learning how to run a high-tech company, and we learned a lot together. We were very fortunate and it's been a wonderful relationship ever since."

Carlson wasn't just learning how to run a high-tech company, but how to run a company, period. "We were able to recruit people with computer backgrounds from IBM and General Motors," he says of the early days of XYCOM. "I had worked with these people. I knew they were great people, so I recruited 'em on to my team. And within a matter of six months, under my leadership, I had that team of people functioning at the level of retarded chimpanzees."

Clearly, not all experiments succeed. "It took me a while to figure out what Peter Drucker meant, and I got this from Peter Drucker and I'm paraphrasing, when he said the only thing that occurs naturally with any group of people—work group, family group, sports group, church group—is friction, disorder, and malperformance, like weeds growing in your garden. You work hard to plant the vegetables, and what grows naturally? The weeds. And if you don't know how to tend the garden, the weeds choke off the vegetables, and they can do it without any help from you. Friction, disorder, and malperformance are the natural weeds in the human garden.

"So what you're trying to develop in a Hewlett-Packard-like company is really an unnatural environment, where people cooperate and communicate and help each other and love doing it. And to create that environment is a real skill. It took me 13 years, the whole XYCOM era, to learn how to do that, working at it real hard."

It's also an environment from which fear has been banished. "Deming said that," Carlson notes. "It's easy to say and extremely difficult to do. And it's not a few things, it's a thousand things. Give people the key to the building. Give them stock in the company. But even more than that. I can remember one time at Perceptron..."

This was in the late 1980s, when that company was undergoing a "very, very difficult period," he says, in the wake of some Big Three maneuvers. During the emergency, all-staff meetings were held weekly instead of monthly, as had been the custom.

"I would get up in front of all the people in the company and say this is Wednesday, we have a payroll on Friday, and I don't have a clue how I'm going to make it," he says. "The only thing I can tell you is I've never missed one."

At one of these sessions, a company veteran named Joe Camilleri rose to speak.

"Dwight," he said, "you're the founder and you've been the CEO of this company since the beginning. We are losing a tremendous amount of money. We're working our asses off. This is no longer any fun. And I think you should be fired. Why shouldn't you be?"

Carlson said he wouldn't mind all that much because he wasn't having a lot of fun, either, but it was really up to the board of directors. In retrospect, he says, "The significance of that event was the fact that someone could stand up in an all-team meeting and tell the founder/CEO/president that as a result of how the company is doing, he should be fired, and then have an open discussion on that point."

Camilleri, he says, is still at Perceptron and, far from suffering reprisals, continued to receive promotions. "There was nothing that I could have done which would have driven fear out of that organization more effectively than what Joe Camellari did in that all-team meeting," says Carlson. "In our culture, it's really hard to do that."

His admiration for, and zeal to implement, the precepts of "a Hewlett-Packard-like company" are conspicuously consistent components of Carlson's career. "I had the experience of seeing Hewlett-Packard in Palo Alto in the late '60s, when I had worked at Buick for six years," he says. "I saw young people loving their company, loving their management, loving their products, loving their customers, and essentially life was a ball because they were working at Hewlett-Packard. You can imagine contrasting that with the culture that I experienced at Buick Motor Division in Flint. It didn't take a genius to figure out that my role on the planet was to create Hewlett-Packard-like working environments in Michigan."

Nor, perhaps, did it quite take a genius to figure out how, but the ratio of actualizing to visualizing resembled Edison's formulation of genius as one percent inspiration and ninety-nine percent perspiration.

"I experimented at XYCOM for 13 years, putting the company at the edge of bankruptcy several times, to figure out how to create that high-performance culture where people were working very diligently and loving it," says Carlson. "It was real tough to figure it out. I found it wasn't a few things, but it's a ton of little things that add up to the leadership clearly articulating what the mission is, what this company is all about, and what success is going to feel like when we get there, and then having the trust in people that they will figure out the best way to get there, for them. No one else can do it my way. They will be successful when they do it their way, but as a leader it's my job to articulate where it is we're going, as clearly as I possibly can."

He also can articulate, on a personal level, what turned out to be the nub of his "experiment." "I spent 13 years learning to be a leader, not a manager," he says. "Managers learn how to do things right. Leaders try to figure out the right things to do. Everyone has to do a certain amount of both, but they're different skill sets. If you get your experience in early-stage companies, then you're figuring out what's the right thing to do all the time, and if your experience in life has been in a big company, you've been learning how to do things right. If you happen to get good at figuring out the right things to do, then you get enjoyment out of doing that, and you have a tendency to want to spend time doing what you enjoy."

As clear as his vision was of the kind of company he wanted to build, he now admits to areas in which his marketing insights were somewhat cloudy.

For example, the technological keystone of XYCOM's success was that, as Carlson says, "We were the first to incorporate I-O (input-output) devices with a microcomputer chip to have an industrial computer."

There were numerous applications besides vehicle emission testing. "We were the first ones to put microcomputer chips in self-serve gas pumps," he says, "and we had a number of other first applications of microcomputer chips."

They also passed on some, "things like pinball machines," says Carlson. "We concluded, along with the rest of our pinball buddies, that taking the mechanics out of games and making them electronic games was a dumb idea. The other idea that was tested early on in those days was that some day there would be microcomputers in your home. Having struggled with putting computers in manufacturing our entire career, we could not imagine a more hideous thing to do than to bring one of those unreliable, frustrating machines into your home. It was such a distasteful thought."

But the hits have outweighed the misses, and Carlson is always delighted when his methods confound the experts. "Every time I've attempted to do market research, or had someone research what I was thinking about doing, they've always come back and said there is no market for that," he says. "And then we set about creating the market. There was no market for self-serve gas stations until we created it."

And when Carlson founded Perceptron in 1981, "There was no market for putting lasers, cameras and computers in automotive body shops," he says. "In fact, in that case, the customers definitely did not want that type of technology in those shops. It was so unthinkable that you would have that level of technology in a body shop. The market research I did said there was absolutely no need for laser-based, non-contact, wheel alignment machines. Is the customer always right? It's a long trip before that customer comes back and says, 'You know, you're right, Dwight. We do need these lasers and computers and stuff.'"

Carlson had a motive more powerful than technological innovation, or even flummoxing marketers. He wanted to know if he really had learned how to create and sustain the kind of work environment he had seen in Palo Alto 15 years before.

"I mostly wanted to figure out if we'd figured it out," he says, "and it was nice to be able to start from scratch, with a clean sheet of paper. Six or ten of us started the company, and we were on a definite mission to implement what we had learned to create a Hewlett-Packard-type working environment."

Even the initial stages reflected that commitment. "Everyone had a key," he says. "In Silicon Valley, that's not a big deal. In Michigan, it was a big deal. The tradition was a mentality where there are owners and there are workers and only the owners had the keys. That's so screwed up it's unbelievable.

"We met almost every evening over pizza and beer," he recalls. "Working from the Hewlett-Packard business philosophy, we created the Perceptron business philosophy. We'd add a person to the core group and keep going; we probably ended up with 25 people in the room by the time we finalized it."

And when it was finalized, he says, it "addressed all the key issues relative to what markets we would enter and why, why the company would grow, why the company needed to grow, how we would treat people, how we would treat customers, essentially the role of the company in the community. And we proceeded to create that culture. Several times, we had people who were experienced with the Hewlett-Packard culture visit Perceptron and say, 'This is more like Hewlett-Packard than Hewlett-Packard.' We were real zealots."

Successful zealots, too. "It really worked," he says. "We impacted the lives of a lot of people. Everyone had stock that they got in the pennies. We went public at 6, then it went to 36 and split and went up to 39. So a number of people made out."

The fundamental tenet of the philosophy, says Carlson, is to "delight customers by creating products that are unique and provide a tremendous amount of value. As a result, you create high margins and good return for shareholders. And you do this in an environment that emanates trust for people. For many years, Perceptron had no policies. Everyone had a key to the building. Everyone had stock in the company. Everyone understood the entire business philosophy and could recite it out loud, and did. We had a very clear mission—create a great company, make a hell of a lot of money for the shareholders, and love doing it. In doing this, you create a very, very high-performance environment."

It's an environment, he says, in which "people are not told what to do, they know what to do, and they are self-motivated to take it to the limit. Many people observing from the outside assumed that I was running a very loosey-goosey operation. It was anything but. If you create this kind of an environment, you do not have to worry about people taking advantage of the company. On the contrary, this environment can take advantage of people. This environment can be so high-powered, it's dangerous. Young people can get so excited about what they're doing, working with computers and technology, that the senior people have to be very vigilant to make sure that they get the proper amount of rest, eat the right kind of food, get the right kind of exercise. They have to require them to take time off, to make sure they don't burn themselves out."

To find the source of this motivation, look no farther than the nearest stadium, arena, rink, diamond, or playground. "Americans will do the Australian crawl in mud up to their shoulders to be on a winning team," says Carlson. "You see it every Saturday. You see it in sports all the time: people really break their butt and sacrifice. Everybody's that way. People like to win. And seldom in their life do they get an opportunity to be on a number-one team, no matter what it is. It's the most important compensation you can give Americans—create a number-one team that they can be on. It's a tremendous high. The question is, can it be sustained? Can you sustain that culture as you grow?"

Carlson believes his role model provides the answer. "A few years ago, I was reading the Hewlett-Packard annual report," he says. "Their sales were over $40 billion, and over half of that was from products that were less than two years old. At $40 billion a year, Hewlett-Packard was a lot more entrepreneurial than Perceptron ever was, a lot more creative. It's a tremendously creative, innovative culture."

Of course, the Perceptron environment produced a product, or there wouldn't have been a company in the first place. Simply put, "Perceptron focused laser, computer, and optics technology into changing the way the process of assembling automobiles was performed," says Carlson. "The challenge of automatically assembling

approximately 300 stamped parts into a unibody construction has mind-boggling complexity, and until
Perceptron technology came along, which enabled people
to be able to measure the process performance, it was virtually impossible to manage that process."

Perceptron changed all that, and the echoes rippled
through the production line and into the executive suites.
"The frustration of being unable to manage the process
was evident in the workforce and in the management,"
says Carlson. "Once we perfected the technology, so that
we could give reliable measurement information on that
process, once we could do that, you could see the tremendous impact you could have on the people."

That would be the people at the Chrysler Jefferson
plant near downtown Detroit, where the Perceptron "2
mm program," i.e., the reduction of variations to a maximum of 2 mm from the mean, was first implemented.
"Once we could show the people that they could determine the mean of the process on critical dimensions and
how much part-to-part variation was in the process, then
they could manage it," says Carlson. "Working with
Professor Sam Wu at the University of Michigan, we went
into facilities and worked with the United Auto Workers'
skilled trades people and empowered those teams and it
was tremendous."

The support of what Carlson calls "very knowledgeable
leaders" was critical: Bob Lutz, the president of Chrysler;
Dennis Pawley, the company's executive vice president for
manufacturing; Tom Brenizer, the plant manager, and
Chuck Kowalski, the body shop area manager. "They
developed in-depth knowledge of exactly what we were
attempting to accomplish," says Carlson. "Their total support was critical to our success."

Thus, he adds, "We were able to reduce variation in the
plant to the 2 mm target, and it fully empowered the first-
line workforce so they maintained and improved it from
there. It significantly changed the lives of those people.
Several of them mentioned to me that they had worked for
Chrysler for 30 years or more and never had enjoyed get-

ting up in the morning and going to work until then. Work can be very enjoyable. Work in the Chrysler Jefferson plant became very enjoyable."

The workers aren't the only ones whose fortunes rise when variations fall. "It's the best thing you can possibly do for the shareholders," Carlson says. "When you reduce the variation, you eliminate waste, you improve quality, and the facility actually gets quieter because the equipment runs smoother. The tooling to frame the body is supposed to be a framing station, where you lightly put metal together, where you hold it and you weld it. If there's a lot of variation in the metal and everything else that's going on in the process, it becomes what's called a forming station, where you're crunching things together. As a result, you need heavier equipment and a lot more power in the crunching. When you reduce variation, you have less cost, less maintenance. Everything gets well."

Carlson cites three essential elements that created the Chrysler Jefferson success, and can do so elsewhere. "The first was knowledgeable leadership," he says. "The second was technology that was robust enough to work literally 100 percent of the time. In metrology, you can't doubt the data. And the third thing is empowered teams in the plant. It's a combination of the knowledgeable leadership, the robust technology that gives them the information, and empowering the teams, trusting the people to manage the process.

"Over the years, I've had the opportunity to work with Asian manufacturers, European manufacturers and U.S. manufacturers. When you look at the most important variables, it always gets back to those three things—who's got the most knowledgeable leadership; who has the most robust technology and techniques; and who can put together and empower the best teams."

Carlson retired as president and CEO of Perceptron in 1996. "After 27 years of doing that same job, 13 at XYCOM and 14 at Perceptron, it was 'been there, done that, got two T-shirts,'" he says. But he is far from retired from the business of enriching the entrepreneurial environment in Michigan and the United States. In a way, it's a natural evolution, and his views on the proper role of government—state and federal—in creating that environment have also evolved. Late in 1998, he became chairman of one facet of that environment, the Michigan Manufacturing Technology Center.

"Like most entrepreneurs, early on in my career, I made speeches that said the best form of government is no government," he says. "Then, about 1980, someone—probably Ted Doan—submitted my name to Governor Bill Milliken and I received this letter which said, 'Greetings, you're part of the Michigan Small Business Advocacy Council.' I can tell you, the last thing I wanted to be doing was volunteer work for the state of Michigan."

But work he and his colleagues did, and they began to make some surprising discoveries. "There were 12 of us that were CEOs of small companies," Carlson says. "We decided if we were going to do this, we weren't going to write any reports. We were basically going to see how much we could get done. And I was quite amazed we could get as much done as we did. We modified workers' compensation, improved the Single Business Tax, and passed Act 55, which liberated 5 percent of the state pension fund for investment in venture capital.

"I learned from that experience that the relationship between government bureaucrats and entrepreneurs is a tremendous relationship," he adds. "One doesn't expect people who have worked for government to be risk-takers; we don't expect them to be very creative, 'idea people.' But what I did find in Michigan is that they are honest, hardworking, good citizens. When you combine them with entrepreneurs like myself, you have a very effective relationship. The entrepreneurs love taking risks, love thinking about creative new ways of doing things, and their absolute downside risk is being fired from a non-paying job. What's very stimulating for the government bureaucrats is that they can work in a creative environment, taking risks, and the entrepreneur is willing to take all the heat. If we screw up, the governor can fire me from this job and I have no problem with that. For the entrepreneur, it's a great opportunity to exercise your entrepreneurial muscle. I found it to be a great training and development ground for both entrepreneurs and government bureaucrats."

Two governors and almost 20 years later, he still hasn't been fired.

"During the Jim Blanchard administration, we came up with the concept of a strategic fund which would enable the governor to make strategic investments," says Carlson. "Michigan is the second largest state in the nation for industrial research and development, following California, and third or fourth in the nation in university R&D. This equates to Michigan being the number one state in the nation in research, and research itself is very important. But what we learn from the folks in California and Boston is that leveraging that research into economic development in the community requires a community team effort. I acquired a keen appreciation for the role of the governor in developing that team effort. Whatever the governor in a state sets as a priority, he can recruit a number of private sector volunteers to accomplish that. Michigan has struggled to turn this research and development acorn into a flourishing oak tree, as the Silicon Valley and Route 128 communities have done. The Michigan team made this type of contribution earlier in the century in the creation of the auto industry and the Dow Chemicals and the Upjohns and the Kelloggs."

He thinks perhaps it's time for that torch to be passed back to the heartland. "Just look what Silicon Valley has done for the world," says Carlson, "and you know what? The research capability in Michigan is better than the research capability in California. What's weak is the entrepreneurial culture, the risk-taking culture. We have become way too conservative."

As a member of the state Jobs Commission under Governor John Engler, Carlson helped pave the way for the creation of the Michigan Technology Board, a panel of seven entrepreneurs, including Carlson, and the presidents of the state's four major research universities. Its function is to "provide private sector leadership in creating an entrepreneurial community in Michigan," he says, yet it was spawned by the public sector. "I now appreciate more the role of government and government leaders in stimulating the creation of an entrepreneurial culture within a community and within a state," he says.

Carlson has also had the opportunity in the last decade to get involved with the federal government, as well. "Contrary to popular belief, there is intelligent life in Washington," he says. "In fact, when it comes to people who are motivated to public service, Washington is the major leagues. As a result, this nation has a tremendous brain trust located in Washington."

The problem, again, is a misperception of that level of government's appropriate role. "The best idea in the world cannot be pushed from Washington," says Carlson. "It must be pulled by enlightened private sector leaders in the states. There probably was a valid concern 20 or 30 years ago that things had to be done at the federal level because all states were not capable of performing a lot of the government functions. But I believe that has changed, and states are more capable of doing a number of government functions, and we can reduce the size of the federal government and concentrate more on the efficacy of the states."

A conspicuous exception, in Carlson's view, is research support. "By any measure, we as Americans can be very proud of our federal government and the way it has managed to develop the research capability in America," he says. "That's one area where the federal government has done a great job, and we should capitalize on our successes."

Another exception, one that rescued XYCOM on a couple of occasions, is government lending.

"The first seven or eight years of XYCOM's existence, every payroll was an exciting event," Carlson says. "One time, in 1972, we were doing vehicle emission test systems for the auto industry, and we had just successfully beat out IBM for the torque monitoring business. We were hiring people, growing rapidly in Flint, and the Arab oil crisis erupted. For the first time in the history of the modern auto industry, General Motors canceled purchase orders. We had two-thirds of our backlog canceled in one week. We would have been a casualty of the oil crisis had the people of Doan Associates and ourselves not gone to the U.S. Small Business Administration and got a $600,000, five-year term emergency energy loan at 6 percent. We repaid every penny, kept the company in business, and were able to recover after the oil crisis to go on and grow the business. If the federal government hadn't had an SBA program, and if they hadn't quickly implemented emergency energy loans, small businesses like XYCOM around the country would have been going out of business left and right."

After XYCOM moved to the Ann Arbor area, Carlson and his colleagues had another positive experience with the feds' flexibility and responsiveness. "XYCOM was heavily involved in electronic systems for self-serve gas stations," he recalls. "The business was outgrowing its capital availability and I had negotiated a deal with Citibank and the office of the U.S. Farmers Home Administration in Lansing. The structure of the deal was that Citibank's venture capital group, for which one of my board members and investors worked, was going to put in a million dollars equity and the FHA was going to put in a million dollars in term debt. After the deal was agreed upon, I left to go with the sales team on an off-site.

"While I was gone," he says, "I received a call from Bob Mitchell, who ran the FHA office in Lansing, telling me that Citibank had reneged on the deal, and that I had best get my butt back to Michigan as soon as possible to see if I couldn't put the deal back together."

As Carlson scrambled to get back home, he grew increasingly curious about Citibank's motivations. "I called New York and was informed that Citibank wanted to significantly improve the terms—their terms—of the deal, to the detriment of the other investors and, of course, the employees of XYCOM," he says. "Upon arriving in Michigan, I called my local banker and we had a very solemn drive to Lansing, knowing that we had our backs against the wall with little alternative other than to accept the onerous terms of Citibank."

But their mood changed when they met with Mitchell. "We began to explain to Mr. Mitchell what we had learned and the situation that we were in," he says, "but he had already analyzed the situation correctly as one in which a big corporation was taking unfair advantage of a small company in Michigan, upon which he said, 'Screw 'em, I'll put in the two million.' When my local banker and I got back to Saline, we called our director and informed him of what had happened. Six weeks later, I received a call from a high-level Citibank executive, apologizing for their behavior. So when I look at government, I have a warm spot in my heart for some of the people who work in it."

Carlson says his experience has taught him that, indeed, the citizens are the government, and it will be about as good or as bad as their participation and education dictate.

"Over the years, as you get exposed to the American system, you start to understand how great this government is," he says. "It's truly a government of the people, so if the people, especially the entrepreneurial leader types, want to make a difference, this government facilitates enabling them to make that difference. The more people volunteer, the leaner and more effective government gets. That's government the way it was supposed to be, with all of us volunteering to make it work. You can't abdicate your government responsibility."

Or, at least, you do so at your peril, in his view. "Those people that are not involved in their government get the government they deserve," Carlson says. "To really understand why you should vote requires the time to understand the system of government we have. That's the commitment that too many people aren't willing to make. I think there should be more education in the early grades on the government, how it works and what it's about. It's appalling, the lack of understanding of Americans about their government."

Not to mention the sources of new jobs. "Essentially, all new job creation is the result of small businesses, and small businesses start in communities that encourage the creation of new businesses," Carlson says. "That's a real challenge for Michigan. We have so many successful mature businesses, whose competitiveness we are working to maintain, that starting new businesses is a lower priority in the community. Michigan was very entrepreneurial earlier in the century and very successful, and then became very conservative and has not participated in the new waves of industries that you're seeing develop in other parts of the country. In that respect, it's been very much a victim of its own success.

"You realize that what changed the world back in Henry Ford's day was the changes in the workplace," he continues. "We're having as significant a change going on now in the world and it's also driven by changes in the workplace. That drives change throughout the whole system. To the extent that you can put together a vision of how that is going to occur and what it's going to look like out there in the future, then you can make a big contribution to the community."

One flaw in the currently prevailing vision, he says, is "the habit of talking about 'months and years,' while the rest of the world talks about 'days and weeks.' The unfortunate part of our community is that there are big companies and big universities that are so big they can get away with 'months and years' for a long time and it feels okay. But the fact of the matter is there are a lot of opportunities that are going away to people who think in terms of days and weeks."

Sports metaphors pepper Carlson's conversation, so it's not surprising that he describes international business competition as "a team sport. The basic understanding you have to develop in the community is that capital today can go anywhere," he says, "so therefore capital is going to be invested in those communities that recognize the importance of the process by which you invest capital and talent and the rewards are shared by the shareholders, the people, and the community. That needs to be articulated by government leaders, educational leaders, and community leaders. It's an educational process."

The results, too, will be spread around. "The reason that I'm active, even though I'm in retirement, in working to develop a more entrepreneurial, creative culture in Michigan is the same thing that I saw when I visited Hewlett-Packard," he says. "If communities are creative, dynamic, spawning new companies, researching new technologies, solving market problems, making good returns and creating wealth for shareholders, they become much more enjoyable. I contend that if you had a community made up of Hewlett-Packard-type companies, it would be a great place to live."

"Thou shalt not develop further away from home than a five-iron shot."

Don Chisholm

When he decided on a career, Don Chisholm had to make a tough choice.

For one thing, there was the music, a lifelong passion. He would still rather talk about a budding talent he heard at the Bird of Paradise than any deal he might be involved in. His mother, with whom he spent most of his childhood, was a talented pianist and teacher. Unfortunately, while he inherited her love for making music, he didn't inherit her talent. Fortunately, he did inherit skills from his father's—and Uncle Collin's—side that enabled him to make a good enough living that he could indulge his passion without depending on it.

Don learned how to deploy his gifts to see opportunities. Through music, he learned how to put together the pieces needed to make a deal, to coordinate and balance the requisite institutions and individuals. "It's like conducting an orchestra," he says. Soon a path opened before him that could have led to riches, but, as he says, "If I wanted to make a lot of money, I could have gone to Chicago and worked with (college pals and later enormously successful entrepreneurs) Sam Zell and Bob Lurie when they were doing their big things in the '70s." But he liked being in Ann Arbor, and seemed to have a feeling for the place that not only gave him an edge in knowing what and where to develop but also a sense of responsibility to the community for the results.

"That's the goal—to do it right and be an asset to the community and not lose money in doing so," says Chisholm. "Notice I never said to make money. You want to survive, although you always hope that you're savvy enough to be ahead of the economic tide so that the project is profitable."

He even had a chance, while he was a lieutenant in the Army's Medical Service Corps in 1957, to work for one of President Eisenhower's golfing buddies, a heady proximity to power for a youth of 23. The man was the U.S. Surgeon General, who paid a two-week visit to Ft. Sam Houston, Texas, where Chisholm was stationed. Chisholm was "assigned" to him and "We got along real well. He said he could have me assigned to Walter Reed, and when he said he could do something, you could believe him. I was tempted, but I didn't do it."

Chisholm had already decided to go back to the University of Michigan Law School under a program that allowed him to end his two-year hitch early if he were enrolled in a degree program, although he eventually applied his law school credits toward his master's in business administration.

"My underlying Chisholm influence was you don't work for big organizations," he says. "I guess I saw the fence post story. And, by then my dad had an office building, almost on one of the prime corners of Bonners Ferry, Idaho."

Bonners Ferry—or, more precisely, 20 miles outside of Bonners Ferry, just south of the border with British Columbia—was where Chisholm spent the summers of his youth on his father's ranch. Hugh Chisholm was a native Idahoan who had met Margaret Sloan, Don's future mom, in Seattle. The couple was living in East Orange, New Jersey, by the time Don was born, then soon moved to Chicago. Then Don and his mother lived with a family friend in Albany, New York, for a while, then they went back to Chicago, where mother and son remained for a few years—after the marriage ended and Hugh went back to Idaho—before moving to Detroit, where Chisholm spent the rest of his childhood.

From September to June, that is, when he lived in a big city with his mother, who taught piano for more than 50 years until she died at "approximately 80." Her brother worked for Pittsburgh Plate Glass for 37 years, one of his two sons for Ryerson Steel for 42 years, and the other for Johns-Manville for 37. "It was 'get in with the company and stay for life,'" says Chisholm.

Ah, but in the summertime, he was about as far from Detroit-and the conservatism of his mother's family—as he could get. He hung out with his dad and his dad's older brother, Collin, who remained a lifelong friend and influence. Hugh ranched, sold cars, started companies, dug logging roads and, during his eras of prosperity, flew around the country inspecting his holdings in a private plane, often with little Don, as young as 10, as his co-pilot. He parlayed a load of pigs into an empire of lumber yards, mills and real estate. He also fell as dramatically as he rose, eventually losing most of his fortune, drifting away from his son after remarrying, losing a bid for the Idaho State Senate, and dying at age 47.

"They called him 'One-million, two-million Hughie' because he always had big ideas," says Chisholm. "He'd go up fast and come down fast. Maybe he had a little deficit in his risk/reward analysis. Maybe I got a little of each." His record certainly shows he is no foe of dependability (as contrasted with routine), but it also testifies to a strong streak of Chisholm-ism.

Hugh's father walked with a mule train from Nova Scotia to Idaho in the last decade of the 19th century. Hugh's mother died when he was 12, and he got a quick course in self-sufficiency. He financed his education at the University of Idaho by selling cars when they were still almost a novelty, worked for General Motors for a while (Don thinks that's what he was doing in New Jersey when he was born), and created an inventory control and prospecting system for auto dealers that was used widely in the 1940s and '50s.

He also drank too much and was careless with his money, frequently having to rebuild some fortune he had gone through.

"I remember once when I was in Idaho, and he was broke but he'd raised a load of pigs," Chisholm recalls. "We took 'em to Spokane to sell. He was going to take the money and buy some fence posts because he heard about a guy in Montana who wanted a load of fence posts, and they had real good cedar around there. So he bought enough for a boxcar and shipped them to the customer. Of course, that's a commodity and very low markup. He made $100 on the boxcar, so he asked the guy if he had any friends who needed fence posts. Once he had a couple of orders in hand, he got guys to make the fence posts, load 'em and ship 'em. The Chisholm Cedar Company became the world's largest shipper of fence posts. That led to construction, because they had to get roads into the woods to get cedar, then to airports and dikes and retail lumber yards and mills."

Next enters the airplane. "My early business training was flying with him or riding with him to jobs," says Chisholm. "He was very good with numbers, and I also had that aptitude. He would say some project would be good because we could get our money back in four or five years, in other words a 20-25 percent annual return. I think when you listen to that at an early age, you get some background that they don't teach in business school."

He got that from his uncle, as well. One precept that he's remembered and employed he calls "a Collinism."

"He told me he often reflected on that Odessa Lumber Yard," Chisholm says. "It was located on a piece of downtown real estate in Odessa, Texas. We lost money on operating that lumber yard most of the time, but we were able to sell the real estate to make up the cumulative losses. So the real estate was the answer, and that's been our history. Real estate, yes; operating businesses, no, unless you develop eight stores and get advertising and buying power. You can't do a 'onesie' in Ann Arbor and think you'll make anything except maybe wages for the manager. At best, they can pay you for working there, but they're not an investment. That's what I've learned."

There was also some reinforcement from the Sloan side of the gene pool. "My cousin Bob used to baby-sit me in Chicago," Chisholm remembers. "I must have been in either kindergarten or first grade, and to keep me busy—this was before TV—he made up little flash cards. Two times three, four times two, pretty soon it was 16 divided by four. Since the flash cards, I'm inherently numbers-oriented."

After the Army, he returned to his job as an economist and market analyst at Owens-Corning Fiberglass Corp. in Toledo. "I was traveling and doing great," says Chisholm. "I was so lucky that when I got to go to New York, I'd run into Paul McCracken, then the chairman of the President's Council of Economic Advisers, at the airport. I took the cab in with him twice from LaGuardia. Here I was, 24 years old, a young MBA, and I'd go in and say to the Owens-Corning people, well, Paul McCracken said this and Paul McCracken said that. All of a sudden, it was like 'How to Succeed in Business Without Really Trying,' which was playing in New York then."

Corporate life soon lost its charm for Chisholm. The solution he proposed was to quit his job, and move back to Ann Arbor with his wife, Betty, whom he had met at U-M and married just after joining the Army.

"We both wanted to live in Ann Arbor and Betty had a teaching job," he recalls. "I could work for nothing, so I thought I'd go into real estate, where it's all commission and I could be my own boss." Predictably, his idea divided the two sides of his gene pool like the Red Sea.

"When I was going to quit my wonderful job at Owens-Corning, all the staid people on the Sloan side of the family said, 'How can you be so silly?' But Collin said, 'Of course, you go work for nothing; how else are you going to make anything of yourself?'," Chisholm says.

The only other vote in his favor from the previous generation came from a real estate developer in San Francisco who was married to a friend of his mother's. "He said, 'Do it, do it now.' It was two against the world. That was enough."

So Betty taught early elementary school in Plymouth and Don went to work for Hobbs-Schmidt Real Estate, where he shared a desk and a phone with another young guy named Joe Savarino. As it happened, he also shared Don's passion for music and was a gifted pianist and golfer. In the coming quarter of a century, they would share a great deal more, but their first meeting, as Chisholm remembers it, was inauspicious, if characteristic.

"Hey, you're new," said Savarino. "I've got a builder open house this afternoon. Can you cover it for me? I've got a golf game."

That sense of—shall we say "proportion"?—infused both their relationship with each other and their approach to doing business. They worked hard but they also had fun hard, their keen senses of humor ever near. They were as dedicated to their pleasures, their music and their laughter, as they were to their livelihood. The result was a spiritual symbiosis, a melding of the men as well as their boundless interests, and a partnership that only death could end.

"Joe got his master's in music from the U-M Music School, studied accompaniment and accompanied the Glee Club the first time they won an international festival in the '50s," says Chisholm. "Joe was in that world-class league. He was a sight reader, and he could do terrific things in classical and even jazz. He could imitate Errol Garner to the note."

In his own version of "Is it live or is it Memorex?",

Chisholm used to challenge his friends to sit in another room and determine if they were listening to Savarino or a Garner record.

In golf, Savarino had eight holes-in-one in his career. Thirteen years after cancer claimed him at age 54, he still shared the course record of 64 at Washtenaw Country Club. "He was always optimistic," says Chisholm. "The day before he passed away, he called and said he finally was on an uptick and had just ordered a fancy new wrist watch."

Almost 25 years earlier, on December 4, 1960, the two had formed Ann Arbor Associates, along with Dean Koelling, the broker who "recruited" Chisholm for Hobbs-Schmidt, and Malcolm Dale and Charlie Stacy. One of numerous Hobbs-Schmidt spinoffs, the partnership eventually began buying parcels of land for which Chisholm saw a future that had seemed clear to him ever since he did a business school project on where Ann Arbor was likely to grow.

"I did a very simple thing," Chisholm says. "I drew a three-mile radius from the Michigan Union, and the whole town was built up within it except for this wedge down here. The reason for that was it was in Pittsfield Township, and it was clay soil so you couldn't get a septic permit. Pittsfield didn't have sewer and water; Ann Arbor did."

What was needed, in addition to the land itself, were the appropriate political arrangements between the two jurisdictions that would deliver those services to the land. The city eventually annexed township land north of I-94, which meant it provided sewer and water, which meant "development could happen," says Chisholm.

"Development," as in Bechtel Tower, Hidden Valley Apartments, Wolverine Tower, Waterworks Plaza, the three Burlington Office Centers, and the necessity for and construction of Eisenhower Parkway. What his old friend Sam Zell said may be true—"What the hell, you can see everything Chisholm's ever done by the light of a candle; State and Eisenhower, it's all here"—but he was the major player in the creation of a virtual second downtown with a center of its own at State and I-94.

In the late '50s and early '60s in Ann Arbor, "development" usually meant buying a lot in a residential neighborhood, tearing down the house if one were there, and building a student apartment building. "In those days, they would spend $3 a square foot for the land whether it had a house on it or not," says Chisholm. This created an attraction that predated the availability of water: a stunning disparity between the price of property in the township and the price of property in the city, which Chisholm saw as inherently unstable.

"If you came down State Street by Yost Field House and there was a building built in the southernmost block before Stadium, that would be $3 a foot," he recalls. "Then you crossed under Stadium and within a mile, you could buy farmland, admittedly not very usable at the time, for $4,000 an acre, or less than 10 cents a square foot. It didn't make sense to me, that 30 to 1 difference within a mile. It needed to get in balance, and it didn't take long after the annexation, once the sewer and water were in."

Chisholm and Savarino had already been doing fairly conventional real estate deals. "We started with a two-family, a five-family, another five-family," says Chisholm. "We bought the first one with only a hundred dollars of our own money."

By 1962, however, they were beginning to assemble the parcels that Zell's candle would illuminate. Perhaps the light wasn't as good then, but they were still able to see the commercial potential in those farms and woods.

"How could we own a piece of ground without a lot of money?" was the question, Chisholm says, and they answered it in the usual way. "It was probably in '62 that we bought a piece of ground on State Street where Englander Triangle is now," he says. "We were able to buy it with a low down payment and make payments. That was on 12.2 acres, which was a big parcel of ground. We put a golf range there and named it Tee and Ski, because we needed to do something with it in wintertime."

But the business was a placeholder; the land was the focus. "I started with why Ann Arbor would come this way, south, so Joe Savarino and I acted on it," says Chisholm. "When the next farm down became available from a fine real estate old-timer named Clarence April, we formed a partnership and bought it, which was 52 acres. Then the one next to that became available at a much higher price, so we formed another partnership and bought that. We also bought the American Metal Products site with a different group. Since we didn't have any money, we might be only 10 percent partners in these things."

The next thing was a parcel across State from Tee and Ski—two single-family, deed-restricted houses, each on an acre, surrounded by eight acres. Chisholm and Savarino acquired the latter, then waited. "When each of the houses became available, we bought them," he says. "It took us a couple of years to put that piece together, but once we had it all, we could remove the deed restriction."

Now they could start some serious horse-trading. Their newly completed tract was immediately north of the Edwards Brothers printing plant. The company needed to expand, and preferred to go north rather than south, even though it already held about 30 acres of vacant ground in that direction. "We said we've got the 12 acres there that could be available for industrial if the city would approve it," says Chisholm. "Edwards said, 'We want that.' We said, 'We're just young real estate guys; why don't we just trade with you? Since ours is more valuable for your use, give us your southernmost piece,' so they traded us 18 acres for 12, and made us a loan on top of that that helped us keep going."

It probably didn't hurt that Savarino's sister, Rosalie, was married to Marty Edwards, one of the Edwards brothers. But no influence was sufficient to expedite the leisurely pace of Ann Arbor bureaucracy. "That 18 acres eventually became Hidden Valley Apartments, after years of fooling with the city planners," says Chisholm. "They held us up about three years because they always wanted to cut a cross street diagonally from State Street to Main behind Edwards Brothers. After a couple years of that delay, we said why don't we move the project back and leave the front vacant until you decide? And, of course, they never did, but that's why Hidden Valley is set back."

Almost 25 years later, Hidden Valley remains both one of Ann Arbor's most attractive apartment complexes as well as one of Chisholm's favorite projects. "We beefed up everything," he says. "I don't think you'll find many apartments in town built with all masonry, masonry floors, walls, fireplaces in every unit. Even though they're small, they had a lot of quality features that were probably overdone, but it turned out to be a good thing in the long run." Don Van Curler was the architect and partner with Chisholm and Savarino.

"Many people 'back into' developing," Chisholm says. "If you're stuck with land in a partnership and nobody will buy it, then you think maybe if you put a building on it at least you can get some income out of it." Hidden Valley was quite premeditated.

"In the '60s and '70s, development made sense; it would work," he says. For one thing, the atmosphere was more relaxed. "The contractor was Don Butcher and Jake Haas was his new partner," he says. "We did the deal on a handshake at my kitchen table. Those were the good old days."

The same was true of financing. "We started when Jay DeLay started Huron Valley National Bank," says Chisholm. "We'd go get our apples and do loans with him. He'd have his promissory notepad in his pocket, and he'd say, 'Good boys, good boys, what do you want?' and it would be done. It doesn't work that way anymore. We need more Jay DeLays and fewer big banks."

Of course, it could also be said that Chisholm laid the groundwork, so to speak, for the conditions that attracted the big banks and the outside developers.

"All I can say is the big-city developers invariably make mistakes coming to Ann Arbor because they think we are a big market and we're a small market," he says. "We could have built 62 units at Sloan Plaza (the premium downtown apartment and office complex he named for his mother) and we did 32, and it's a good thing. There are many, many cases of that. We're a quality town, but we're still 110,000 in Ann Arbor and 300,000 in the trading area."

The interlopers also violated another Chisholm commandment: "Thou shalt not develop further away from home than a five-iron shot."

"Most of the catastrophes were pyramiders," he says. "They typically do one good deal here, then let's do two more in Detroit, and since that's so good, let's go to Kansas City. As soon as we get the first draw (loan installment), we won't wait for the project to be completed, we'll do two in Dallas. And they all go down. If they had done one at a time where they knew the area...but, of course, if they knew the area, they wouldn't do it. When you're in a small town, you're like a general store. We've gone from student houses to six units to 12 units to residential to some industrial, then to office buildings, and then back to residential and golf. Each one was dictated by the market, and you don't try to force your specialty on the market."

Chisholm describes a developer as "a cross between a Broadway producer, in that he arranges financing for the performance, and an orchestra conductor, in that he brings the musicians together. He does not necessarily have the artistic ability of any of the people who work with him, but he does have the ability to get them to work together. You need a lot of talent of different types; in the developer's role, it might be the engineer, the land planner, the lawyers, the architects, marketing people. That's the orchestra, and the developer is there to try and make it something harmonious and hopefully in good taste."

Like the conductor and producer, the developer needs to know his audience as well as his orchestra. And like the producer, the developer needs not to lose money because "if you lose money, you can't play again."

Merely having the opportunity to stay in the game has

had to sustain developers for some time, he says, quoting his friend Sam Zell that "he doesn't know of any develop- er office projects in the country after '82 that have made money."

"That's a shocking statement," says Chisholm, who says it applies to him as well. It is a major reason why Ann Arbor Associates, of which he is now the sole owner, shift- ed its emphasis to property management around 1990. "People think the dirty developers are gouging and rich and so forth, but something happened to costs, which include financing costs and the delays brought on by (to be polite) bureaucratic procedures. A lot of projects went under and then they were purchased at less than repro- duction costs by people who did make money. If you wanted to be the boy developer and start from scratch and build your pretty building, they generally didn't work."

And, as Chisholm points out, another function of the developer is "to take the risk. The lenders want security and somebody has to step up to bat, and that is the devel- oper. It would be the common perception that developers are just greedy SOBs trying to exploit everybody, and the developer group is populated with some of the former. They end up giving properties back and not paying their bills. Some of the out-of-towners here, and there's a lot of them along State Street, just come in and hit and run. I hear about caterers still not being paid for some of the fes- tive openings. The difference with us is we sell things and scrimp and save in order to preserve our good standing."

What hurts, he says, is the attitude his less responsible colleagues induce in the government bodies with whom they all must deal. "One of the problems with the indus- try is the officials take the lowest common denominator and they treat everybody like they are one of...those," he says. "And maybe they have to, but it certainly is not pleasant."

Chisholm's record clearly belies the developer stereo- type. Not only has he made esthetic appeal and sensitivi- ty to the surrounding area's "big picture" among his high- est priorities but also, true to his own guidelines, none of them has ever lost money and most of them were profitable for investors. The champ, he says, was the State Road Development Company, "where the $120,000 partner's equity turned into a $1.8 million payout in less than four years."

This, despite contravening one of the precepts he taught students during the four years he taught real estate finance as an adjunct faculty member in the U-M Business School. "The investment principle of diversification was violated by concentrating along a strip of land on the south side of a small Midwest town," he says. "Although there were many problems concerning delay and regulatory restrictions, the long-term patient investment in a known area where good planning could be enforced proved fruitful."

Indeed, beyond the commercial potential his school project illustrated, Chisholm zeroed in on the south side precisely because developing an entire area "from scratch" would make such planning possible. Also, there weren't a lot of not-in-my-back-yard neighbors to deal with, which Chisholm says is why he has shied away from downtown development.

The one conspicuous exception, of course, was Sloan Plaza.

It all started when Chisholm had lunch one day in Seattle, while attending an Urban Land Institute meeting, with the developer of the Opera Plaza Condominiums on Van Ness Street in San Francisco. "I said, 'I'm going to go down there. Can I see it?' It was a big, full block of buildings, and two blocks from the symphony hall and the opera building," Chisholm recalls. "Van Ness was a little blighted at the time, so they got some government financing to clean up some stuff. I talked to a couple of people in the lobby and asked how come they moved here. They said some friends who lived there had invited them to the symphony, and they had a drink at their house, ate at a restaurant, walked to the concert, walked back."

Chisholm was pretty sure he knew of another place where such a "location, location, location" could be a selling point. "Icerman, Johnson and Hoffman, the accountants, had this site on East Huron Street and had been talking to me about it," he says. "I came back and told them, 'I've got the use for your site.' They said, 'We don't want to do it; why not you?' And I thought, 'Oh, no, downtown.'"

But, he says, "my gut told me" it would work "because there was a need for something near the entertainment district," and his own affection for and interest in the arts had convinced him that their quality and accessibility were important attractions for the market he would be targeting.

"I talked to Joe O'Neal because I wanted a good, knowledgeable high-rise contractor," he says. "I talked to Dick Black because I wanted a good architect with a local feel."

And he talked to his ailing mother in San Francisco, for whom it would be named and who he expected would move to Ann Arbor as one of its residents. "We told her we were naming it for her brother, the solid rock of the family," he says. "She had an apartment picked out, and she called a few days after Christmas in 1984 and said, 'Remember the motto—stay alive 'til '85.'"

She did, but just barely. She went to her friend Frances' house on New Year's Day to watch the Rose Bowl. When Frances came back from the kitchen after getting a cup of coffee, Margaret Sloan had passed away.

But her monument, in a sense, is one of the most visually striking buildings in downtown Ann Arbor. It's also one of the projects her son is most proud of, partly just because it survived.

"Joe O'Neal and I were the developers, and we didn't lose and we didn't go under, and that was the first time in Ann Arbor that a high-rise was constructed that didn't go under," he says. "And for contribution or influence to the community, Sloan Plaza would be my favorite because it did something downtown, and every owner there has done well with their apartments."

Apartment 307 in Sloan Plaza is a guest suite used primarily by visiting musicians, principally pianists. Within it resides Margaret Sloan's 1928 Steinway, and virtually every great jazz pianist (with the exception of Oscar Peterson) has stayed there over the years and enjoyed her instrument.

Sloan Plaza would have fared even better had it been all residential, Chisholm believes. While the apartments sold briskly even before it opened in 1987, sluggish demand for its office space doomed its overall profitability. "We wanted the office space so the parking could be used for guests after the office workers went home at five o'clock," he says. "That's what turned it from a plus to a wash or a slight loser."

On the other hand, the response to its residences confirmed his theories about the town's appeal. "We put an ad in the Michigan Alumnus saying 'downtown living, two blocks from Hill Auditorium, on Huron Street,'" he says. "We had 31 responses and a couple of sales out of that one ad. It wasn't just the Ann Arbor market, and that was a big deal because we had just started the Washtenaw Development Council, and we were trying to get people to share our quality of life in Ann Arbor. We had one buyer from Windsor, one from Midland. A fellow named Bob Hoffman, who had been vice president of Marshall Field, moved here from Chicago and became the first president of the residents association board. He and his wife were going to buy a condo in Hilton Head, but they were here for a football game, saw our ad, and said, 'We always wanted to be here; why don't we move back?' It was worth doing the deal to have Bob and Fran Hoffman come here."

This was during the time Chisholm taught in the business school, and his students were understandably interested in the project. "They kept saying, 'What was your marketing plan for Sloan Plaza?' They grilled me so much I finally said I really did have a marketing plan: If you can ever find a site within a block of the newspaper office, where the sun sets behind it and they're looking for something out their window at deadline time and they could take a picture at five minutes to five and run it at 10 the next morning, that's your marketing plan. They had pictures of Joe O'Neal's festively decorated crane at Christmas time, which helped, so there's some truth to it. I think we were on the front page of *The Ann Arbor News* five or six times in the two years we were building it."

Another Chisholm favorite—and it should be noted that he singles them out as reluctantly as a parent would with his children—is Waterworks Plaza, a 70,000-square-foot office building that nestles almost invisibly off State Street near I-94, a bucolic island in the midst of the intersection's bustle and a success both esthetically and commercially.

"Again, it was Dick Black's creativity," he says, "along with the work of a great artist in town who happens to be in landscaping and road building, Don Cunningham. He created the stream through the middle of the building with a bridge over it. It follows my theory of real estate development that you get the best creative artists and get out of their way."

It also fits his definition of "a good working deal. It was done in '80, did not get in trouble, and offered the investors— and I'm only 12 percent—a return over the years."

Aside from some personal satisfaction, however, the deal called Stonebridge might fit the definition of a nightmare, despite a few heartening rays of sunshine and Chisholm's persistent optimism. The plan, launched in 1988, was to develop 655 acres of farm land in Pittsfield Township into an 18-hole golf course and an 18-acre lake surrounded by 711 home lots. Firstate Financial, a savings and loan association in Florida with ties to Sam Zell, was going to back it.

"They had experience in golf course communities and they were going to do this venture," says Chisholm. "And they would have. They were not in bad shape like other S&Ls. However, they were hit by the same flak when the S&L industry collapsed, and the federal government drastically reduced the amount an association could loan to any one borrower. Their loan limit went from $20 million to $2 million. Our project would take in the neighborhood of $10 or 12 million. We were right in midstream, waiting for a draw to proceed, when they said, 'Send us back our money.'"

Suddenly, he and Myron Serbay, his partner in the venture who had developed a similar project in Brighton, were obliged to come up with $4 million just to stay out of debtors' prison. "That caused us problems we're still trying to smooth over," says Chisholm. It also produced one of those rays of sunshine, although the necessity was regrettable, when Sam Edwards rode to the rescue. The president of Beacon Investment Co., an Ann Arbor money management firm, Edwards had also invested personally in various Chisholm projects and knew him as a friend. He organized a pool of his clients to provide a mortgage on the project that was sufficient to repay Firstate and start construction of the golf course.

"It got to where I had to work harder than ever, and so far for nothing because of the financing problems," he says. "When the township bureaucrats give us delays, I say I've been working on this since 1990 now and I still haven't had a pay check or an interest payment on my debt, and I'm becoming one of the largest lenders there."

However, Stonebridge also gave him the opportunity to get out of the way of some more creative people, including Cunningham, master planner Richard Magnuson and golf course designer Arthur Hills, in addition to scratching a unique niche in the market and attracting interest from an upscale audience throughout southeastern Michigan.

"It's too big a project for Ann Arbor," says Chisholm. "I violated my own rule. But we're getting there. We've never missed a payment with anybody, never been tardy, because somehow or other I was able to do something to cover whatever the company couldn't. The whole housing market is active now, the economy's good, interest rates are down. If we can have two more years at it, we might come out all right."

Most enterprises with which Chisholm is associated do come out all right, be they public or private. In addition to his ongoing involvement in the local arts scene, he was one of the founders of the Washtenaw Development

Council and was elected its first chairman in January 1983. "The economy was such that everybody was desperate for something to promote jobs and investment," he says.

The WDC became a key player in the community's efforts to foster economic growth, but not before a bit of a shakedown cruise. "They then had a very large board (19 members), in order to have the various governmental entities involved with the private sector and maybe foster some dialogue," Chisholm says, "but they'd get these bureaucrat thinkers, and a few years later a banker got involved, and they spent most of the year planning their plans. And every day was scheduled."

Chisholm has always favored a high ratio of action to preparing for action, and a delicate balance between having a plan and staying light on your feet. "Everybody's obsessed with long-range plans," he says, "and how can you have long-range plans if something happens, you name it, whether it's an El Nino or an earthquake or the Asian crisis or all of a sudden the Japanese economy goes down, and all of your long-range plans are out the window. You've got to be flexible and have your one- to two-year plan, but you have to be ready to pitch it at any time."

That was particularly true with Park Place for Business, a stretch of 11 industrial office lots on either side of Oak Valley Drive in Pittsfield Township. Chisholm never had to pitch his plans but, to say the least, the way things worked out was a little ironic.

The day of the evening that the Pittsfield Township Planning Commission was to vote on final approval of the Planned Unit Development, Chisholm met Mary Lindquist, the founder and guiding light of Arbor Hospice, through a mutual friend, Mary Reilly. "She was helping Mary Lindquist at Arbor Hospice, and I had worked with her on Downtown Development Authority and Ann Arbor Economic Development Corporation projects," he says. "Mary Lindquist had said to her, 'I have this dream, but I need some real estate,' so we went to see her."

When Chisholm heard her requisites—a rural, pastoral

spot with a slope to the back so guests could see flowers and trees from their rooms, along with easy access to the interstate—he said, "I have the place for you." One of his Oak Valley lots filled the bill with an almost eerie perfection. But still, as he says, "She had her dream, but I had to temper it with realities," the chief ones being water, sewer and zoning.

"The sewer and water's there," he told her, "but it isn't zoned. I'm going to the zoning board tonight."

"We had been talking about a 'typical' business park," he recalls. "I had in mind a Route 128 in Boston or a Palo Alto high-tech thing. The township had said you can either make it a business park or, if you want to make any modifications, we might approve them. So I said that night that I wanted to add indoor recreation, I wanted to add a day care center, as an amenity, medical care in-house, such as a nursing home, and a drive-in bank. They were all approved as designated uses in the Planned Unit Development."

And, so far, they are the only uses to which the sites have been put. "We have the Ann Arbor Ice Cube, Arbor Hospice, Gretchen's House Childcare Center, and Tutor Time," says Chisholm. "Then we've got indoor soccer next door. Where is the Super Instrument Co., the XYZ Technology? We haven't gotten one yet."

He's happy to point out, however, that both Arbor Hospice and the Ice Cube are "fabulous facilities, world-wide models." It's consistent with his interest in creating quality of life facilities in his adopted town, not only from affection but also because, quite frankly, it's good for business.

Much to his surprise, one of the arts entities he's been most closely identified with also turned out to be a good business: Kerrytown Concert House. "There was a case where it was said you have no chance, you're crazy, but Deanna showed us," he says. That would be Deanna Relyea, the founder and director, whose charming and intimate facility has been one of those grace notes for 15 years.

"Joe O'Neal got me into that," Chisholm recalls. "I thought it was a noble effort but the feasibility just didn't seem to be there because of its limited capacity (perhaps a hundred or so seats), but she knew there was a niche there and that's one of the secrets—you've got to find something nobody else is doing."

Besides Kerrytown Concert House, Chisholm has been president of the Michigan Theatre Foundation Board of Trustees, a board member of the Arts Foundation of Michigan, and a director of the Ann Arbor Summer Festival. He received the Annie for "Outstanding Business Support of the Arts" from the Washtenaw Council for the Arts in 1990.

Chisholm believes arts organizations owe it both to themselves and the town to tighten up their business operations. Ironically, he finds them falling prey to the same misperception that has plagued out-of-town developers.

"If you look at Ann Arbor, the story is basically quality of life," he says. "It's what we have that other small towns don't have. It's important for the University Musical Society and the Michigan Theatre and the Summer Festival to all prosper and develop, but when I get involved with them, I find one of their common mistakes is that each one wants to grow exponentially. They don't understand that this is a small market, and they eat each other up."

Even something as simple as a master arts calendar would be an improvement, he says, using as an example the U-M football schedule for 1998. "September 5 was an away game, then there were three home games before they went on the road again October 3," he notes. "Every arts organization in town had an event on October 3 and thought they were being original. Those of us who are real fans can go to two a night at most, and we'd all have to go to six to keep them going. Then they say they need a donation. I'm not disputing that, but I'm an advocate for them to do smart things, too."

It could be argued that Don Chisholm has changed the

face of Ann Arbor, or at least moved it south a few miles, as much as anyone else in the last three decades, but he's kept the sense of humor that gave Monopoly names to most of the streets and properties east of State and north of I-94, starting with Boardwalk.

"Just before going to the planning commission, we found out that the city couldn't approve the 60-acre area plan until we had a name for the road," he recalls. "Betty said, 'You two are always goofing around. It's just a game to you, anyway; why not call it Boardwalk?'"

So it was that the game had its start while the three of them sipped a libation and listened to music together.

And he eventually managed to merge some roads that once appeared so disparate. The Burlington Atrium and Sloan's Apartment 307 blend business with performances, community activity spaces...and a place where the greats can play Margaret Sloan's Steinway.

"If you make them want to buy, you don't have to ask for the order."

Herm Deal

In the midst of the carnage that was World War II, Herman Deal was affected by a single death.

"He was a peach of a guy," says Deal. "The Russians killed him. That hurt me."

Deal doesn't often talk about hurting. He talks about good luck, good breaks, having friends instead of customers, the half-full glass. But this hurt him, the killing of a German prison guard, officially his enemy, by Russian soldiers, officially his allies. He and the guard had worked out a relationship during the months Deal had spent in a Nazi prisoner of war camp. They had become friends, official positions notwithstanding.

Half a century later, this man who doesn't keep much memorabilia still has a copy of a book privately printed by one of his fellow internees, a man named Ben Phelper. Ironically, Phelper died in an auto accident shortly after the end of the war, shortly after he published this book, *Kriegie Memories*. (A "kriegie" was a prisoner.) The book has two pictures of Deal's friend—one of him smiling, and one of him dead.

World War II veterans learned an abundance of hard—and often sad—lessons. Herm Deal learned most of his as a POW, which is how he spent virtually his entire overseas service. But, on the whole, he saw it as a positive experience. That's Herm Deal for you.

"I'm a salesman, nothing else," he says, "but I've never asked for an order. I have no claim to fame other than being able to work with people. I study what I can do for them and if it works, maybe they'll give me an order."

Working with people has been the constant theme of his life, from a hardscrabble boyhood in Georgia to a prison camp in Germany to 13 years with Michigan Consolidated Gas to the acquisition and expansion of Huron Valley Sales to the daunting task of apportioning what he has created among his offspring.

Yes, he is only a salesman...who has made much and given much away, always considered himself lucky, and worked hard because he was trained to and likes to. He's also one of the godfathers of the car wash industry. Wait a minute...the car wash industry?

Typically, he has no illusions about that. "People say, 'Car wash industry? What's that?', but they're a very sharing, giving group of people, the most giving group of people in the world," says Deal. "They have no trade secrets. They give what they know to everybody." Also typically, the highest praise that occurs to him is to say that they're generous.

"I just attended the funeral in Indianapolis of Larry Harrell, a man who was in the industry and died suddenly at 59," he says. "There were 150 people in line to sign the guest book and more than a thousand at the funeral. He touched so many lives."

Deal proposed establishing a memorial fund to provide college tuition for the children of industry families. The first 44 phone calls raised $40,000. All but one of the people he called pitched in.

When Deal speaks of the exception, he is as close to unkind as he ever seems to get. He told his staff before he called that the man would not give. "He is a man worth $20 to 30 million who said he 'couldn't afford it.' I said, 'Don't tell me that. Tell me you didn't like the guy, or don't tell me why at all. But don't say you can't afford it.'"

Where Deal grew up, on a "two-horse" farm in Bulloch County, Georgia, with his parents and five younger siblings, it was understood that folks helped each other.

"You had roughly 60 acres of land and that's what you lived on," says Deal, whose father's parents were share-croppers. "You grew all your food and got very little other than that." They also butchered, canned, and cured their own meat, made their own lard, and raised cotton, peanuts, tobacco, corn and soybeans. They didn't have electricity, or plumbing, until Herm was 16.

But they were far from deprived. "This was a community where everybody shared," says Deal. "You moved from one farm to the other to do chores and whatever had to be done. You couldn't afford to hire labor so everyone worked together. We used to put up 200 half-gallon jars of toma-toes a year and gave them to the people who worked for us. My parents were sort of leaders in the community and gave much to anyone in need, loans and material and labor for people needing help. I saw a lot of giving at home, both to their family and to the community as a whole."

For a while, the Deals raised chickens as a cash crop. "We had 1,000 and my chore when I got home from school was to shell the corn, feed the chickens, and pick up the eggs."

Hard work was not his only fowl legacy. One day at his grandfather Deal's house, little Herm climbed over the fence to get a pomegranate and found a territorial rooster instead. "He got me before I got back over the fence," Deal remembers. He still has a two-inch scar on his bottom where the rooster spurred him.

Life changed in a hurry after Deal enlisted in the Air Force and left Georgia for the first time in the fall of 1942. In 18 months, he went from Savannah, where had been working in a shipyard; to Boston; Willow Run (where he met Helen Ellis, his future wife); Laredo, Texas; Salt Lake City; Tucson, Arizona; Blythe, California; Clovis, New Mexico; Langley, Virginia; Westover, New York; Norfolk, Virginia; Casablanca; Algiers; Tunis; Sicily, and, finally, a town in the heel of the Italian boot called Mandura.

It was a wild ride, almost as wild as his first flight at gunnery school in Laredo, when he failed to properly tighten the strap on his parachute. After Deal fired the first 100 rounds, the pilot took the open plane into a roll and "I was hanging out with a .30-caliber machine gun in my hand. I think it scared him more than it did me."

After all that training, then service as a flight engineer instructor, then escorting a boatload of 3,500 American soldiers "who had gotten in trouble" across the Atlantic to a work camp in Casablanca (a trip that was supposed to take seven days but took 29), Deal was finally about to fly his first mission.

D-Day was just over a month away, and the Allies wanted to soften up the French coast. "The line had just moved up in Italy, about 50 miles ahead of where we were stationed," says Deal. "On April 29, 1944, we were to bomb Tulon, France, so I volunteered for a makeup crew. En route to our target, the Tulon Submarine Yard, we were hit by fighters over the Adriatic Sea and very heavy flak (anti-aircraft guns) as soon as we reached the coast of France. We had one distinction—we were the first airplane of the 15th Air Force over the target, and we were the first one down."

The first of many; intelligence hadn't briefed them about the anti-aircraft base on the side of a mountain near Tulon. "The flak was so heavy at 25,000 feet, it looked like you could walk on the clouds," Deal says. "We took a direct hit on an engine, and right in front of the co-pilot's feet. The airplane blew just as we bailed out. I landed in a tree with Germans shooting at me all the way down. It was only an hour or two before they captured me.

"My thought was that I had been a very expensive soldier to train, with one plane completely destroyed in a crash landing in Tucson, losing a nose wheel in Langley

Field, and now a bailout."

He and 18 other American prisoners were taken into town, jailed overnight, interrogated, and then subjected to an experience that was shocking even by wartime standards.

It seems the commandant of the German air base there had been a prisoner of the Americans in Africa. He had been well treated and, says Deal, "This was his first opportunity to repay them." The debt was settled like this: For two days, the 19 prisoners were guests at his lavish home in the middle of the base, complete with servants and an indoor swimming pool.

Says Deal, "They put two of us in a room and said, 'Have anything you want; just don't try to get away. The place is surrounded by mine fields and soldiers. Just enjoy yourself.' The only thing he insisted on was if he wanted anything to drink, all 19 of us had to drink with him. He was the most interesting guy I ever met, spoke nine languages, a very unusual person."

Deal and company got another shock a few days later, when the train carrying them to an interrogation camp pulled into Frankfurt. "The day before we arrived, Frankfurt had been totally bombed out," Deal says. "The people there were very upset at the Americans, and if it hadn't been for the German soldiers protecting us, we wouldn't be here today."

He strictly followed the rule about revealing only his name, rank, serial number, and home address, but soon found "they knew more about me than I knew about myself. They told me where I trained, lived, grew up. I could not believe it. Their intelligence had to be second to none."

Deal spent four weeks there, giving the same answer over and over. "I was never roughed up but you were threatened with everything in the book," he says. "You'd be in a cold room one day, a hot room the next, but there was never any abuse. It was a long four weeks."

Also long was the week in a boxcar that followed, especially since Deal was now suffering from pneumonia and the Allies periodically shelled the enemy train. The prisoners were being transported to a POW camp at Krems, Austria, on the Danube River northwest of Vienna. Upon arriving at camp, they were marched up a hill to a long, low building. Their hair was clipped, they were ordered to undress, their clothes were taken away, and they were herded into another chamber. "When vapor started to come out of the walls, a lot of them lost it, but it was just delousing," he says. Deal didn't, and doesn't, suspect that it was psychological warfare.

"It was just a coincidence that it had been used as a gas chamber, but it was quite a shock to everybody," he says. "They were just soldiers doing their job, which was to get us deloused and our clothes clean."

Deal continued to see being a POW as just another handful of lemons that life had handed him, a whole bunch of blessings in disguise.

Why, when he got to the camp, he ran into an old buddy from high school, who had the connection to get Deal a camp job. The camp had both college professors and books, so a school had been set up and he ended up earning 17 college credits while he was there. "All you had to do was go do it," says Deal, "but only about 10 percent of the 4,200 prisoners took advantage of any of it. I probably learned more there than I would had I been in college because you had to concentrate on what you were doing."

Talk about your lucky breaks. And then there was the time he got caught in a tunnel digging—"for somebody else"—and spent two weeks in solitary. "Everyone tucked cigarettes and soap in me (for bartering with the guards), so I got any food I wanted while I was in there," he says. "I gained 18 pounds."

In general, he says of his captors, "I think they did the best they could do under the circumstances." He was so appalled when he went to a reunion of the former inmates a few years ago that he and Helen left early. "It really kind of surprised me, the attitude of the others," he says. "These were the ones who, when they were in the camp, sat and did nothing, played cards and complained. I personally didn't have time to do any of that. I was busy all the time."

Not even Deal would claim it was all gin and bananas. In fact, the cuisine was distinctly meager; food was not something an army about to lose a war is likely to lavish on prisoners. "Hot water for breakfast, beetley-bean soup for lunch and bread for dinner," he says. "That was it. And the water was on for only about two hours a day."

Nor was his wardrobe extensive. "I didn't have any shoes for about three months," he says, "and we'd have to fall out for inspection in the snow and stay out there for hours sometimes while they went through the barracks. It was a little chilly."

What about Ben Phelper's reference to the guards opening fire indiscriminately into the barracks? "That only happened once," Deal says. "And somebody asked for it."

In January 1945, the Russians advanced through Czechoslovakia and neared Krems. "We could see the flashes at night," Deal says. "They got orders to move us out. The only reason was to get away from the Russians, because they were afraid of the Russians. So they started to move us out in groups of up to 200, each with four guards."

That's when the soap, cigarettes, and D-bars (high-energy, concentrated chocolate bars that arrived in Red Cross parcels and became camp currency) that he and his buddies had hoarded came into play. "Five of us pooled everything we had, and drew straws to see who would go out and do the bartering," says Deal.

Deal and a fellow prisoner named John Hester became the emissaries. They made arrangements with the guards and went out to the local farms and villages to barter for provisions during the march to freedom. "We always came back with all the food we could carry," Deal remembers. "We all fared pretty well."

It was, again, a people experience for him. "The first thing you had to do when you got to a farmhouse was have a drink of hard cider," says Deal. "They were very pleasant to us. That was partly because they knew the war was over, but I think they probably would have treated us the same anyway. As long as there weren't any German soldiers in the area, it was no problem. And if there were, they'd hide you. It wasn't pleasant, but I enjoyed the people."

They covered 10 to 20 miles a day, slept on the ground at night, and finally reached Braunau on May 8, after a three-and-a-half month march. It was one week after Hitler's suicide and eight days before the Third Armored Division liberated them. They eventually ended up in Le Havre, their point of embarkation for the United States, where Deal spent three weeks in a hospital "just getting acclimated to food."

Still, he says, that year of his young life "was a very educational thing from a people standpoint, for learning to live and work with people."

After three weeks in Le Havre, Deal sailed to New York, then took a train back to Georgia. There were two things on his mind: finding work, and the girl he met at Willow Run. He spent a week at home, then four weeks in Michigan visiting Helen, who returned home with him to visit his parents. Then Deal and Helen separated again. Helen was secretary to John Airey, chairman of the board of King-Seeley in Ann Arbor. Deal got a job at a Coca-Cola bottling plant and soon became its manager, in addition to going to school part-time.

There wasn't much to managing the plant, he says, because sugar was rationed. "You could only get enough for two days' bottling, then you'd clean up and do the accounting for one day, and then a day of making deliveries, four days of work and one of in-house duties," he says. "I didn't have plans. I was just floating, you might say. The Coca-Cola plant might have been a good place to stay, but I wasn't happy with the environment."

Actually, he did have one plan—to marry Helen—"so I moved to Michigan, without a job, just before we got married." He arrived in the state to stay on April 1, 1950, and soon was working as a door-to-door salesman for Michigan Consolidated Gas, selling appliances in

Ypsilanti "where they had just brought natural gas to the city."

After a year in Ypsilanti, a retirement created an opening in Ann Arbor and Deal filled it. "I worked 18 hours a day," he recalls. "I worked the showroom during the day, then called on people at night to close the sale. I got to where I was making $15,000 a year, a lot of money in those days."

Four years later, his sales manager was transferred to Detroit and the job was offered to him. "I turned it down twice because I was afraid of it," he says. "I was the youngest man there, and directing a force of about 35 people was a big challenge for me. They finally talked me into it, and cut my salary back to $7,200 a year, but there were enough perks to make it worthwhile. In a few years, I was above where I had been before."

Not surprisingly, he describes his years as sales manager as "a real learning experience, working with people. I took advantage of every school offered in the country. I took anything that would help me advance in the gas industry, and I had a boss that would let me do it."

At that time, Deal says, MichCon operated as five virtually independent districts, one of which was Ann Arbor, so his boss had the authority to do that.

There were other forms of education, too. Deal says he quickly learned there was one "secret" to success in sales, and it was a secret he had been raised to know. "Work," he says simply. "Seeing people. After I became sales manager, I did a study on sales calls. I ran the program for four years continuously with every salesman there. They had to account for every call they made, whether anyone was home or not. And the man who made 1,200 calls a year would average $6 a call in commission. The man who made 2,200 would average $6, so it was a matter of seeing and exposing your wares to the customer. And it did not vary 25 cents in four years. It's just volume; it's seeing people.

"Yes, there are certain attitudes and approaches that play a part, but we had seven salesmen who worked the sales floor and they were all types. If they made the call, they made the sale. In my opinion, there's no such thing as a real good sales person when it comes to trying to close an order. My whole theory is you make them want to buy; you don't have to ask for the order. You create a situation where this is something that they need and want."

Thanks to the relative independence of MichCon's districts, Deal had a pretty free hand in developing his tactics, and the company could hardly quarrel with the results. "I had one boss and one budget and whatever I wanted to do with it was left up to me," he says. "We always had something going on, a challenge or a contest to keep everybody going. We were the top district in growth every year, and we had a lot of fun in doing it."

A couple of those "somethings" stick in his memory. One was a gas dryer promotion for new mothers, and the other a sales campaign targeting blue-collar workers.

"At the time gas dryers first came out, there was a public service radio program on WPAG, announcing the babies born the day before," says Deal. "I knew the sales manager at WPAG, and the owner, too, so I called him about letting us sponsor the program."

Not only did MichCon sponsor the show, but also every new mom received a package from the company that included a down payment for a dryer, a layette with diapers and powder, and a 30-day free trial offer. There was also a note: "You wouldn't think a two-day-old baby would insist on a gas-dried diapers, would you?"

"That just took off," says Deal. "We never took a dryer out."

A more substantial, even historic, achievement was convincing the city of Ann Arbor to buy natural gas, rather than electric engines, to pump its water supply. "This was a major accomplishment as far as MichCon was concerned," says Deal.

It was also a bit of a cliffhanger. The City Council had actually approved the purchase of electric motors, on the night before the state Public Service Commission approved a rate for natural gas engines that was considerably lower than the standard commercial rate.

"I called Bud Abbot, the director of the city water department, and said, 'Don't sign that purchase order until we talk.' I was in his office in five minutes," Deal recalls. "I took his department to some water pumping stations in Arizona, Illinois and Louisiana. We were finally able to convince Bud it would be a good move."

Convincing City Council was another story. It took 14 months, including three of what Deal calls "debates" with Detroit Edison, but the deed was finally done, and "They still use them," he says.

But two converging circumstances were about to end Deal's MichCon career and point him in the direction of what became his life's work. The first was the persistence of a man named Harlan Bird.

"He sold Ruud water heaters to the gas company," says Deal. "I was a buyer in this case. He had started calling on us in 1957. I was sort of a renegade, and he always got a kick out of some of the programs we ran. 'When you get ready to get out of here, come buy me out,' he would say. He asked me that every time I saw him for seven years."

The second event was a shift in MichCon's management philosophy. "I probably would never have left there," says Deal, "but they brought all five districts under one head. I lost all my independence. So I called Harlan in and said, 'Let's go today,' and that was that."

The company Deal bought was Huron Valley Sales, and it was the only time it went into debt under his ownership. "When we bought the company, it was worth $206,000," he says. "I had a $50,000 investment and borrowed $167,000 from the National Bank and Trust on a seven-year note on future business, inventory, etc."

At the time, the company consisted of Bird, a sales person, an office assistant and, now, Deal. "All Bird did was sell water heaters to the utility," says Deal. "We had the eastern side of Michigan, a line through Lansing to Sault Ste. Marie. He had done a good job, sold 6,000-8,000 heaters a year, and made $12-14 on each. But I took it as a challenge to go into areas where they had not had any growth."

Little did he dream at the time what some of those areas might be. He was simply approaching his current challenge the same way he had its predecessors: with hard work, a sunny outlook, and a knack for connecting with people and connecting people with each other.

After four months at Huron Valley Sales, though, all he was connecting with was restlessness. "I was very discouraged because I didn't have a challenge," he says. That all changed the day Bob Glen, whose office was up the street from Deal's, stopped by for a chat.

"He was a distributor for one of the car wash companies, Robo-Wash," says Deal. "He didn't like the equipment that the company was providing him, so he came down to us to develop a system for him that would better suit his needs. A month later, he was back for another system, and also asked us to contact his supplier, Robo-Wash, in Kansas City. We had recently completed an agreement with Raypak, Inc., a commercial boiler and water heater manufacturer, to handle their product in the state of Michigan and neighboring cities south of Michigan, but we had no authority to sell elsewhere. However, we had been asked to negotiate so we could sell Robo-Wash, so we met with that company several times.

"They felt our price was too high, however, until they had problems, as we projected. They finally ordered two systems. With both installations, we were put to the test and won their confidence without lowering the price. We determined that the car wash industry was positioned for tremendous growth, so we made a presentation to Al Whittell, president of Raypak, on the potential market, and he gave us the car wash industry for North America."

The dogged Deal swung into action. "At that time, everyone involved in the business was trying to sell equipment to the car wash industry," he says. The packagers and assemblers of the complex machinery that cleaned the vehicles needed suppliers. "Any assembly maker who ran an ad in *The Wall Street Journal*, I would call and ask where's your closest one to Detroit. Wherever it was, I would go there and do an engineering study. Often, there was no professionalism; they were seat-of-the-pants, unsafe and very expensive installations. Then I would come back with a proposal to do a better job for less money."

The first account he landed was particularly instructive.

"The Walter Kidde Company had put in an installation in Flint and I spent about three days there trying to work something that was better," he recalls. "Then I arbitrarily went out to the plant in Vermillion, South Dakota, which was the wrong thing to do, because they had nothing to do with decision-making there. That was in Zanesville, Ohio."

Deal then made an appointment to go to Zanesville and meet with one of their engineers, "a German guy, very sharp." Deal showed him the drawings he had made of the layouts.

"He looked at them and said, 'Where did you get all the information?' I said I had been to Flint and studied the system. He pushed a button on his desk and called somebody in and said, 'Would you buy 25 of those for me?' I thought, 'Well, that's got to be the way to do it.' That was my incentive to keep going with *The Wall Street Journal*."

That, and paying for the company. "The first year after Bird retired and I had purchased the company, the car wash industry was just starting to grow, but I was quite concerned when I went and paid Harlan," Deal says. "On September 1, we were $100,000 in the red, and on November 30, the end of our fiscal year, we had a profit of $16. But we averaged 20 percent compounded growth a year for several years after that."

Deal signed up a total of 19 accounts that first year. "One-third of Raypak's production went to the car wash industry through us," he says. "So we got their attention."

And, of course, they also got the attention of the car wash world. "Because this was a small industry, we were able to dominate the market completely," he says. But dominating even a small market requires constant attention to the customers' needs, future as well as current. That meant "basically just service, service, service, service," says Deal, and it also meant innovation.

"One of the first things we did was design a system to keep ice off the floors of self-service car washes," he says. "Ice was very hazardous, and a liability issue. We put in our first one in Wisconsin, and from that time it took off like you wouldn't believe. Both the self-service and the high-pressure automatic operations needed this application, plus they needed hot water."

In addition to dominating the market in the nascent industry, Deal quickly involved himself in car wash politics. Within two years, he was on the board of directors of the Coin-Op Car Wash and Laundry Association. He served six years in two different terms on the National Coin-Op Car Wash Association board. When the NCWA merged with the International Car Wash Association, the group of tunnel operations where cars are pulled through on conveyor, he was elected to the ICWA board.

Eventually, in 1995, he was named to the Car Wash Hall of Fame, the industry's highest award. Deal's indifference to memorabilia is such that there are only a couple of mementos that he truly cherishes. One is the 15-pound, 40-inch steelhead trout he caught in British Columbia in 1990. The other is his Hall of Fame plaque.

"I probably spent two months a year working for the association," he says. "Doing that, you just got exposed to people."

And they got exposed to him, and found that he was a good fit in an industry where mutual assistance is the norm. "It's a real sleeper, from an industry standpoint. There's no glamour in it. It's all hard work, details," he says. "When it started out, there was such a small group involved, and everyone needed help. There was a sharing of ways of doing things, experiences, even the operations themselves."

He remembers how Larry Harrell, the man from Indianapolis in whose memory the scholarship fund is being established, "would come to a new place when they were starting, stay for three days to help them, then leave, with no thought of payment for his time and expertise. He would just wish them luck."

This was clearly a hospitable environment for a man who says, "I don't have customers; I have friends," and who annually takes his suppliers to his cabin on Georgian Bay in Ontario to unwind for a few days without TVs, radios, or phones. "It's not a customer-supplier relationship at all," he says. "It's how can we help each other get the volume of business we're looking for. Another thing that has helped us from our supplier standpoint is we didn't take on a lot of items. We're not a rep house with 40 items. We concentrated on products that would help the car wash industry."

But don't get the idea that Deal credits himself with some grand, visionary strategy. "Whatever we tried to do was successful," he says. "We couldn't do any wrong. In my case, it's been a lot of luck."

Another challenge had nothing to do with competition and everything to do with managing to survive as the result of—almost a reward for—his business practices. People who weren't in the car wash industry may not have noticed, but as the '80s drew to a close, there was a three-year period when it rained almost every weekend in the central United States.

Thus it was that Deal had to write off more than a million dollars in bad debts over that span, including $671,000 in 1990 alone. "We're a weather business," he says. "It took out so many operators. They couldn't make any money, so the manufacturers couldn't sell anything, and most of the major ones went bankrupt. No one could control it. It brought them to their knees. The people that went out were unbelievable, and they took us with them."

Well, not quite. "We've always been a cash company, except I had to borrow some when I first bought it," he says. "And we never spent any money. What we don't give away, we put back in the company. Nobody got any big bonuses that year, but we survived it without a problem because we're so strong. And we paid all the employees a two-year bonus the following year."

As the above illustrates, part of the company's strength is in his relationship with the people who work for him. You could almost paraphrase his comment about customers and say, "I don't have employees; I have friends." Mere employees might not have been as willing to take a few short-term hits in return for the long-term health of the enterprise.

"I've always taken the philosophy that whatever we make, I didn't do it," he says. "It was all the people that supported me, the employees that were there. We have a profit-sharing program and we have always given away most of the money at the end of the year. We pay them a living salary and, at the end of the year, divide the profits, leaving just enough to handle our projected growth for the next year. I never felt I had to grow a big company, just enough to support growth. I've been more interested in supporting the people who were already there."

One year, when the company fared particularly well, he sent the whole workforce—along with their spouses and significant others—to Disney World for four days. "Helen and I went down and ran the business, just answered the phones basically," he says. "This has always been my philosophy. I don't earn the money; you've got 20 other people there doing the job and they've got to be rewarded. If the money is there and it's available, let's do it."

Not surprisingly, there isn't a lot of turnover at his company. "They retire," he says, "once in a while. We had one who retired three times."

Between good luck and good employees, Deal almost edits himself out of his own success.

"I got a call about eight years ago from a man at Hexagram, a company out of Cleveland that had developed a remote meter-reading device," says Deal. "He would not tell me who referred him to me. He said, 'You know the utility business and you're a pretty good marketer.' He wanted me to take the device for the world. I told him I hadn't been in the utility business for years and turned him down twice. The third time he called, I got excited about it."

Deal then invoked one of his principles, as well as another personal relationship. "I've always believed in selling from the top," he says, "so I called Robert Stewart, a man who at that time was president of Primark Corp. in McLean, Virginia. They own MichCon and a lot of other companies, and lease UPS airplanes. He had worked for MichCon when I did. I said, 'I want to come down and see you. I've got something I want you to look at.'"

"I flew down and met with him at 5 o'clock that afternoon," Deal recalls. "I said I just want your opinion. He looked at it for 15 minutes, got up and went into the office next door, and got on a conference call. He said, 'I'm sitting with Herman Deal. I'm sending him back to you. Buy the goddam thing.'"

Three weeks later, Deal had an order for $15 million. "It ended up being $35 million over a six-year period," he says. "It was one of those things I took on the outside, nothing to do with Huron Valley Sales. I just made a straight commission. We ended up moving quite a bit of it."

Another major stroke of luck, in his view, benefited his company. "Valley Die Cast Company did the chrome plating for Chrysler Corp. and manufactured car wash systems," he says. "On a cold call from an ad in *The Wall Street Journal*, I found they had a serious misapplication of a boiler they were shipping for installation through the USA. That day, we engineered a proper application and they ordered ten 1,500,000-BTU boilers. Before I reached the office the next morning, they had placed three more 10-unit orders, to be shipped ASAP. Not bad for one call."

He does admit to spending "an awful lot of time with the manufacturers and their distributors, training them on the engineering and sizing and applications and radiant heat systems. We just became the standard.

"It was a good way to dominate a niche market," says Deal. "It certainly worked for Huron Valley Sales, and Raypak had the vision to give us the territory and support to make it happen. To this day, Huron Valley Sales handles 70-80 percent of the radiant heating market in car washes, and 50-60 percent of the water heating market. For 21 consecutive years, HVS was the top Raypak distributor, receiving many awards."

Deal's biggest challenge came after the runaway success of his business enterprises. Not surprisingly, it involved his children, a common enough circumstance for anyone who has had them. But someone who is so proud of his children (six sons, two daughters, and 22 grandchildren), and equally proud of forging relationships with other people, may feel it more keenly if that skill sometimes seems to desert him when his own offspring are involved.

He places the onus on himself, not them. "I really feel bad that I did not know my children," he says. "I did quite a bit of work in scouting with them but other than that, it was Saturday noon until Sunday night. We always went to church every Sunday, always there on time and dressed properly. But Helen was their teacher, not me. It's kind of sad that I don't really know them the way I should."

It also created unforeseen difficulties when Deal began considering how to divide what he'd built, both the enterprises and the proceeds, among his tribe. "We made good money," he says. "Now we had to figure out a way to keep it going for future generations.

"Helen and I have been very fortunate that none of our children have ever been in any trouble or created any serious problems," Deal adds. He describes them in chronological order, starting with the oldest:

"Howard is an electrical engineer and independent consultant to Chrysler. Mitzi is a homemaker and teacher, and with her husband, Eduardo, owns Mila Marble, a distributor of imported marble products. Jeff is president and owner of Hamilton Engineering Company, a distributor of water heating and heating products for the laundry, greenhouse and motel markets. Jim owns Dillon's hair salon in Ann Arbor.

"Alan is president of Performance Engineering Group, a

distributor of water heating, heating, and allied products to the general construction and utility market, with radiant floor heating being one of their fast-growing divisions. Doug is president of Huron Valley Sales and a good replacement for me. Doug is respected for his knowledge of the car wash industry and has a tremendous following. Alice is now a homemaker and personal athletic trainer. She was formerly a banker and she and her husband own Ahearn Enterprises, a printing and sign business.

"And Rob, the youngest, the 'last Deal,' is national sales manager of commercial products for Turtle Wax. We've all been very lucky that they had a mother and teacher like Helen."

The two sons who cast their fate with the family business were Alan, a mechanical engineer, and Doug, who began working there while he was in high school. Alan worked with outside engineering firms for several years before joining the company. He was in the commercial and industrial side of the business, while Doug was in the car wash side.

"After several years of trying to determine the best way for the company to continue into the next generation," says Deal, "we created a separate company and divided the assets according to the percentage of business in each division."

Thus, Alan became president and part-owner of Performance Engineering Group, and Doug is president and part-owner of Huron Valley Sales. "Both companies are doing well and growing," says the proud father.

"The last four years have been devoted to getting this company separated and hopefully on its way so I can somewhat retire," says Deal, "but I can never sit still. I have to be involved in something, community work or volunteer work. I could never go and read or wait to die. So many of our good friends from the gas company, when they retired, lived six months or less and worked themselves up into a heart attack and that was the end of them. I can't fish every day and I don't play much golf. I think a lot of health and living long is keeping your mind active and your body active."

Between the war and being in sales, this is a man who's done a lot of traveling that was hardly recreational, but he seems to have developed a taste for it anyway. It's certainly been one of his favorite ways to keep the mind and body active.

"The last few years, Helen and I have taken quite a few tours, anywhere from 10 days to three weeks," he says. "We've covered a lot of the world, and I've enjoyed all of it. If I were a young person, I would head for the gold coast of Australia right now—fantastic climate and fantastic environment, very clean. Australia and New Zealand would be my favorites, and Ireland. The best fishing trip I ever had was in British Columbia a few years ago, getting there by helicopter, up in the Canadian Rockies, 800 square miles leased for fishing rights. It was unreal."

He catches fish, but he feeds birds. His back yard is practically an aviary, filled with trees that are filled with feeders. He says he buys about 1,000 pounds of bird seed a year.

But, then, they aren't really birds; they're his friends.

"The potential for a better life."

Jack Dempsey

More than half a century later, Jack Dempsey still remembers the night vividly.

He and his older brother, Carlyle, were living with their maternal grandparents and great aunt back in Corry, Pennsylvania, where they were born, while their mom and dad suffered through one of their frequent bouts of marital instability in Buffalo.

"I remember a gentleman coming to the door in the evening and my brother and I were shepherded off to the kitchen," says Dempsey. "My grandfather was in a discussion with a life insurance man. I felt that, somehow or other, there was something important going on. In those days, it was the 50 cents a week being collected for debit insurance just to cover burial costs, but it did leave an impression."

His awareness of life's uncertainties was deepened a few years later when his father died at 41—"and I think the cause of death would be lifestyle," says Dempsey. Then his stepfather, Philip Houck, died suddenly at age

50 when Jack was a junior in high school, an event which Dempsey feared might doom his ability to attend college. It's no surprise then that security became a central issue in the youngster's life, and one that eventually provided his life's work.

Dempsey was born in Corry, a factory town of 12,000 or so, 25 miles southeast of Erie, on Christmas Day, 1935. His parents, Rex and Lila Hinman Dempsey, separated, then reconciled when Jack was age 4, moving him and his brother, Carlyle, age six, to Buffalo. Three years later, the parents divorced, and Jack returned to Corry to live with Carl and Lucy Hinman, his mother's parents, and his great aunt, Ola Young, Lucy's sister, who was a first grade teacher.

Despite the apparent turmoil, Dempsey remembers his childhood fondly, and has always been grateful for the genetic blend he inherited from his parents.

"I was born to an Irish Catholic father and a Methodist mother, and I was exposed on the Irish Catholic side to a lot of music, warmth and fun, and on my mother's side, to a very strong Protestant work ethic," he says. "The Hinmans lived on Maple Avenue, and the Dempseys lived up on the Hill, on Mead Avenue. What I would hear from the Hinmans and my first teacher, Great Aunt Ola, would be 'A busy boy is a happy boy.' From the Dempseys, I would hear 'All work and no play makes Jack a dull boy.' They both had good messages, really, and I absolutely split the difference; it's carried through my life.

"I take my work and my career and my family very seriously," he says, "but I'm also able to let go, play the piano on occasion, and hit the golf ball on more than an occasion. While I didn't have the ideal circumstances, nevertheless I didn't feel shorted. I did experience love and nurturing, and I established a value system early in life."

His early history with the piano is almost a parable of the different sides of his nature. "My father was a wonderful piano player," says Dempsey. "He played by ear, and he played very well. I still have a record. His sister was also a piano player. It was up on the hill in Corry where I first got exposed to music. But the music lessons, the discipline of music, those were started by the Hinmans. It was one thing to enjoy music but it's another thing to pay some prices and start learning what you're doing. I hated those lessons, but I did 'em. And then when my mother remarried, she got me started with a music teacher named Carl Bach, and he taught me chording."

For a while, anyway, and then the Dempsey genes resurfaced. "I took lessons from him for about a year while I was in high school," he recalls, "then I have to confess I took the money my mother and stepfather gave me for the Saturday morning piano lessons and used it to enter competitive jackpot bowling. Then, one day, my mother had a reason to call my piano teacher because there was something going on at home, and he allowed as how I hadn't been there for a year. It was an interesting session when I got home."

Obviously, Dempsey needed discipline and structure in his life. That was provided in those relatively stable times in Kenmore, New York, from the seventh grade through high school. Those early Corry years were also critical in Dempsey's development. His grandfather was a carpenter who worked at Raymond's, a local factory. Although he was not well educated, Dempsey remembers him as well read, and vehemently opposed to attempts to unionize his workplace. He was also an avid sports fan, an interest he nurtured in his grandson, and sport fisherman, an interest that was indirectly responsible for introducing young Jack to Chautauqua, one of the most powerful influences on his life.

So, in a way, was Raymond's, even though Dempsey admits he "didn't have the foggiest idea" what the company made. He did, however, visit his grandfather there a couple of times "and I had a fear that some day I would have to work in a factory. That wasn't very inviting."

It was at the summer-long Chautauqua Institute at Lake Chautauqua, just 20 miles away across the New York state line, that Dempsey got "my first taste of the potential for a better life."

It was pretty eye-opening for a seven-year-old. "It was a gathering place for religious leaders, educators, musicians," he says. "It was kind of a diversified Interlochen. It had an awful lot of culture. My Great Aunt Ola went there because a lot of teachers gathered there. My grandfather went there primarily for fishing with his son Al and my brother, but fishing wasn't a very exciting sport to me, so the problem was what do we do with Jack? The answer was to bus me up the road to the Chautauqua Institute to get involved with the day camp."

At first, he only went for a couple of weeks a year. By the time he reached his teens, he was spending entire summers there. "Most of the culture I got from osmosis because I was more interested in golf and baseball, and I was working," he says. "We'd sweep out the amphitheater in the mornings when they were going to have church, plays, and concerts. During the day, we'd sickle grass. Further down the line, I wound up becoming a guide at the gate. I would ride with visitors and hope to get rewarded at the end."

During these tours, he would point out the homes of prominent families along the route. His exposure to such people shaped him more than the culture, or the golf. "The names that ring a bell are the Campbells, the Heinzes, and the Samples—Mr. Sample was chairman of Murphy Five and Dime," recalls Dempsey. Affluent and influential Pittsburgh families they were, but "these were people who were not splashy," he says. "The Samples, in particular, were very, very open and very nice people to be with. They didn't hold it against you that you didn't come from similar circumstances. I sure liked the quality of their life. They were not only affluent, they had real class."

Dempsey's mother remarried when he was 11, and he and his brother went to live with her and their stepfather in the Buffalo suburb of Kenmore. "That was another kind of blossoming," he says. "I was a big fish in a little pond in Corry and a little fish again in Kenmore. I think our class alone was 400-500 people. It was an excellent school system; I got a very good grounding in English, math, and history."

He also began to set his sights on college; specifically Cornell, his stepfather's alma mater. But then his stepfather died. "My brother, who wanted to be a pharmacist, dropped out of the University of Buffalo," says Dempsey. "I was absolutely certain I wasn't going to be able to go to college because there had been no provisions for us."

Although not quite as dramatically as Pip's benefactor in *Great Expectations,* a man named John Pennington now appeared in Dempsey's life. A Cornellian like Jack's stepdad, and active in alumni affairs, Pennington took an interest in the youth. "He essentially planted the seed that it would be possible for me to go to Cornell if I could demonstrate that I had the will, and find a way to find jobs," Dempsey says. "Scholarship aid was available, and so were student loans. And it was really a combination of those, along with the fact that it happened to be a state-supported school, so acceptance there was a scholarship in and of itself."

And attendance there was, as he puts it, "another mind-expander." This was even vaster than Kenmore High School, and far more daunting. "The first time I ever saw it was the first day of school, and I was just overwhelmed," he says. He was also, thanks to the accident of his birth date, a year younger than his classmates. "I had a lot to learn, a lot of maturing to do," he says.

His academic performance was fine, and the enormity of the institution was offset for him by the fact that he was enrolled in the relatively small and close-knit School of Industrial and Labor Relations. It was in the arena of social skills where he had "some catching up do to." Extroverted and outspoken, he found some of his colleagues were not always as eager to hear his opinions as he was to share them. Dempsey got an example of this when he entered the Woodford Senior Oration Competition, at the encouragement of his speech instructor at Cornell. "I wrote a speech on conformity because I had been told by my fraternity brothers that I was too friendly, that I somehow should become more conservative or whatever, and some of that hurt. I also learned many positive social lessons from the fraternity. In any event, I wrote this thing on conformity, and the title of it was 'The Charcoal-Gray Mind.'"

He tied for first with a student who spoke about the Yalta Conference, and they shared the $150 first prize. It enabled him to go to Florida for the first time at spring break. That was the same year he was defeated for re-election as class president, a post he won as a junior after being class secretary the year before.

"It isn't important that I was class president," he says. "What's important is that the person running against me in my senior year really built a platform on what I hadn't done. It was what today is called negative campaigning. I found that I was sensitive, very sensitive, and still am today. While I had considered a legal and political career, I realized that I was too thin-skinned to be involved in that way. It was one of the best decisions I ever made."

Between waiting tables, working as a dorm counselor, school break jobs (milk and laundry delivery in the summer, and mail at Christmastime) back in Kenmore, and loans and scholarships, he managed to make it through Cornell. And, oh yes, he sold a little insurance. Very little.

"I think I fared better having had to work than many of those who had an easier road," he says, but his first steps on what became his lifetime's path were hardly auspicious.

It seems John Pennington was a general agent for State Mutual Life, of Worcester, Massachusetts. "He sensed there might be potential for me in the life insurance business," Dempsey recalls. "He had me licensed while in college, when I was 18 years of age, and I made a couple of sales, but it was a kind of scary experience. I wasn't really convinced that this was for me."

Upon graduation, he thought maybe IBM was for him, and quickly accepted a job offer. "At that time, it was considered a real honor to be selected by IBM," he says. "I was with them for 90 days, a 90-day wonder. They wondered why I was there, and I did, too."

The theory apparently was that he ought to know how to wire whatever product he was going to sell. "It was highly technical," he says. "Here's a guy with a liberal arts background with some business components, and they're talking about input and output and working with these large machines...they actually wanted us to learn how to wire these boards! I was just completely out of my element. It was really a confidence shaker."

And the training period would be two years. By now, Dempsey's theory was that he didn't choose to devote that much of his life to wiring boards if it turned out he didn't have an aptitude for selling in the first place. He asked to go out in the field, preferably accompanying one of the company's top salesmen on some important calls.

IBM assigned him to a man named Glenn Johnson, Buffalo's top data processing salesman, whose answers to some questions Jack asked at lunch one day changed his life.

"I asked him if he had the choice of staying with IBM or going into the life insurance business, what would he do?" Dempsey says. "He was very candid. He said he had friends in Rochester, New York, who had gone into the life insurance business who were doing better economically than he was. He said these corporations have a tendency, once you make a large sale, to re-describe how you're going to be compensated. There was a roof; there was a lid. His thinking was that in the life and health insurance business, there was no lid. That was a tremendous appeal. And I was in a large corporate environment. I wanted a chance to develop my own business."

Enter Mr. Pennington, again. "I thought I might go to law school," says Dempsey. "He was encouraging me to consider the life insurance business. He said you have to decide whether you want to spend more time with people or with books."

The new graduate opted for the former, and signed up with State Mutual in August 1957. "It was the beginning of one of the toughest years of my life," he recalls. "The training was next to nil. They would say, 'This is your prospecting list' and hand you a phone book. So I started really from nowhere, except for maybe calling on a few high school friends."

And his fraternity brothers. "The only thing that saved my butt, frankly, my first year was going back to my beloved Beta Theta Pi and starting the seniors and those about to graduate on their first life insurance programs," he says. "Without capitalizing on that, I would have failed."

More consistent success came with a more coherent plan. "I started to focus on the medical market: young interns, residents, University of Buffalo medical school students," he says. "One reason is you usually find that the markets you function best in are those markets where people are within five years of your own age, and a lot of these medical students were exactly there, and they also were beginning in their careers, as I was, so we had a lot of empathy for each other. About the third or fourth year, I finally started making a livable income.

"But the most important thing that happened in my life at that point was meeting Barb," he says. And that happened on St. Patrick's Day, 1960, when they met at an Irish pub called Crotty's while they were both playing hooky—Dempsey from his CLU (Chartered Life Underwriter) studies at the University of Buffalo law school, and Barbara Bentley from her job with Bell Telephone as an editor.

"My intent was to go back to class," he says, "but then you start getting into it and enjoying yourself. I met Barb and there was instant chemistry. We made plans to meet again after work and went to the University Club, a place that I could barely afford. I demonstrated that I could play the piano and we just had a wonderful evening. That began a relationship that ended with marriage in August of that year."

The relationship almost began three years earlier. "I had just graduated from Cornell," he says. "She was walking down Main Street and I introduced myself and tried to get a date. She allowed as how we hadn't been properly introduced. It was ironic; the timing wasn't right, either."

Clearly, things change. Less than a year after Dempsey and Barb were married, their daughter, Kim, was born. "It was then that I really began to get serious about business because of the responsibilities," says Dempsey. It was also then that he came down with a blood disease called ITP, resulting in a serious compression of platelets.

"I was laid up for six months on very strong cortisone-oriented drugs that ultimately, we thought, took us out of the woods," he says. "But during that period of time, instead of lamenting the fact that I was disabled, I completed my CLU studies at home. When you take this cortisone stuff, you get so hyped up, you have all this energy. I was studying at night and able to complete my studies and get my degree at the tail end of that six-month layoff."

He was also able to spend more time than he could have otherwise with their new baby, Kim, who eventually became a major figure in the evolution of his business. Barb quit working when she became pregnant, and the family was kept afloat by State Mutual's disability income plan. "It was a very, very frugal period, to say the least," he recalls. It was also his first experience with turning the lemons of misfortune into lemonade.

Just a year after earning his CLU designation, he qualified for the first time for the Million Dollar Round Table, "an organization that has had an immense impact on my life."

At that time, in 1963, "the number of people qualifying nationally for MDRT was maybe in the area of 3,000, out of 200,000 in the field," says Dempsey, "so it was an achievement, and it was something that was important to me. I would read the MDRT profiles about successful people in the life insurance business, and I wanted to meet these people, I wanted to be with them, and I wanted to adapt the parts of what they did that would fit my personality so that I could be assured that I could be with them every year, and that has been the case."

Since he's now a 36-year Life and Qualifying Member, it

will continue to be. "It's a very nurturing organization," he says, citing "the feeling of belonging, the acceptance by your peers. People outside the industry don't attach the same significance to it that the people in the industry do. You begin to learn who the professionals are. It's a small fraternity, in that sense. There's always been a heavy emphasis in my career on making sure that I'm advising and assisting people as I would want to be advised. It's not only the CLU creed; it's what we've lived. The importance, I've always felt, is to form relationships that are built on trust."

Within the next three years, trusting a fellow Cornellian uprooted him from Buffalo and deposited him in Ann Arbor, and trusting his own judgment kept him there to build a business.

The Cornellian was Bob Safford, also from Buffalo, who had been in the class ahead of Dempsey at the School of Industrial and Labor Relations. "While in college, I sold Christmas cards for him on a couple of occasions," says Dempsey. "He was going to be the marketing head of a new life insurance company to be formed in Michigan. The name of that company was Alexander Hamilton.

"Barb and I visited them in Michigan and I didn't really feel like they had things together," says Dempsey. "We opted not to come. But, a year later, we made the decision, and hindsight says it was a pretty gutsy decision on her part and mine, to leave our roots and friends in Buffalo and come to a new town, Ann Arbor, where we knew no one, and start with an unknown company."

Like his introduction to life insurance, it was another inauspicious beginning, even more so than he anticipated. A month after taking up residence at the Ann Arbor Y while Barb stayed behind to sell their house, his ITP reappeared. "It became even more of a challenge," he says. "This time, I knew I was involved in a life-threatening situation."

First, he went back to his physician in Buffalo, "hoping he would encourage me to stay because that would be a comfortable decision. Instead, he said I should go on with my life." That is, if he had one. He was told by Dr. John Nixon at St. Joseph Mercy Hospital that "if they can't lick it with cortisone, then they remove the spleen, but in about half the cases, the people still have the problem."

Dempsey returned to Michigan for the surgery. Ironically, Alexander Hamilton had recruited him to work in the area because of his experience selling life insurance to doctors, of which there were, and are, plenty in Ann Arbor. Their profusion and quality were now paying unexpected dividends.

"Dr. John Nixon was one of the kindest, most informed people that I ever met," says Dempsey. "He really helped me through this. He helped me understand the disease, and I came out on the right side of it. With it being a 50-50 proposition, I went from being uninsurable to becoming a preferred risk."

His experience with Alexander Hamilton was less eventful. "After two years working with Hamilton, I had serious reservations about the product and about what they represented," he says. "What I was observing was more sizzle than steak, and some greed. Hamilton today is a very respected company, but these were promotional stages, early stages, and there were some things going on that I wasn't comfortable with."

So, in 1966, he made a two-pronged decision: to become an independent agent, and to focus on business insurance. The latter was inspired by two other significant considerations: that there was an unfilled niche in the local market, and that Dempsey wanted to spend more evenings with his growing family instead of visiting potential clients.

"At that point, I felt that I would absolutely have a reduction in income, that I was going to lose some residuals," says Dempsey. Instead, "the year after I made the decision to return to my professional instincts, my income doubled. That was partly because of changing to the business market, but it was also because, once again, I felt 100 percent professional."

Maybe that helped clarify his vision. "As I was marketing and selling to businesses, I found that there weren't many people in the area working in the group insurance arena," he recalls. "The large insurance brokerage houses were more interested in the big deals, and most of the local people were concentrating on personal insurance. Benefit planning for small, medium—and even some large—businesses became a marketing niche; a marketing strategy, really. And I had the very good fortune to connect with some significant companies early. That was the beginning of our group life and health business."

It was also the beginning, albeit a small one, in the pension area; an entrée for the relative newcomer into the local business community, and further confirmation of the theory that it is most effective to sell to people approximately your own age. "I felt that until I was over age 30, I would not get the respect, or the attention, of owners of businesses who might be 10 years my senior," he says.

But now the time had come, and he painstakingly laid the foundation for what, he says, "eventually became, in the true sense, marketing. I would establish a base of companies, then from there I would go back to the business insurance aspects of key man coverages, buy/sell coverages, the different kinds of funding that are necessary in business. It was a good decision, but you first have to make the conscious decision. It all involves forethought and planning and pursuing a plan. Fortunately for me, it worked."

Fortunately, as well, he had linked up with a company called Bankers' Life of Iowa, now Principal Life. "They had a great small group product," he says. Perhaps just as important, he adds, "I really saw a marriage with a company where I could identify with their culture and their work ethic. We shook hands on it and a year later, we sealed our deal with them as a general agent and it's been a wonderful two-way street ever since."

That was also the year Dempsey, Inc., was born, a major stage in the evolution its founder from sales person to business person. "Once you prove that you're someone who's really interested in the community and in the customer and the clients, you're beginning to get established," he says. "You also make that transition some-where in there. I really consider it a business maturing process. It isn't just about money; it's really a lot about job satisfaction. It should be part of your job description, for any business person, that if you are benefiting from a community or an industry, that you should give back to it. That becomes a definition of not just a business person but a whole person. There are many of them in many businesses. Those are the kind of people, frankly, that I've gravitated to."

The importance of incorporation was itself one of the lessons he learned from his clients. "We were the first life insurance agency to incorporate in Washtenaw County," he says. "It just wasn't heard of at that time. By doing that, we were able to implement the same kind of plans we were recommending to our clients.

"There were tremendous tax advantages that corpora-tions enjoyed that individuals did not," Dempsey says, "including primarily the ability to set up sheltered retire-ment plans. All of those—the establishment of deductible medical and disability and benefit packages, not only for ownership but also for staff—could be implemented in a C corporation, which is what we were and still are. From day one, 1968 on, we have never missed a maximum con-tribution in any of these retirement plans. That really happened because we incorporated.

"More importantly, it happened because we were disci-plined in the handling of money. I don't think it takes any skill whatsoever to spend money. Where the skill comes in is in the discipline of saving, of any kind. Equally impor-tant, as the savings grow, is the ability to invest and prop-erly manage those assets. That is so important, and it's not simple. The world is full of chasing bigger and bigger homes and toys, so there's a lot of temptation out there."

Clearly, as he says, "I've never been into the 'keep up with Joneses' mentality. I can recall a real estate lady approaching me at a Chamber of Commerce meeting and saying, 'I understand you're doing well in business. You should consider a larger home.' My response was that if she could guarantee more happiness with this larger home, I would be pleased to entertain the idea, and that was the end of the conversation. It was kind of a smart-ass comment, but I thought she was being inappropriate."

Dempsey would never pretend to guarantee happiness, but he could guarantee that he and his company bought the same products that they sold, and that they held themselves responsible for more than just their selling. "It's much easier to sell if you in fact are a buyer yourself," he says. "I never advise people to do something I wouldn't do myself. Not everybody's circumstances are the same, but I have long held a strong belief in the value of life insurance and its inherent tax advantages. Therefore, I'm a significant owner of life insurance, and it's funded primarily through the business."

As for the service component, it is in many respects his true "product."

"In our business, there's very little to differentiate us from our competitors because of product and pricing similarity," Dempsey says, "so the only way you can differentiate yourself is to bring something to the table that is what is called 'value added.' I think real service is what defines professionalism. There's an attitude that gets projected."

It is also an attitude that needed to be projected as Dempsey's business, and the peers with whom he dealt, matured.

"In the advanced markets, the emphasis is to be on the leading edge, to be totally aware of and on top of developments within the tax law," says Dempsey. "My business has evolved from a business insurance practice to an estate planning practice. You are working in tandem with very astute accountants, trust officers and attorneys, and you better bring something to the table that's meaningful and that they can use to benefit their client. You better know what you're doing."

Dempsey must have known what he was doing when he hooked up with Bankers' Life because, he says, "They became leading-edge in the 401(k) arena, which is really what my son Mike has focused on. That's his doing; I want to emphasize that. I take a great deal of pride in what he's accomplished, but it's his accomplishment, as it was previously my daughter's."

Yes, Kim, the same daughter he spent recovery time with when he was ill and studying for his CLU designation. Maybe she absorbed something through osmosis when she was an infant, but when Dempsey needed to add staff to diversify his practice, it turned out he needed to look no farther than his own house.

"I had always been able to find people to help me handle the demands of the group insurance," he recalls. "The repricing that's involved, the annual reviews and all that, can become very tedious. I didn't wish to get involved in that because I was concentrating on the other things I enjoyed more. Kim heard a conversation I was having about this with Gary Albrecht, an old and dear friend in the business, in the back room at my house. After I was done, Kim volunteered that maybe she could help. I hadn't even considered it. It never dawned on me, really. I unhesitatingly took her up on her offer.

"Initially, she came in as a staff person, and then it turned out that she had a very strong interest in the marketing side. Over the next seven years, she was dynamite. She tripled that base group business. My philosophy was more that I just wanted the group revenue to cover the overhead, but she turned it into a real profit center.

"People just gravitated to Kim because they knew that she genuinely cared," says her dad. "She became, for a number of smaller firms, kind of their substitute insurance and risk department. A lot of these new firms don't have the money to develop in-house operations like you have with big companies. She became a real resource for them. A 70- to 80-hour work week was nothing for her. And I think she paid a price for that. She not only had drive, she had overdrive."

And then she developed Chronic Fatigue Immune Deficiency Syndrome, and became unable to work at all. "Unfortunately, she was never really able to celebrate the victories," says Dempsey. "It was a heartbreak to see her leave, but in her place she gave us a gift of Mike."

She prevailed upon her younger brother, then in sales training at Johnson Controls, to take up where she was being forced to leave off. "Mike had a good future there," says Dempsey, "but Kim made him an offer he couldn't refuse. I essentially had given Kim ownership of that part of our business and she, in turn, offered that ownership opportunity to Mike, as well as a decent starting compensation package. They worked out a formal buy-sell arrangement between them, with some moderate guidance from me. It really was their deal, their call and, from that point on, their business, even though we're under the same umbrella."

Mike took Kim's base of business and grew it as fast as she did. "They're both quick studies," says their father. "They had to be, because anything they learned from me was strictly by osmosis. I was not a teacher; I never had the patience or the aptitude. I could be perhaps an example, but I'd rather be sitting down with clients, working out problems, than working with personnel on their problems. Without their achievements, I couldn't with good conscience say that Dempsey, Inc., would survive beyond my active business life."

The importance of that cannot be overestimated. "My most outstanding achievement from a business standpoint is the continuity of Dempsey, Inc.," he says, "and I really take little credit for this. That credit belongs to Kim and Mike. It's satisfying to know that Dempsey, Inc., will extend beyond my life. And that's also important from a service standpoint, because many of the estate plans that we've put in place will come to fruition perhaps beyond my life. It's the old idea of having a conscientious attitude about long-term service, because these are long-term contracts."

That he feels so indebted to his children reflects the healing that has occurred in his life in the area of family, perhaps even more than the financial security he's been able to build.

As Kim had for him, Mike offered the opportunity to John, the youngest sibling, to join the business. "He worked here for about a year and a half and really decided to pursue his interests elsewhere," says Dempsey, "and that was fine. John's instincts are more artistic and less business-oriented. He has a tremendous skill there. The other two children were blessed more with numbers skills. Mike felt that John should have the same opportunity that he and Kim had had, but different people have different aptitudes and interests and skills."

What the Dempseys do share are values.

"We've been without money and we've been with money, and I certainly subscribe to the idea that it doesn't buy happiness," he says, "although there's no question that when you come from some insecurity in your background, there is this desire to somehow have financial security. The ultimate goal, I would think for most people, is not to be dependent on money. We've been fortunate."

Barb never knew her mother, who died when she was a few months old. Her father remarried a couple of times, but "to his credit," says Dempsey, "given all that instability, he sent her to Loretto Academy in Niagara Falls, Ontario, and that really was her salvation. She probably had her 'Chautauqua' there, her educational exposure to very upscale people. That was a real break for her.

"And I feel blessed in the sense that being financially secure has helped mend some of the insecurity that Barb and I both experienced in our childhoods."

Not that the road has been without detours and construction zones. "It isn't as if I sat back and laid out a plan because the Man Upstairs has other plans and sometimes they knock you right over," says Dempsey, "but the importance is the getting up again. I'm really a strong believer—and I get very emotional about it—that every adversity we face has a greater benefit."

He can even say that about what appeared at the time to be the biggest investment disaster of his career: the ill-fated purchase of the Goodyear building in downtown Ann Arbor.

"There was a period, let's say up to the point where I was just about 50, where I'd been doing the same thing for a number of years and felt I should diversify," he says. "I'd had some real estate experience and I thought it would be a way to develop net worth and broaden my business acumen. I made some good decisions with regard to personal real estate properties or properties that we would have some control over, and then I made a major mistake, taking a few good friends with me, in the purchase of the Goodyear building.

"It was a mistake, but mistakes are what we learn from. I asked four friends of mine to join with me as general partners to see if we could make a go, initially as a repeat of the old Goodyear's on a retail basis. All of us were inexperienced with regard to retail, but we always felt we could have an office building there, that it would be a natural fallback if retail didn't work. We underestimated, we really underestimated, the overbuilding that had taken place in the office arena. Frankly, we didn't do our homework. So for the next 10 years, we spent significant sums to keep that building afloat. Now, I'd be remiss if I didn't say that I can't think of better guys to be involved in a bad deal with. We all stood up like men and paid our dues and it didn't impair our friendships or relationships. Now we're out of the woods, but it was a tough 10 years.

"So the message from me to someone else is, 'Shoemaker, stick to your last.' Even if you get a little bit bored doing the same thing over and over again, it may be the absolute best thing to stay with what you know. If you are going to diversify, by all means do your homework. That little bit of friendly advice might save some future Jack Dempsey a tremendous amount of money and pain."

Adding to the pain was the media coverage. "It's the only time that I'd ever gotten any unsolicited press," he says. "That's the sensitivity side again. All *The Ann Arbor News* was interested in was how we hadn't done a market study. It's one thing to fail, but it's another to have people rub it in, and to have that be the way you're measured.

Why didn't I have similar inquiries about the growth of Dempsey, Inc., throughout that period? And that says something about society, really. There's a certain side of some people's nature where they like to watch the lions kill the Christians or Clinton make an ass of himself."

One answer may be that the newspaper, by its nature, is focused on the day-to-day, while Dempsey has tried to persevere in the longer view. "The people that interest me the most are the milers, the distance runners, not the sprinters," he says. "We have a lot of sprinters in business. They're enjoying some quick success, but I think at some point these people are going to have their comeuppance. This community has spawned a number of very fine companies that have been acquired and the successful acquisitions or mergers, where you see additional growth going on afterward, are the good stories, I think. Those that no longer exist, or move, those are painful. I do think there's too much emphasis, even at very high levels, on short-term achievement."

The long view, and his commitment to his practice, have contributed to his longevity in Ann Arbor. So have the charms of the place. "I cannot think of a better place to have landed than Ann Arbor," he says, "given our interest in music and sports, and the proximity to travel. People who've been here a long time may take it for granted. It's still a place where there are younger and older people and a sense of community."

For Dempsey—and he has come a long way, spiritually as well as geographically and professionally—the path of business has also been a voyage of self-discovery.

"I was fortunate to be born with a competitive instinct," he says. "The challenge for me has been how to channel that drive constructively and positively. Sometimes it's important to just simply say nothing. You can have your thoughts, but you kind of learn that you're not the only source of wisdom."

In this, as in so many other ways, he finds an appropriate metaphor in his beloved game of golf. "You do come to a point in life where you say this is who I am, just accept me, warts and all, and let's have a little more fun along the way," he says. "Golf can be a very intense sport that sometimes brings out the worst in people, or it can be an absolute blast. What I've had to do is step back, trying to remember that it is a competitive game, but it is a game. I'd like to think I've been able to do that. I also like to think people enjoy playing golf with me."

"My approach is to try to make an improvement."

Bill Dobson

They say golf is a humbling game. Perhaps that's part of its lure for Bill Dobson. Humility would be one of the first of his qualities that might come to an acquaintance's mind. Courtesy, civility, and a sense of responsibility would be near the top, too. And, if you ask him, this elder statesman of the insurance industry would say that his early experiences working on the course at Barton Hills Country Club instilled a perspective that he might not have found otherwise, and would certainly have missed.

"My two older brothers, Russell III and Jack, and I worked one summer on the course with the greens crew," Dobson recalls. "My father was chair of the greens committee and instructed the greens superintendent to do us no favors, so he worked our tails off. They wouldn't let us use any power tools. Barton Hills now has a tennis complex and swimming pool, and that was the old source of sand. My brother Jack and I opened a sand pit that summer. We would shovel it by hand into a truck, then drive the truck onto the course and put it in traps. (The traps didn't have very much sand in those days.) That was hard work. We replaced a lot of divots, raked a lot of traps. You see a golf game from the other side when you work on a course. I saw how the other half lived."

And he never forgot that lesson, despite growing up in the cozy arms of affluence. Ever since he was a small boy he had been playing golf at the country club that his grandfather, Russell Dobson, helped found. The senior Dobson also founded The Ann Arbor Trust Company, helped to finance Hoover Ball Bearing, and owned *The Ann Arbor News* from 1915 to 1921, along with a good deal of downtown Ann Arbor real estate, including the historic building that now houses the Dobson-McOmber Insurance Agency.

"He was also good in the stock market," says Bill Dobson. "And he did it with an eighth grade education. His father died early and he and his brother had to support their mother. The classic story."

Prior to moving to Ann Arbor from Akron, Ohio, in 1913, a year after his only child, Russell Jr., Bill's dad, graduated from the University of Michigan Law School, the senior Dobson had also owned newspapers in Akron, Youngstown and Canton, Ohio. He came to Ann Arbor with money to invest, and quickly established himself as a force in his new town. He was already a formidable force in the family.

"A born entrepreneur" is how Dobson describes his grandfather. The same could not be said of the second Russell Dobson, who soon gave up practicing law to become what Bill discreetly calls a "jack of all trades" in his father's multiple enterprises. None of those trades involved much heavy lifting; Russell Jr. might have been more interested if they had.

"He had been talked out of pursuing a professional baseball career when he was approached by a leading minor league team to sign a contract," says his son. "He was an outstanding pitcher, and had earned $50 per game from semi-pro teams in Michigan and Ohio. But his parents influenced him against signing the contract.

"He liked to work physically but not mentally," Bill Dobson adds. "He was a good father, I'll say that—he read to us when we were young, and joined us in sports activity—but he never had to produce anything, with my grandfather taking care of all the finances. He wasn't a playboy or anything else, but he was never encouraged to work too hard. My grandfather was a very dominant person, and as long as my father kept him satisfied, he could play a lot of golf and hunt and fish. He was an only child and a bit indulged. My grandfather made all the decisions and he just executed them."

Ironic, perhaps, that such a parent also provided the lesson of the greens crew. In many other ways, at least by his own accounts, young Bill's life was cruising along much like his dad's.

"I took up golf when I was eight or so," he says. "My father would drop my brothers and me at the course at 8 or 8:30 in the morning and pick us up at the end of the day. We'd get in two or three rounds. I just lived on the golf course in the summer, both playing the game and earning money by caddying."

Dad was at least making regular appearances at the office of the insurance agency that bore his name. He had founded it in 1927, but it was primarily a vehicle for the title insurance work on mortgages he was already doing for his father's Ann Arbor Trust Company. "He'd go to the office because he liked to go," says Bill Dobson. "It wasn't a very active agency because my father didn't put much time in it. You'd have to try pretty hard to buy insurance from him."

Popular and athletic, the 6-foot-3 Bill was a basketball and track star and president of the student council at University High School where, as a senior, he caught the eye of freshman Molly Hunter.

"Her family moved from Detroit to Ann Arbor in 1935 and her brother, John, was a good friend of mine," Dobson remembers. "I met him through neighborhood sports and picnics. We included Molly in whatever we did, and the romance developed. They had a swimming pool and a tennis court, so we used to spend a lot of time at their house."

They continued to date after Bill enrolled at the University of Michigan, where he took pre-law courses and was, he says, "a run-of-the-mill quarter-miler" on the track team, where brother Jack was a teammate. "I always ran second on the mile relay, where I had three world-class quarter-milers with me," he says.

When the United States entered World War II in December 1941, Dobson was just a few months from graduation. He enlisted in the Navy, which allowed him to finish school provided he added some math and science to his curriculum. He says he also "dropped out of track and started to party. I knew I might not get that opportunity again for a while."

Such fatalism was common and perfectly reasonable. That Dobson saw as much action as he did and returned home unscathed was little short of miraculous. That the very experience of being, while still in his early 20s, the gunnery officer on a 2,100-ton destroyer would awaken a hitherto dormant zeal for hard work was much more than a bonus.

Dobson was commissioned as an ensign in the Navy's V-7 program at Northwestern University and, after advanced training at Norfolk, Virginia, and Washington, D.C., he boarded the *USS Bullard* on April 23, 1943, 15 days after his 23rd birthday. He would spend almost all of the next three years in the Pacific, from Tarawa to Okinawa, getting a lot of sunburn and seeing a lot of combat.

"I had the responsibility for the operation and maintenance of all the ordnance equipment," says Dobson, "which included 5-inch guns, torpedoes, depth charges, and 20 mm and 40 mm machine guns, as well as training the men who used them. Other than when we were on radar picket duty (i.e., shooting at the many kamikazes who buzzed their ship), we were always with a task force of aircraft carriers, battleships, and other destroyers. The destroyers would form a ring around the task force, because the Japanese were always trying to get the carriers."

Dobson and his gunners shot down 18 Japanese planes during the war, four of them in one brutal battle at Okinawa, when the *Bullard* was subjected to 16 separate air attacks. And then there were the submarines.

"We got hit once, very lightly, by a kamikaze northwest of Okinawa during radar picket duty. He hit us on the port side, bounced over the ship, caught the life lines and a 20 mm gun, then hit the water and sank. The bigger ships never had sound gear. They counted on the destroyers to protect them from subs, so we had torpedoes, depth charges, and sonar."

In that same action, another enemy pilot, his plane a mass of flames from direct hits, tried a last-ditch dive and missed the ship by fewer than 20 feet.

Near the end of the war, Dobson says, "We fired three shore bombardments on Honshu, Japan, which was kind of unusual. It was more for our morale than the damage we did with our light guns. They were the biggest guns we had, but we were fast enough that we could get around and get closer to shore than the bigger ships. The whole idea was to blow away what little morale they had left, which was effective. But the bomb, I think, was the most effective."

That would, of course, be the atomic bomb, which ended the war in the Pacific. It wasn't over yet for Lt. Dobson, however. Only hours after Japan agreed to surrender on August 14, 1945, the *Bullard*'s guns blazed one last time, bringing down just a few yards from the ship a kamikaze who either hadn't heard the news or didn't accept it.

Nonetheless, Dobson says he was "very glad I volunteered. To see our Marines go marching in through that surf, carrying their rifles above their heads, was no sight of joy. By contrast, Navy service is a pretty clean life, physically. And very satisfying. It didn't have the discomfort of living in a foxhole."

It did, however, cost him part of his hearing. His battle station was right in the open, and the sponge rubber that lined his earphones was apparently no match for the roar of the artillery. "That's what the doctor told me, 10 years after the war," he says. "It was a nice way to make me feel pretty patriotic. I didn't get a Purple Heart or a pension; I'm just glad I got back."

He came home once for a week in 1943, while the ship was in San Francisco for repairs and the installation of advanced radar, then didn't see Ann Arbor again until December 1945. In the meantime, Molly had earned her B.A. from Michigan in 1944, then spent the rest of the war as a WAVE in Washington, D.C.

"Our ship was back in San Pedro, California, for decommissioning, and I got a week's leave to come home and get married," says Dobson. "Molly and I were engaged, but I didn't know when I'd get back to the United States. We put a wedding together in a hurry, and were married at First Presbyterian Church in Ann Arbor."

Then it was back to the West Coast for four more months of demobilization before returning to Ann Arbor for good. But instead of entering law school ("Too demanding," he claims), he pursued an MBA, which he still calls "the best thing I ever did. All the original professors who started the school in 1925 were still teaching, really first-class professors.

"Also, the University was very patriotic, so they found some interesting ways to give you credit for military experience," he says, with characteristic self-effacement. "There were so many GIs back that they had to process them out somehow. But I'm very grateful for the education I got."

In particular, he's grateful to Clayton Hale, a member of the business school's first graduating class who had gone on to a successful career as an insurance agent in Cleveland. Hale commuted by train to teach at his alma mater in 1946 and 1948.

"We had the class on Tuesday, Wednesday and Thursday, so Professor Hale could come up on Tuesday morning or Monday night and go back after class on Thursday," Dobson recalls. "He taught me you can be professional and be in the insurance business, which many people to this day don't believe. He set very lofty standards for his classes. He was a real high-quality, experienced person, and he did a lot to lift the image of the business to the students. I don't know how it is today, but in the old days when *The Ann Arbor News* would run birth announcements, the parents used to be pestered by life insurance agents calling to ask if they wanted insurance to protect the newborn. It was thought to be a kind of peddler operation. Clayton Hale showed it was an essential occupation, and that it could be done professionally."

At the same time, several other factors were converging to carry Dobson into the profession that has occupied him for half a century. One was his Navy experience. While Dobson was in business school, he started working part-time in his father's agency...as a janitor. "They needed one, so it was a place to start," he says. "I was so used to working, thanks to the Navy, that I didn't know there was any other way of doing it."

Another was the influence of his mother, Angela, whom he describes admiringly as "an early activist." Dobson's father may have lacked ambition or drive, but he did serve two terms on the Ann Arbor City Council in the late 1930s. But Angela Dobson was the energetic parent, with a dazzling array of civic and community activities. Among other things, she was an originator and president of the Ann Arbor Thrift Shop; a board member of the National Conference of Christians and Jews and the Ann Arbor Women's City Club; a founder of Ann Arbor Civic Theater; a delegate to the State Republican Convention; and a member of the Citizens Council, the Washtenaw County Court House Committee, and the New County Building Committee.

"She set a good example for her children," says Dobson. It was from her, he believes, that he inherited what his father dubbed his "Atlas complex," one of his most pervasive and conspicuous qualities.

"My father used to call me that because I carry the

weight of the world on my shoulders," he says. "He felt I worried unnecessarily about things that didn't concern me, but I do. If I encounter a problem, rather than get annoyed at the person involved, I try to help correct the problem. Most people say, 'Just don't go there again,' but my approach is to try to make an improvement.

"I was cursed with being a perfectionist and I'm very critical of myself, because I know how people should be handled and I try to do it that way. I set high standards for myself, and I'm also the first to recognize when I fail to meet them."

By 1948, when Bill Dobson had completed both his MBA and a year as a janitor, there was plenty of room for improvement at the Dobson Insurance Agency. As he decorously puts it, "I saw a need for some input. There was an obvious place for me. My father had lost interest in the business. He had a very competent secretary, Virginia Riddle, but in those days women weren't accepted as professionals, so the company needed me to get involved. I'm glad I did. I've had a very happy business career and what I learned as an MBA was directly applicable to the business."

Also applied to the business was a summer of "insurance school" in Hartford, Connecticut, then the capital of the industry in North America, as well as a decade or more of 70-hour weeks. "I wasn't very popular at home but I felt it had to be done," he says. "The insured are entitled to service, and when they call for it, you can't put it off until it's convenient. You've got to do it then, so I got more and more immersed in that. You don't just sell it, you service it, manage the claims, see that they're paid promptly."

And when the business begins to grow, you see to it that the people you hire place the same premium on service that they place on sales. In Dobson's view, "You always have to start any business with the sales, but there are still people who emphasize the sales, and a lot of people have been very successful in the business in the sense that they've sold a lot, but they often haven't reinvested some of their money in providing better training for their employees and in improving service."

It's clear that the sense in which Dobson defines success is somewhat larger. "We're a poorly understood business, and it's our own fault," he says. "You've really got to know a lot. We use the term 'risk management,' which means that you identify what risks you have in your life or business or personally, and analyze them and see where they can be eliminated. Risk management does a lot of work in loss prevention. It's a strange business, it really is. An awful lot of people who are in it don't understand it. You can do it responsibly, but it has a generally unprofessional reputation."

That would be less likely to be the case were Dobson's credo more widely practiced: "Treat others the way you'd like to be treated. Putting the customer or potential customer first is the best way to do business because, in the long run, what's best for the purchaser or customer is best for the agency as well. You can live with yourself if you do things that way. If you do it the other way, sometimes you're just not going to be happy with yourself."

Recognizing the prevailing attitude toward insurance, his approach has been to educate his clients. "Almost nobody ever seems to read a policy until a loss occurs, and then it's too late," he says. "We think people have to devote some time and get a presentation on what the coverage is and is not, and how value is measured. You just can't take an order. You've got to do some probing and informing and try to educate people, because they just don't think insurance is worth mastering. They don't want to fool with it."

Dobson understands his business well enough to have taught courses about it at the University of Michigan Business School. That was in the days before a chair in the field had been endowed, the result of an effort he spearheaded. He can render insurance comprehensible to the lay person in just a few sentences, the first of which will often be about how misleading some vendors' emphasis on pricing can be.

"There are now companies—I hear them three or four times a day on the radio—pitching everything to a 15 percent savings on premiums. It makes people very conscious of the price, but they don't realize that every price that you pay is regulated by the state you're in. You can't charge a rate that isn't approved, and the rate is mostly determined by the losses paid. We've always lived with price control."

Insurance is, in fact, as heavily and minutely regulated as public utilities. "You hope to make what you call an operating profit, where the losses are less than the premiums," he says. "Companies are allowed to make only a 5–6 percent operating profit on their underwriting, but that's harder and harder to do. However, they hold a lot of money until they pay a loss, so their investment income is a very important aspect of an insurance company's operations. Many times, the only profit comes from the investments, so they're very skillful in investing."

He estimates that his company's business is about 60 percent commercial, and the rest personal. Much of the commercial activity stems from a niche Dobson targeted early on.

"We probably are the only agency in this area that is really knowledgeable about the surety bonds that contractors must provide when they bid on public work," he says. "As far as I know, we're the only ones that really know that business in this area, although there are plenty of people in Detroit that know as much as we do. It's a narrow field because it applies only to contractors doing construction, or anything else that requires a bond in order to bid it. Then if the contractor gets the job, he must provide a bond guaranteeing performance of the contract. It's a demanding type of business. You have to know a lot of accounting. Anybody can do it, but very few of them have ever specialized. We have always been very heavily involved in the construction field as a result."

The Dobson Insurance Agency became part of the Dobson-McOmber Agency, Inc., in 1956 when Dobson teamed up with another Ann Arborite whose dad had founded his company. "Ted McOmber's father was a field man for a large insurance company and his territory was Michigan," says Dobson. "He traveled by train to call on agents, which is what his job was, so Ann Arbor was a convenient place to live."

In 1893, the senior McOmber decided to quit riding the rails and start what may have been the first insurance agency in Ann Arbor. Sixty-some years later, his creation combined forces with its newer and suddenly resurgent rival.

"Ted and I are the same age, and we both grew up in the greater Burns Park area," says Dobson. "I knew him in grade school and college, although he went away to boarding school in between. He graduated from U-M in 1942 and didn't go back after the war."

In most important respects, however, their similarities were more than geographic or chronological. "We were competitors, but we had a lot in common and knew each other and trusted each other," Dobson says. "Ted also taught in the business school after the war for a short period of time. He was very professional and knew the business, and he was trying to do it the way I thought the business should be done: without putting pressure on people."

There were tactical advantages, as well. "You've got to have size," he says. "The business is diverse and complicated enough that it's really impossible for one person to master it and keep up with it and provide the service that is really necessary. The merger was ideal for both of us. He handled a lot of the inside management, accounting and related work."

And the whole became greater than the sum of its parts, although the Dobson part was much the larger before the merger.

"We have 50 people here now, and when we started there were two of us, Virginia Riddle and me," says Dobson. "Out of 50 people, I'm the only one that doesn't have a computer on his desk. And that's the way it's going to stay."

In non-technological arenas, however, Dobson has always lived in and for the future, tirelessly engaged in managing risks, cutting losses and improving the lot of society at large. You might say he treats the community where he has lived all his life as if all its members were his customers.

One achievement of which he is particularly proud, and which is (as any development officer will tell you) the kind of gift that truly keeps on giving, is the establishment of the Waldo O. Hildebrand Chair of Risk Management and Insurance in the University of Michigan Business School.

"It's named for a man who was the longtime manager of the Michigan Association of Insurance Agents," says Dobson, who was the Association's president for part of that time. "He had to drop out of U of M in 1925 when he ran out of money, and he worked 30 years for the Association. There were 1,000 members at that time, more now, and his job was to manage their legislative efforts and joint advertising and to negotiate solutions to problems with companies and the state."

The chair filled what Dobson saw as a long-standing vacuum, one that local professionals had done their best to fill on an almost ad hoc basis. "When I got an MBA, the three classes in insurance had 40 or 50 students," he says. "When my son came back from Duke to get his MBA, he had seven in his last insurance class. The present professor is getting 50 students enrolling. We just had that void."

But no longer. One reason for the subject's popularity is industry's demand for insurance-savvy executives, which is also why Ford and General Motors, in addition to about 100 insurance agents and companies, contributed to the endowment. "The whole idea is that everybody benefits by having a higher quality of insurance knowledge," says Dobson. "Insurance and Risk Management is a marvelous subject to have studied, whether you're going to be in personnel, marketing, finance or any other kind of management position."

It also dovetails nicely with the UM's renowned program

in actuarial mathematics, "which is essential to insurance but isn't a broad enough subject to provide good skills for what you need in the business," says Dobson. "The actuarial mathematicians are the statisticians, but they and the business school never intermingled much before."

Does this mean there's a degree program on the horizon? "We got the professor," says Dobson. "That's what I was after."

And it certainly took long enough. "We started in 1985," he says, "and he just went to work September 1, 1997. All the intervening years were used raising money."

The next item on his to-do list could take even longer, and is certainly less susceptible to a clear-cut resolution. "My current 'Atlas project' is to try to offset the loss of open space and the spread of urban sprawl in our area by getting some philanthropic support for adding to existing parks or starting new ones," he says. "I'm talking to people who are in the park business, with the city and the county. I had lunch with a young lady today who is in the Potawatomi Land Trust; I didn't realize how extensively it operated in Washtenaw County, and I think in Ann Arbor you could raise some funding for this.

"It would be pretty hard to find someone who doesn't like parks and open land," he says. "I've got a lot of knowledge to gain before I can be helpful, but I'd like to see if we can't get a movement started, at least to expand existing parks."

Dobson's community activities reflect his grandfather's entrepreneurial spirit, his father's amiability, and his own "Atlas complex." It's the one area where he admits to a quality that's a stereotype in his business. "I would never get on someone's tail and hang on until they bought insurance or told me to get the hell out of there," he says, "but I get overcommitted to a lot of community activities. That's where I'm really dogged. I'm trying to finalize three campaigns right now."

Even a long list of his pro bono activities is incomplete: He helped found the Ann Arbor Area Community Foundation and served as its president. He has been a trustee for Greenhills School. He is a major donor to the University of Michigan. He was instrumental in establishing the Washtenaw United Way Leadership Giving Association. He's been an active supporter of the Boy Scouts of America (although never a Scout himself), Ann Arbor Affordable Housing (working with a private non-profit corporation that built 156 units of same), and Planned Parenthood.

He and Molly fund scholarships for business students and child care at Washtenaw Community College, where the agency also supports a scholarship. In 1995, as a 50th anniversary present, Molly endowed a business scholarship at WCC in Bill's name. They have also created a scholarship fund at the University of Michigan Center for the Education of Women.

In addition to saving open space, his other current passion is saving hearing, a subject he obviously knows more intimately.

"I got my first hearing aid 20-some years ago," he says. "I didn't know enough to be critical of them at all, but the testing consisted of someone getting behind a screen and then asking through a microphone, 'Did you hear it?' and then repeating it. It was pretty crude; there was an obvious need for research."

And still is. "People aren't jumping up and down to give money, even people who have hearing aids," he says. "It's admitted that there's need for improvement, but you can't get funding from government because it's not dramatic like AIDS or cancer. We're stuck at $100,000, and that isn't going to pay for much research. This hasn't gotten attention from the normal sources of medical research funding."

Nor has Dobson had much luck with more creative approaches. "I think the people that would be interested are insurance companies or manufacturers who have noise problems that create hearing problems for employees, but we haven't been able to get far with that," he says. "We hope insurance companies can help, but we have a very limited number of people involved in the fundraising."

Just having Bill Dobson involved carries a multiplier effect. Sometimes it seems he really could be Atlas. Then again, his penchant for self-criticism almost compels him to confess some sin: he doesn't go to church often, "particularly during golf season.

"I've lived such a disciplined life," he says, "that I kind of like occasionally not doing what I should be doing."

"Four generations in an honorable business."

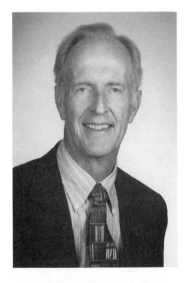

Marty Edwards

It was not an auspicious time for major financial investments, but Marty Edwards' father had made one, and he was bent on making it work.

The year was 1929, and the Great Depression was about to cast its shadow over the land. Just before it did, Marty Edwards' father Bill (actually John William, or JW, but no one called him that) put a lot of money into changing his family's business from mimeographing, which had been its focus since it was founded in 1893 by Thomas and Daniel Edwards, to offset lithography.

The original Edwards brothers were law students at the University of Michigan who mimeographed and sold their lecture notes. When they finished school in 1899 and went into practice in Washington, D.C., they turned their budding business over to their other brother, John, or JJ. He ran the company until 1920, when his health began to deteriorate and he turned to Bill for help. Two years later, JJ was dead and Bill and his brother Ward were in charge.

"My dad was a real fighter," says Edwards. "He played

all kinds of sports around Ann Arbor. He set the shot put record at Ann Arbor High, and he was a little guy, probably weighed 160 pounds at the most. He also played professional football on Sundays and college football at Michigan, Eastern Michigan, or the University of Detroit on Saturdays."

Edwards is quick to point out that "he went to all those schools, too. But that competitive nature that he had is what saw him through all those ups and downs."

It probably was also part of what compelled him to act decisively on his vision of the industry's future. "He jumped into the early phases of lithography, just as the Depression arrived," says Edwards. "He and his brother actually parted company over that. Ward started Edwards Letter Shop, which was over Moe's on North University for years and eventually became ELS Lithographics. My dad built a building on John Street, where Fingerle Lumber is now, in 1929. He bought new presses, got himself in hock up to his eyeballs, and managed to get through that. I suppose it was being at the cutting edge that saved his butt. He was really hanging out there. But they got through, and they built a business."

The difficulties and heartbreaks were not exclusively financial. In 1935, when Marty was three years old, one of his older brothers died of leukemia at the age of six. "My dad paid the nurse who was there when Tommy died with his last gold coin," says Edwards. "That was it. That was the money. My mother told me that story years later when I was old enough to understand it; that was her way of illustrating the depths."

But the heights were not far off; Bill Edwards' reinvented business spun off enough other companies, directly and indirectly, to make Ann Arbor the short-run publishing capital of the world. Just a few years after Ward founded Edwards Letter Shop, Carl Braun and three other former Edwards Brothers employees started University Lithoprinters. In 1948, Bert Cushing and Jim Malloy left Edwards Brothers and launched Cushing-Malloy. When they came to a parting of the ways in 1960, the latter founded Malloy Lithographing. Meanwhile, Braun left University Lithoprinters to start Braun-Brumfield in 1950, which spun off both Thomson-Shore and McNaughton & Gunn in the 1970s. Bookcrafters, which began life in 1965 as Lithocrafters, was founded by former Braun-Brumfield staffers.

Not only are they all offering about the same product, but "they're all kind of working on our model," says Edwards. Is this the proverbially sincerest form of flattery?

"Well, it worked," he says matter-of-factly. And just as the Edwards Brothers' alumni learned from watching how Bill Edwards did business, so Mary Edwards learned from watching how his father kept it. "Jim Malloy and Bert Cushing tried to buy the business from my dad right after World War II," he says. "He was in his mid-50s then, and he said no, I'm passing this on to my sons, and that's when Jim and Bert chose to go out on their own. So that was the model—I watched his passion to build the business so he would have something to pass along."

Of Bill's four surviving sons, three joined the business, and two—Marty and his older brother Joe—made it their life's work. "I suppose it was a certain expectation on the part of my dad that was communicated to us all," says Marty. "I was always tracked. It's what I wanted to do. I worked in here as a kid in grade school and high school. There was ink running in my veins even then."

But Sam, the youngest, went into investment banking right out of college and built the highly successful Beacon Investment Company in Ann Arbor. "Sam's just a bit of a contrarian," says Marty. "He didn't dislike this business; he just wanted to do something on his own. He didn't want someone to tell him, well, you had a silver spoon. Or, as one of my sons says, he's a member of the lucky sperm club."

As for brother Bill, "the seed didn't stick with him," says Marty Edwards. "He left around 1960, got into allied activities, and died unexpectedly after routine back surgery."

Joe and Marty, however, didn't fall far from the tree at all. "All you have to do is talk to someone who's been in a family business, who's gone through those ropes," says Marty. "You'll find a little camaraderie. They know what it is. The expectation is that you will succeed. If you do, you should have. If you didn't, you're a bum. In some ways, there's a lack of gratification and public acknowledgement, I suppose. That never meant much to me but I could see where it could mean something to some."

He also knows the business grew and changed enormously under his direction, a healthy scratch for that entrepreneurial itch. "When I came into this business, it was maybe a million-dollar business, which in those days was a good-size business," he says. "But we got close to $70 million in 1998, and we employ almost 800 people in three plants and eight sales offices. And that's a lot of changes.

"We don't start off and say let's go into a new business. We're not on that side of the entrepreneurial game. The side we're on is continuous reanalysis, reappraisal, upgrading and expanding the quality and quantity of one's efforts. It's that kind of entrepreneurial stuff, as opposed to just sitting there and milking the cow. And we know there are people who do that. But this business has changed a lot, physically and in its character."

Edwards attended the late University High School in Ann Arbor, playing football, basketball, and golf, "only one of which I do anymore," he says. After spending a year at Notre Dame, he came home to earn his bachelor's and master's degrees in business administration from the University of Michigan. "My father said you're going to Notre Dame," says Edwards. "He wanted me to go out of town. You get so inbred in Ann Arbor. The military and the one year at Notre Dame did me a world of good. You learn that Ann Arbor isn't the only place in the world."

The Army stint began when he volunteered after finishing his MBA. "I didn't want to sit around waiting for my number to come up because I knew I was dead meat," he says. "I went in as a private, went to Fort Ord for basic training, crawled on my belly like everyone else did, froze my fanny. But I got classified as an auditor, and was assigned to the Army Audit Agency. I've had a life full of good breaks and that was one of them."

At first, his job called for him to audit suppliers to the Army. Many of them were located in and around Detroit, so he lived in Ann Arbor and commuted. "They'd send us a bill for $20 million, say, and we'd go into their offices and go through all their vouchers and labor system to discern in our opinion if that were a legitimate bill."

After about six months, he was reassigned to Europe, and to auditing the Army itself. "You'd go to a place where they had training activities going on and make sure their inventories were accurate, audit their business practices, make sure they were following the manual of instruction, those kinds of things. Boy, that was thrilling. But, again, it was a lovely assignment. It was a 9-to-5 job and I was really kind of separated from being an infantryman. And after my two years were up, I came home."

That was in 1957, and he immediately returned to the family firm. His brother Joe, who had been there since receiving his own BBA shortly after World War II, was already president.

"When I first came into the business, a big percentage of our work was the individual author writing his own book, usually a lab manual to supplement a textbook," he says. "We also did school yearbooks and some government printing. It was lots of onesies and twosies, lots of mail order work. It didn't have a lot of momentum."

Like his father before him, he set about reinventing the business. The yearbook business—at their peak, they did as many as 300 a year—was history by 1970, as was most of the government printing and individual author business.

"Instead, we've focused on book and journal publishers," says Edwards. "They don't do their own printing; they go to hired guns. But what you find with these publishers is, if they do one, they might do 21 or 101 this year, so you get into the stream with them. Suddenly, your sales effort is leveraged."

And its personnel were fanned out, thus leveraging the effect. "When I came into this business, we had a salesman in New York, period," he says. "For most of my career until 1975 or so, I was in sales, and we took that sales force and started to deploy it in territories where the book publishers were to be found. We opened offices in Chicago, Washington, and San Francisco, and now we have an office in Boston. We went where the customers were and established offices there. We now have offices in Atlanta and Raleigh, and we have salespeople working there, too. With a field sales force of 20 people or thereabouts, we've made a determined effort to put ourselves in those markets and in front of those buyers. That's where the publishers are, in the big cities."

Like so many other successful business people, Edwards learned early on, and at the cost of some discomfort, not to let any single customer become too big a piece of the company pie. "Happily, not one of our customers represents as much as 5 percent of our business," he says. "I learned a lesson there back in the early '60s, when we lost a U.S. government contract that represented about a third of our work. Let me tell you, that's grim. And that's a lasting impression. We don't really say we won't allow someone to get 5 percent or 10 percent, but if somebody's going to grow that much, we better grow the rest of the business around them."

Knowing what parts of the business to shrink is also vital. Just as his father saw the future in lithography and abandoned mimeographing, so Edwards gradually withdrew from the typesetting business.

"That's another example of how the business has changed over time," he says. "We probably had 100 employees in that area who no longer get their paychecks from us. When we were in the mimeograph business, we were cutting our own stencils with typewriters. That was how we typeset. In the 1930s, we were the largest consumer of IBM typewriters in the world. My dad pioneered the idea of sending the typewriter home with the pregnant woman.

We had a cadre of home workers; we'd get the manuscript to them one way or another. That typesetting department was a pretty good-sized department."

As recently as 1990, Edwards Brothers bought Impressions, Inc., a typesetting firm in Madison, Wisconsin, and consolidated the two plants' operations. Five years later, they sold it back to the original owner. "We print a lot of the work he typesets," says Edwards.

He became general manager of the company in 1968, president in 1979, and chief executive officer in 1985, when his brother Joe retired. Marty ("actually, the bank," he says) then bought out his brothers and the company's other stockholders and it became privately held again for the first time since 1930.

"That was a defining event," he says. "Going private was a whole new world. This company had been very well financed, always had cash in the bank, kind of flush; suddenly, that all disappeared. It's been a different kind of business to run since then. I don't think that's bad."

One recent example was in 1998, when Marty's oldest son, John, became president and chief operating officer while Marty stayed on as chairman of the board and chief executive officer. Handling the handoff to his son was eased by some advice from his board of directors, which he had initiated upon the return to private ownership.

"They've really done a terrific job for me," he says. "They don't always make all the meetings because they have full agendas but, boy, they can be very helpful. I'm not afraid to take any question to them."

The transition was a case in point. "At our November 1997 meeting, I said I wanted to make John the chief operating officer. He was 37, he'd had 15 years with the company, I was lightening up and he was accumulating more responsibilities, so it was a good time to talk about it. They listened and talked about it, and came back and said, 'You're not doing that right.' I said, 'What do you mean? It sounds good to me.' They said, 'If you make him COO, period, you're not giving him the authority that goes with that responsibility. You better make him president.' I wasn't even thinking that way. I was going to dole it out, a morsel at a time. But we made him president and chief operating officer, and I think their wisdom was correct.

"They've come to this with great experience and great backgrounds. They know a lot about what's going on and they can be very helpful to me, and now my son, in keeping this business run professionally and smart."

The "professional" part really came to the fore after World War II, not that the operation or its principals up until then had been amateurish. "There was professionalism going on then," says Edwards. "We just tried to expand on it. Like I did later, Joe came into this company with a bachelor's degree in business administration, so he had some awareness of how businesses are run that would be different than just learning at your daddy's knee.

"We wanted to become a professionally managed family company, whereas I think my dad was just a guy trying to keep all the pieces in place. He was a college graduate and a bright guy, but one day he'd be selling, the next day greasing a press, the next day at the bank, the next day chasing a receivable. He was the proverbial one-armed paper hanger. We decided that, by golly, we're going to figure out how to run this company professionally, and we've tried to engage a professional management force ever since."

Of course, as Edwards points out, "That just raises the bar, but as the expectations of our customers go up, we better raise the bar. The kind of workmanship that sold 20 years ago doesn't sell today."

Or even 20 months, for that matter; the pressure for higher quality, in all of its definitions, almost seems to increase geometrically. Even the traditionally staid book business is feeling the heat. "Just look at the bookstore changes, what Borders and Amazon.com and Barnes & Noble must be doing to the little stores all over the country, the independents," says Edwards.

Not that he's nostalgic for the good old days. To him, many of consolidation's advantages are clear. "The hope for our customers, the publishers, is that these big retailers will in fact improve the distribution of their books, and there is some evidence that that is going on," Edwards says. "They can list in their systems anything that's printed. You or your computer can walk in there for a very obscure title, and your search ends there. You don't have to go to this little guy or that little guy and hope he can find it. One customer who publishes a lot of short-run books said it was clear already that he was getting more back orders for stuff in his warehouse that he thought he might die with, so he was applauding what he views as improved channels."

Improving distribution includes improving the industry's traditional returns policy, a policy some call quaint. "The book publishing business is the craziest business you ever saw," he says. "A retailer can send it back two years later if it didn't sell. I was talking to a guy here in Ann Arbor, a religious publisher, and he said he was getting 25 percent returns. Well, you kind of thought you sold it, and it comes back. And 25 percent is not uncommon. But the professional distribution people are better at returning what doesn't sell. They do it quicker; they don't let it sit in the warehouse and gather dust. The mom and pop shops may be inclined to hold on to it a little longer."

Such issues are of vital concern to Edwards' customers, whose wares are fairly specialized. "If there's success in this company, it's been because we focus on trying to do the medium- and short-run book and journal," he says. "We don't try to do a hundred thousand copies of this and half a million of that. We don't try to do the multicolor jobs. We just try to serve that community that needs the product we're good at."

How best to do that is always open to improvement, but the picture can be complicated by the charms of technological change. Edwards says it's important to remember that just because you know how to do a new trick doesn't mean you must.

"Suddenly, you get a new technology and somebody says now we can do this," he says. "Maybe we shouldn't and maybe we should. Being able to do it doesn't mean doing it well."

Edwards calls the process "bumping the edges of the niche. It's trial and error." For example, acquiring a press that can print four colors "does not mean that suddenly we're a four-color printer. We've tried it, and it's just not our bag. That's not the best equipment for it anyway, but we can provide supplementary four-color off that press as well as covers and dust jackets."

Another case in point is the company's Digital Book Center, opened in 1997, which is used for ultra-short reprint runs—50 to 250 copies—of books previously printed by Edwards Brothers and others. "We knew publishers had a need for reprints in very short quantities, and we knew that the pricing we would give them from lithography wouldn't cut it." says Edwards. "There were people out there using this Xerox technology, so we finally got Xerox to make us a special-size machine to accommodate the special-size book we wanted to do, and found the right kind of equipment to produce it out of this plant in Ann Arbor."

But with the added capacity to do more and different tasks came the urge to exploit that capacity for its own sake. "Right now, in that Digital Book Center, we basically produce only books of a certain trim size," says Edwards, "so the dimensions of those books are six by nine. Because we print other trim sizes, some people want us to do those sizes in the Digital Book Center. Others say we're good at that six-by-nine, let's stay put. My inclination is to stay niche-focused. And I think that's really been our salvation. It sounds like we're not innovative and willing to try things, and my response to that would be, that's right, but we want to innovate like crazy in how we do what we do."

It might or might not be considered an innovation, but the decision to open facilities in North Carolina was certainly a break with tradition for a company that had done business only from Ann Arbor for the first 86 years of its existence.

"1979 is when we pulled the first trigger on our North Carolina operation," says Edwards. The company acquired an operation called The Graphic Press, located just a few blocks from the Capitol in Raleigh, to provide additional pre-press, press, and soft bindery capacity. Four years later, the renamed Edward Brothers Carolina moved to a newly built plant in nearby Lillington.

"That's when we really got into some decent business down there," he says. "That was a long, hard struggle to make that a going show."

He cites two major reasons for the foray into the mid-South. One was the Ann Arbor plant itself. Built on South State Street in 1956 and enlarged on several occasions, the last in 1973, it had just about reached its capacity. Another site was in order if the company's growth were to continue. The other issue was "the size of the labor pool," says Edwards. "Ann Arbor always been a tight labor market. The irony of our North Carolina decision is that everyone else made the same decision at the same time, so that labor market is just as tough as this one right now."

Still, Edwards Brothers Carolina has grown significantly. It now accommodates two plants on its Lillington site, one for softbound product and the other for hardbacks, with more than 100,000 square feet of space (about half that of the Ann Arbor plant) and annual sales in excess of $30 million (more than 40 percent of the company's total). It would appear to be a success but, after all, it's only been around for 20 years. Says Edwards: "I think the jury is still out on how smart a decision that was."

On the other hand, the jury didn't have to deliberate for long on the value of treating employees well. "We've never had a union," says Edwards. "We've worked very hard at staying union-free. We just feel that that third party at the table on every decision is counterproductive, and our customer isn't going to pay for that. He'll find someone who doesn't have that hassle. Almost 100 percent of East Coast book manufacturers no longer exist because they got organized and became unproductive. Union-free shops in the Midwest just killed them."

And the road to un-organization is paved with "a little bit of the golden rule," he says. "It's getting people involved. We don't want a bunch of robots out there. We want folks who are interactive with the business, with the customers, with each other, with the management. This is where they spend most of their waking hours. We want it to be a place where they want to be."

This has meant action as well as talk. "We've been heavy on benefits over the years," he says. "I think it was back in the '30s that we had our first life insurance plan for employees. In the '40s, we started a pension plan, and in 1949, we started our profit-sharing plan, a cash payout plan independent of our pension plan. This is where I think people play games, and we try real hard not to. A lot of people have what they call a profit-sharing plan, but the truth is the profit-sharing plan is used to fund the pension plan. It's a defined contribution plan, so the contribution is defined as the profits to be shared. That's not what we're doing. We have two separate plans."

This, too, is an area where ongoing improvements are mandatory. "A very interesting thing occurred here about 10 years ago," says Edwards. "We kept looking at what inflation was doing to profit-sharing and, particularly, future pensions. If you project that a person retires at age 65 and lives another 20 years, his pension is probably fixed at his 65th birthday, but his cost of living is going to go up. So we got into a 401(k) plan, most of which our employees fund themselves."

The response has been gratifying, to put it mildly. "It's astonishing to me how much money our employees have put into their 401(k) plan on their own for their future," he says. "It's absolutely wonderful. I would guess, after a very slow start, that in 10 years, our people have put nearly 10 million bucks in that plan. And it's all in one kind of market or another. They've taken on the responsibility for part of their retirement costs. So our people have a three-legged stool: pension plan, Social Security, and 401(k). We have a very high participation level."

Distributing the wealth, of course, is impossible without the continuing creation of same, which for Edwards Brothers is predicated on the continuing demand for its product. In the current and foreseeable technological environment, this is by no means a given.

"That's the big debate," says Edwards. "What is the future of the book? There is no lack of opinion on that. We obviously have a huge investment in the book business, so for us it's pretty frightening to think about this going away. It's your typesetter story in spades."

Nonetheless, Edwards does think about it, and talk about it. Like a movie director who starts with a cover shot and then slowly moves in on the subject, he begins with the big picture.

"Information is what you're talking about, and how do you get information from one person to the next," he says. "Publishers are presently kind of the content providers. They're at the crossroads of information transfer, and they use us to accomplish a good deal of that. There are all kinds of variations on this theme of moving the content around: the newspaper, television, radio, and now the internet and the e-book.

"In its defense, the book is very cheap; it's probably one of the best buys going. With an e-book, it may be real cheap to get it downloaded into my personal computer, but all the steps that have to be taken to ready that content for book production probably also have to be taken to ready that content for downloading. There's not a big savings there. The e-book and a lot of this other information transfer is getting a free ride right now because all of that stuff has already been prepared for distribution via print. So it looks easier than it is."

If the e-book takes over the entire process, "there's going to be some numbers crunching going on that's going to scare some people," says Edwards. "The cost of printing is a fifth or less of the price you pay in the bookstore. The rest is shipping, copy editing, royalties, marketing, shelf space—there's a lot of money there."

There's also a lot of speculation. "Publishing is really

entrepreneurial," he says. "You've got to have that book in hand before you know if it will sell. How many Clancys are there, or Grishams? So then it comes down to the user's preference. Is he comfortable with electronic data transfer or does he like print transfer? There's going to be continuation of both for the foreseeable future."

It's even possible that the rising tides of populations and of literacy levels will expand the information market sufficiently to float more providers' boats. "We may get a smaller and smaller piece of a pie that's growing," says Edwards. "At least, that's our rationalization. We don't really know. If this goes away, what do we do? And we don't have an answer to that."

That "we" is not merely rhetorical. The company continues to be very much a family business, and it seems likely to remain so even if the traditional book does, indeed, "go away." The fourth generation, three of the four children of Marty and Rosalie Savarino Edwards, now works there. Laura Edwards Ottenwess, a marketing specialist, is the twin sister of John, the president and chief operating officer. Their brother Jim is a regional sales manager.

Rosalie Savarino was born and raised in Hillsdale, Michigan, and was working toward her master's in music at the University of Michigan when she and Marty met. "If she were telling you the story, she'd say, 'See, I'm much younger than he is.' Which is true. She was a junior high teacher for a while until we started having children rapidly."

The twins arrived first, followed by Stephen, a composer of film music in Hollywood, and then Jim. At last count, the potential labor pool in the fifth generation numbered eight, although the oldest was only six years of age.

"Rosalie has been a wonderful balance wheel," Edwards says. "When I was working all those hours and traveling all that much, she was right there in the trenches with those kids, seeing to their schooling, seeing to their music education, doing all the stuff that moms do. She didn't get a lot of help from me, and she always has had an interest in things outside the home.

"Rosalie taught piano and flute in the home when she was raising the children, then she went back and was on the original Greenhills School faculty as a music teacher." And then, as he puts it, she "got hold of the University of Michigan Women's Glee Club," building the long-dormant ensemble's forces from 12 voices to more than 80, and enhancing its stature commensurately, in the dozen years she led it.

She has also, not surprisingly, been a bulwark for Stephen, the musician in the next generation. "She was so encouraging to him through all those grim years when he was alone in California," says Edwards. "She was his fan club and his booster and his confidante. It's a remarkable thing, how she's kept that going. Fortunately, Stephen's wife is smart enough to know that, and she and Rosalie have just a wonderful relationship."

Still, Edwards is pleased by how many of his offspring have opted to follow their ancestors' footsteps. It's not just family pride, but also because he happens to think it's a fine and honorable business to be in.

"I always liked what we did," he says. "We didn't do everything right, we made our share of mistakes, but there was always this idea out there that this is a wholesome business, this is a good business, you can hold your head up, you don't have to duck or alibi. That always made it fun. If I was out of town on vacation for a week, I couldn't wait to get back. I couldn't wait to get up in the morning to get here. I'd stay late. I put in lots and lots of hours, lots of weekends, traveled a lot, but I never thought I was doing anybody a favor. It was what I wanted to do."

It worked out for him, and he wanted his children to have a shot at it working out for them, too. "I tried not to give them the do-or-die message," he says, "but if they wanted to, I wanted to have it here for them. As it turns out, two full-time and one part-time, that's a pretty good batting average."

In addition to his work for the company and related service to numerous industry associations, Edwards serves on the board of trustees of Hillsdale College and the advisory board of the Mackinac Center for Public Policy. While soft-pedaling the significance of the latter ("It only meets twice a year," he says), he is effusive about Hillsdale.

"I like what they're doing," he says. "They believe that you stand on your own and you do your own thing and you don't lean on Uncle Sam to do anything for you. They're militant about that. If you've got a scholarship, they won't take that money if it's got government strings on it. I think that even means the GI Bill. They've gone out and raised money so they can match those scholarship funds that Hillsdale students may lose, if they want those students."

His commitment to education also included his role as co-chair of the fund-raising campaign for the new Father Gabriel Richard High School building. "That's a big job," he says. "It's going to take a lot of time, and I'm in the fortunate situation where I think I can make a contribution."

Faith, family and business are inextricably intertwined for Edwards, nourishing and inspiring each other. "I think life is not what's here, it's what's hereafter," he says, "so you have to live your life in a way that you hope will get you to the hereafter. You have to be honest and ethical in your business, practice the golden rule, respect people. And you want to infuse that into your kids. That's the constant struggle one is on, to do those kinds of things. Gaining fame and fortune has been a helluva lot less important to me than being a good Christian, a good Catholic, which to me means following the Ten Commandments and practicing in my business my faith life and practicing in my family my faith life."

Far from being inherently contradictory, he sees the concept of the Christian businessman as essential. "If you don't take care of your customers, you don't achieve your objectives," he says, "and you can't take care of your customers by stealing from them and you can't provide them with good services by beating up on your employees or cheating on your taxes. It just doesn't work, not if you want to be 106 years old. There are probably some people who are hit-and-runners and maybe they don't much care. I think if you're going to be around for the long haul, and if you want to look in the mirror every morning, you've got to care. I want to honor my father and what he did and honor my employees and what they did and honor the industry we're in. It's a wonderful business to be in, transferring information and knowledge from one place to the other. That's a good thing. It might be a little harder for me to be that altruistic if I were selling cigarettes, but the ones who do that have to come to terms with it."

He cites a couple of recent examples of how that philosophy is expressed on a day-to-day basis. "It's a five-and-dime item, but somebody overpaid us the other day for what we did and we sent the difference back," he says. "I don't know if we get a gold star for that or not, but it's the right thing to do. Just recently, another employee came across some critical information about a competitor. He said to John, 'Do you want it?' John said, 'No, just throw it all away.'"

Edwards credits his involvement with Legatus, a national organization of Catholic CEOs and their spouses that was launched by Domino's founder Tom Monaghan, with making him more public about his faith.

"I think a lot of us who are Catholic have been taught to keep our faith under our hats, to keep it quiet," he says. "I went down to a company-wide dinner meeting at our southern plant one time, and a pressman stood up and said the prayer before the meal. We'd been having those kinds of affairs for years and years and years in Ann Arbor, and we'd never done that. Following that example, we do it here now."

Even though it meant a fairly major deviation from the norm, Edwards says "one of the things I'm proudest of that we printed is the catechism of the Catholic Church, when it was recently rewritten. Uncharacteristic of us, we must have printed a couple of million of those. It was published worldwide pretty much simultaneously, and we were the U.S. producer."

Not that he takes any particular credit, here or elsewhere. "If I have any skill, it's probably persistence," he says, "just hangin' in there."

"I'd see whether I could come up with a solution."

Chuck Gelman

Chuck Gelman learned early on that the way of the bureaucrat was not going to be his way.

It was 1953. He was 21 years old, working at the U.S. Army's Chemical Warfare Center in Edgewood, Maryland, and car pooling from Baltimore, about 60 miles away, where most of the people lived who worked on the base. This was his first job after earning a degree in chemistry from Syracuse University. He had taken almost as many courses in international relations as he had in his major but, as he says, "At the time the State Department did not employ Jews. Maybe that wasn't officially the case, but everybody knew that wasn't the place for a Jew to seek a career."

His only thought, he adds, was to "get a job someplace and earn a living. I had no idea what to expect." It's safe to say his employers were in the same boat. When he was assigned to a fairly high-budget project to develop new methods for measuring and testing for nerve gases as a defensive weapon, he headed for the library. The key, he felt, was an enzyme called colinesterase that was sensitive to the gas, but so far it had proven impossible to stabilize it at the appropriate temperatures.

"My boss got very upset with me because they had funded this project for two years with a pretty large budget, and I spent like six weeks in the library," says Gelman. "He kept saying, 'You're not doing any work, what are you doing up in the library?' So then I came down and worked in the lab for about two weeks, and he said, 'There are no requisitions for equipment.' I said, 'All I need is 24 eye-dropper bottles.' And after those two weeks, I had this new invention put together."

Gelman had found something in a surgical journal about how colinesterase was stained for visibility in tissue culture slices, and then found an article in a journal in entomology about how to stabilize it so it could be stored for long periods of time. Why entomology?

"I kept looking through the literature trying to find if anybody had been successful in stabilizing this enzyme," he says. "The place where there was the highest level of colinesterase was cockroaches, so I found it in a cockroach journal. With those critical pieces of information, I was able to come up with this new invention. I didn't have to do a lot of development and basic study. I went into the lab with a 95 percent chance of being successful with the knowledge I had gotten out of the literature and by putting together some unrelated pieces of information. Once I had the key to stabilizing the enzyme, and the technique of colormetrically visualizing it from the tissue journal, that was the ham and eggs."

His supervisors found it hard to digest, however. "They wanted you to follow the rigid procedures," he says, "but the people who followed their procedures are people who worked there for 40 years and never came up with anything meaningful." Gelman's procedure, so to speak, was what he calls "free thinking, seeing the connection between what other people might say are unrelated happenings, of seeing how it could be useful in a product or useful to customers."

Gelman's test kit worked so well that it is still in use today, and there was one other long-term effect of his time in Maryland: He met a young microbiologist named Rita Specter who worked in, of all places, the cockroach lab. She has now been Gelman's wife for more than 40 years.

"Rita was dissecting cockroaches under a microscope," Gelman recalls, "but we didn't meet on the base. We met at some social events in Baltimore. She had grown up in Baltimore and gone to Goucher College there."

It is supremely ironic that Chuck Gelman later became famous, albeit unfairly, as a polluter, given that much of his early career was spent in search of a venue for his services that was as committed to public health as he was. The next stop in this quest was Louisville, Kentucky, where he would work on a U.S. Public Health Service study of air pollution, and where further lessons awaited him.

"I went from the Army to the Public Health Service because of the feeling that I really was almost doing something wrong to promote chemical warfare, for a variety of reasons," he says. "First of all, I believed the likelihood of an enemy using nerve gas was so remote that this whole thing was a waste of time and money. I also felt that this wasn't a socially useful pursuit of science or a benefit to mankind. I had all this expertise in measuring marginal contents in the atmosphere, so I thought I'd put it to good social use."

In the mid-1950s, air pollution was still a fairly arcane subject. This study was the first that attempted to measure the effects of an industrial community on a municipality; it was being done in Louisville partly because the federal, county, and city governments had agreed to cooperate in funding it, and partly because one of the federal government's largest monitoring systems was already in place there.

"The local citizens felt rather strongly that the industrial community on the edge of Louisville was the cause of all their problems, so they agreed to contribute to the study with the expectation that this would a hanging committee for the rubber plants," Gelman says. "The results of the study—and this is where the politics got rather heavy—clearly indicated that the culprit was the alcohol industry right in the middle of town and a garbage dump across the river. But this didn't meet the political objectives of the local community, so the report came out saying nothing when it was quite clear from a scientific point of view that if they're going to solve the problem, they had to go to the two sources of the problem."

There was a little problem with methodology, too, the discovery of which did nothing to further endear Gelman to his supervisors. In studying particulate contamination, "We'd collect the particulates on glass fiber and extract it and measure what was extracted from the air," he recalls. "I was fresh out of school, and they had taught me in analytic chemistry that the first thing you do is a background, to establish the limits of what you're trying to measure. So I did some backgrounds and checked different lots and wrote that there was so much variability from lot to lot that the measurements we made were totally meaningless, and our four years of data simply reported variations in manufacturers' equipment and had nothing to do with air pollution. They threatened to fire me on the spot."

His boss came to his defense and he wasn't fired, but he did get the message. "At that point, I decided that the Public Health Service wasn't quite what I had expected it to be," he says. "They weren't looking for truth and science. It was great fun that I prevailed and destroyed four years of extremely expensive data. I was like a kid with a room full of firecrackers, but I also knew I didn't create the basis for a long career."

Gelman concluded that if his skills were to serve humanity, "going into industry was more logical." For someone who had flirted with Communism as an adolescent, this was a stunning turn of events. "I had this picture of businessmen as the leeches of society, profiteers, so I was very much anti-business," he says. "I didn't think business was an area that I would ever in any way want to go into. It wasn't until I actually was in business for myself that I felt there was anything socially useful about businesses or businessmen."

Still, he was less resistant to evidence than were, say, the bureaucrats at the Public Health Service. "I decided I'd go to graduate school and equip myself to be an industrial hygienist or for some other work related to public health," he says. "At least there was a given task to do as an industrial hygienist—measuring exposure and seeing how it complies with acceptable regulations."

It came down to a choice between the University of Michigan and the University of North Carolina. "They both offered me some sort of graduate scholarship, and North Carolina also offered a small supplement," he says. "I couldn't picture myself at Chapel Hill, North Carolina, which at that time was pretty much the Deep South. I hadn't been down there enough to really know what it was like, so I chose the U of M, which probably turned out better for business."

Not that business was what he had in mind when he headed for Michigan, although business soon came calling. Rita went to work at the U-M's Kresge Institute to help make ends meet, including the rent on a house they found in Chelsea. There was even more than the usual shortage of affordable living space in Ann Arbor, and Gelman also wanted space for a workshop in case "I might want to play around some with building some more gadgets."

It was, however, an earlier gadget that lured entrepreneurship to his door. A device he left back in Louisville had, like the Timex watches of yore, kept on ticking. Due perhaps to his inconvenient principles, he had been assigned an overnight (midnight to 8 a.m.) shift monitoring emissions from a creosote manufacturing plant. As fond as anyone of a good night's sleep, and a newlywed besides, he invented an automatic sequential air sampler to do the work for him. After he got to Michigan, he got a call from his old boss, the one who had stuck up for him.

"He said, 'We're still using your machine, we'd like to buy it from you, and by the way, we'd like another dozen,'"

Gelman remembers. "I said I'll call you back. I called him back with a price, he said, 'That sounds fine, I'll get you the orders.'"

The orders helped him get a bank loan for $5,000, and, in 1958, the Gelman Instrument Company was born. Gelman invested $300 to rent a booth at an air pollution convention in Philadelphia, where he demonstrated his machine. "I had the idea that the sequential sampler could be used as both a gas and dust sampler," he says. But sampling dirt particles required 12 filter-holders whose total price was more than that of the entire machine. Gelman needed a way to lower that price.

"I went down to the local screw machine shop and showed the owner, William Thomas, what was on the market," he recalls. "He had been manufacturing manager of Federal Screw Works and started his own company. He said, 'This is not the way to make 'em. If I run 'em a thousand at a time, I can make 'em for you for three dollars apiece.' I said, 'Gee, that sounds terrific. People should jump at buying these for 10 dollars apiece (about a 10th of the prevailing price), and that would be a nice profit margin for me.'"

"Shall I run a thousand for you?" Thomas asked.

"I can't take a thousand," Gelman replied. "I don't have that kind of money."

"You look honest," said Thomas. "I'll tell you what I'll do. I'll make a thousand, keep them in my inventory, and you buy them as you use them."

"What if I can't sell them?" Gelman asked.

"I've taken other risks," he said. "If you sell them, I have a good customer. If not, it's my problem. I'll give them to friends as paperweights."

Soon the orders for the instruments were running into many thousands. Some customers were ordering a hundred at a time. And many customers were asking for the filters to go along with the instruments.

"They were saying, 'We have to buy the filters from somebody else and they're not very good,' so I started looking around for sources for filters," says Gelman.

He imported membrane filters in sheets from the Sartorius Company in Goettingen, Germany, for a while, cutting them up into different sizes and selling them under his Polypore registered trade name. Soon he was in danger of being a victim of his own success: his supplier had trouble keeping up with the demand.

"They said they had to go to another production machine and somebody had to pay for that, so our prices were doubled," says Gelman. "I started to explore the possibility of making our own line of filters."

Gelman and Donald Churchill, the first chemical engineer he had hired, went to work. It was back to the literature again, and again Gelman's non-standard procedures paid off.

"I didn't feel we had the luxury of five years to develop a line of filters, so I was looking for whether the technology might already be in the literature," he says. "I found that, in the literature from 1900-1920, there was a series of publications that spelled out pretty much how to make these things. Other people hadn't gone into this because there's this tendency to think that whatever is done in the last 40 years is as far back as you have to go, that before that, nobody developed anything useful. This was 1960, so most people would figure before 1920 was the dark ages. In this case, there was some sophisticated technology. In fact, in the case of membranes, the first membrane publication went back to the 1860s. We came up with a way of making membranes, tried it out, and it worked okay."

To say the least. That technology, gleaned from dusty bound volumes of arcane scientific journals, enabled Gelman to convert a battery separator membrane that the company had recently acquired into a filtration membrane, forming the basis for the giant conglomerate that Gelman Sciences, Inc. (so renamed in 1979), would become.

That key acquisition began with a phone call from Brooklyn. It was from a Mr. Prince, the general manager of Niemand Brothers, a manufacturer of lots of spiral tubes and a few battery separators. As it happened, the latter were sold under the trademark Polypore, and the company's lawyers had prevailed upon him to call Gelman about the trademark infringement.

"Apparently our lawyers had investigated laboratory devices when they searched through trademarks, but not battery separators," says Gelman. "The membrane they were using in their battery separators was fabric-reinforced, which I felt would be a step forward because the membrane we and others were producing was very fragile."

As the call went on, Gelman's ears were attuned to a couple of subtexts—this was a product that had the potential for wider applications, and his caller seemed pretty half-hearted about making it, "so I asked the guy, 'What the hell are you doing making filters? They're so unrelated to your core business.' He said, 'You're damn right they're unrelated; these filters stink and I don't want to make 'em; I'm just doing it as a favor to Mallory (now called Duracell). I got sucked into this in the first place.' So I saw my opening."

Prince's customers were large companies like Mallory and Sara Lee, who used his tubes for packaging and shipping everything from muffins to toys. He was doing $20 million a year in tubes and $100,000 in battery separators.

Gelman offered to come to Brooklyn. Prince agreed. "When I visited there, he made it clear from the very start that his battery separator represented nothing more than a nuisance for him. I seized the opportunity, even though it presented itself as coincidence."

By 1961, Gelman's company had gone public, offering 25 percent of its stock. Its product line had increased to more than 200, and its clients included Dow Chemical Company, General Electric, Stanford Research Institute, and the U.S. Air Force, Army, Navy...and Public Health Service. It was also still located in a storefront on North Main Street in Chelsea, and it was in the downstairs bathroom there where the company's first membrane filters were made by hand.

"After careful mixing to get just the right consistency, the membrane was poured onto glass plates, then rinsed in the bathtub and hung out to dry on laundry lines," says Gelman. "It seemed a lot like making candy, because it was critical to get the consistency and the thickness just right."

The application of the redefined technology, Gelman points out, "revolutionized our businesses. It allowed us to fully automate our membrane casting process and to cast the membrane onto a substrate. This was extremely important because it allowed us to pleat the membrane and encapsulate it in a much broader range of configurations for more applications."

In 1963, Gelman and his staff of 48 moved into a new, 14,000-square-foot facility in Scio Township, just west of Ann Arbor. In 1968, the company opened its first subsidiary, in Canada, and also its first overseas office, in Hawksley, England. Another first that year was the company's first Presidential "E-Star" Award from the U.S. Department of Commerce for export achievement. Gelman's undergraduate work in international politics was being put to good use, even if it was not for the State Department.

The parade of new products, many of which also opened up new markets, continued: Acrodisc®, the world's first disposable syringe filter in 1972; the Preflow® membrane filter in 1974, and the first polysulfone membrane in 1975. The company's Ann Arbor facilities had grown to 85,000 square feet and sales hit $20 million in 1977, the year of another "E Star" Award.

And Chuck Gelman continued to listen to his customers. In 1978, on a visit to Cobe Laboratories, the leading manufacturer of kidney dialysis machines, he inquired about the possibility of using filters similar to the Acrodisc as a barrier to contamination passing from patient to patient during hemodialysis.

"They indicated that they didn't need a filter, but there was another problem," says Gelman. "Blood kept backing up into the dialysis machine and clogging the transducers. What was needed was a hydrophobic barrier. Our company was at that point just beginning to market our hydrophobic Versapar membrane. I offered the client a handful of samples, and almost immediately afterward received an order for 25,000."

Then the U.S. Food and Drug Administration mandated the use of the device for each dialysis patient. Then there was an order for a million. By 1996, annual sales for this one application reached more than 40 million units.

Although it might look like luck, "it wasn't accidental," Gelman says. "I was trying to sell filters and the customers weren't interested in filters, but I came up with the proposal that the same filtration device could be used to protect dialysis units and that the customers were interested in, or this particular customer."

Beyond listening to customers, and listening to opportunity, the story illustrates another approach that has served Gelman well. "Quite often, in going out to see customers, I wouldn't talk at all about a product, but we'd discuss their operations and try to find out what their problems were," he says. "Then I'd see whether I could come up with a solution to a problem that they had, that hopefully would incorporate some form of filtration. My approach wasn't, 'Gee, I have a wonderful filter, you ought to buy it,' but 'Gee, I'd like to know about what you do, what you find difficult to do, would you like an easier way to approach it?'"

And he would be sincere about solving the problem, even if it meant sounding a bit like Kris Kringle in *Miracle on 34th Street.* "Sometimes I've said to people that what we manufacture is too expensive," he says. "There's something simpler that a competitor makes that can solve your problem more easily. I've killed the sale but it establishes a relationship."

The prodigious success of Gelman's entry into the health care market necessitated a site expansion to 54 acres, including a new, 19,000-square-foot Medical Device Building. A record 35 new products were introduced in 1981, the Medical Device Building was expanded, and a 53,000-square-foot warehouse was constructed.

The next year, Gelman implemented a management decentralization plan that reshaped the company into autonomous profit center groups, as well as research and development, finance, marketing, and manufacturing. "It also was an attempt to give employees more control," says Gelman, "so you didn't have interdependent divisions and enormous amounts of committee work to make sure decisions would work for each one of the divisions."

Gelman admits the management structure had previously been "very centralized and top-down. And I had always been accused of being very autocratic, although I don't think I was." Now he was also able to focus on strategic planning rather than organizational detail.

The new system, a precursor in many ways of highly publicized strategies of the '90s such as Total Quality Management, stayed in place until the company was sold to Pall Filtration in 1996, when Gelman retired. "It was helpful," he says, especially a few years later, in 1987, when employee loyalty helped bail the company out of one of its toughest spots.

"The Bank of the Commonwealth had induced us to borrow from them and then, when they were in trouble, gave us 90 days to pay it all back," Gelman recalls. That meant both reducing inventory and maintaining production in order to lower costs and meet customer requirements.

"I told the researchers, when I have to lay people off, I would rather lay off research which we'll need in the future, but I'd like you to work on the production line for six months," he says. "Then, if we've made it, you can go back to your old jobs. If we haven't, we'll all be out on the street."

The researchers enthusiastically agreed. "They actually were proud of the fact they were able to achieve a higher work output than the production people," he says. "Each week, they would fight to get the lower reject rate and higher output. So that's a situation where we were asking people to help and cooperate and it did pay off."

In more ways than one. "That probably was great training for the researchers to be more sensitive, in developing product, to what the problems in production were," Gelman says. "And it was critical to our survival that they were willing to volunteer to do that. One of the guys in that team wound up staying with the company for 30 years. He retired when he was in his 50s and the value of his stock options was something like $4 million."

Gelman estimates at least ten of his employees have become millionaires, a form of being "socially useful" that would probably have stunned his youthful Communist compatriots.

"For a while, we became a conglomerate," he says. "As long as it was scientific and it related to removing articles, we'd buy another company."

In 1986, Gelman Sciences' sales passed the $50 million mark. The company was cited in the book *The 101 Best-Performing Companies in America*. Gelman himself received the first annual "Trailblazer Award" from the Detroit Science Center for his contributions to the scientific community. Everything seemed to be coming up roses, but another unhappy encounter with government was lurking just around the corner.

Before revisiting Gelman's protracted battle with the state of Michigan over groundwater contamination, however, it might be instructive to go back to the beginning, the fifth-floor walkup in a declining neighborhood in the Bronx where Gelman spent his earliest years. It was the depths of the Great Depression, Gelman's parents had separated when he was two years old, and he and his mother were living with her parents, brother and sister.

"When I was maybe 10, my mother found out where my father was and that he had a draft exemption, probably based on the fact that he had a family," says Gelman, "so she ratted on him to the draft board and he got drafted into the Army."

This was 1942, shortly after the United States entered World War II. Gelman had a newspaper delivery route, his mother worked as a stock clerk, his grandfather washed windows and cleaned medical offices, and his 15-year-old uncle went to Stuyvesant High School and worked at Barnes & Noble. The teen became a father figure to the younger boy.

"He'd buy books, bring stuff home, and we'd talk a lot about literature, about the house," Gelman says. "He'd tell me, 'You have to realize that we're both growing up in a snake pit.' That was his characterization of the family."

Young Chuck got out of the house as much as he could. The money he saved from the paper route "enabled me to have a little freedom. On Saturdays, I'd take the Hudson Bay liner up to Bear Mountain Park. It might have been a two-hour steamer ride; it was an all-day excursion. The rides up to Bear Mountain would keep my sanity."

Then came one of those opportunities that arrive in the guise of a crisis. After delivering papers one afternoon when he had a cold, Gelman came down with rheumatic fever.

"The doctor came up to the house," he remembers, "diagnosed what I had and said, 'This child must immediately get to the hospital.'"

The physician quickly reassured his mother that, since the boy's father was in the Army (thanks, mom!), the New York War Fund, which was established to care for the dependents of those in the armed forces, would pay all of Chuck's medical bills. Gelman was admitted to the prestigious Columbia Presbyterian Hospital, where he was treated by leading specialists, and then sent to a convalescent hospital in Greenwich, Connecticut.

"It was me along with the Rockefellers," he laughs. "There never was any question of money."

But his health-related luck was just beginning. While he was in Greenwich, the doctors told his mother that regularly climbing five flights of stairs was just too risky for his potentially damaged heart. He would have to live somewhere else.

"She went around to different Jewish agencies and found this place that was called an orphanage, but was really a boys' boarding school for kids from broken families," says Gelman. "Of 80 boys in the school, only one or two were actually orphans."

The place was called Homecrest, and Gelman remembers it with understandable fondness. He was on his way up, and out.

"I felt a tremendous relief to get out of the house," he says. "It was a funny coincidence that my mother's craftiness managed to get me out of the city and into an upper middle-class environment. The school was in Westchester County, and it was the equivalent of a very fine boys' finishing school. We went to Roosevelt High School in Yonkers, we had counselors. Wealthy people from Westchester would take us out on their boats or to the opera. It got me out of the city and I saw a different aspect of life that I never would have seen had I stayed there."

And the director of Homecrest, a man named Reubon Koftoff, became a kind of surrogate father, even as Gelman rediscovered his relationship with his biological dad.

"He very much encouraged me, since I was good at academics, to do well in classes," Gelman says of Koftoff, "and assured me that if I did well, he would find ways for me to go on to college. He'd get one of the ladies' leagues to come up with the money to finance it for me. So that turned out to be a very lucky circumstance, because I don't know if I would have gone to college had I lived in the city."

By the time the youngster was in high school, his father was back from the Army and had, as it happened, a wholesale dry cleaning route through Westchester. "He would visit me once or twice a week, and we started to develop a pretty good relationship," Gelman says. "We'd go out for coffee and talk; I don't even remember what the talks were about. I had to sort of keep contacts with him under cover from my mother. She was aware that I would see him but she was resentful that he hadn't been around while I was a child. She thought I shouldn't even see him, that he deserved punishment for having abandoned the family."

The father-and-son chats gradually revealed a different picture of events. "I knew there was more to the story

than what my mother had told me about simple aban-
donment," he says. "My mother was a very difficult person, very controlling. I could understand how she could
have driven anybody crazy. My father and I didn't talk
very much about the reasons why he left the house. They
both probably were too young to have gotten married in
the first place. She says she was 17, so he must have been
about 18. My mother had a very bad relationship with her
father and was anxious to get out of the house. She recre-
ates that in any relationship she has, including with
myself, so I assume it was the same with my father."

Gelman maintained contact with his father until his
father's death in 1968.

One of the supervisors at Homecrest, who was part of a
group of people Gelman socialized with, was connected
with the Communist movement. "He invited me to come
down to their social evenings in Greenwich Village,"
Gelman recalls. "They had hootenannies, the old labor
hootenannies. It was fun and it was interesting to experiment with what they were talking about."

But it was also perilous, as Koftoff pointed out in a
fatherly chat. As Gelman remembers it, his mentor said,
"I'm not going to lecture you. I know you're going to
Greenwich Village. I don't really approve of the philosophy
but it's pointless for me to get into a debate with you
about social philosophy; you're going to have to work that
out for yourself. So all I can caution you is to be safe,
don't sign any petitions, don't affiliate. We're getting into
an area where there's going to be a witch hunt for
Communists. At some point, you may want to work for the
government. If you get your name on a list, you're going
to limit your choices. I'm not going to spy on you, do what
you please, but let's agree I'll be generous if you promise
you'll never sign anything."

Given that his first job out of college was with the Army,
"it turned out to be very wise advice," says Gelman.

So was Koftoff's urging that he continue his education,
although it turned out that he didn't need his mentor's
help, at least financially.

"They came up with the cash," Gelman says of Homecrest. "In fact, they pushed me to apply for Harvard. They really wanted to have one of their graduates go to Harvard, but I got a New York State Regents Scholarship, and Syracuse matched the regents scholarship with a tuition scholarship, so I had a full room and board and tuition scholarship."

Four and a half decades later, he had a company whose profits for the year were $2.7 million. In between, he learned lessons beyond those of the classroom and laboratory—about listening to customers, seizing opportunities, empowering employees, doing business in diverse cultures, and keeping his mind open to possibilities and away from boxes and boundaries.

When you do business in other countries, he says, "You have different rules, so you've got to know by what rules you will be expected to operate. The worst part of it is the problem of bribery. In the United States, if a supplier suggests that he's going to offer a bribe to get business, you consider it illegal or unethical. Ninety-nine percent of the people would have nothing to do with it. In other areas of the world, well, what else is new? Who else would you do business with but family and friends? How would you know whether to trust them?"

When you develop a product, it better be useful to customers. "A lot of developers, especially in the technical fields, come up with beautiful creations that they think are the greatest invention and nobody's interested," he says. "There's a market of one."

When you make a deal, keep the other side's needs in view. "Whether it's buying a piece of property or buying a company, I think a lot of people go in and try to get the lowest price possible," Gelman says. "They focus on their objective and then the deal is killed because somebody offers two percent higher or 10 percent higher."

Better, he says, to "try to figure out why the person is selling, and if you really match the reason why the person is selling, you may have a deal that's unbreakable because you've established a non-monetary match. Assurance that there won't be capricious firing of employees may be far more important to a founder than 10 percent or 20 percent more in the price. But usually companies acquiring companies don't even bother to find out how important are the non-monetary factors to the people who want to sell the business. Somebody may be focused on keeping the name, on keeping certain employees, there may be a lot of things they're focused on that if the acquirer finds out about those, it can make a much better deal for both parties."

And, oh yes, when you deal with government, watch your back, and your front, and your flanks, and be prepared to dig in and fight long, expensive battles.

In 1986 the Michigan Department of Natural Resources found in the groundwater surrounding Gelman's plant what it considered to be potentially hazardous amounts of 1,4-dioxane, an industrial solvent used in the company's manufacturing process and a suspected animal carcinogen. In 1987, the DNR put Gelman Sciences second on its list of the worst polluters in the state, and sued the company in an attempt to force it to clean up the contamination. Gelman countersued, and a flurry of legal actions followed.

The company's position was that the DNR lacked rules for either its ranking or its enforcement procedures, that the plan it insisted on was unreasonably expensive and would put the company out of business, that it had disposed of the dioxane in conformity with its permits from the DNR, and that, in any event, the concentrations in the groundwater were far too small to threaten human health.

Time after time, the company won in court, including the settlement of the DNR's original lawsuit in 1992, but the struggle took its toll. Gelman and his company were demonized as polluters. Stock prices tumbled. Almost overnight, it seemed, he had been transformed from the founder and grower of a major industrial enterprise—that employed hundreds of workers and plowed much of its profit back into the community—into an irresponsible poisoner of his neighbors' wells.

"I don't feel ashamed of the exercise," says Gelman, "but I do feel it was a lot of, to quote Shakespeare, 'sound and fury signifying nothing,' a lot of nonsense and nothing ever happened out of it."

Not in terms of solving the problem, which Gelman says was his focus and intention all along. Pall-Gelman, the company formed when he sold the business to a larger competitor, is still battling with the city of Ann Arbor over how much dioxane can safely enter the sewer system, even as the allegedly contaminated plume continues to spread.

"The pollution could have been cleaned up rather quickly if the state had sat down with us and agreed to a reasonable plan and then convinced the neighbors that the plan was reasonable," Gelman says. "The neighbors were panicked. They were told that three parts per billion of dioxane in the groundwater was lethal, when in fact you could safely drink something like 3,000 parts per billion. The state wouldn't sit down with them and explain what all these different numbers meant. So the position of the citizens was here's a wealthy industry, they can afford to clean it up to zero, and we don't believe anything the company is saying or the state is saying.

"Had the state done its job, sat down with parties interested and come up with a workable plan, this whole thing could have been settled and cleaned up 10 years ago at a fairly modest cost of something like $3 million," he continues. "Instead, the company spent $15 million in legal fees, maybe another $10 million so far on cleanup, and probably has yet to spend another $25 million because the pollution has gotten so diverse that it can't be controlled."

Even after a decade, there's a trace of disbelief in Gelman's voice when he talks about what happened. "We were charged with criminal pollution, irresponsible pollution, even though we had followed the directions of the state," he says. "In fact, they had given Japanese groups tours of what we were doing to show how advanced the state of Michigan was in technology. Meantime, the contamination was no longer a problem because we had been connected to the sewer, and for a period of time we had a deep well where we were injecting this stuff 5,000 feet underground."

But political considerations surfaced, just as they had in Louisville so many years before. "At the time, Governor (James) Blanchard was making a big statement about how he was going to clean up the environment, so it was the position of his administration that they should go heavily after industrial polluters," Gelman says. "We were put on the list of polluters as number two in the state of Michigan, which was an administrative error. Later on, we were changed to number 120, but by that time all the damage had been done. There were headlines around the state. The attorney general had vowed to put these companies out of business. We were targeted. The neighbors wanted us out of the area, wanted the plant burned down, and wanted the officials burned at the stake."

Not to mention the $100 million fine and the $50 million cleanup plan to be imposed on a company whose net worth was $10 million. "We discovered we had insurance that would pay for our legal defense and technical defense, so there really wasn't much choice. The state wouldn't negotiate anything reasonable in terms of cleanup, so we had to defend ourselves. We looked at the possibility of selling the company, but no big company wanted to buy us because all they would do is inherit a problem, and the state would have found someone with deeper pockets to go after."

In addition to the lawsuits, Gelman launched what might be called an information assault. He commissioned a study from a University of Michigan professor that found dioxane in 35,000 consumer products, including baby shampoo. His staff members sifted through mountains of DNR records and discovered state-owned sites with vastly higher pollution levels than Gelman's, a story that was furnished to the press "out of public duty," he says. The company even offered to drill new, deeper wells for any neighbors whose water supply was found to be contaminated. Gelman proposed holding discussions with those neighbors where top scientists would explain the risks and the company could explain its own cleanup alternatives.

"The answer was 'No, you have such powerful science that you'll overwhelm us with reason, so we won't even talk to you,'" Gelman recalls. "They believed that we were liars, that the scientists that we would bring to talk to them were whores. These were people like the head of the Society of Toxicology. 'Of course,' the critics said, 'you can afford a very expensive whore. Of course, he has a reputation to protect; imagine how much money you had to pay him.'"

It looked, for a long time, like a no-win situation. "The first five years took a very heavy toll because most people in the community figured there's so much noise about it, he must have done something wrong," Gelman says. "There were cartoons in the paper about midnight polluting. Employees' children were told at school, 'How can your parent work for a community polluter?' I think at some point, Rita even said to me, 'Now tell me truthfully, what really happened?' People weren't interested in discussing what we did as a company. They were interested in talking about the pollution."

Now, he says, the community is less interested and besides, he sold the company in February 1997 and founded Palladium Associates, a consulting firm that discharges nothing anywhere.

"I think the media have somewhat gotten off it," Gelman says. "They no longer go after the company hammer and tongs. And there's a turnover of reporters, so that the articles change somewhat as a new reporter comes in, whether they are familiar with the history or not. The community at large, I think, has just gotten tired of hearing about the subject. To some extent, a situation like this may be peculiar to Ann Arbor and its attitudes. But it's also an indication of how things can get when people just dig in and don't look at reason at all, or at what they ultimately would want."

Strange as it may sound to his critics, Gelman's background inculcated in him a strong sense of social responsibility, which preceded the bad publicity and is now out-
lasting it. "Judaism places a lot of emphasis on giving to
charity and community service," he says. "If anything, I'm
an agnostic, but I'm active in the synagogue, and we celebrate the Jewish holidays." Two of his and Rita's four
children are Orthodox, and one of them, a Hebrew day
school teacher in California, is publishing books on training children in the Jewish tradition.

The Gelmans' community service has taken many
forms. They made a major contribution to The Ann Arbor
Hands-On Museum's capital campaign, he serves on the
advisory board at Peace Neighborhood Center, and they
fund an annual seminar at the University of Michigan
School of Public Health on risk appraisal and public
health.

But the primary recipient of their pro bono energy and
resources is the Charles and Rita Gelman Educational
Foundation. "We are focusing on elder care in the community, outside of the medical area," says Gelman. "We're
looking at programs in the community that enrich the
lives of people over age 70, and where are the lacks that
prevent people from taking advantage of existing programs, or the gaps where there aren't programs for them.
We find the lacks are more in the area of any kind of
buddy system, any kind of community support to regularly give them visitors. The problem seems to be mostly
with the detachment of older people from the community,
that they feel nobody cares for them, other than their
medical needs, so that most of the elderly population
looks to the medical community as their friends, social
workers, caretakers. Which is a very expensive form of
support group. Our premise is that the country could
save billions and billions of dollars if you had a system
with churches and synagogues and Y's giving the kind of
support that used to be available from the family."

Gelman recently addressed a class at an institute in
London that is run by Syracuse, his alma mater, and

reflected on the importance of family. "You can be extremely successful," he said, "yet find yourself holding an empty bag. If you are so dedicated to business that you lose sight of family, you may end up very wealthy, but also very unhappy."

When asked what he's most proud of in his life, he says without hesitation, "What some of my children have done."

Steve, the oldest, is a marketing executive for technology firms, running innovative programs for more than 20 years for companies including Gelman Sciences, Future Medical Technologies, and RELA, Inc. He was president of a small technology company in Boulder, Colorado, where he has lived for three years. He has earned two master's degrees, and is working on his PhD in business administration.

Eric began his career representing Gelman Sciences in China for five years, where he learned to speak Mandarin fluently and negotiated a major manufacturing deal with the Chinese government. When he returned to the United States, he managed the Gelman Sciences International Department for several years, then organized and ran an import/export company selling sporting goods. When he sold that, he used the proceeds to attend the University of Connecticut, where he earned a master's in biotechnology, then went to work for a large, multinational company.

At 35, Nina has already managed several businesses. She was editor of the *Washtenaw Jewish Times* and ran a bed and breakfast in Ann Arbor before earning two master's degrees at Brandeis University, one in Jewish education and one in management. She's now the principal of a Hebrew school near Santa Barbara, California, running a business that publishes Jewish educational material, and writing a syndicated column on Jewish education published in Jewish community newspapers.

Rebecca, the youngest, is an architect and designer who chose and installed the decor in what he calls his "executive play pen" high above South Main Street in Ann Arbor. "I guess I feel she's carried on some of my attitudes of life: If a problem comes up, it's not a problem, it's a challenge," he says. "In spite of the fact that she's very comfortable economically, she hasn't taken this as a license that she should just spend the money she gets, but she has a program of achievement. All four of the children have picked up the entrepreneurial spirit and are willing to experiment and go off on their own."

That tradition, that spirit, is obviously important to Gelman, who has often cited its disappearance as a major factor in his decision to sell the company he spent most of his adult life building. "As the company grew, it became more distant from the original sense of adventure," he says. "At one point, the idea of being head of a worldwide establishment with a billion dollars in sales and several thousand employees seemed very glamorous. But as we got bigger and bigger, the ratio of chores to fun things became greater, chores like preparing talks to stock analysts and bankers, especially when you know that a lot of what you prepare is nothing better than a guess. But you can't tell them.

"The fun part of it was coming up with a new product, figuring out the problems involved in manufacturing a mass. But the reality of building a business is that it needed to focus on the bottom line and make more and more money, plus quite often what you knew was the right thing to do in long-range terms wasn't a practical thing to do to satisfy Wall Street and the bankers."

In long-range terms, Gelman had a vision that transcended practicality; however, the purchasing company, Pall Corporation had other priorities. Gelman says, "Pall proceeded to dismember the company to achieve financial synergies. In doing so, they are destroying much of what they paid for. I don't have a method that could have insured against this."

What Gelman does have is a family, which helps insure against an inordinate measure of business regrets. Chuck proudly notes that Rita went back to school at age 50 and earned a master's in social work. "She's a licensed social worker," he says. "Our foundation puts her background to use."

He also quietly points out that it's Dr. Charles Gelman now. "I did it the easy way," he says. "I got an honorary doctorate degree from Cleary College."

Then he grins just a little. "My mother is at last satisfied."

"I just kept broadening."

Dick Griffin

Of all the jobs he's ever had, Dick Griffin says, "the most awesome one is trying to raise children. And each child is different. And there aren't any experts. Maybe somebody else learned something in raising theirs, but there aren't any experts in raising yours."

This is from a man who bought dozens of companies as a mergers and acquisitions expert, who was a key figure in one of the major communications buyouts in Michigan history, who prevailed in legal combat with the likes of the Kroger Company, who pursued for 16 years the goal—never realized—of being CEO of a major U.S. company.

This is also a man who is quite clear about where the real value in life resides. He lost his father, whom he idolized, when he was 13. Two of his siblings died in infancy before he was born. Two of his own children survived major health scares, and one of the main reasons he abandoned his lifelong CEO dream was so he could be home on weekends and spend more time with his family.

"Money is just a means to an end," he says. "That's all it is. Hopefully, we can show our kids that it's a responsibility to give it where it's needed and handle it properly."

Is it a curse or a blessing? "Certainly, having money allowed my children to go to the colleges of their choice," he says. "I think that's a blessing. And it allowed us to give them a Catholic elementary and secondary education."

That's what Griffin had, and that's what he wanted for his children. He also, of course, wanted them to survive, and it looked iffy a couple of times. The first was in 1972 when Lisa, five years old and the oldest of what were then three, underwent surgery to repair a congenital heart defect.

"Open heart surgery was sort of an unproven thing at that point in time," he says. "In fact, another little boy was in the hospital having heart surgery the same time she did and we got to know the parents. The boy had a valve problem, which was much more serious. The doctors came back and told us our daughter was fine. They came back and told them their son had died."

Six years later, Kevin, the youngest, who had been born only a few months before, fell ill at the family's lake cottage in the Irish Hills.

"He became sort of lethargic and had a fever," Griffin recalls, "so we came in to Ann Arbor and went right to our doctor. It was a weekend, so our regular doctor wasn't there, but somebody was on call and met us at the office. He took one look and said better get him into Mott Hospital."

The diagnosis was bacterial spinal meningitis, and he and Ruth, his wife, spent the night at the hospital, praying. "As soon as we got him to Mott, they started giving him massive doses of antibiotics," Griffin says. "It was crucial to get those antibiotics in there before the damage was done. Drugs are overused in a lot of different ways, but if they need one and they've got the right one, it's almost like a miracle."

It seemed like even more of a miracle when Griffin got

home early the next morning to update the other children before they left for school. While waiting for them to get up, he thumbed through the mail and found a letter from Dr. Trent Spolar, a physician friend who had been a Notre Dame classmate.

"I don't even know why I opened it," he says. Catching up on correspondence was the farthest thing from his mind, but this turned out to be painfully relevant. "In the letter, Trent informed me that his daughter had spinal meningitis and it had caused severe retardation.

"It put a scare into me," Griffin admits. "I don't cry often, but I sat down and cried. I thought if Kevin lives, he'll probably be retarded. You fear the worst. The reason it ended up in retardation for my friend's son was he didn't diagnose it fast enough and get his child on to the proper drugs. He felt really at fault, I guess. He's gone through life with that hanging over his head."

Like his sister, Kevin pulled through just fine, but such experiences reinforced a hierarchy of values that Griffin had started building early in life.

As a youngster growing up in East St. Louis, Illinois, he could hardly be pried away from the baseball diamond or the basketball court. "Perhaps sports consumed too much of my time and effort," he says, "but sports taught me a great deal—teamwork, doing your best, setting goals, playing by the rules, how to win and lose. Many of those principles have stayed with me."

He earned seven varsity letters at Assumption High School, co-captained the basketball team, and pitched a no-hitter (missing a perfect game because of his own throwing error) in baseball. His preoccupation didn't seem to hurt him academically: He was valedictorian of the class of 1956.

Four years earlier, he played for the St. Patrick Grade School team that won the city's CYO basketball tournament and then appeared in an all-star game. It was on a Thursday night in March. "I played in it and came home," he says, "just another regular night. When I woke up in the morning, my mom told me my father had died of a heart attack during the night."

It was as sudden as it was traumatic. A successful civil engineer who had just turned 65, Emmett P. Griffin hadn't been ill, had no history of heart disease, and was still active and prominent in civic affairs. He had created the East St. Louis park system ("both politically and in terms of designing it," says his son), served on the Illinois Planning Commission, chaired the St. Clair County Housing Authority, and once ran for mayor. He was also devoted to his family.

"Even though he died when I was real young, I still have good images of everything about him," Griffin says. "One of the things I will never forget about his funeral was the large number of blacks and people with handicaps who attended. They were people who worked for him. I had never noticed that before."

Although they would undoubtedly be labeled differently, he sees some consistency between his father's views and his own. "He was a Democrat," says Griffin, "and a Democrat is normally considered a liberal, and he was liberal in the sense that he wanted to help the underprivileged people. I consider myself rather conservative, but I still want to help those people, too. The question is how you go about helping them. I wouldn't mind at all paying taxes to the government if the money wasn't wasted, but the great majority of it is. If it actually reached its destination intact and achieved the goal, we'd be all right. But it doesn't. Just go back to what my dad did. Our government's way of helping those people has been to give them money. He didn't give them money; he gave them a job. They worked as hard as anyone else for their money."

Griffin had to start working hard, too. His mother suffered from depression—"she would have what we called in those days nervous breakdowns"—and he and his two brothers, three and eight years older than Dick, took on significant household responsibilities. "Growing up without a father and with a mother who had an illness, it would have been easy to head in some wrong directions," Griffin says. "The example that my brothers showed me—

the way they took on responsibilities, the balance they had in their lives of academic achievement and sports—was a big help in keeping me pointed in the right direction. They were just good role models." After his freshman year in high school, he also took on his first summer job.

"My uncle was the vice president of a glass bottle manufacturing company," Griffin recalls. "I went to see him and took my two best friends, expecting that he would give us jobs and that we would work together. Instead, he gave us swing-shift jobs and put each of us on a different shift; I didn't get to see much of them all summer."

He did get to see life in the trenches of manufacturing. "I gained a lifelong respect for those men and women who make their livelihood by toiling in factories," he says. "I also learned that I did not want to spend my life doing that."

That meant college, and that meant Notre Dame. There was never any doubt, then or now. "I was the typical Catholic grade school kid interested in sports, so I sort of followed Notre Dame in football and had some knowledge of Notre Dame athletics," says Griffin, "but my brother going there gave me exposure to it as a school. When I went there and visited him, I just loved it. The place had a magical attraction for me. I had to go there."

Not that he had any clear idea of a career—other than not working in a factory—but he had been good in math and chemistry in high school, so he chose to study chemical engineering. And although he says "the days of academics coming easily for me ended abruptly," he eventually graduated second among the 40 or so chemical engineering students who remained from the original group of 150. That was good enough to earn a fellowship for graduate work at Northwestern University, where chemical engineering became the second item on the list of livelihoods to avoid.

"I had two degrees in it, then decided that it wasn't what I wanted to do," Griffin says. "I wanted something broader. As an undergraduate, you're doing a lot of things other than your major. There are the social aspects, the broad education you're getting, but when you're studying for a master's in chemical engineering, that's your entire focus. You've taken a step away from all your undergraduate friends and you're into the chemical engineering system. The intensity of that just got me thinking—hey, this isn't where I want to spend the rest of my life. What should I be thinking of for the future? It took five years of college before my focus really got on the business world."

It was the breadth of the opportunities there that appealed to him. "I wanted to keep my options open," he says. "If you get boxed in to a real narrow job and you stay in that for a period of time, then you don't have a lot of options in terms of branching out. I feel sorry for people who get into those situations where they don't have alternatives. As I went through my career, I just kept broadening and broadening and creating more options for myself."

His first move was to New York City. He had accepted a job as an economic evaluation engineer with the M.W. Kellogg Company, an engineering and construction firm, and headed there just a few weeks after completing his master's.

"My best high school friends threw a going-away party for me in East St. Louis and I left for New York," he remembers. "All my belonging and I were in a VW bug and I drove 24 hours straight. As I approached the Lincoln Tunnel at dawn on Labor Day, 1961, I thought to myself, 'What the hell am I doing here?'"

That feeling intensified after he checked into a YMCA recommended by his new employers and decided to refresh himself with a shower. The first thing he saw when he walked into the shower room was one man giving oral sex to another. This was a long way from East St. Louis, or even South Bend. "I wanted to jump back into the VW bug and head home," he says. "I didn't."

For one thing, he wasn't a quitter. For another, he had chosen this job because he wanted to beef up his business skills, not only by assessing the economic, as well as technical, feasibility of new chemical processes, but also by taking courses part-time at New York University.

"I knew NYU had a good business school which was oriented toward evening students," he says. "And New York seemed interesting to me. As a young bachelor, it seemed it should be a good experience."

He also began to discover the benefits of blending engineering and business. "There are some technical things you learn in engineering that are helpful in any business," he says, "but it's more the analytical approach to solving problems that you learn as an engineer that is very applicable to business. So it ended up being a good decision to go to New York on my first job."

But the New York days also brought the end of his bachelorhood. One evening, he and a senior colleague at Kellogg, an amateur artist who was also a fellow Notre Dame alumnus, boarded a flight in Newark for Charleston, West Virginia, where they would meet their clients at the Union Carbide Company.

"He was scared to death of flying and normally, if he had a chance, he would take an overnight train to get there," says Griffin, "but this was sort of a short-notice meeting. He got to the airport about an hour and a half early and fired down some martinis, then he had a couple more on the plane."

When he was sufficiently relaxed, he began using the cardboard tray left over from dinner to make sketches of one of the flight attendants. "When she had some free time, he would ask her to come over," Griffin says. "While he was sketching her, I struck up a conversation, found out she lived in New York City, and got her phone number. The first couple of times I called for a date, she was not available. I thought I was getting a message there but I wasn't accepting it. The third time I called, she was available, we went out on a date and things progressed from there. Once we started dating, it went pretty fast."

On October 2, 1965, Griffin and Ruth Klaboe, the stewardess and a native Minnesotan, were married in Minneapolis. "We met when we both lived in New York City, but we shared common Midwestern values," he says.

Not that they had much opportunity to share them during their courtship, thanks to an ill-fated ski trip in Vermont. "She broke her leg in two places," Griffin says. "I felt real bad. I had to put her on an airplane and send her back to Minnesota to recuperate, so for much of the time we were engaged, we were separated."

There was another change at about the same time— Griffin left Kellogg to become manager of commercial research at Nicolet Industries, a manufacturer of industrial products in Florham Park, New Jersey. "Kellogg was a large company and my job was mostly engineering-oriented," he says. "Nicolet was a small company and my job was mostly business-oriented, determining the market potential for new and proposed new products."

During his three years with Nicolet, the Griffins' first two children were born and they bought their first house, in Morris Plains, New Jersey. But it soon became clear to Griffin that, since most of Nicolet's products were asbestos-based, their long-term outlook "was not very bright. The industry was starting to get painted with a pretty broad brush, and it looked like it would be tough just to survive with all the litigation they were going to get pulled into," he says. "I thought there were greener pastures elsewhere."

He went back to work in New York City, as manager of commercial development for Reeves Brothers, Inc., a maker of textile, rubber, and plastic products. "I was responsible for analyzing the market for new products and for the evaluation of acquisition candidates," he says. "This was when I developed a keen interest in the merger/acquisition business. I just like all the ingredients that go into that kind of work. Every day, you show up and there's something new. You get to meet a lot of different people in a lot of different industries. You learn about a lot of different industries. You see how different companies function and what separates the good ones from the bad. It involves travel, which I once enjoyed, and the thrill of making a deal.

"It's like pitching that no-hitter. You make that deal and

everything falls into place and it just gives you a great feeling. There's an outcome, a closing. But it's really an opening. Because now you own that company, and it has to produce the results that you had projected it was going to produce."

But with the job at Reeves Brothers came the need to commute an hour and a half each way. "I was really tired of it," he says. "I guess that was the main thing that made me receptive to a different opportunity. They said you get used to it, but I'd get on the train every day and see guys with their hats pulled down over their faces, and they didn't seem very happy."

His next job was a gamble that came tantalizingly close to paying off handsomely, then went sour. He joined Advanced Technology Consultants Corporation in Wallingford, Connecticut, as a vice president, in charge of venture capital and merger/acquisition consulting and institutional investment research, and moved his family to nearby Trumbull. "I was given significant stock options and the company planned an initial public offering of stock to finance its growth," he says. "I almost became instantly wealthy, but not quite."

The IPO market cooled off, the offering was called off, and the focus became financial survival. "I was exposed to more new businesses and industries, and we did some excellent work for our clients, but we had great difficulty generating cash flow," he recalls. The remedy proposed by the chairman (and major shareholder) and the company's other officers was that they would be paid partly in cash and partly in stock.

"Then I found out that the chairman was continuing to take his full salary in cash," says Griffin. "I resigned on the spot and walked out of the office mad as hell. We now had three kids and I was out of a job. And then I got introduced to the legal system. I had to hire a lawyer to sue for, and collect, my back pay...less the 33 percent kept by the lawyer."

His eyes were opened further during a brief period of free-lance consulting, during which he analyzed investments for a stock brokerage firm and acted as an acquisition intermediary. In the latter capacity, he midwifed a transaction in which an individual buyer acquired a division of a West Coast conglomerate in a leveraged buyout.

"He had me jumping through hoops to put together a deal for him," says Griffin. "He was a Harvard Business School graduate, you know. Out East, Harvard Business School is the school. At that age, I thought if I were dealing with someone from the Harvard Business School, he would be moral and responsible and pay his bills, particularly when the deal I put together for him was a helluva deal."

But instead of the finder fee of $105,000 that was due him, Griffin got a check for $5,000. His client refused to pay the rest, so Griffin sued him. It took more than five years for the case to come to trial, and only three days after that for the judge to call the parties into his chamber and tell them to settle for a compromise amount, because that was how he was going to rule anyway.

"I was flabbergasted," says Griffin, "but my attorney told me that's the way the system works." And the Harvard Business School guy knew how to work it.

"He made out," says Griffin. "In the end, he paid me only half of what he should have paid me, and it was seven years after he was supposed to pay me. He saved half the money, minus whatever he had to pay his lawyer. You have a number of people in business who know how expensive, bad, and time-consuming the legal system is, and use it as their strategy to get things. You can't avoid it."

It was even harder to avoid after he began acquiring manufacturing companies and commercial real estate in the late 1970s, but he still had two jobs to go before reaching that point. The first was director of corporate development for the world's largest maker of abrasive products such as sandpaper and grinding wheels, the Norton Company in Worcester, Massachusetts. The second, as director of corporate planning and development for Booth Newspapers, involved him in Booth's sale to S.I.

Newhouse, brought him and his family to Ann Arbor, and positioned him for a virtual second career in which he applied what he had learned to his own investments.

Much of that expertise was put to work for Norton. "Norton wanted to diversify into faster growing businesses," he says, "but it had a very conservative board and some very conservative large shareholders."

Griffin thought they were on the right track. As he says, "The proper corporate strategy is to have a balanced portfolio of companies in various stages of development. And yet some people and some companies want to build empires and they end up acquiring things at the wrong price or for the wrong reasons. They want to make a deal, not a good deal. A lot of companies have been destroyed by mergers and acquisitions, and a lot of people lost a lot of money by doing the wrong deals."

An excessive zeal for deals was not one of Norton's problems. On the other hand, it would take just the right approach to get them moving on that track despite their reservations about tactics.

"Norton did not have the appetite for major acquisitions," Griffin says, "but they would buy into the concept of a series of smaller acquisitions that would give them a leading market position in a fragmented industry. I isolated the industrial safety products field and spent about three years acquiring eight companies which, combined, gave Norton the second leading market position in the industry."

He describes his experiences at Norton as "exhilarating, thrilling, and productive," but after three years without a promotion, he was willing to listen when a headhunter approached him about becoming director of corporate planning and development for Booth Newspapers. It looked just about ideal—a chance for him and Ruth to get back to their Midwestern roots, a highly profitable industry that he hadn't been involved with previously, and a company within it that was ideally suited to benefit from his skills.

"It looked like a great opportunity," says Griffin. "The

newspaper industry is great, in terms of profitability and ease of management, and Booth had some great newspapers. The company was very well off financially and had the wherewithal to do mergers and acquisitions. It had a bunch of cash cows, semi-monopoly newspapers generating a lot of cash, but there were also a lot of trends going on in society. Newspaper readership was in decline; it was basically a mature business. And Booth did not have the growth businesses where they could take the cash generated by the cash cows and feed them. It makes sense to go that way, and that's what we started off trying to do at Booth."

After considerable study and planning, the decision was made to target the cable television industry. "It had a high growth rate, reasonable acquisition prices, and required substantial capital," says Griffin. "It was fragmented, and there were numerous acquisition candidates."

If the plan had been executed, he believes, "Booth would have been a helluva company today in newspapers and cable TV. And probably by now, since cable is getting mature, we would have gone on to another field to use the cash generated by cable and newspapers to fund development in other areas."

But the profitability of newspapers was no secret, and other players were eyeing Booth covetously even as the company planned its development strategy. "We became involved in a takeover battle before we could implement our acquisition program," says Griffin. "Whitcom Investment, a New York money group, had obtained a 17-percent stock interest in Booth a few years earlier when Booth acquired Parade Publications. The Booth family was not really active in the management of the company, and the family control ownership position was spread among many third-generation family members."

When Whitcom sold its interest to communications giant S.I. Newhouse, the battle was joined. After a year of long hours, extensive travel, quick decisions, sudden shifts in direction, emotional highs and lows, and 2 a.m. board meetings, it ended in a flurry of activity over one

memorable weekend. In the midst of it all, Griffin was promoted to vice president and chief financial officer of
Booth.

"You have to be opportunistic and pragmatic," he says.
"If someone throws you a curve ball, you have to be able
to hit it. Once you see that you're 'in play,' you want to
make sure you get the best deal for your shareholders and
your employees. So we fought hard and had the best
lawyer in the country and succeeded in getting the price
up to three times what it was when we started out."

The lawyer was Joseph Flom, the nonpareil
merger/acquisition attorney. "I don't know how many
companies put him on retainer at $40,000 a year and had
him do nothing, just so nobody else could hire him and
take them over," says Griffin. "They didn't want him on
the other side."

Board meetings were sometimes held in the middle of
the night to accommodate Flom's schedule; often the only
time he was available was for a stopover between New
York and Los Angeles, or vice versa. Griffin recalls one
such occasion when he played liar's poker at 2 a.m. in the
hallway with Flom; John Shad, vice chairman of E.F.
Hutton and later chairman of the Securities and
Exchange Commission; and Thomas Murphy, CEO of
Capital Cities/ABC, while the directors met inside the
board room. But the result justified the effort. "Flom said
he had been involved in a lot of doubles [of stock prices]
but this was the first triple he had seen," says Griffin.

At one point, the four top officers of Booth, including
Griffin, were going to acquire the company in a leveraged
buyout.

"We had the financing all lined up and everything," says
Griffin. "That served to get the price higher. Then the
Times-Mirror Company of Los Angeles came in and
topped us, and Newhouse came in and topped them. By a
wide margin."

The officers' bid was $35 a share. Then, on a Friday in
late October of 1976, Times-Mirror bid $40. "We flew out
to LA," says Griffin. "First we tried to buy it ourselves,

then we supported Times-Mirror, then Newhouse went to Chemical Bank of New York on Saturday and arranged a $300 million line of credit. They must have considered him a good customer."

Newhouse's bid was $47. "Why he went to 47, I don't know," Griffin says, "but Joe Flom called on Sunday and said, 'Boys, when you go from 40 to 47 in one bid, the game's over. We have only two things to finish up—your management contracts and my fee.' We said, 'Joe, we'll be in New York on Monday morning.' The involvement with Flom was a once-in-a-lifetime experience. He is the most brilliant business strategist I have ever met, in spite of the fact that he's a lawyer."

Within seven months, the honeymoon with Booth was over. "Running a division was not like running a public company," says Griffin. "The Newhouse management style was nepotistic, autocratic, and did not emphasize planning. I was like a fish out of water. I just didn't like working there anymore, and I've got to like what I'm doing. I've always had fun in my various jobs. I really feel sorry for people who have to go through life not liking their job and not have any fun at it. You spend so much time at it. I guess I've been very fortunate that way."

Griffin and his cohorts were driving to a retirement dinner for Bill Kulsea, the longtime head of Booth's Washington bureau, when he had an inspiration. "We had like five-year contracts," he says, "and there was a clause that said if there were an unprivileged removal, they had to pay off your contract. I said to Jerry Miller, who was our vice president for administration, 'I'm gonna get me one of those unprivileged removals.' He laughed and said, 'You'll never get one of those.' I said, 'No, I'm going to go to Jim Sauter [Booth's president] and show him that Newhouse could save money if I leave and they pay me 80 percent of what they would have paid me if I stayed here.' Jim said, 'I'm sorry to see you go but I understand and I'll take that to the Newhouses.' Then the other officers said, 'Hell, if he gets that, I'll take it, too.' And Newhouse was very fair with us.

"So we had golden parachutes when we left there. It wasn't anything compared to the golden parachutes some of the top corporate executives get today, but at that point in time, to me anyway, it was quite a bit of money. It gave us some financial independence."

It also ended Griffin's quest to become the CEO of a major U.S. corporation. "I wasn't completely sure of it at the time, but leaving Booth ended my professional corporate management career," he says. "There were opportunities for me to continue my quest, but we liked living in Ann Arbor. Our kids were in a great school (St. Thomas) and we didn't want to pick up and move again. The Booth experience had exposed me to the trials and tribulations of top corporate management, and also I was tired of the travel. But most of all, I wanted better balance in life. My kids were growing up. I wanted to spend more time with my family. I also wanted to be more involved in community and school activities."

They bought a cottage in the Irish Hills, less than an hour from Ann Arbor, and used it as often as they could. Griffin coached the fifth and sixth grade basketball teams of each of his three sons and joined the board of directors of the Father Gabriel Richard High School Booster Club, which funded all of the school's athletic program. He and Ruth were instrumental in forming the Notre Dame Club of Ann Arbor, and he served as its first president. In 1986, he was elected to a three-year term on the national board of directors of the Notre Dame Alumni Association.

But the siren call of commerce also needed to be heeded. He got an office in downtown Ann Arbor, set up Richard P. Griffin Investments, and began looking for them. One of the first was also one of the worst, at least initially, but it turned out to be both educational and profitable.

"I should have done better homework," he says. "I had just left Booth, had a bunch of money, and everyone said you have to get a real estate tax shelter, so you're scurrying around looking for a deal that's a tax shelter and I threw like a hundred grand into Woodcrest without looking into it, which was different from what I'd done my whole career."

That bought him a 6 percent interest in the limited partnership that owned Woodcrest Villa Apartments, a 458-unit complex in Westland that, he soon learned, was "headed south. The next thing I know, I'm managing it, just to try to save it."

He convinced another partner who, happily, owned 80 percent, that they needed to take over operations. Griffin became president and CEO—"the easy way," he says—of the management company they formed. Roofs were fixed, units upgraded, new personnel hired...and their management fee deferred. The situation slowly turned around, and by 1984 they sold the property to another syndicator for $15 million.

But Woodcrest was not out of his life yet. "We took part of the sale price as basically a second mortgage note," Griffin says. "Then this guy proceeded to run the complex for five years and took out all kinds of fees, didn't put anything into it, and eventually went bankrupt. The turkeys—that's what he called his investors—lost all $5 million that they put in. He made out okay on the deal because he got a big up-front fee and then, when the well went dry and he couldn't suck any more fees out of it, he stopped making payments on the debt, and strung it out a little longer by going bankrupt. The way we got it out of bankruptcy was we paid all the attorneys. He didn't even pay his attorneys."

They got the property back in 1990. "Conditions were bad but not as bad as the first time around," says Griffin. "Within a year, the complex again became a real nice place for people to live and work." Three years after that, they sold Woodcrest again, this time for $17 million.

"We stuck with it, that's the point with Woodcrest," he says. "Sometimes you get into situations that aren't easy and you need that stick-to-itiveness to ride it through the tough times and play out the hand that you're dealt."

Two other properties dominated Griffin's business time, in part because of legal complications, in the 1980s and

'90s. One was the Tel-Ford Shopping Plaza in Dearborn Heights, purchased by a limited partnership assembled by Griffin in 1983. The 72,000-square-foot shopping center is located at Ford and Telegraph Roads, one of the busiest intersections in Michigan, and things went well at first.

Then, in August 1990, Kroger bought Meadowdale Foods, which operated the Great Scott supermarket in the shopping center, representing almost a quarter of its leasable space, and immediately closed the store. Kroger wanted to keep the space vacant—"dark," as it's called in the industry—in order to force consumers to other Kroger stores in the area. After the partnership filed suit, Kroger assigned the lease to Foodland Distributors (50 percent owned by Kroger), who in turn assigned it to an independent operator who opened a supermarket at the location the following January.

"After the lawsuit was filed, Foodland called and asked to talk settlement," says Griffin. "On Christmas Eve, 1990, I went to the Foodland headquarters to meet with a top vice president. I had prepared a one-page settlement proposal that I placed on the table in front of him. Without looking at it, he shoved it back to me, looked me in the eye, and said, 'You had better drop this lawsuit and save yourself a whole bunch of legal fees.'"

Griffin and company decided to go to trial, which meant a two-year wait. The jury deliberated only 20 minutes before returning a unanimous verdict in favor of the plaintiffs, but a slew of motions and appeals still had to be endured. "Kroger and Foodland finally threw in the towel and paid us in late 1997," says Griffin. "The whole thing was a very unpleasant ordeal."

As much for Kroger as anyone else. In addition to the $718,000 in damages the company paid the partnership, they were hit with a $36 million judgment, including interest, to the grocer who had leased the space. He claimed, among other things, that they neglected to tell him about this little dispute with the landlord.

To Griffin, perhaps the most amazing aspect of the story is that his Notre Dame connection didn't work.

"While we were in the midst of this lawsuit, I noticed the CEO of Kroger was a Notre Dame alumnus, class of 1961, a year after me," he says. "So I just wrote him a personal handwritten note, saying I don't think you would be happy with the way your employees are behaving. I left my numbers and addresses and said please give me a call at my home or my office and we'll solve this as one Notre Dame man to another Notre Dame man. I was prepared to fly down to Cincinnati and resolve this, one way or another."

He never got an answer. "Not only did they lose our litigation but the guy they brought in there nailed them for $36 million," he says. "If this guy adds up all his legal fees, he's looking at $40 million he might have saved if he'd just given me a phone call."

When he left Booth, one of Griffin's goals was to acquire at least one manufacturing business. Nine years passed before "the right deal hit my desk," he says. "A business broker brought Park Metal Products and Park Electric to my attention, and I knew almost instantly that I wanted to buy the companies. Park had been in business 40 years and had a good niche market position in the manufacture of electrical distribution products."

It also had two plants—in Detroit and Armada, Michigan—in good condition, an experienced labor force, a good profit history, and a 76-year-old owner, Walter Staskowski, who had founded the company and was now ready to sell it. Unfortunately, he had not developed a second-line management team and, as Griffin told the broker, "the demands of my other businesses wouldn't allow me to manage Park full-time."

Not to worry, said the broker, and introduced him to Rand Overdorf, an electrical engineer who was also interested in Park but wanted some assistance with the financial side. "It was one of those matches made in heaven or something," says Griffin. "Having a business partnership is somewhat like a marriage in a lot of ways, and we've just had a wonderful relationship. Being partners with Rand Overdorf has been an extraordinary experience."

Their skills have been as complementary as their personalities. "He's a real entrepreneur and he likes to run the business," says Griffin. "I said, I want you to run the business. I'll give you whatever advice, make sure the books are kept right, get financing, but you're running it day to day. A product has to get out, you'll get it out. I'm not going to get in your way, and I haven't. He has a little different style than I do but it works and I'm not going to cramp it. I did what I said I would do and he's done what he said he would do and it's working."

As hard as he is on the legal profession, the judicial system, people who don't take responsibility for themselves, and the dishonest, Griffin also sets the bar pretty high for himself. "My relationship with God has affected the way I do business," he says. "I want to do it on a moral, ethical, honest basis. And believe me, there are a lot of people out there who don't do business that way. They tell you one thing and do another. They lie to your face. But you can't bring yourself down to that level. Then they've won."

And it's clear Griffin likes to be the one who wins as well as the one who plays by the rules. That's why he wanted to be a CEO for so long. "To succeed in business is to be the CEO," he says. "That would be the height of achievement in business management, so it's just sort of a goal you set. When you're in a game, you might as well set it high."

Following the right path, however, is ultimately paramount. "I sleep good at night," says Griffin. "I know I haven't screwed anybody. I've treated employees fairly, I've treated customers fairly, I've treated suppliers fairly, I've treated shareholders fairly, and I've treated partners fairly. And I think that's my reputation. If Griffin says it, you can bank on it. You'd have a lot of difficulty in business if you became so cynical you didn't trust anybody. You'd have a real problem."

∞

"Jenkins is lucky,
that's what Jenkins is."

Phil Jenkins

Phil Jenkins figured he and his wife were doing okay in raising Lee, their daughter and only child, the day he overheard her talking to a couple of friends of hers who were visiting the family's summer place at Harbor Springs, Michigan.

"Lee was a product of her era, when having some money was almost a stigma," he says. "She and her girl friends went through the place and out the front door, which faces on a marina, and there were these huge boats. I heard one of the girls say, 'God, Lee, all these people must be rich.' Lee must have been embarrassed, because she said, 'Yeah, we're a poverty pocket here.' I told my wife, we've done a good job there, we've got her convinced."

Like many another successful entrepreneur, one of Jenkins' principal challenges these days is "how you keep from spoiling your kids and grandkids. You're tempted to give them things, but my argument, and I've said this to my granddaughters—although my grandson is still at an age where it's hard to talk seriously with him—is that I've never seen a happy rich kid. I've had that place at Harbor Springs for 30-some years. There's a lot of what we call trust fund babies there, people 50-60-70 years old who have never worked a day in their life. They're not happy campers, most of them. It's really sad."

Think of a stereotype about millionaires and Jenkins belies it. He's shy about giving advice, shuns the limelight, attributes his success more to luck than virtue, doesn't believe he works all that hard, and has quite a clear sense of what he can do, and even what he can't—like serve on committees.

"When they built the swimming pool here (in Dexter, where his businesses have been located), they wanted me to be on the committee," he says. "I said, 'I'll give you some money but I don't work real well in a committee format. I wouldn't mind running the thing but I don't want to be on the committee to run it.' That's kind of my problem."

If it is, indeed, a problem, it's been a most productive one for both Jenkins and his community. For example, it was not a committee that transformed Jenkins Farm Equipment, his father's post-"retirement" company, to Dumpster and then to Sweepster, Inc., the world's leading purveyor of brushes mounted on tractors for highly specialized applications. Nor was it a committee that gave birth to Generations Together, the intergenerational day care center across the street in Dexter from where the Sweepster office was long located.

"After my mother had a stroke and I'd been around nursing homes, I thought that every little town should have a small nursing home, a lot of volunteerism and what have you," says Jenkins. "I thought we could do it cheaper and better."

That was probably true, but apparently impermissible. "If you've ever tried to get through the nursing home permission and rules and what have you...I got disgusted," he says, and recounts a conversation he had with a state licensing official:

"We're doing this to protect you, Mr. Jenkins."

"Protect me from what?"

"From losing your money."

"It happens to be my money and what the hell difference does it make to you? Is the object of this agency to lower the cost of nursing home care?"

"Oh, yes."

"Let's say I put my beds in in Dexter and nobody comes to rent my beds. What do you suppose I'll do?"

"I don't know."

"I'll lower my price, and somebody from Saline will come over and take some of my beds, and somebody from Whitehall will take some, and then they'll lower their prices, too. Won't that be a good thing?"

"Oh, yes."

"So where will I go to get a permit?"

"Oh, no. We still have to do a survey of need, and that takes two years."

"I know there's a need. I knew it with my mother and my mother-in-law."

He had heard about the concept of intergenerational day care centers, where children and the elderly are accommodated in the same space, "and thought I'd give it a try." He also thought the process might be less burdened by bureaucracy.

"There's no problem with building one of these," he says. "You have to get licensed for the kids, but we could have these old people chained to the floor and nobody'd ask us a question. I don't think there's any regulation on day care for adults. They have regulations up the kazoo for the kids, which is probably good, except that some of them are ridiculous. One of the things that's done it to us in this country is this fear of lawsuits. We're a paranoid nation. The legal profession has got us all living in another world."

Nonetheless, Jenkins persisted in trying to improve conditions in this one for people who need help in caring for their families. "I went through nine years of it," he says, from the time his mother suffered her first stroke, which ended her working career at 79, until her death. "What happens is that taking care of the incapacitated person is really harder on the caregiver than it is on the sick person. I know this, the old people light up like a Christmas tree when they come in here with the kids. The kids really make it for them. This becomes a place they don't dread coming to. They're not just being warehoused, they're coming to live and mingle with the kids."

His most notable commercial enterprise has been Sweepster, but he's done his best to focus on other projects in the decade or so since he "got out of the day-to-day thing" there. "It's run by Don Socks, and he has a board, if you will, of which I'm not part," says Jenkins. "I stay out of that, or try to. I'm too closely associated with that business. I don't want people to come to me; I want them to go to him. It's a very difficult thing to do. It's like not giving your kid advice, especially after they're 16, when they know everything."

Sweepster had its origins in the Jenkins Equipment Company, founded in Dexter by his father, Ralph, shortly after the end of World War II, about the same time that Phil, Ralph and Lena Clemons Jenkins' only child, went to work for Caterpillar as a sales engineer trainee after graduating from Purdue University. Except for five years in Minneapolis, Phil had grown up in Detroit, where his dad was general manager of Gar Wood Industries, a builder of truck bodies, when he retired.

"He was pretty well licked," Jenkins says of his father. "They did a write-up on him in Fortune magazine. His picture was on the cover with a caption about 'gearing up for post-war business,' and that's about when the old man retired. He always wanted to be in the farm equipment business. He grew up on a farm. I don't think he got beyond seventh or eighth grade, but he studied his whole life. Every night of the week, he was reading. If the company got involved in a patent lawsuit, he'd buy a set of patent law books and read 'em."

Not long after Jenkins Equipment was founded, he got a call from his mother. His father's appendix had ruptured, he would be hospitalized for several months, and could Phil come back and run the business in the meantime?

"She wanted to know if I could get a leave of absence," he says. "I'd only been working at Caterpillar a couple of months, and I always say they were probably happy to get rid of me. So I came home and never went back."

When he was just starting at Caterpillar, Jenkins was introduced to the vice president of marketing. "He got called out of the office and I'm looking at the desk and his family pictures," he recalls. "He couldn't have been much more than 45. I figured I was probably going to have his job in a few years and the poor bastard would be out of work. That's how a cocky young kid thinks. But the whole thing about it is I never would have fit in a corporate culture, I don't think, and it's too late to find out now."

Besides, running the company would put him on a faster, and certainly more direct, track toward an unstated but persistent goal. "I guess subliminally it was a competitive situation with my father," he says. "I always wanted to succeed at something because I figured, Christ, if the old man could become general manager of a $50 million corporation, which would be $500 million today, with a grade school education..."

It also helped steer him toward engineering. "My dad had great faith in what engineers told him," he says. "I think that rubbed off on me. I felt they were the chosen people, engineers. I don't know what else it could have been. Everyone in those days seemed to hold engineers in awe. There weren't a lot of them, just like there aren't enough now. Why that did it to me, I don't know. Hell, I had none of the prerequisites or skills or anything else."

He first enrolled at the Massachusetts Institute of Technology, "which was really laughable," he says. "Then a friend of mine came home from MIT after one year, and he'd lost 20 pounds. He said, 'They think you've already had differential calculus, so they start you on integral calculus.' I said, 'What did you do?' He said he learned differential calculus nights. So I canceled MIT. I took a look at Cornell, but I liked Purdue because of the farm environment."

By his own admission, and to his long-term regret, he says he "skated through. I told people I wouldn't have made a pimple on a good engineer's behind when I graduated. I learned how to play the system, which was as soon as I came to the class, if you were the professor and you were 30 years old, I would go right to registration to transfer out. I wanted old guys, because the old guys couldn't help themselves. When they came to something that was going to be on the exam, I could hear it in their voice. I used to sit there and not put down anything until they came to that sentence, and then I'd be scribbling frantically. I got through class that way but at the end I knew nothing. It was a shame. I should have gone to business school, that's where I belonged, but I didn't have sense enough to know what I should do. I wasted my father's money."

When Jenkins' father recovered (from his illness, not the waste of money), he decided to retire for real and leave running the business to his son. "I guess he made up his mind that he really didn't want to work like that," says Jenkins. "That's a tough business, still is. That's why I got out of it."

It took a while, however. For the better part of a decade, he simply operated the company his father had envisioned, selling farm and construction equipment and making a few specialized products for those markets. "My mother handled accounts payable, so I knew the checks would be okay," he says.

Then one day a friend from high school named Bob Moss, who had a Jeep and Mercedes dealership on Livernois Avenue in Detroit, called with a question. "He wanted to know if I could put a sweeper on a Jeep," says Jenkins. "He said he could sell a hundred of them, and I laughed because everybody says they can sell a hundred of whatever they want you to make."

But a friend is a friend and what the heck. "He sent a Jeep out and we made a sweeper for it and, by God, he sold 80-something the first year," Jenkins says. "That started us in the sweeper business."

What helped keep them in it was a skill that Jenkins doesn't deny. "The only thing I do reasonably well is sell," he says. "I took the sweepers to International Harvester and we put 'em on their Scout vehicles. Their tractor division got a hold of me and wanted them on their Cub tractor. Everybody in the tractor business was a customer then."

Over the next three years, Jenkins Equipment phased out its retail business and phased in accessory manufacturing. "It was not a big jump, as it would be nowadays, to go from retail to manufacturing," he says. "In those days, there were no service shops like there are now. You had real people who were real mechanics and learned it by skinning their knuckles. We built things to go on tractors and manure spreaders, so we had cutting and welding ability, turning ability, lathes, things like that."

It wasn't long before the company's expertise attracted the attention of customers who not only needed fairly specialized gizmos but plenty of them. "We like to say that we don't build sweepers, we build solutions to problems," he says. "We've got a jillion little niches in all these goofy markets. That's why we don't have much competition. Most people, if they've got any brains, don't want to get into these niches. But by now, we have an accumulation of engineering and paperwork and what-have-you in all of them. I can remember one time, 10 or 12 years ago, someone questioned me when I said we make any kind you can think of. We figured out we fit 259 different makes and models of tractors. We make a sweeper to go on the front of a switch engine. Dow Chemical has one, for instance, and they sweep their switches so they don't have any derailments in the yard; it keeps the rocks and debris from building up. The Chicago Transit Authority has our sweepers; that hundred-year snow that cost the mayor his job, the next year they bought 16 of them."

According to Jenkins, he didn't have to dream up applications for his sweepers; his customers did it for him. Two examples come readily to his mind.

"In strip mining, they remove the dirt, then they go in with a sweeper and sweep across a horizontal vein of coal before they start taking coal out, and that gives them a higher purity of coal," he says. "The only trouble was, nobody made a sweeper strong enough to do that. They bought our sweepers but smashed them up in three days, so we flew some guys down there and looked at what they did. Everybody that operated one of these sweepers was a bulldozer operator. It wasn't the sweeping on the coal that hurt them, it was when he hit the wall of dirt on the other side. The sweepers were too delicate for that, so we built a coal-heavy model for that.

"Then a guy down in Florida came up with using our sweepers for back-filling trenches. They trench across your lawn to put in a gas line or water line, and when they go to back fill that trench, they come in with a tractor, they tear up your grass, and you have to spend money to fix up the lawn. They tried one of our sweepers, and because it swept at an angle, the dirt followed it into trench. The only problem was our sweepers were made to run too fast, so we had to redo that model. That one company down there had 22 of them at one time. It was a hell of a market."

Having been moved by a chance event to attach a sweeper to a tractor, Jenkins was now selling them to all sorts of customers he had never anticipated. "Accidentally, we were geniuses," he says. "It's a helluva lot better to be lucky than smart, I can tell you that. I'm a very good example."

Wasn't he at least smart enough to give the people what they wanted? "I was asked," he says. "I would never have gone into the sweeper business unless somebody had asked me to. I'd probably still be making truck bodies."

Not only that, but he insists the really essential people in the operation were Art Doletzky and Jim Klapperich, a couple of long-time employees who are memorialized on a plaque outside the Dexter Intergenerational Day Care Center because, says Jenkins, "They made this building possible."

"Jim was a farm boy out of South Dakota. He had 10

kids and had to work two jobs," he says. "I finally bought him out of the second one. There again, it was luck. Here was a guy with about a fourth or fifth grade education, couldn't spell—we had one girl to decipher Jim's writing and type it up for him so he could tell engineering what he wanted—but he was an absolute genius at understanding hydraulics. To this day, there's only a couple of guys at Sweepster who know as much about hydraulics as Jim did innately. He just understood it; it came to him. And electricity. He was unbelievable. I can't even imagine what he would have been with an engineering degree.

"Art came to work for me when I was in the farm equipment business. When I started making stuff, he said, 'I ought to get out of your way.' I said, 'Why don't you handle the purchasing? It's no different than selling, it's just the opposite. You're the buyer instead of the seller.' He did just an unbelievably good job for us. If he was alive yet, I wouldn't need computers. He could keep it all in his shirt pocket on a bunch of cards."

Jenkins has only one criticism of the duo—they didn't live long enough, barely 60 years apiece. "Art, the stubborn ass, needed a bypass and wouldn't listen to the doctors, wouldn't let 'em cut him," he says. "Jim wasn't much better, damn him. He had a heart problem and overate and smoked. I tried to get him to quit smoking; he'd quit in front of me and sneak it.

"I rode in on their backs."

At first, Sweepster was set up as a separate corporation from Jenkins Equipment, then the two were merged, "then we finally dropped the Jenkins Equipment in the late '80s, which we should have done 10 years before because it was confusing."

Another confusion, and another bit of what Jenkins would call luck, arose because of the company's dominance of its "little niches"—mail intended for competitors was sometimes addressed to Sweepster because it was the only name the sender knew. "They'll start describing our competitors in their letter," says Jenkins. "We never tell them they got the wrong place."

By the mid-1980s, its original site on the southern edge of Dexter had become "the wrong place" for Sweepster; it had simply outgrown it, and Jenkins bought a former Chrysler plant on the Huron River at Zeeb Road in Scio Township for the company's new digs.

"We ran out of room," he says. "We had 100,000 square feet in one location and another 100,000 in another. We don't use much more than 250,000 or 300,000, but it was split up. It was inefficient. We had the airport people [a large share of Sweepster's brushes clean airport runways] down on Grand Street and then the offices and inventory on Main.

"I can remember telling the employees, 'Look, we can buy this plant. Yes, it's too big for us, but hopefully we can rent out some space in it. What do you guys think?' This one guy says, 'Jeez, I don't really want to move, Phil.' 'What's the reason?' 'Hell, how'm I gonna watch the girls go by here going to high school?' I said, 'No, dammit, be serious.' They couldn't come up with a good reason except they were scared. It's a helluva big factory.

"Then I learned something about our employees and human nature in general. About six months later, the water tower still had Chrysler's name on it. I wasn't going to paint it; it would cost 25,000 bucks. I didn't care whose name was on the damn water tower. Well, we were going to have an open house for the employees' families. They said, 'Phil, we can't have Chrysler on the water tower for the open house.' I said, 'What difference does it make? It's not Chrysler, it's Sweepster. Your families know that, don't they?' But by God, they wanted it painted, so we painted it."

Even today, when he visits the plant, everyone calls him Phil. "I had two German businessmen here one day and when we walked outside, two high school kids were cleaning up the parking lot. One of them said to me, 'Hey, Phil, where do you want this stuff put?' We got back to my office and one of them looked at me very seriously and said, 'You allow your employees to call you by your first name?' I said, 'I don't know how to stop them.'"

But eventually, the company itself became "the wrong

place" for Jenkins, or at least one that had become less well suited to his talents. Organization, he says, is not among them. "My desks are an absolute shambles," he says. "I know where most of the things are on them, but that's my inadequacy, that organizational ability, being structured. The guys that fought with me the most wanted structure. 'Phil, we're going to go to hell, I don't have a job description.' I said, 'I don't have one either. Mine is to do whatever needs to be done.' As soon as I got a guy in there that gave them job descriptions, the first thing they did was come to me and say, 'I can't do this and I have to do that.' I said, 'Hell, you're the one who wanted the job description. Now you've got it.'"

Which doesn't mean Jenkins is opposed to the concept. "It works," he says. "They just have to learn to live with it."

Turning the business over to a more management-minded group worked, too, Jenkins says. "They went into a manufacturing resource planning mode, which I knew we needed and tried to put us in even before we left. I had a man who understood it and knew how to work it, but he didn't have the ability to sell it. It has to be sold. You have to get people to buy into it. Everything is done on that damn computer. Nothing moves in the shop that isn't tracked or traced. You call up as a customer and want to know do we have a left-hand widget in stock? Yes, it's in such an area; no, we're out, but we'll check with production and maybe we can steal one there for you. They've cut their inventory in half since I got out of the way. It's phenomenal, really; profits skyrocketed."

Another factor in that success, he believes, is the motivation created by employee ownership, through an instrument called an Employee Stock Ownership Trust. "A guy named Kelso was the father of ESOT," says Jenkins. "I think ours was one of the first ones he had ever done. I liked the idea. It was a question of how do you involve employees? You get them into ownership of the company, and it works."

Jenkins dropped in to visit the shop one day after a hiatus of several months. "I said to Don Socks, 'Damn, the shop is filthy.' He said, 'Do you want brushes or do you want a clean shop? We're running three shifts a day, seven days a week.'"

Shortly thereafter, Jenkins found "office people working another shift or half a shift, making brushes after their regular job, just to catch up on the orders, because it's to their benefit. I saw a technical service fellow working on a lathe. It was after four, he had finished his shift, he'd been on the phone all day, so he goes out there and works four more hours."

Employee ownership also necessitated another explanation for some of Jenkins' overseas business associates. "We were entertaining a couple of Indians from Calcutta, and Bob Doletzky [son of Art and currently vice president of Sweepster], was telling them about who owns the company. 'How does that work?' they asked. A little while later, I came in, and he introduced me. One of them turned to me and said, 'I understand, Mr. Jenkins, the employees own 44 percent of the company. That's very interesting. What will happen when they get 50 percent of the company?' Doletzsky said, 'They'll throw his butt out in the street.' I said, 'Now you see the reason they don't get 50 percent.'"

He may worry about the effects of material wealth on his offspring, but he's been pretty consistent in bestowing the riches of time. Even though he wishes he had been with Lee more when she was growing up, "She and I got along pretty good," he says. "Still do. I took her to work with me a lot, spent quite a bit of time with her, but the one regret I've got as I've gone through life is that I didn't spend more. The way I see it, the only child grows away from you and away from the need for you faster than, like Lee's kids now, they go to their mother, they go to their father, they need them, even the 16-year-old, much as he thinks he knows."

He says it's "my conscience that keeps me spending so much time with my grandchildren." There are five of them, three girls and two boys, ages seven to 20, and they provide some of his best stories.

"I took the oldest one to see Baryshnikov," he says. "She was taking ballet; I'd never been to a ballet in my life. I came back and told my wife, Lynn, I figured out how to pick up women. You rent yourself a little kid and take her to the ballet. You never saw so many single women in your life, admiring the kid. 'Oh, are you the father?' I used to kid with the oldest one. I'd tell her, 'You call me Uncle Phil, not grandpa.'"

Besides conscience, he may also have wished to replicate the quality of his experiences with his own grandparents, much as he sought to emulate his father's business success.

Jenkins' father was the second of 10 children, including three sets of twins. "He said one thing he remembered about his mother was seeing her with one on the breast and rocking the others with her foot," Jenkins says. "His dad had the best job of all. He was a guide in the Adirondack Mountains. He guided for the Whitneys and Vanderbilts and Carnegies and those kind of people, up at Lake George. As he described it, he hunted and fished and lived off strangers."

Young Phil spent a couple of months one summer with that grandfather and "an ungodly amount of time" throughout his childhood with the other one.

"My mother's father was probably the biggest influence on my life," he says. "He matched teams of horses for breweries up and down the East Coast, trying to get them as close to identical as you could. He always had a hundred or so horses in the barn. He used to go out West and bring back carload of horses. He had an eye; he could look at a horse and say, 'I have two or three to go with that,' and match 'em up for some brewery. He was a farmer. I think he liked horses better than humans. And he had the patience of Job. He could train a dog ... honest to God, if he were a young man today, my advice would be go to Hollywood and train dogs for these commercials. I left my dog with him for six weeks when I was trying to teach the fool to roll over. I came back and the dog could do half a dozen tricks with no bribery, nothing. All my grandfather said was do it, and he did it. His explanation to me was you had to be smarter than the dog to teach him tricks."

Jenkins was still quite young when his grandfather sold his farm and business and moved to Detroit. "He took the money and bought, I guess it was a city block, in Brightmoor, a subdivision of small homes. He started by building himself one, then he built one next door and sold it, then next door to that. My mother and dad bought that and lived there for a couple of years. He went right around the block, some he sold, some he rented, and that's how he lived until the day he died. That was prior to Social Security. He made his own Social Security."

When his folks traveled, Phil usually stayed with his grandfather. "We drilled a well when I was 12 or 14," he says. "He showed me witching for water and that kind of stuff. He was a great old guy and a great influence on me. The only trouble was, like every kid, I didn't listen enough."

One night in 1953, Jenkins was playing poker at Detroit City Airport with a bunch of pals who were General Motors pilots. A man with a date on his arm stopped by to collect some money that one of the pilots owed him. "The guy's date and I got to talking while they were talking," Jenkins recalls. "I got her phone number. It took a year, I guess, and we got married."

They still are. "Lynn thinks I should go play golf," he says. "I'm not going to, though. I played golf until I was 25 or so, but it's too slow a game. I'm waiting until I get old enough to take it up again."

Likewise with fishing. "I got fished out as a kid," he says. "My dad would rather fish than eat, so I fished every weekend for the first 10 or 12 years of my life."

He also played football and ran track at Cooley High School in Detroit. "I was 6-foot-1 and skinny, so I guess I was an end," says Jenkins. "Then I ran the half-mile and the relays for all the years I was in high school. My biggest mistake was I didn't keep running."

He compares himself, unfavorably, to his friend Red Simmons, who was women's track coach at the University of Michigan for a number of years. "Red comes in, throws a leg over a chair, and says, 'How ya doin', guys?'" Jenkins says. "He's the youngest old man I ever met. He's 88 and I could take him anywhere and he'd pass for 60. He runs every day of his life, has since he ran in the Penn Relays. He just never stopped. The problem is, you take care of your body and your mind goes and what the hell good is your body? You wish to hell you had a body that would quit."

At age 76, Jenkins shows no sign that either body or mind is about to quit. He's been absorbed in a career's worth of projects since he more or less retired from Sweepster.

"I'm just doing what I like to do," he says. "I invest in companies and work with them. It's recreation to me." His "recreations" have included developing mobile home parks, including the 1,000-unit Scio Farms Estates; developing and virtually filling Parkland Plaza; building the Dexter Intergenerational Day Care Center, which his daughter Lee runs, and owning a company called American Augers that makes him almost vibrate with excitement.

American Augers is based in West Salem, Ohio, and makes horizontal drilling machines. "Michigan Trenching must have a couple million dollars' worth of those things," he says. "That's a market growing at 35 percent a year; it's exploding."

Among the applications so far—in airport pollution cleanups, for laying pipe under river beds instead of on top of them, and to deploy fiber-optic cable. "They keep finding new uses for the damn things every day," says Jenkins. "Every airport in the country is polluted because for 50 years they paid no attention to glycol runoff and fuel runoff. These machines drill horizontal holes underneath the airport, they pump air in one end, suck it out the other, and bring out the pollution. For remediation, it's become a hell of a market. In China and Japan and Russia, we're selling them for that river-crossing market."

He credits himself with no great prescience for his other

pursuits. "I bought the Bibikoff farm, where Scio Farms Estates is, and my son-in-law, Steve Tracy, and I built it. We've been involved in others, Steve and I, but we weren't the main developers."

After the park filled up at a breathtaking rate, "People said, 'Jenkins is a genius,'" he says. "Jenkins is lucky, that's what Jenkins is. I had no idea. Oh, I probably had it in the back of my mind (that the park would succeed), but I'll tell you how smart I was. I spent $5,000 on a company to give me a survey and appraisal of that property as a mobile home park and how fast would it fill up. They came in first-class air fare, hired a Cadillac, checked in to Weber's for three or four days, and wrote this beautiful report that said it was a good site for a park, and it could fill up at a maximum of nine lots a month, but probably closer to four or five."

That sounded reasonable enough, but Jenkins still wasn't sure. Meanwhile, his daughter and son-in-law had moved back to Ann Arbor from McCall, Idaho, where they had been schoolteachers since their marriage. "I asked Steve if he wanted to build a mobile home park," Jenkins says, "so we started going around looking at some, and then went ahead and built the thing."

And stood back to avoid getting run over as it filled in record time, or at least "a rate faster than anyone had ever seen a park fill," he says. "We had 550 of them filled in the first 10 months," a mere six times the maximum rate predicted by the consultants. "It was unbelievable. We used to have traffic jams of homes coming in there. We sold it a couple of years ago, and it's up to about a thousand now."

Naturally, Jenkins had little or nothing to do with it. "It was just pent-up demand for low-cost housing in the area," he shrugs.

Then there was Parkland Plaza, a commercial strip along the burgeoning Jackson Road corridor in Scio Township, "which again was a partnership," Jenkins points out. "I guess my wife and I have 75 percent of it and the rest of it is (Ann Arbor insurance leader) Bill

Dobson and several other people. It's pretty well filled now."

But just as his dad longed to sell farm equipment, Jenkins' agricultural genes also sought expression. "Like my father with the farm machinery business, I like farming," he says. "I had a dairy farm at Rapid River in the Upper Peninsula with a partner from International Harvester, the head of the agricultural division. We had 150 dairy cows."

Along with business destinations—and there are many when "you need the whole world to add up to a market," as Jenkins has said of Sweepster—the farm has been a regular stop for the grandchildren, his boon companions, over the years.

By contrast, the uses to which he's recently put his 200 acres on Park Road in Scio Township are more indicative of his creativity, or perhaps what Jenkins would call his luck, than of farming expertise.

"I used to spend a lot of time there, but I don't anymore," he says. "I rent it to a farmer who the taxpayers pay not to grow things. I found the golden chain."

Also attracted to it were the hunters. "Friends of mine from the city would say, 'Hey, you have that farm. Mind if I hunt out there?' Pretty soon, on opening day of deer season, there'd be an army out there shooting at each other. My neighbors were all mad at me. Then the hunt club came along and wanted to know if I'd be willing to rent it. They'd pay so much per hunter and never let more than three be on the property at the same time. I made a few enemies the first year or two when my friends would go out and it was posted. But my neighbors have never called me since, and the rent's now up to a couple thousand bucks a year."

He waxes rhapsodic about the farmhouse on the property. "It was built by an old German family, and all the oak in the house was cut there on the farm," he says. "It was just beautiful. I would have loved to have lived out there. But my wife never would. There were times when I was traveling a couple of hundred days a year, and she didn't want to be out there by herself."

The next best thing was sprucing it up for his daughter and son-in-law, which he did, and they lived there for several years. Jenkins shrugs off the suggestion that such a level of spare-time activity might indicate that he's, oh, a little driven.

"Everybody at my office thinks I'm a workaholic," he says, "but I'm not really; I just give that impression. I read constantly. To this day, I must read 20 trade magazines a month. I don't sleep a lot, five or six hours is all I've ever slept. I can get by on four or five without any problem."

In addition to Lee and their grandchildren, Jenkins and his wife Lynn have been deeply involved in the lives of five other young people—exchange students from Brazil, the first of whom has called Jenkins "dad" since her own father passed away shortly after she returned to South America.

"Our daughter came home one day and said could we have an exchange student and we said sure," he says. "She picked out the one she wanted, which turned out to be Celia, and she was an absolute jewel: affectionate, smart, great kid, loved the snow, loved to ski."

And loved to help others. "She's a doctor in Brazil now," says Jenkins. "She runs a charity cancer hospital in a poor area of San Luis. Her husband's an ophthalmologist and they live off his income. She's up here pretty near annually, or I'm down there."

Like one's own children, she's not shy about sharing her opinions. "When my wife told her 'the darn fool bought another company (American Augers),' Celia said to me, 'When I come to America, I look inside your head. You're crazy. At your age, why do you buy another company?'"

His answer, to her and anyone else, is "because that market is so exciting. It's the only time in my life that I have regretted my age."

∞

"The bottom line is health and safety."

Nina McClelland

Given her father's attitude, Nina McClelland is just as happy that she hardly knew him. In fact, although she grew up without a natural father in her life, she finds it hard to imagine a warmer, more supportive environment than the one in which she lived.

Whether or not that environment nurtured her lifelong commitment to public health can be left to the psychoanalysts, but she remembers her childhood as "a question of which lap do you want to be on now," she says. "I'm sure I was badly spoiled, but I'm more sure that I was loved. I had a family of four wonderful parents."

She lived with her mother and her mother's youngest sister and their parents since she was 16 days old, not long after her father, who had desperately wanted a son, suggested that his wife "leave me on a doorstep," says McClelland. Needless to say, she didn't, and Nina's parents—both students at Ohio State University—soon divorced.

A few weeks later, the stock market crashed. The nation was plunged into the Great Depression, and so was the non-traditional Toledo, Ohio, household.

"The only person in the family who was working was my aunt, Fern Mervos," says McClelland. "She was supporting us. She was a professor of mathematics at the University of Toledo, an absolutely brilliant woman who did her PhD in mathematics at the University of Michigan. I remember her teaching nothing less than differential equations, and she had a profound influence on my early years; in fact, on my entire life."

But the biggest influence of all was McClelland's mother. "I owe my mom an awful lot," she says. "I was an only child, she was a single parent, and she worked very hard to make sure I had enough money for my education. She was probably my best friend, too. And when we did a little international travel together she was the most cost-effective interpreter in the world. During her teaching career, she taught six languages."

When McClelland started school, however, her mother had a job at an ice cream shop, working six days a week from mid-afternoon to midnight. "Her day off was our day," she says. "We always did something together—go to a show, the art museum, downtown."

Sometimes their joint forays were less pleasing, although not because of her mother. "I still remember going down to the agency where child support payments were to be made, and going up to the window with my mother, and being told 'there's nothing here' because my father had defaulted," she says. "Some of those days, I was walking in shoes that had holes in the soles. I guess, by today's standards, one could say it was a poor childhood. But perhaps when I got things I appreciated them more. I was always jubilant over a new pair of shoes. It still makes me realize, when I look in my closet, that I should be sharing more of what I have now."

By the time McClelland was in the eighth grade, her mother had earned enough additional credits to get a teaching certificate. She took a job in Gibsonburg, about

30 miles from Toledo, and Nina's graduation from Gibsonburg High School marked the last time her father surfaced in her life.

"When we were in Gibsonburg, we rented an apartment above a German couple who became adopted grandparents," she says. Like her father, they had been invited to her commencement. When she went over to say hello while they were sitting in the auditorium before the ceremony, they told her a man they didn't know had come to the house asking about her.

"Just then, a stranger came into the auditorium, stood at the head of the stairs and looked around. I walked up to him and said, 'Excuse me, are you my father?' He said, 'I don't know; are you Nina?' I said, 'Yes, I am.' He said, 'Yes, I'm your father.'"

He asked her to come out to his car and "see your brothers and sisters." He showed her an 8-by-10 photograph of them.

"I want you to go home with me tonight," he said.

"I can't do that," she replied. "I've got a party in my honor."

"He ruined the evening for everyone, and I vowed that was the last time I would see him," McClelland says now.

And it was. He never had occasion to ruin anything else for his daughter. Four years later, she had a degree in chemistry and biology from the University of Toledo and a job with the Toledo Health Department. She was at the beginning of a career distinguished as much for its high standards as its commercial success.

In her 12 years with the city of Toledo, she honed her skills, rose through the ranks, and met her mentor, Walter Snyder, the former head of environmental health there. She began her employment with the city in the laboratory at the health department, then transferred to the laboratory at the wastewater treatment facility.

That move, like the move she made several years later from Toledo to Ann Arbor, illustrated the law of unintended consequences.

She was working at the health department as a chemist

bacteriologist when an opening for a chemist came up in the water department, and her boss suggested she test for it. "The pay at the water department and the wastewater department at that time was far higher than it was at the health department," McClelland says. "My boss asked me if I would mind taking the examination for the open position to see if she could use that as leverage to get our pay scale raised. The upshot of that was that I was offered a position at the wastewater plant."

By 1963, she had another degree from the University of Toledo—an interdisciplinary master of science—and was chief chemist and head of industrial waste for the city. "At that time, that was very important," she says. "If any of the industries in town had high-strength wastes, they were eligible for surcharges. This was another source of revenue and control for the city."

Equally important, "I was very happy there," says McClelland. "I liked my rut." But she was about to leave it.

"I came to Ann Arbor because of Walter Snyder," she says. "He was the person who really founded NSF [known through most of its history as the National Sanitation Foundation] and I always considered him my mentor. Walter persuaded me to get into the doctoral program at the University of Michigan. He made all the arrangements—I had a stipend and all of the good things that it would take to get someone to leave a stable job and go back to school.

"The city gave me a leave of absence to get my master's in public health, and I fully intended to return to Toledo at the end of a year. But when it came time to make a decision, I decided to stay at Michigan and complete my PhD."

Much to her own surprise, it must be added. "It was very hard for me to move to Ann Arbor," she says. "I was alone in an apartment after being so close to my family in Toledo and having wonderful friends down there. I didn't think this was my world at all. I was quite sure I would go back."

The day came when she had to call the city manager in

Toledo with her decision on a new, highly attractive job offer, one that was much better than the position from which she was on leave. "I came into school thinking I would make the call and accept the job," she says. "But when I made the call, I refused the job, and I still don't know what happened to make me do that."

It was either destiny or Walter Snyder, or perhaps they were the same. She ran into Snyder in the hall right after the fateful phone conversation and was, she recalls, "feeling very uncertain. 'By the way,' I said to him, 'I should tell you I rejected that job in Toledo.' He had already started walking away and said something I didn't catch. 'Pardon me?' I yelled after him, and he turned around and said, 'Damn good thing you did.' 'Why is that?' I asked. 'Because if you hadn't, I would have called up and lost it for you,' he said. And he was absolutely capable of doing those kinds of things."

Two years later, regrettably, he passed away, a victim of leukemia. A grieving McClelland moved in with his widow, Doris, with whom she would make her home for the next 30 years. Then McClelland's own life almost ended.

"I had a diverticulum that ruptured," she says. "I had emergency surgery, then contracted peritonitis. There were all the signs and symptoms of something that wasn't recoverable. Obviously, I did, but it put me behind a lot. I lost time and developed a pretty negative attitude about completing the PhD program."

Her self-assessment notwithstanding, she not only completed her doctorate in 1968 but also, during the last two years of her program, taught an evening class in environmental chemistry at the University of Toledo's engineering school.

Meanwhile, NSF had been contacting her periodically since Snyder's death. As she drew ever closer to wrapping up her degree, their overtures intensified. The company was hoping to get a major grant from the U.S. Environmental Protection Agency for a water quality monitoring project, and McClelland had been involved in both writing the proposal and in a site visit by the agency.

McClelland decided to go with NSF because it was a good fit on other counts, too. McClelland was a scientist who had devoted her career to public health, and NSF was a nonprofit corporation dedicated to serving public health through science.

Not incidentally, it was also Walter Snyder's brainchild. "When he was head of environmental health for the city of Toledo, it became obvious to him that people who were building and operating restaurants were required to satisfy the whims of the local sanitarian," she says. "There were no uniform standards. No one had bought into the idea of a piece of equipment that would be adequate for use anywhere."

Snyder's idea was that there were certain basic standards that could be applied anywhere, that a consensus on those standards could be reached by the interested parties (not only restaurateurs but also food and beverage companies, glass and pipe manufacturers, government and, of course, the end users). He believed that those parties would benefit mutually from having the standards in place, and from using products that were certified as meeting them. He saw NSF as a neutral third party, bridging the gap between—and trusted by—all of the stakeholders.

Underwriters Laboratories had been developing electrical and fire safety standards for years, "but nobody had standards for water and wastewater and food and food equipment—anything that was in the health and environmental area," says McClelland. "Walter had decided that was something that should happen."

The short version is that it did, and an ironic twist, considering where McClelland's mother had worked years before, was that the first standards NSF ever issued were for soda fountains.

Her first title at NSF was director of water research, and her first assignment, which lasted several years, was the monitoring project with the EPA "to build very sensitive, on-line monitoring equipment that measured, as I remember, some 16 parameters of drinking water quality," she says. "That resulted in a mobile water quality monitoring unit, actually a van that said NSF and EPA on the sides. We tested this equipment in Chicago, Detroit, and Philadelphia, and when it was fully refined, the van was delivered to EPA. To my knowledge, it was operated by EPA for quite some time. The instrumentation was so sensitive that you could pull up to a house, connect the monitor through the hose bib on the outside of the house, and measure the quality of the drinking water in that system. It was also so sensitive that when we ran it in Philadelphia, which draws its water from two different rivers, we could tell when the water plant would switch and take more of the Delaware River or more of the Schuylkill into the treatment system."

After that project's successful completion, wastewater was added to McClelland's responsibilities, then she was named director of technical services. "That meant that oversight of anything done in any of the laboratories or any research—chemistry or engineering or any other kind—was my responsibility." In 1978, she became vice president for technical services, and was almost immediately involved in a crisis that she believes played a pivotal role in her eventually becoming the company's president, chairman, and chief executive officer.

These were the days of double-digit inflation, but Robert M. Brown, McClelland's predecessor in the top spot, decided one year that there would be no salary adjustments. More or less simultaneously, he finished paying off—only three years after incurring the debt—the Plymouth Road property where the company's new headquarters was situated.

"That was not popular," says McClelland. "The result was that many of the employees responded favorably to advances made by the Teamsters Union, and we got two bargaining units. One was the regional and lab employees, so that was a professional unit; the other included the clerical, custodial, and the skilled employees. On the day that the employees were balloting to decide whether or not to become unionized, I came back from a trip and

I walked into the president's office, just to say I'm back and how are you. There was a man sitting there who I had never seen before. It turned out that he was our labor lawyer, Martin J. Galvin, who was on site for the election."

McClelland and Brown chatted while Galvin listened. "Afterwards," she says, "I learned that when I left, Marty said to Bob, 'Who was that?' When Bob told him who I was, Marty said, 'If you get a union, she and I are negotiating the contracts.' I learned a great deal from Martin. We entered into the final agreement the day before he was getting married, so I was alone to do the handshake with the Teamsters and to commit NSF to that agreement."

The contracts were for 16 months, "a very non-traditional time frame," McClelland admits, "but Bob wanted it that way because he wanted to know if we were going to have a union for another period at the time when he was setting prices and budgeting for a new year."

The answer was no. McClelland used those 16 months to orchestrate what she dubbed the "Bring Back Teamwork" campaign. The company's relationships with its employees were significantly improved, and the employees elected to decertify the union.

This was fresh in the minds of some of the board members when they gathered at the Detroit Athletic Club to pick Brown's successor. Three NSF vice presidents remained in contention.

The union experience "was fundamentally favorable to me," says McClelland. "I think it had to be important in considering whether or not one could be capable of running the company. I also had a lot of people contacts. I worked the Washington scene. I made a lot of friends there, both on the Hill and in the federal agencies, and I know that those people spoke up on my behalf and supported me."

But still, she says, "When we were called back by the board, at the end of a long and difficult meeting, and I was announced to be the candidate of choice, no one was more surprised than I. I didn't believe I really had a chance."

Now she had much more: she had a company to build.

One of her first goals was to reconstitute the board itself. At the time, its membership consisted largely of former members of another NSF advisory group, the Council of Public Health Consultants. "To me, it wasn't the right mix," she says. "We were a not-for-profit business. We had to make contacts with business people; our clients were mostly business people. I felt that in order to develop and meet our growth objectives, we needed people who understood business. My perception was that the board ought to be principally business people, and the professionals in public health ought to sit principally on the council."

There was also, in her view, a subtler peril in the existing arrangement. "The president of NSF, in my opinion, could not be held accountable for his or her business performance when the board had little or no knowledge of what business performance really was," she says. "When I took over at NSF, it was 1980. NSF had been chartered in 1944, and it had taken all those years to get, almost, to a $3 million corporation."

One of the few business people on the board then was Jervis Webb. "Shortly after I was elected, he called and asked if he could come by and talk to me," McClelland says. "The chemistry was good between us. He asked how he could help and I said, 'Get me some more business people on the board.' He said, 'Who do you want?' I said, 'I don't know.'

"He then gave me two names. One was Dick Tullis, who was chairman of the Harris Corp., a $3 billion aerospace firm in Florida, and the other was Martha Griffiths, who was about to be elected lieutenant governor of Michigan. I said, 'You bet I want them; can you get them?' And he did, and that was the start of reconstructing the board."

She also saw, perhaps earlier than most, the need to globalize. "You couldn't just focus on the United States of America at a time when everyone was looking at how to eliminate barriers to trade," she says. "Our customers needed to buy and sell outside the U.S., so we needed to become a global business. And we did. We opened an office in Brussels. We had one in Ottawa. Then we signed partnership agreements in Asia and Europe so that we could do business with and through other organizations."

But, she says, her principal legacy to NSF was the water quality additives program, precipitated by amendments in the early 1980s to the federal Safe Drinking Water Act. "Responsibility for regulating the quality of drinking water was shifted from the treatment plant to the consumer's tap," says McClelland. "Stop and think what this would mean to the EPA. The states and the communities were already monitoring the treatment plant, but quality could be affected by products in contact with water between the points of treatment and delivery to the consumer. This was a massive change for the regulators.

"I went and talked to the people at the EPA and said how in the world are you going to do this?" she recalls. "They didn't know. I said, 'You can't afford to do it.' They said, 'You can't, either.' I said, 'Yes, I can.' That's what's neat about this third-party system. I can collect the fees that I need to cover my expenses from the people who are going to gain most from our program, so the affected industries—not the taxpayers—would really be the people who would bear the burden of cost."

And there were plenty of affected industries. "Now there was responsibility vested by Congress for the delivery of quality drinking water to the consumer at the tap," says McClelland. "Anything that came into contact with drinking water during its treatment had to be part of the monitoring process. That included pipes, paints and coatings, storage tanks, piping in the home, treatment chemicals, and even household faucets."

The task was complicated by the tumult of the Reagan-era EPA. "The agency was undergoing a real transition," she says. "Just about the time I would persuade the people it was a good thing to put this in the private sector, there would be a change in the EPA and the whole process would start from the beginning. Finally, EPA agreed to a concept that involved a number of parties. NSF, because of its experience and expertise in writing consensus standards, and its experience and expertise in certifying products for conformance with standards, would be the lead organization."

NSF was joined by the American Water Works Association and its Research Foundation and the Association of State Drinking Water Administrators in a consortium "to develop and implement the standards that were necessary under the requirements of the revised act," says McClelland. "Two standards resulted: one for direct additives, i.e. those that are deliberately placed into drinking water for treatment, and the other for indirect additives, i.e. all the products that come into contact with drinking water during its treatment, storage, and distribution."

It was a classic case of doing well by doing good. "This was potentially a very huge activity, and it became the largest revenue program at NSF," she says. "We had an important public service that became a thriving business as well, but only in that order of priority."

Another benefit, for both NSF and the public, was the large toxicology program that spun off from the water quality additives effort "because NSF is making cutting-edge decisions about contaminants that are not regulated but could have adverse health effects," she points out. "The neat thing is that the EPA continues to play a very strong role as a stakeholder in this effort; it has never bailed out of its responsibility. The law says that if anyone has to be punished for doing something wrong, EPA has to do it. NSF is in no position to punish anyone. NSF has control through its contracts for service, but enforcement comes through the regulatory authority of EPA and that was never abandoned. It's a wonderful partnering between public and private sectors to achieve a health benefit. And you can be sure I'm very proud of it."

Having expanded the notion of what nonprofits can do in general, as well as the fortunes of the particular one she oversaw, her views are both pertinent and informed. "Nonprofit industry today is really being challenged," says McClelland. "You've got to be state of the art. You've got to make money. If you took a continuum and you put for-profits on one side and not-for-profits on the other, the amount of money the latter have to make—'gain,' if you will—is about the same, or even greater, because they have to reinvest so much to stay current."

During her tenure, NSF experienced impressive growth. "But you've got to consider the basic tenet of why you exist as the most fundamental priority you have," she says. "And in the case of NSF, it's the health, safety, and environmental well-being of the public; it is not the bottom line of the business."

It was also far from being all her doing, McClelland quickly points out. "Much of the credit for this success goes to an outstanding and dedicated staff," she says, "and to Eugene E. Jennings, the Michigan State University professor emeritus of business management. He was always there for guidance or to answer questions when needed. His expertise is so tremendous. He was there, really by my side, throughout the entire experience."

She retired from NSF in 1995, but her pace has hardly slowed. Her expertise is widely sought by scientific societies, community service organizations, the World Bank, and academe.

"One of the things I do that's both satisfying and gratifying is to serve as an elected director-at-large on the board of the American Chemical Society," McClelland says. "The ACS is the largest scientific organization in the world, with over 150,000 members. It has two national meetings a year, registering 10,000 people or so at each of them, and also some international meetings. It advocates for research in science and technology and has been, I think, a principal motivator for seeking a commitment from the federal government to double its research appropriation over the next five years."

Not surprisingly, she's also on the board of the American National Standards Institute, a federation of government agencies, private companies, consumer groups, and other organizations that focuses on the development of consensus standards and the accreditation of conformity assessment activities for products, services and quality systems. "The direction is toward getting all of the national standards to be international so that there are uniform global requirements," she says.

As a member of the board of visitors for the School of Public and Environmental Affairs at Indiana University, she is involved with "an academic program that's unique," she says. "It has programs in public health, environmental science, public policy, and criminal justice. It's one of the few programs at the formal academic level that begins to educate people to understand that if you're going to have good public policy, you have to base it on sound science."

She also serves on the board of Cleary College, "and I'm very proud of that," she says. "It's a great institution, very progressive and very competitive in the sense of being first on the street with something that's new. Cleary makes it possible for you to do what you need to do; it was one of the first institutions in the area with an accelerated degree program, so a student can get a degree in two years instead of four years of on-site study."

She also recently represented the World Bank in a project in Mexico. "My responsibility was to assess the current status of MSTQ (Metrology, Standards, Testing, and Quality) there, to determine where Mexico wanted to go with MSTQ, to recommend where Mexico should want to go with MSTQ, and to help the World Bank determine how best to help it get there," she says. "The World Bank had an appropriation of $300 million for this science and innovation project, about half of which was for technology (innovation). It was established very clearly that Mexico had not kept pace with its trading partners in the North American Free Trade Agreement and the World Bank wanted to try to remedy that. It's pretty clear that MSTQ is critical to barrier-free trade, so I was sent to meet with top people in government, academia, and industry to get their input. It's my understanding that the $150 million that was available was awarded, and that much of the award was based on the recommendations in my report. I hope that's true."

One thing she knows is true is that keeping busy has helped her survive a string of devastating personal losses. Within the space of two years, McClelland had to cope with the deaths of her uncle, Nick Mervos, who married her aunt and became an important part of that semi-extended family; Doris Snyder, with whom she lived for 30 years, and then her mother.

"That time in my life was devastating," she says. "I'm very lucky that I've had the friends and family support that I've had and that I've had the professional activity I've had since leaving NSF. I think they've been the difference between sanity and insanity. I knew when I retired from NSF that I needed to stay professionally active, for both my mental and emotional health. I realized that the family I was so close to was older than I, and I was aware that my losses could be extensive and consecutive and I would need to be able to sustain myself through them."

Now her family consists of her aunt, her aunt's three children and their immediate families, a beloved woman named Shorty (her real name is Lavone Witting), and their two dogs. McClelland has been close to her cousins, the offspring of her Aunt Fern and Uncle Nick, since childhood. Bob Mervos, the oldest, is an electrical engineer and lives in Lancaster, Pennsylvania. He and his wife, Phyllis, have a son who's a senior in high school and, like his father at Purdue University, plays in the band. Mary Jo Gibson is a gifted dancer and computer engineer; she and her husband, Ed, have a 12-year-old daughter, Lindsay, who is McClelland's goddaughter. Joy Benedek, the third cousin, is also her goddaughter. She is married to John Benedek and manages the telecommunications business her father started in Pennsylvania which her mother now owns. Her son, Matthew Galeza, is a freshman at Penn State University.

"Shorty and my mother and I made our home together in Toledo before I came to Ann Arbor," says McClelland. "I met Shorty when I went to work for the city. She was a nurse, and she was in charge of pediatrics at the health department when she retired. She and my mother stayed together after I came up here to school. She is an adopted family person whom my family loves very dearly, and she continues to be a very dear friend. She's been just a great help to me throughout my life and my career. For years, Doris and Shorty and my mother and I spent as many weekends as we could together, either at the lake or at home, because we really enjoyed each other's company a great deal."

Although Shorty still maintains the home that she shared with McClelland's mother in Toledo, she spends a great deal of time in Ann Arbor with McClelland—and, of course, Reili and Corky.

"Shorty fell down the stairs at our cottage and broke her leg very badly," McClelland explains. "She nearly lost her life. The recovery from that was very difficult and very prolonged, and at one point it seemed like she really needed an incentive, and that might be a puppy. That's when we got Reili. We had her for 10 minutes and I said, 'This dog is going to live the life of Reili, so why don't we call her Reili? But since she's a little kraut, we should spell it like Heidi.' Then Corky, who is Reili's niece, came along when Doris was beginning to fail. We got Corky for the same reason; Doris really needed an incentive and an attachment and Corky provided that. So now Doris is gone, my mother's gone, and it's Shorty and Nina and two dogs, and not in that order. It's Reili and Corky and Shorty and Nina."

McClelland puts herself last in such formulations, but she has never been shy about taking the lead when her sense of justice is provoked. For example, the first board that McClelland served on after coming to Ann Arbor was that of Peace Neighborhood Center "and I still have a strong attachment to it," she says. "Rose Martin is an absolute saint. It is the organization that is most responsible for the relative lack of crime on the west side of Ann Arbor. The job PNC does for the city of Ann Arbor is absolutely incredible."

So was the job McClelland did for the center when Washtenaw United Way declined to include it in its funding. "When the federal block grant program went away, it looked like Peace wasn't going to make it, so we wrote a grant application for United Way and it was rejected," she says. "When I asked why, I was told that money was going to be very scarce that year and they were just going to have to give only to agencies that had been in the program for a long time. I said it seems to me you have to do something for the people who can't survive. Maybe you can think of some unique concept for organizations that are mature and might be able to get funding some other way. There probably are many families in Ann Arbor who have a Boy Scout and would sponsor another Boy Scout. Then the Boy Scouts wouldn't need their entire allocation for a year and we could help other groups to stay alive."

Her argument was eloquent but unpersuasive. Her next move was more compelling. NSF and its employees had long been major supporters of United Way—making large corporate gifts, offering payroll deductions, and encouraging employees to visit, on company time, the agencies in which they were interested.

"I called all the employees together and said, 'If you want to give to United Way, that's fine, but it's only fair to tell you I'm not making my usual contribution. There are other agencies who won't survive without help, and that's where my personal and our corporate gifts are going.' The second time that happened, the United Way people made an appointment to see me, honored the grant proposal and took in PNC, and it's been there ever since.

"I still think I have something to contribute," she says. "I hit the big Seven-Oh this year but I don't think my ability to think straight and be helpful has diminished."

Nor has her vision been clouded. "To me, community is important," she says, "and anybody in business ought to partner with the community because the community is clearly partnering with them."

∞

"Timing is everything."

Larry McPherson

Larry McPherson is known to say "timing is everything," especially if someone is trying to give him credit for some achievement.

Like getting a full, four-year football scholarship to Clemson University in 1963, or becoming, in 1996, the first American ever elected to the board of directors of NSK, Ltd.

At the time of the former, schools in the South were in the final throes of segregation. "There was an Indian, but I don't remember any Afro-Americans on the team at that time," says McPherson. "I was a big, slow quarterback, but I had a very strong arm and I was Caucasian. Of course, today things have completely changed. Timing is everything."

Today, a major college football program would never look twice at an honorable mention high school all-stater from a small community like Lisbon, Ohio, regardless of pigmentation. As it was, although he did not earn a varsity letter, he did receive more important ones: a B.S. in EE (bachelor of science in electrical engineering).

In the case of NSK, "Individual recognition is fine," McPherson says, "but it's more important that the Japanese have shown they understand the importance of a non-Japanese contributor to the company. Again, I was the right person at the right time to be given that opportunity."

Ironically, given his undergraduate experience, he was a sort of Jackie Robinson. Some other major Japanese corporations, he was told, acknowledged both the wisdom and justice of NSK's move. "I've been told that, in some respects, other Japanese corporations were envious," McPherson recalls. "They know it's the right thing to do, but they're not in a position to change their company's culture, or they haven't found the person to use as a Jackie Robinson, if you will."

Long before he became a trailblazer, McPherson learned to be a survivor, more like Oliver Twist than Jackie Robinson. His family was supportive but it took everything they had to keep their noses above the waves. That included a strong religious faith. "We were in church every Sunday and participated in church activities," McPherson recalls. At Clemson, he says, the church was his "fraternity"; he didn't belong to any others.

Homer McPherson owned one feed mill in Lisbon and another in nearby Salem, buying crops from farmers and processing them into flour and livestock feed. "I still remember shoveling corn cobs in the dust," says son Larry. He was only five or six when a fire destroyed the mill in Lisbon, and Homer McPherson's modest but comfortable livelihood along with it.

Grace, Homer's wife and Larry's mother, went back to teaching school after 40 years of parenting and helping with the business. Homer became a free-lance truck driver. The three youngest boys essentially monopolized local delivery of the *Cleveland Plain Dealer* and the *Pittsburgh Post-Gazette*. And still, says Larry McPherson, "There were many times when our house had a sign in front of it from the government, saying that if we didn't pay certain things, the house will be taken over, repossessed."

Fred, the oldest, joined the Marines. Almost miraculously, the other three all went to college and earned degrees. First, though, they had to get up at 4:30 a.m., seven days a week, and fold and deliver those newspapers. "We took over the whole town," says Larry McPherson. "On Sunday morning, there was a bigger paper and none of us could drive, so my dad would get us up and we would run back and forth from the truck and deliver the papers. From that, we got an appreciation of money."

After Carl, the second son, enlisted in the Air Force (he eventually graduated from the U.S. Air Force Academy), Larry and Dave, the youngest, continued the delivery business through high school. Dave went on to the U.S. Naval Academy and a Navy career, and Larry had a chance to go to West Point and make it a service academy hat trick, "but I did not like the idea of a military commitment afterward," he says. "Fortunately, I was given a full scholarship to Clemson but," he laughs, "prior to going there, I didn't know where the hell it was."

McPherson speaks glowingly of the lessons he learned at the South Carolina college from sports: leadership, teamwork, discipline. At Clemson, he also learned the humility of being the same-sized fish in a bigger pond. "I remember my mother driving me down for orientation," he says. "At that time, there was a freshman team and a varsity team. They showed you a depth chart, and there were 20 different teams for freshmen, 10 each for offense and defense. Here I am, a football hero from a small town, and I couldn't find my name. I think I was number six. It was probably the biggest shocker of my life. I played quarterback my freshman year, then in the following spring practice, I was moved to the offensive line and played center. Instead of taking, I was giving."

Of course, he was also giving his best all along, and taking an education in return. "My athletic career at Clemson was not illustrious," he says. "At the time, not winning a letter was very disheartening, but as I look back, things have a way of working out. The good news was I had a four-year scholarship. Out of 120 football players in my freshman class, I'll bet less than 30 percent ended up graduating.

"I guess I chose electrical engineering as a major because of my lack of knowledge of engineering," he says. "I remember talking with a couple of teachers and asking them, based on what I did in high school, what would they recommend? They said definitely engineering, but I don't know why electrical. I just looked at the program. I never changed curriculum from day one. That's what I wanted to do and that's what I did."

But it was more a means to an end than the result of an inborn knack or inclination. "I have no patents," he says. "I was never a design engineer. I enjoyed being around people and I had a knack of being in leadership positions, whether quarterback or clubs, so I never felt I wanted to sit behind a board the rest of my life and be an engineer. I wanted to use the engineering to get a job and provide for my family, but then I wanted to get into the management side."

After graduation, McPherson went to work for the Boeing Company in Huntsville, Alabama. "Boeing knew I was going to be leaving for military service," he says. "They tried writing a letter, but during the Vietnam War that didn't mean diddly."

Upon graduation, he had been commissioned a first lieutenant in the Army Corps of Engineers. He attended the Officers Basic Course at Fort Belvoir, Virginia, then spent 10 months with the corps' Communications Systems Agency at Fort Monmouth, New Jersey. And from there, it was 'Nam.

"I was assigned to the 82nd combat engineering group," he says. "We basically built roads, bridges, and perimeter defenses for base camps out in the jungle. When I first got there, bombs were flying overhead. It was tough to tell what was incoming or outgoing."

Although he claims "I spent most of my time under the bed," he did see some combat in his ten months in Vietnam in 1969-70. "It was our job to police at night, patrol the perimeter, and there were a couple of occasions where the enemy tried to pursue," he says. "There were people in our organization that were shot but no one was killed."

At least, not while McPherson was there. He took advantage of a plan whereby his tour in Vietnam would be shortened if he resumed his education when he returned. "I came out in May," he says, "and my group, at the end of June, went into Cambodia, where we lost several from our organization. Again, I was lucky."

Although it would be an exaggeration to say he enjoyed it, he recalls Vietnam as "a good experience in my life. I've often said I'd like to go back to Vietnam. The amount of money that was put into that—the buildings, roads, equipment, helicopter pads, airstrips. It would be nice to go back and see what happened to it all."

But in 1970, his focus was on getting back to school ... and to his wife and two-year-old son. He and Charleen Lederle had known each other since junior high and were married during McPherson's junior year at Clemson, right after she graduated from Ohio State University with a degree in nursing. Her family had been as active in the Catholic church in Lisbon as McPherson's was in the Protestant. They continued to attend their own churches when they were first married, but "when I found out she was pregnant, I said, 'Okay, there can't be that much difference,' and I became a Catholic," McPherson says. "We've continued to support the values of the church."

Charleen was the youngest of three daughters. Her father, Chuck, was a barber in Lisbon and her mother, Rose, was a cook at the school cafeteria. "I used to work in her mother's kitchen, washing dishes," says McPherson. "I got to know her mother through that. She would come in and I spotted her early, let's put it that way."

She also contributed her share of hard-work genes to the pool. She worked while her husband finished school, earned a master's from the University of Virginia, "and wherever I've moved, she's always found work," says

McPherson, "most of the time in the academic area, and while parenting our children. After we moved here, she worked for Eastern Michigan, then she went back and took two years to get her nurse practitioner's license, and today she is a nurse practitioner within the St. Joseph Mercy System."

After Vietnam, McPherson had decided to pursue an MBA at Georgia State University in Atlanta. Just as his football prowess had paid for his undergraduate education, so the GI Bill would pay for graduate school. The pattern of Charleen's support was also already well established.

When McPherson finalized his educational plans, "she was living with her parents, our son, and a dog," he says. "She went to Atlanta by herself, found a job, found an apartment, everything. When I got back, I basically picked her up and started school."

Eighteen months later, he finished, and went to work for Kaiser Aluminum and Chemical Corp. in Ravenswood, West Virginia. "I did well," he says. "I was hired as a maintenance engineer, but became a maintenance supervisor and then a general foreman very quickly. It was good experience."

The problem, he says, was that "Kaiser at that time was a huge organization." There was a lot of ground, and a lot of people, between McPherson and where he saw himself going.

Then he got a call from "this company called Hoover Universal Ball and Bearing." It was headquartered in Ann Arbor, Michigan, but the plant that had the opening was in Malvern, Arkansas.

"My wife and I flew out in November 1973. When we got there, we kept asking people where this Hoover plant was," he recalls. "By the time we found the place, before I even talked to anybody from the plant, we knew we didn't want to stay in this community."

Apparently, there were no hard feelings; Hoover called again several months later. The job of chief engineer at its division in Erwin, Tennessee, had opened up. Says McPherson:

"They told me that the general manager of the division, who would be my boss, 'is a maverick character but the good thing about him is he makes money.'"

The character was Dick Ennen, and the description "was absolutely true," says McPherson. "I think his degree was in psychology, and he was a fraternity brother of Don Shula," he adds. "I found him fascinating to work for. We parted on not the best of terms, but as I look back, it's like somebody once told me about Warren Avis—you could put Warren Avis in the middle of a field today, stark naked, and a year from now he'll be worth a million dollars. Dick Ennen was in the same mold. He had an uncanny ability for just good business sense. If he was after a business, he went and got that business. It wasn't unethical; he was just committed to getting that business."

For example, cylindrical rollers. Although it was then called the Ball Division, Ennen "basically sold the fact that we'll also make rollers, which was interesting because we had no capability of making rollers, yet he went and got the business," says McPherson. "So one of my most significant accomplishments there was going from literally no experience to setting up a total manufacturing process to supply rollers to the oil drilling industry. We didn't have time to order new equipment, so we bought old equipment off the used equipment market, and we hired consultants to help us develop this process. It was seven days a week, we were working constantly to make the schedule, we had tremendous problems all the way through, but over time we got 100 percent of that business, and it was profitable in less than a year.

"Dick was a very unusual guy, brilliant, a very devout Catholic, extremely smart," McPherson says. "I remember at staff meetings, if we missed a schedule, he'd get very upset and say, 'Let's go out and see the process and see what's happening.' To be successful, you have to focus on doing things right every day. There's no mystery to success, just a lot of hard work and consistency in meeting the expectations of consumers."

After a year as chief engineer, McPherson became manufacturing manager, then plant manager, then operations manager for plants in Charleston, South Carolina (which he started), and Cummings, Georgia, as well as Tennessee. By 1980, the annual sales of what was now known as Hoover Universal's Ball and Roller Division had increased 280 percent since McPherson joined the company. Also by 1980, he and Ennen were both on the way out the door.

To put it briefly, there was a new chief, Dan Carroll, at Hoover in Ann Arbor and he and Ennen got along "like oil and water." When Ennen hired his brother as McPherson's human resources director, he says, "Dan Carroll came down and said you can't have family members working for one another, and Dick said, that's fine, I'll quit. Dick left to start his own business, and it went downhill from there."

When Carroll brought in "40 or 50 young people from Chicago, I took a vacation," says McPherson. "I was so relaxed on vacation that I realized I didn't like what was going on, flying around the country, spending money, meeting people you didn't have to meet to know what they looked like and how they acted. I said life is too short. So basically I quit. I didn't have a job, and I wasn't looking for a job."

But splendid as it was, idleness couldn't charm him indefinitely. "I remembered a guy who had hired me at Hoover," says McPherson. "I contacted him, and ended up working for a division of Armco Steel called National Supply Company."

The place was New Iberia, Louisiana, and the gig was building offshore oil drilling rigs. "At that time, the oil industry was booming," he says. "One of our challenges was how to find 100 to 200 people a week because business was so good. A lot of people were coming from the north because there was no work there."

Another challenge was "I didn't know anything about drilling rigs," he says. "There was a lot of welding and fabrication, which I knew nothing about."

Neither challenge was his problem long enough to be

resolved. "Within nine months after I joined them, the question became not hiring enough people but how fast can we get rid of them?"

An always volatile industry had rapidly overbuilt in response to the energy crisis, and one of the people National Supply got rid of was its production manager, McPherson.

"We now have three children and a brand-new house in New Iberia," he recalls. "What am I going to do?"

The Hoover connection came through again. "Hank Wallace, the human resources manager at Hoover when I was there, was now human resources manager of a company called Hoover-NSK," McPherson says.

Hoover-NSK had started in the early 1970s as a joint venture between NSK Corporation of Japan, the world's second largest bearing company, and Ann Arbor-based Hoover Universal, which became its U.S. presence. By 1975, NSK had bought the entire operation, and immediately built a second plant in Clarinda, Iowa. "NSK wanted to become a major player but they didn't want to be an importer," he says, "so their philosophy forever has been to manufacture in the home country."

Ironically, the Hoover name was retained not only because of its reputation but also because "frankly, many people would not buy from Japanese companies at that time," McPherson recalls.

He came to Ann Arbor for an interview and quickly realized that this was a different climate than the one he had known for 18 years.

"After the interview," he says, "I called my wife and said I would be delayed coming home—I think it was April 1— because there was snow. Despite that, I felt it was a good opportunity to run a plant and I liked the business, so I joined the company."

It was now the spring of 1982. "I was getting back into a business I was familiar with, and working with some people I knew," says McPherson. "Roughly 500 people worked in the plant, manufacturing a variety of different bearings."

Its later luster notwithstanding, his career got off to a rocky start. "I'll never forget it," he says. "I started in May, and in July I had to lay off a number of union people because business was so bad. That fall, I ended up laying off salaried folks because business was so bad. But since that time, we've turned it around and been very successful."

McPherson's rise paralleled NSK's in many respects. After two years as plant manager, he was appointed vice president of manufacturing for NSK's Bearing Division, which at that time included a plant in Clarinda, Iowa, as well as the one in Ann Arbor. He became president of the division in 1988 and president and CEO of NSK Corp. in 1990 before his election to the board of NSK Ltd. in 1996.

During that time, NSK Corp. grew from two plants in the United States to six, from 500 employees to 1,800, from an annual capital budget of $600,000 to more than $50 million, and from importing 70 percent of its product to manufacturing 70 percent domestically (and, obviously, the total market had grown).

McPherson outlines three phases of NSK's activities in the United States. "At first, it was simply an acquisition, from the Japanese standpoint," he says. "Just send some representative people and let the locals do their thing. Then the economic situation got much tighter, and performance maybe suffered a little, so NSK said, 'We're going to become a more active owner in this business.' Then there was a transition to identifying and trusting management capability in the United States.

"When I joined Hoover-NSK, they had five or six people in senior management positions and I happened to work for one of them. When things got tight and the Japanese got more involved, some people left the company. I was in the right spot at the right time, and through this transition period, they saw some value in what I brought to the table."

In other words, guess what? "Timing is everything," McPherson says. "I was fortunate to be there at the right time."

But there was a bit more to it than location. As he himself says, "We had some major hurdles at the plant," including virtually reinventing the way it functioned, which meant labor negotiations, job classification changes, a rethinking of what the jobs were, and a physical rearrangement of the plant to accommodate them.

"We went from a department-type operation to a cell concept, in-line manufacturing," he says. "Instead of having a department where everyone does the same thing sequentially, and each worker is responsible for a particular process, now they were responsible for the total product."

This necessitated the physical overhaul. "Over Christmas one year, all we did was rearrange the factory," McPherson says. "We did some basic things with old equipment to try to improve the process."

When that got results, NSK became more receptive to McPherson's ideas. "Once we understood each other and had confidence in each other, they start making significant investments in the United States," he says. "About 1986 or '87, we formulated the plan for what we needed to do, and I was given the opportunity to carry it out. The Ann Arbor plant was 40 years old, so we gutted it, completely reconfigured it, and we built another plant in Iowa."

Three more in Indiana soon followed. Over a 10-year period, NSK spent more than $500 million in the United States on plants and equipment. But at least as important to McPherson were the gains in product quality, customer service, and cost control. The plaques and awards from happy customers that festoon NSK's Ann Arbor office lobby attest to them.

"That recognition by people of what we have achieved in the last few years is as gratifying as anything I've done," he says. "Go to Ford, Chrysler, Emerson Electric, Black and Decker, and mention NSK, and the response is 'very quality-conscious, very service-related, and very committed to doing the job.' Some awards are much more difficult to get than others because the quality audit the company does is much more in depth, but the meaning of all of them is that NSK is recognized by many, many global companies as truly number one in the area of quality. That's not saying we don't have quality problems at times, but how you respond to those quality problems is most important."

The company's growth made it more challenging for McPherson to sustain the personal touch that he feels is an important part of his managerial approach. "I feel very comfortable being with people, so it's not my style to distance myself because I'm president or CEO or whatever," he says. "At one time, I prided myself that I knew everyone in this company. Unfortunately, we've grown so fast it's difficult to do that presently."

His solution has been to spend the first six weeks of every year meeting with every shift at every plant to brief employees on the state of the company. "My philosophy is you cannot communicate enough to people about basically everything, whether it's financial success or financial failure, opportunities, or challenges," McPherson says. "As an executive, I think that's one of your primary responsibilities. You can have the best machine, you can have the best product, you can have the best computer system, but unless you have well-informed team members who are highly motivated and challenged to bring continuous improvement, rather having the attitude that 'my job is to produce so many parts a day or so many data entries a day,' you're not going to be successful."

At these meetings, he updates attendees "on how well we did, our expectations for this year, the challenges, the risks, the expectations for individual plants," he says. "I think, over the years, people appreciate that you take your time, and it's very time-consuming. But it's worth it to go out and meet people. That personal touch means a lot more than sending a video or posting a printed statement."

It can also lead to some lively and enlightening discussions. "Many of these people are very astute, interested in business, and they ask some very thought-provoking questions," he says. "I recently was in a meeting in Clarinda, Iowa, and I think it was on the third shift some-one asked me, 'Two or three years ago, you talked about the Buy America campaign and the importance of pro-ducing domestically, and today you're talking about the globalization of the bearing industry. What happened to that Buy America campaign?' Basically, I told him that the dynamics of the world have changed. It's not impor-tant from a consumer standpoint today where that prod-uct is made. In many cases, it's being driven by price, so people are willing to source products from anywhere in the world."

But communication means much more than McPherson's conversations; it means everyone's, which is one of the reasons that he's so strongly in favor of rela-tively small plants. "I believe there's a maximum size for a plant to control the effectiveness of the operation, whether it's communication, productivity, or employee morale," he says. "Say 500, plus or minus, that's a manageable level."

He shakes his head. "The main aisle at the Willow Run plant is a mile long," he says. "Some of these plants employ thousands of people. I think it just complicates the communication. One of our sites has a hundred acres and employs roughly 450, a very nice, state-of-the-art manufacturing facility, surrounded by farmer's fields. Farmers actually grow crops on part of our property. Some people say I could put another building there. I say, 'No, no, we have 450 people and that's a nice, manageable size. Let's go somewhere else and build a factory.' That's what we've done in the Midwest, rather than focus our attention on one entity."

About 45 percent of NSK's business is automotive, with industrial OEM—electric power tools, steel mill bearings, dental drills, manufacturing of precision glasses—com-prising most of the rest. "Our strength is in high-preci-sion, high-quality ball bearings," McPherson says. "That represents about 75 percent of our sales in the United States."

Perhaps ironically, given the extent and nature of NSK's

growth, "it's a very mature business," he says, "yet wherever there is motion, some form of bearing is required. There's been nothing developed that replaces it. So in some terms, it's a pretty stable business."

That makes globalization an increasingly compelling challenge, and puts a premium on new applications and incremental product improvements. "We've invested heavily in the United States and one of our priorities is to continue to use that investment at a very high rate," says McPherson. "At the same time, the world is getting smaller and smaller. We've done a very good job in growing NSK Corporation in the United States. We also want NSK Limited, the parent company, to be a global company. The real challenge that we face is how to continue to hold our high marks in service and engineering and quality and at the same time continue to expand our support for overseas operations here in the United States."

But, not surprisingly for a self-confessed "people person," McPherson always returns to the preeminence of human resources. His own rise, he believes, is an example of how they can be deployed in the future. "It's nice for me," he says, "but what's truly nice is it tells everyone else in NSK that it doesn't matter what race or creed you are, there are still opportunities in Japanese companies.

"We have many Japanese people working all over the world," he says. "What we want to do as a company is allow non-Japanese people those same opportunities, to take someone here who wants to and let them work in Europe in a key position, or maybe go to Japan. The organization chart is getting flatter and flatter, so we need to broaden it. Taking an engineer here and saying, 'Why don't you go to France for two years?' is another way of strengthening and diversifying the company.

"I haven't found a glass ceiling in this company," he adds. "There are many Japanese companies today where there truly is one, but the good news for anyone associated with NSK is it does not exist here."

Nor does penury, or an exclusive focus on the bottom line. Or it may be that McPherson defines the bottom line a little differently.

"When I became president of the company, I took it upon myself to make sure that NSK became totally committed to supporting the community in many, many different ways," he says, "whether it was nonprofits, charity, fund-raising. That was one of the primary missions of this company."

Not a frill, but a mission.

"Some people think, okay, once you get in a financial situation where you've got something extra, then you can consider contributing to these areas," says McPherson. "It's 'let's make some money and then give some back to the community.' I felt that this was one of our responsibilities. Regardless of our financial situation, if we were going to be a public citizen, this was an obligation we had to the community, a cost of doing business.

"I can't honestly say I had a mentor," he says. "It's just something I personally felt we needed to do."

Maybe the mentor wasn't a person, but a fire, or a football team, or a foreclosure sign on the front lawn. When it came to hard work, the mentor could have been the paper routes.

And when it comes to his children, he doesn't mention the possibility that he and Charleen have been mentors. They've just been lucky.

"Our oldest son, Brad, is in business for himself, McPherson Sales and Associates," says McPherson. "Our daughter, Traci, is married, lives in Williamsburg, Virginia, and teaches high school mathematics. Our youngest son, Nate, is at Purdue University, majoring in mechanical engineering.

"You look at situations where the kids don't end up the same way, and you wish you could write a Dr. Spock book on how to do it, but I don't know what it is. Our kids were allowed to do a lot of things that my mother and dad or my wife's parents would never have allowed us to do, but times change. Fortunately, we were blessed and got three good kids. How it happened, I can't honestly tell you."

McPherson's house is in Stonebridge, next to the golf

course. One day, a golfer rode by and saw him out wash-ing his car. "The man said, 'Beautiful home, prettiest home in Stonebridge,'" McPherson recalls. "Then he came back, played another nine, and I was mowing grass. He says, 'Now I know how you can afford this home.'"

"Believing and building."

Dick Sarns

Noah couldn't have learned more from the Ark than Dick Sarns learned from the Boat. It deserves capitalizing, at least once, for all the lessons, values and perspectives that flowed together in its building...and its keeping.

This was in Mt. Clemens, Michigan, where Sarns grew up in the years when America was sliding from the Great Depression into World War II. Sarns' dad, also named Dick, had been an engine installer and test pilot for the Hacker Boat Company, which supplied the recreational needs of the wealthy. The Depression sank that enterprise, but not his zeal for boats.

The elder Dick went to work six days a week, as a foreman for an automotive parts service company. On the seventh day, he and his two oldest sons, Dick and Bill, would work on the 26-foot vessel that was slowly taking shape in the family garage.

First, of course, they had to build the garage. "It probably cost about a hundred bucks," says Sarns. "It was all

used material. Back in those days, we reclaimed everything. The kids would take nails out of used lumber and
straighten them to build the garage, I remember that. Then
my dad bought a wrecked Chrysler, took the engine out,
water-jacketed the manifolds, tested it, made it into a boat
engine, put it aside, and we proceeded to build the boat."

And not just any boat, either. "This was a cabin cruis-
er," says Sarns. "It would sleep six, had hot and cold running water, a flush toilet, a galley, Lincoln Continental
upholstery. It was super deluxe, made mostly from all
these bits and pieces his friends gave him."

Using lumber from a large live oak on a nearby farm,
and clear mahogany boards from a closed covered wagon
plant, the project fairly dominated the domestic landscape
for three years. "One half of the garage was the workshop
and the other half was the boat," Sarns recalls. "The rear
of the garage was removed so the boat projected out the
back. Boats out of water look like monsters, especially
this one. When people came into the garage, they would
stand there with their mouths open."

In addition to space, materials and immense patience,
the enterprise also required tools. "A band saw, a rip saw,
lathes, grinders…we had a very complete workshop in the
garage," says Sarns, "and my dad designed and made
most of the machinery in it."

He had done that work in the Sarns Machine Shop,
which was opened in 1904 by Maurice Sarns, the elder
Dick's dad. It was clear the gene pool had persisted, as
Dick Jr. and his brothers learned to use the equipment
their dad had built in their grandfather's shop.

"One thing my parents did was give us a heck of a lot of
freedom," Sarns says. "Once we got our schoolwork done,
we had a lot of projects going. My brother Bill and I
designed and made toys on a production basis, a couple
dozen at a crack. We built them in the shop, then took
them door to door and sold them. We had a little woofing
dog you pulled on a string and the legs would articulate
and the tail go up and down, rubber guns, bird houses,
all that stuff. We sold a lot."

But one thing the family did not sell was that boat, dubbed Gertie (Sarns' mother Blanche's middle name). "We had maybe 1,500 bucks into the whole project when we got it done," he says, "not counting thousands of hours of time, and then a wealthy man in town offered my dad $6,000 cash for the boat. We had a little family crisis about what to do. Our house cost $3,500. We lived in a pretty nice side of town, too. Anyhow, the decision was not to sell the boat. It stayed in the family for 20 years. It was priceless at that point."

Beyond focusing on the big picture, beyond designing the proper tools and using them effectively, beyond understanding the value of quality, young Dick Sarns also learned what was beyond the power of money.

The intense reinforcement of many of those lessons began five years later. He graduated from Mt. Clemens High School in December 1944, and was in the Navy three months later. Luckily for him, the war was over by the time he completed boot camp and engineering school at the Great Lakes Naval Training Center and shipped out as an engineer/technician on the U.S.S. Frontier, a destroyer-tender or "a mother ship for destroyers," as he puts it.

"The destroyers would actually tie up alongside us, shut down all of their power plants, and we would fuel them and furnish them with fresh water, steam, electricity, and shore boats," he says. "We had a hospital on board, we had dentists, repair shops; it was like a little floating city. We carried over a million gallons of fuel. Right after our shakedown, we were part of the North Pacific Fleet and went on to Japan. That was quite an experience.

"I was ship's company," he says. "I was just a kid, but I was in charge of the fuel handling in addition to standing top watch in the engine room. Not only myself, but all of us had a lot of responsibility." Especially for a boy who had never been outside of Michigan.

And a fair amount of excitement, war or no war. "We got involved in a major storm en route to Japan," Sarns says. "We took the Arctic Circle, and just south of the Aleutian

Islands, we got into 60-70 mph winds that lasted for several days. Our ship was 600 feet long and the waves were, peak to peak, the length of it. Then we had a little catastrophe because we lost power and the ship broached and we rolled around in that storm for four or five hours before we could get back on line, get our power back, get steam back. Meanwhile, the ship was tearing itself apart. We had quite a time of it. Luckily, it didn't capsize."

One of the phrases that falls frequently from Sarns' lips is "good fortune," as in "We had the good fortune to (fill in the blank)." This was a case where it would be difficult to fault the usage.

His time in post-war Japan—his ship was at anchor just north of Hiroshima—also opened his eyes to just how bad fortune could be. "We witnessed the aftermath of war, and people walking the streets who were very seriously wounded," he says. "Despite the devastation, we gained a perspective on why the decision was made to drop the atomic bomb. Just being in Japan and seeing the topography of the country, which is about 70 percent mountains. Had the Allies invaded that country, there would have been carnage on both sides. It's a very difficult place to get around, even to this day."

Sarns returned to Mt. Clemens to work in the Sarns Machine Shop after his discharge in 1948, and started taking night classes at Lawrence Technological University, then located in the former Packard Motor Car facility in Detroit. "I was eager to learn industrial engineering, just preparing for the future," he says. "There was always quite an emphasis on education in our family. That came first, before boats. Schooling was something my dad had been deprived of and he pushed that."

One evening in the fall of 1949, a classmate from Mt. Clemens High fixed him up with a date, a girl named Norma Dubuque from L'Anse, in the Upper Peninsula. Norma was a freshman at Michigan State Normal College (now Eastern Michigan University).

"We hit it off right from our first date," says Sarns. Three years later, they got married and set up housekeeping in an Ypsilanti apartment; Norma was finishing her degree in business education and Dick went to work as a product design engineer at Argus Camera Company in Ann Arbor. A year after that, they bought a house in Ann Arbor. By then, Norma was teaching in the school provided by the University of Michigan Hospital for youngsters who were long-term patients. She was also pregnant with their first child. And she wanted some clear answers from her husband about the future course of their partnership.

"She suddenly asked me some very serious and provocative questions," Sarns vividly remembers. "'What are our long-range plans for the future? What are our personal goals? What do we want to accomplish in life?' She pressed the question of our goals for the future, and it took me aback. I stumbled around.

"After some thought and discussion, we decided that we wanted to form a business and make useful products we could be proud of. They should be electro-mechanical with high value added."

Sarns' sigh of relief that this had been settled was short-lived. "Norma wasn't done," he says. "She said, 'Okay, how do we prepare for this? What skills and training do we need?'"

It became clear that only a varied palette of experience and education would do. They would take jobs—and change them, if necessary—on the basis of the job's contribution to the long-term goal, the gaps in training that the job could fill. And they would take classes in engineering and business, at the University of Michigan.

Thus began a seven-year stretch in which Sarns changed jobs four times, including a second stint at Argus. "It was definitely strategic," he says. "I wanted to have experience in designing products, and also in managing. There were quite a few jobs in there." He quickly adds, "I wasn't fired from any of them."

He was also going to night school again, this time at U-M, for the first three of those years. But it was a night when he and Norma went to a party that proved to be memorable. It was a "people from work" party, and most of Norma's colleagues on the teaching staff were married to doctors.

"Frankly, I wasn't looking forward to it," says Sarns. "I was worried that I wouldn't fit in with the doctors, that I would be the 'odd man out.'"

Much, perhaps, to their mutual surprise, they found a great deal to talk about. The doctors were researching and developing an array of surgical procedures that would require, for the most part, devices that didn't exist yet. And, lo and behold, here was an engineer in their midst.

"There was no such thing as 'biomedical engineering' as we know it today," Sarns recalls. "Doctors would actually go to hardware stores looking for tools that could be adapted to surgery."

By the end of the evening, he says, two things had become apparent to him: While these cutting-edge procedures eventually would create a need for new surgical tools, medical devices and materials, the clinicians' lab work was still several years away from that point.

So he continued to collect skills and earn pay checks from his various engineering jobs, while spending the rest of his waking hours building a house for Norma and their two little boys.

One of his jobs was managing the manufacturing department at Strand Engineering Company, which was building radar equipment for a federal defense station in Alaska, near the Arctic Circle. He had previously enriched his skills by working on the massive machines that fashion and quality-inspect automobile engine blocks (at Buhr Machine Company) and designing and building an automated lens grinding machine (in his second stint at Argus).

But the most valuable experience of his time with Strand may have been his attendance at a conference of the Society of Manufacturing Engineers at St. Joseph Mercy Hospital in Ann Arbor, instigated by Dr. Clarence Crook.

"The doctors made the presentation to the engineers and they outlined their instrument needs in pretty fair detail," Sarns recalls. "There were maybe a dozen devices that they needed, and they were quite clear about them. However, they had no money for product development. They were reaching out for contributions from companies and free services from engineers to create working prototypes which could be used to advance their lab work."

He also recalls their attitude: "We're in the space age. We've got people flying around the stratosphere. Where are our good tools?"

Sarns figured he could answer that question. "I was one of the guys that started working on medical devices," he says. And if it took some time, well, heck, he'd spent three years working on a boat, hadn't he? And if they had no money, well, heck, he had a day job and...

"It was a pioneering time," he says. "The doctors were developing the techniques and they needed new tools and new instruments to help them perform their work. You could make a contribution."

The house he and Norma had designed themselves and built by hand included (surprise!) a large, walk-out basement and a complete workshop, outfitted with metal-working tools, a drafting table and an office.

"While keeping my day job," says Sarns, "I began working with area doctors to design and build a variety of surgical devices."

Without having a formal name for it, he was "transferring technology," not in the sense of moving it from the lab to the marketplace, but in applying the skills of the practicing engineer to the domain of health care.

The key, he says now, was "that transfer of technology. More important than the basic science or basic engineering was knowing the materials and the components, and putting them together. It was knowing resources, where to get things done, and getting them done very quickly. That was my role. I was invited into the laboratory and even the operating room. I would stand next to the surgeon and observe. We would be talking all the time he was working. The goal was to come up with a device that would solve his problem or meet his needs."

One early success that illustrates this technique was a sternal saw he developed that is still manufactured by a company run by Sarns' brother Ted. "I read where the Oster company had come out with a new, wood-cutting saber saw that was vibrationless, smooth," he says. "I called the company and found out they had this saw in South Lyon, so I bought one and ran it, took it apart, and reverse-engineered the saw to make this surgical tool. The feature of this is it's very smooth and runs at an extremely high speed. This is a lesson for other people: How do you design things? You can start from ground zero, or you can take some other idea, capitalize on it, reverse-engineer it, and adapt it for the job you're working on. I built a prototype and it worked. Dr. Joe D. Morris, a surgeon at both St. Joseph and U-M hospitals, used it in his laboratory, then took it to the operating room, and that was the launch of the sternal saw."

Just as he did with engineering, Sarns acquainted himself with numerous domains. "Urology, plastic surgery, organ preservation, and then cardiovascular surgery—I was bouncing around in all those areas."

And he came to rest in the realm of cardiovascular medicine. His first purchase order was from Dr. Herbert Sloan at the University of Michigan, for a disc oxygenator. "Our design used less blood to prime," he says, "and it was more efficient and easier to clean."

In the middle of 1960, he changed jobs again, going to the Electronic Assistance Company in Dexter, Michigan. But the "spare time" work on medical devices was growing as fast as the open heart procedures that used them. Both St. Joseph and University hospitals had ordered his heat exchanger, "the device that heats and cools the blood in the heart-lung bypass system," Sarns explains. "Ours also incorporated a bubble trap."

In November of that year, Sarns, Inc., was incorporated. Seven months later, in June 1961, Sarns quit his job to devote his full time to the new company. Before that year was out, two "milestones," as he calls them, in its history occurred.

The first was a meeting of the American Society of Thoracic Surgeons in Philadelphia. This was an era that now seems longer ago than it actually was. Not only were commercial exhibitors only grudgingly tolerated (especially compared to their presence at such conventions today), but also the meeting room itself "was just filled with tobacco smoke," Sarns remembers. Prevention was much lower on the agenda then than it is now.

"I had a blood oxygenator, heat exchanger, sternal saw, blood access cannulas and a few other items," he says. He was also, on opening day, exhausted from the long drive and sweaty from assembling the booth.

"My stress level was at an all-time high," he says. "I was really shaking in my boots at this meeting, exhibiting our products for the first time. I remember one surgeon from Alaska looked over my exhibit, grabbed me by the arm, and said, 'You look pretty healthy. Let's see if you're around in a couple of years, and maybe I'll buy something.' That was a time when the surgeons made the decision to buy the instruments, either personally or as an advocate within their institution."

But what Sarns got that made the Philadelphia story a milestone was not sales or exposure but a piece of advice.

One visitor to his booth was a fellow Ann Arborite, Dr. Cameron Haight, chief of thoracic surgery at the U-M Hospital. He scrutinized Sarns' wares, then stepped back for a look at his sign, which simply said, "Sarns, Inc."

"What is Sarns, Inc.?" he roared. "And who the heck is Sarns?"

Sarns was appalled. Then Dr. Haight smiled. "I don't mean to be offensive, Dick," he said. "I want to make a point. You're brand new in this business. Nobody knows your name, and it'll take years before you can establish it. My suggestion is to put 'Ann Arbor, Michigan' up there in big letters, because that is a place that people all over the world recognize as a leading medical center."

"That," says Sarns, "was a very good piece of advice." It was probably also one of the first examples of surgical device marketing.

The second milestone was an order for a complete heart-lung machine, custom designed and built, from Dr. Delbert Neis of Omaha, Nebraska. He had done his residency at the U-M and knew Dr. Morris, who recommended that Dr. Neis contact Dick.

"So we had a conversation," Sarns says. "He had very specific ideas of how he wanted this machine to function. We drew up the specifications, had a handshake and then I got on with it."

Dick had six months to build the machine, including five in-line pump heads, a disc oxygenator, heat exchanger, bubble trap, a large blood reservoir and several other custom accessories. It was all assembled at the Sarns' home and tested for hours using water in the system. Finally, the day came to load the unit into that station wagon and deliver it to Omaha.

"We put it in his lab, it worked there for a day or so, he was satisfied, and wrote me out a check for $12,000," says Sarns. "It was a happy ride home."

Once again, an opportunity spawned a challenge. "The Neis order was major, in the sense that it spun off several subsequent orders," he says. "At the time, we had three full-time employees and some part-time help for the electronics and electrical wiring. We did not advertise or have a sales staff; we relied on word-of-mouth-recommendations."

Which they got from Dr. Neis. However, "Now we were in another crisis. It was a challenge to build these heart-lung machines and to scrape together the monies to finance them," Sarns says. At this time, Sarns Inc. moved out of the basement and into a leased, 5,000-square-foot factory on North Main Street in Ann Arbor. "That was a real neat move," says Sarns. "We were there for six years. Charlie Baird was an ideal landlord. He was a business confidante, a supporter, and a very good person. I even got my U-M football tickets from him."

Behind its unprepossessing exterior, the Sarns plant housed some equipment that was highly sophisticated for the era. Providing a boost to productivity was one of the area's first numerically controlled milling and boring machines, and an early IBM computer, a 402 punch card system, was used for inventory control.

Also inside was the ongoing development of a pump design that would be the most user-friendly (another term that still lay in the future) and, thus, best positioned to survive the inevitable marketplace shakeout. "Our pump competed with a number of small U.S. companies," Sarns says. "Fortunately, large companies—including General Electric, IBM and General Motors—never went beyond their laboratory prototypes, which allowed the small companies to exist."

Another crucial ingredient was the Sarns-designed roller pump—and that finally carried the day. "This was a time when there were several different pump devices, and the marketplace hadn't determined which device would be the standard," says Sarns. "There are a lot of ways of moving blood: a squeeze device like a milking machine, a ventricular bellows arrangement, a piston pump, centrifugal pumps, and vacuum displacement pumps, among others. We chose the roller pump due to its lower cost, noncontact with fluids, reliability and simplicity."

The simplicity was the result of a lot of human engineering. "We focused on the position of the person operating the machine, including visual eye contact of instruments, controls and fluid levels," he says. "Another important factor was the operators' range of motion, as they reach to make adjustments or add fluids. Our control panel had color-coded switches that lit up to indicate the switch mode."

They also caught a break with what Sarns calls "a tremendous advance in tubing. We started out using latex, which was expensive, so the tubing had to be cleaned and reused. It was not a desirable material for a roller pump. Along came advances in the polymer chemistry. They came up with clear plastic tubing that could be sterilized and disposed after the surgery. It had the proper memory characteristics, so it operated very efficiently as a material of choice. Plastics is a major factor in the business, a big, big contributor in the field of medical applications."

What the company needed now was another source of revenue. "We had our house mortgaged to the limit," says Sarns. "We had exhausted our bank financing and we had these orders for heart-lung machines. That gave us a tremendous need for dollars that we didn't have. I reduced my salary to $600 a month; that was our family budget. You just lived accordingly. We were working all the time so we didn't have time to spend anything anyway. I don't want to be bragging, but I don't know how we did all that. We never thought about working hard. We enjoyed it."

Nonetheless, as he says, "one of the first challenges of rapid growth is the need for working capital." That's where Baxter Laboratories came in, a Chicago-based firm with a division that made kidney dialysis machines. Word of mouth had reached some people there about this little company in Ann Arbor whose roller pump might be adapted to their needs.

"They were looking for a small blood pump that would work with their kidney dialysis system," says Sarns, "so we adapted the pump that we had for cardiovascular surgery, scaling it down using the same basic principles, and provided Baxter with a sample to use on their kidney machine. After a few modifications, they ordered a dozen units, and then began ordering on a monthly basis."

It was, he says, "a major breakthrough. We never had any contract with Baxter but over the next 10 or 15 years, we built 25-30,000 of these pumps for them. It was nice, steady business, and it gave us cash flow, continuity in our manufacturing, and the opportunity to work with a large, sophisticated company. That's where we really started to produce product on North Main."

Then Sarns won the bid to produce the entire kidney dialyzer machine for Baxter, incorporating the pump the company had developed. "We built several thousand dialyzers for them," says Sarns, "and again that gave us cash flow. The profit allowed us to put money into research and development in our core business, which was always equipment for cardiovascular surgery."

In the meantime, Baxter's requirements precipitated a need for more space. The Sarnses looked for land on the west side of Ann Arbor, because employees who lived there had told them about a settlement of German families in the area who were being displaced from farms. "Our people were very selective about who they would recommend for employment," says Sarns.

They were right on the mark with the regional talent pool. "We found those people to be fine employees," says Sarns. "They had an excellent work ethic and a can-do attitude. They were problem-solvers, and had the ability to learn and continue to learn. They were so great."

But first, of course, the plant that they would work in had to be built. "One Sunday afternoon when we were out looking for land, we had the good fortune of locating some desirable property," Sarns says. "We talked to a neighbor who advised us to talk to Mr. (Karl) Geiger, the farmer who owned the property. We called on him, and he invited us in. We had a cup of coffee and told him what our aspirations were. He offered the land, fronting on Jackson Road, for $5,000 an acre. We bought five acres on a handshake. The expressway (I-94) had just been built, so Jackson Road was pretty quiet. It was ideal. So we built a 16,000-square-foot facility on that land."

The operation moved at the end of 1966, thanks in large measure to the faith and commitment of Clarence Dubuque, Norma's father. "I not only had a neat wife but also a wonderful father-in-law and mother-in-law," Sarns says. "Norma's dad was president of the bank in L'Anse, a small-town bank. I talked him into building the building and leasing it to the company. In hindsight, he took a helluva risk. He was not a wealthy man. He put his net worth on the line to do this."

The company eventually purchased the building back from him. "Then we got a little nervous about our flanks," says Sarns. "We had open land to the east of our business, so I went back to Mr. Geiger and got an option to purchase that property. Through successive options, we wound up buying 55 acres from Mr. Geiger. That gave us a nice rectangle all the way back to the expressway. It was always a handshake, nothing in writing. And the interest was always at 6 percent."

Through the end of the '60s and the early '70s, the company made other moves besides from one side of town to the other. The Sarns Modular Pump System, for customers who wanted to "start small" and grow their systems, and the Sarns Disc Oxygenator had already been developed. Products that were standardized rather than customized, like the 5000 Heart Lung Console, the Air Bubble Detector, and a variety of sterile disposable instruments, were introduced.

And, says Sarns, "We made a major effort to expand our marketing overseas. We recognized early on that because the U.S. was known as a leader in medical technology, people from around the world were being trained in this country. The new physicians returned to their home countries and asked to buy equipment they were trained on. We were very fortunate in getting some fine distributors. That gave us another order flow and stability and market expansion."

He met one of those distributors, a urologist named Dr. Taro Tsuchiya, in 1967, on his first trip to Japan since his Navy days. "He ran a medical supply company in Hiroshima and invited me to his office," Sarns recalls. "It overlooked Peace Park, the epicenter of the bomb blast. This fellow was very wealthy—his family owned a 400-bed hospital—and he also had a plant in Hiroshima, with more than a thousand employees, making blood sets for the Far East market. He could speak English very well. He said, 'What do you know about the Japanese market?' I wisely said 'not much.'"

A blackboard stretched across an entire wall of Dr. Tsuchiya's office. "He drew the islands of Japan, put in the capital, the principal cities, major hospitals, and which hospital was leading in each area," Sarns says. "Obviously, he knew the market extremely well. I would love to have a photograph of that wall; it had so much information on it. He said, 'We want to be your distributor. We'll buy some of your equipment now, but not much. It'll take five years to build a market.' It turned out that he bought more than he said he estimated; he became our number-one export customer. The relationship with this company continues to this day."

At the same time, Sarns Inc. was establishing itself in Europe, starting with its first exhibit at an international trade show, in Milan, Italy. "That was a wonderful show for us because Dr. Michael DeBakey (the open heart surgery pioneer) was there in person," says Sarns. "Our equipment was used in a display, so we couldn't have had a better reception."

That Dr. DeBakey was a "star" at that show was indicative of the sea changes in the world of cardiac surgery, the tides of which would sweep Sarns and his company to unprecedented opportunities.

One was the introduction of the coronary artery bypass graft (CABG) as an elective surgery—no longer were bypass machines used almost exclusively on gravely ill individuals in the late stages of cardiac disease. Another was the application of technologies and materials developed for the space program to the civilian arena in general and health care in particular. And, finally, the U.S. government, through Medicare and Medicaid, determined that it would pay for these procedures, thus effectively subsidizing the vast majority of them..

Within eight years, the number of open heart procedures performed annually in the U.S. almost tripled, from 70,000 to 192,000. And a good thing for Sarns Inc., too, because the company then experienced what Sarns almost demurely calls "a major event." Baxter had bought a plant in Red Bank, New Jersey, to build its own pumps and kidney dialyzer machines, taking away about a third of Sarns' business; more, he admits, than any one customer should have represented.

"We violated the rule about not being a captive shop for anybody," he says. "That left a huge hole in our little business. We were fortunate that Baxter gave us six months' notice so we could work reduce our inventory."

Layoffs, he says, were "not an option. I don't think we've ever laid off anybody. We'd just go out and get some work."

In this case, though, there was less work. Fortunately, compared to previous flash points, there was plenty of cash.

Says Sarns: "We decided as a company to vertically integrate and to move very aggressively into manufacturing in three areas—precision sheet metal and painting and finishing, precision machining, and then electronics." Like Baxter, they would now make for themselves what they formerly purchased from outside vendors.

The adaptability and skill that Sarns had sought in his workforce helped make the transition work. "We had some real sage advice from Gilford Laboratories, a company in Ohio that we were exchanging dialogue with in terms of management," he says. "They told us not to go out and hire the so-called experts to run the new manufacturing areas. They suggested we train from within. We took our workforce and went through a real crunch training program. We took people literally off the assembly line and trained them to run machines and perform other operations.

"And it worked. It was almost like a paradigm shift. The machines that we brought in were largely numerically controlled, so they had keyboards instead of handles. We had to have smart workers to set up these machines and operate them. They even had a say in the selection of the equipment. Our equipment purchases included training. It was an exciting time. Some of our people even asked to come in on their own time so they could program and test the moves of their machine. Nobody seemed to be intimidated."

Sarns admits that "a little pride" was "probably" involved in wanting to keep the company's workforce intact, but it also, he says, "turned out to be a very good business decision, not only for the employees because they could increase their salaries, but for giving us control over our costs and quality."

When inflation ran rampant in the late 1970s, Sarns was making its devices' componentry in-house, by a trusted workforce, safe from 14 percent interest rates. "It was very important at that time, as it almost became prohibitive to make money with money," says Sarns. "You couldn't stay ahead."

One hardly need point out that quality control is even more critical in the medical products business than in most others, and more challenging to effect when your output is numbered in the dozens or hundreds, rather than millions. As Sarns, ever one to understate, puts it, "Life-support equipment has to be as good as you can make it."

By 1979, the time seemed nearly ripe for completing a kind of horizontal integration. "We came to the conclusion that to be a long-term significant company and contributor, we needed a total system for open-heart surgery," says Sarns. "We had some of the components—the heart-lung machines and some of the instruments that go up on the table—but the key item we didn't have was a blood oxygenator, which is a major product item. This would be a huge investment for us."

At the same time, he says, "We were asking ourselves the tough questions: 'Are we producing the very best product that is possible? Can we be a world-class company? Could we do better if we had more resources, not only technology but also management and finances?' And the answer was 'Yes, if we can find the right partner, the right company.'"

It also had to do with corporate culture, the Midwest work ethic, what the employees would get out of it, and whether the company would stay in Ann Arbor. Sarns expressed it as "Whose team do we want to be on?"

While serving on the board of directors of the Health Manufacturers Association in the mid-1970s, he had gotten to know 20 or so other CEOs, including Lew Lehr of 3M. "He came across as a visionary and a risk-taker," says

Sarns. "We had subsequent meetings at 3M, so I had a chance to see 3M Center, a 650-acre campus with 14,000 people. It's unbelievable."

He knew 3M's health care business, largely invisible to the general public, was "mind-boggling," he says. "They don't acquire many companies." But they didn't have a cardiovascular "flagship," so Sarns held some allure for them, too.

Talks went on for about two years. "The final six months were really focused on a planning blue book, a 10-year plan," says Sarns. "They didn't take anything for granted. They looked us over pretty thoroughly."

The additional land Sarns acquired years earlier now became crucial. "It was so important to have a nice clean piece of property that was expandable," he says. "3M would never have been able to build what they did had we not had the property."

Most important, from Sarns' point of view, was that it was a key to 3M keeping the business in Ann Arbor, always a crucial issue for him.

And, on June 1, 1981, Sarns, Inc., became Sarns 3M, a subsidiary of 3M's Medical Products Division. Dick Sarns stayed on as general manager for five years, as did the rest of the management team. The company soon got its oxygenator (purchased from Baxter Laboratories!) and thus its complete system. This helped to fuel a doubling of sales volume in the next five years. The Jackson Road campus added its third building (the second, for the design and manufacture of sterile products, opened in 1978): an administration and education center that included a completely equipped, simulated operating room, one of Sarns' longtime dreams.

"That was part of the deal," he says, and the new GM was "told to get going on that a.s.a.p. It turned out to be a real positive addition."

Sarns retired in 1986, but only from the company whose products still bear his name. Within a year, he and Norma had founded LifePlus, which in 1997 became NuStep, the name of its most successful product. Having spent most of his adult life in improving the treatment of heart disease, Dick now turned his attention toward its prevention, and the rehabilitation of its victims.

"It's shocking that only 25 percent of the people who have heart disease or cardiac surgery go into any form of rehabilitation," he says. "We wanted to explore the opportunity to make a product contribution in cardiopulmonary rehab and in preventive medicine. What we see around the country is a lot of equipment that's cast off from the gym and into rehab. We came to the realization that the needs are more scientific than that, and that's what we've tried to respond to."

Their first go at it, he says, was "a recumbent bike on which a person would be seated in a safe, comfortable position." For a first go, it wasn't bad. They sold two or three hundred units, assembled from components supplied by a Japanese company, and the concept clearly had potential.

"Next came the 'seated stepper' concept from our son Steve, who has a master's in exercise physiology from the U-M," says Sarns. "I didn't design this product. Mark Hildebrandt was the design engineer on the job. He also has a master's in exercise physiology from U-M."

Their oldest son, David, also earned a master's from Michigan—in business administration—and is enjoying a successful career in investment banking in New York.

Meanwhile, back in Ann Arbor, there was "a long gestation period" for the NuStep, says Dick Sarns. "We built a number of prototypes, from the ground up, of a total body exerciser for users over 40. That was the market segment we were looking at."

Eventually, what we now know as the NuStep was ready to roll out. "We were quite pleased to be able to get a full patent," says Sarns. "We got both a utility patent and a design patent, which is quite surprising considering there's so much equipment out there. It's an extremely competitive market, so to be successful we had to have a unique quality product that really filled a need."

The proof of that pudding is in both its sales—into the

thousands and counting—and its buyers. The Mayo Clinic, the Texas Heart Institute, and the Cleveland Clinic are some of the "big-name" facilities among the more than 500 cardiac rehab institutions that have purchased NuSteps.

NuStep, says Sarns, has been his business focus for the last five years: "Knock on wood, it's another little pioneering expedition." He's president of the company, Norma is vice president, Steve Sarns is sales and marketing manager, and Hildebrandt is the product manager.

"Looking at it from the standpoint of quality of life, and certainly health care costs, I think the next real medical breakthrough is how can we prevent serious medical problems," says Dick Sarns. "Once they occur, how do we rehabilitate and maintain the patient?"

His perpetual concern remains "what's next?".

For the past 20 years, Dick and Norma have served on a number of business and community not-for-profit boards. Dick's volunteer focus has been education. What is next?

For NuStep, it's a building that opened in the fall of 1998, housing both that company and those of the Sarnses' other business, S.I. Company, as well a satellite of the St. Joseph Mercy Hospital cardiopulmonary rehab program. "We're really excited because it puts us across the hall from our customers," says Sarns.

For the workers of the future, it's the recently opened Washtenaw Technical Middle College, which he helped create and on whose board he serves. "To actually be on a board that's delivering quality education is pretty exciting," he says. "We're off to a great start. This has all the ingredients to make a significant difference for a number of our young people, providing them with the opportunities for technical training that they wouldn't otherwise acquire or be exposed to."

For the children of the future, it's a major addition to the Ann Arbor Hands-On Museum, a nationally renowned institution that serves thousands of youngsters in southeastern Michigan. The Sarnses have contributed both time and resources to the enterprise, which was completed in the fall of 1999.

And for Dick and Norma themselves? "We're having fun and very much in business. We're not retired people yet. To be continued..."

"The heart of any community is in its downtown."

Dennis Serras

Dennis Serras pays meticulous attention to the details of his restaurant operations. He researches menus, finesses physical layouts, and maintains an operations manual. It's one of the keys to his success.

There's one exception. He doesn't even know what kinds of alcoholic beverages his restaurants serve, much less what they charge for them.

"I have to laugh when people say to me your drinks are too expensive," says Serras, whose Mainstreet Ventures owns 18 restaurants in four states, each of them unique in concept and all of them uniform in operation. "I'm not involved in the wine list. I don't know what we charge for a drink. In the layouts of new restaurants, I get involved in the location of the bar, but when it comes to the actual functioning and buying, I stay away. When I hear some of the prices we get for a mixed drink or a glass of wine, it blows me away. When I stopped drinking, a glass of house wine was 75 cents."

That was 20 years ago, when he checked into a treatment center in downtown Detroit to satisfy Ellie, his wife of less than a year. "The reason I did it was to con her," he says. "It was over an incident where I thought I was going to lose her, so what I said so I wouldn't lose her was I was going to go get help. I started at Detroit Memorial Hospital, the only place that had an opening. That was the war zone down there, but it was probably the best thing that ever happened to me. They not only had alkies but hard drug addicts, too. That was a little eye-opener. You'd sit out there Friday night and Saturday night and they'd bring in the guys with the DTs and the junkies. It was pretty heavy-duty."

A couple of weeks later, an opening materialized in Saline and Serras transferred. "Not that it wasn't a sobering experience," he says, "but I really was concerned about my wife. Detroit Memorial is in a rough part of town. She was coming down every night after her job and I just didn't want her driving down there."

Serras now professes amazement that Ellie even paid any attention to him, much less married him. "She wouldn't have anything to do with me when she met me," he says. "I was a practicing alcoholic, as opposed to being a recovering alcoholic, so I was pretty obnoxious. I must have won her heart over. She must have seen some good somewhere in me."

He did have a couple of restaurants in Ann Arbor, Maude's and Real Seafood Company. He was charming, in a raffish sort of way. And he quickly began to see for himself the toll that alcohol was taking.

"The more I started to understand what alcoholism is about, the more I knew I had a drinking problem, and had had it for many years," he says.

He still managed to open and run a couple of restaurants because "I was not a daytime drinker," he says, "unless it was a day off. I had a work ethic. You didn't drink and work, but as soon as work was over, there were no holds barred. I'm not blaming the business for being an alcoholic, but you work nights, you work in a restaurant, you get out at 10 or 11 o'clock, and what is there to do? You go to a bar. You have to be careful how to unwind in this industry. You don't have to unwind in a saloon."

Now, he says, staying sober is—and has been for two decades—"the most important thing in my life. When you're a recovering alcoholic, it has to be. It's a very selfish program; it's you, you, you, the most important thing is that you stay sober. I've had 20 years of sobriety, which is a lot of years, but there isn't a day that goes by that I don't think about my sobriety, and I say this in a positive sense. It's another day I'm going to be sober again."

Serras says being up-front about his condition helps both himself and others. "One of the things that keeps me sober is when I'm talking to anybody about the disease," he says. "That builds up the structure of my sobriety. And it helps other people when they understand that there are some very visible people who are alkies. There are a lot of alcoholics in prominent positions, and the biggest problem they have is if they go for the cure, if they go to the tables at AA, it's in their heads that it's demeaning. I had that feeling when I first went into the program. I didn't want people to know. But now I'm not ashamed of it. I share it with people because there are people I've shared it with that it's helped. That's the reward."

Serras grew up in Schenectady, New York, in a close-knit Greek family not long removed from its ancestral home. His father, Louis, emigrated to the United States at the age of 16. His mother, Constance, was born here to immigrant parents. LeGrande and Dennis, their first two sons, were born 11 months apart shortly after the end of World War II. Ten years later, they had two more children, also less than a year apart: a third son, John, and a daughter, Andromache, known as Andrea.

Louis had a restaurant in nearby Troy; Constance taught school. "My dad didn't do as well as I've done," says Dennis, "but he was in the restaurant business all his life. I never saw a father that worked for anyone other than himself. I didn't understand the concept."

Serras' mother, as a teacher, also had more control over

her destiny than most parents of the time. "Obviously, I considered teaching a job," says Serras, "but it didn't fit that corporate image. She had summers off, weekends off, holidays off. I guess I never really thought of it as a 'job-job.'"

All four children spent time in the restaurant business, albeit via different paths, and three are in it today. LeGrande has two restaurants in Albany, New York. After living in Greece for a couple of years, Andrea came back to the U.S. to attend college, did some work in banking, got married, had a couple of kids, and now runs the company deli, open for breakfast and lunch, for a high-tech corporation in Schenectady. "The kids are in school and it's a day job, so she loves it," says Dennis.

John graduated from the famed Culinary Institute of America in Hyde Park, New York, and was rushed into responsible managerial jobs by development companies that didn't know much about the restaurants they had opened. He burned out on the business and is now a registered nurse.

"My dad always said, 'Go to college and get yourself a job with G.E. and get those benefits,'" Serras recalls. "But from day one, I never had any doubt about what I was going to do."

By contrast, the father of Dennis' first partner, Mike Gibbons, was a "corporate guy" who encouraged his son to blaze his own business trail. "He didn't preach to him to do it, but he said, 'Hey, if you can, go do something on your own and be master of your own destiny.'"

The Greek connection brought Dennis' brother LeGrande to southeastern Michigan in 1964 and Dennis followed a year later. The Serras family's parish priest, Father John Kamalakis, had moved to Ann Arbor as pastor of St. Nicholas Greek Orthodox Church. The first marriage he had ever performed was that of Louis and Constance Serras, he had baptized John and Andromache Serras, and now he was about to change the other siblings' lives. During LeGrande's senior year in high school, he and his mother stopped to visit Father

John en route to Chicago. LeGrande was getting ready to attend music school at the University of Miami, but the priest somehow convinced him to go to Eastern Michigan University instead. "Father John took him over to Eastern and that was it," says Dennis. "I also continued my education in Ypsilanti, but at Cleary College rather than EMU. I lived with Father John the first year. The second year, LeGrande and I lived together."

And, around 1970, they parted company. His brother returned to upstate New York, while Dennis stayed in Ann Arbor, tending bar at the Golden Falcon (later Maude's and then Arriba) and Colonial Lanes, making and delivering pizzas for the original Cottage Inn, and cooking at the Brown Jug and the Lamplighter.

"Then I did two years, what I call my formal training in the restaurant business, with Chuck Muer," says Serras. "I opened three of his restaurants in two years. That was 1973 to '75. I like to say I've had one job, other than 'college jobs,' growing up, and that was it. It was only two years, but it seemed like more. It was 100 percent a strategy. Make that 110 percent. I was out to steal, and it wasn't money. It was knowledge. I wanted to know how to run a dinner house."

By 1975, he believed he did, and Real Seafood Company was born on South Main Street, where it's still going strong more than two decades later. In 1977, Serras opened Maude's in the space once occupied by the Golden Falcon on South Fourth Avenue. That a man in his late 20s with limited capital could pull off such transactions was partly a result of circumstances: Briarwood Mall had opened in 1972 and seemed to be draining the retail life out of downtown

"But that's when Real Seafood, Mr. Flood's Party, the Del Rio and the Whiffletree all opened," Serras recalls. "These were opportunities for people like myself. I had a lot of imagination, not a whole lot of money, and a real willingness to work—hours meant nothing. We had what we thought were darn good ideas, and here were rent structures we could handle because there were empty storefronts. What was bad for some was an opportunity for others to come in. When I took over the Golden Falcon, it had one employee, but Seafood had already opened up and was doing land-office business.

"That was also when the first theme restaurants started to appear in the mainstream," he says. "TGIFridays, Victoria Station—this was exciting dining. Even though those restaurants weren't what I ended up doing, my focus, whether I stumbled on it or it was intentional—and now it's intentional—was on different types of concepts that would offer different types of cuisines. It's more difficult doing those than a Chi-Chi's or a Chili's, for instance, where it becomes a cookie-cutter. You just pick the areas with the right demographics, and you punch these things out over and over."

Basically, he borrowed the concept of having a concept, but not the concept of endlessly cloning it. "When I saw the first Victoria Station—and I don't know if there's one left—it just blew me away," he says. "They took four box-cars, put a restaurant in the middle of it, and served prime rib. At Maude's, we took a hamburger basket that was going for 75 cents, put sour cream and olives on it, called it a Russian burger, sold it for $1.75 and packed the joint. We put our salads in glass bowls. We developed a salad with white asparagus and artichoke hearts, named it Tuxedo County, for the wealthiest county in the country, and sold it for much more than the others. We did one called the Diana, after the Greek goddess, and then we sold the ribs."

In effect, he was selling the sizzle as well as the steak. "When they spend the kind of money that we charge, you need to do more than just put a plate of food in front of them," he says. "They want something else that goes with it—the ambience of a place, how it lays out, where it's located. I don't want to say our concepts don't travel; they do. We have these concepts out of town and out of state, but they become harder to run because they're individual establishments. We've learned through success and failures that we operate better regionally. We had restaurants in Richmond, Virginia, and Knoxville, Tennessee, but we left those areas and came back and started strengthening our company in Michigan and Ohio. We still have a restaurant in Charleston, West Virginia, that does very well, but we pretty much focus in Michigan and Ohio. It's just easier."

Meanwhile, back in the late '70s, it was clear that Serras' ideas were bankable, as they say in Hollywood, but his managerial skills were being tested.

"My first restaurant, Real Seafood, obviously I ran," he says. "When Maude's opened, I could sense that things were starting to fall apart a little bit, but because of their proximity to each other, I was basically running both of them, even though I put a manager and assistant manager in each one. Where it all fell apart was when I opened my third restaurant, Mantel's in the Briarwood Hilton. That's when the wheels came off."

Ironically, having three restaurants had been one of his goals. "I didn't want to be accountable for my time, and what I realized early on about someone running their own one place is that its success had too much to do with the individual's personality that owned it. You didn't own the restaurant, the restaurant owned you. I knew that off the git-go; I'd seen it happen. With three, I didn't have to be accountable. In principle, it was right, but it didn't work because I didn't have any organization set up to deal with it, so I was running around in circles. It didn't need to be a big organization, but it did need a structure."

A big piece of that was a procedures manual. "Even though our concepts are different—in this town, we've got four separate concepts—each one has the same manual," says Serras. "Any manager who followed the standard procedures in one place can go to another and already know 75 percent of the operation. The product is different but the systems are the same: how to treat customers, employee policy, the job description of the assistant manager, working with vendors. There might be a little bit of a tweak in how we serve people but the service sequence is the same."

Another piece of the structure was more help for Serras himself. "After I'd opened my third restaurant, that's when I brought in my first partner, Mike Gibbons," he says. "At the time, he was director of training for the Muer Corporation. I met him down in Cincinnati when I opened a restaurant. I was the manager, and he was a student at Xavier University who came in as an hourly worker. The deal I offered Mike was to be a principal in the company, not just an employee of it."

Two years later, Serras tapped the Muer talent pool again for his second partner, Dieter Boehm. "He was vice president of the Muer Corporation," Serras says. "He was actually our boss. We've all been together ever since."

"Ever since" has included "building probably 17 or 18 restaurants, and we probably have 10 through leases," says Serras. It has also included the evolution from being owner-operator of a couple of restaurants in one town to heading a company with dining establishments in several other states, and throughout southeastern Michigan.

The organization he launched to coordinate the operation of three restaurants also served him well as his business expanded. "Organization—that's the word," he says. "If you've got the organization, you can grow. If you don't, you can't. I was approached recently by someone who wanted to take a concept and fly with it and wanted my company to be involved because I had an organization in place ready to do it. That takes a good amount of learning and experience and mistakes and corrections and money to develop. If you were to go out and put the people together that could start the organization for you, you'd probably spend all your money before you opened the restaurant."

But organization alone isn't enough. Says Serras: "What's really important in our company is that the restaurants don't exist for the organization, the organization exists for the restaurants. We're there to assist them in running their businesses. So many times, you find an attitude that the restaurant exists for the benefit of the organization, and it doesn't. If you don't ever lose track of that, then you have success, and if you have success, you've got everything else. Restaurants are the most volatile business in the country, but they'll throw money at you if you've got success. That's the long and short of that."

In Mainstreet Ventures, he says, "Each of the three partners basically has his own areas. Mike does operations, Dieter does construction and marketing, and I do initial site selections and all the financing and administrative stuff. I'm the president and they're vice presidents, but we really never use the titles. I kind of was first but we're really equal partners in the company."

Their harmonious interaction is partly personal and philosophical compatibility and partly the result of years of working together. "I go to work seven days a week, but I don't consider that I work hard," says Serras. "I think we all cover each other. We don't say, 'You've got a week off coming' or 'You've accumulated this much time.' We take what we want, we know what we've got to do, we know what our responsibility is to people, and that's never put aside for our own time off, but we all get as much time off as we want. I go to Greece every year; I have a home there. Mike has a two-handicap, so you know he's got to get out on the course a little bit. Dieter's an accomplished sailor.

"We all work a lot but I don't think any one of us would say we were overworked. I really like coming in. I'm real methodical. Mike says he knows where I am every hour of the day. I've got to get up in the morning and come down here. I never say I'm taking a day off. I might say I've got to do something this afternoon at the house or wherever. I enjoy dealing with the people in the restaurant. I enjoy customers. I like more the mechanics of the place now as opposed to the running of the place. I like to see the managers. I like to see when the managers are really high on the place and themselves."

As fun and profitable as it was, Serras now feels he may have gotten a bit carried away in the go-go '80s when offers started rolling in to create establishments in far-flung locations. "I'm not sure how it happened," says

Serras. "It started with Portside, the downtown Toledo revitalization project that included its own Real Seafood.

"Portside was done by Jim Rouse, who was famous at the time for Faneuil Hall in Boston and Harbor Place in Baltimore," Serras says. "Jim put into words what was always my feeling, that the heart of any community was in its downtown. I was brought up in downtown. That's where my dad's place was. Jim really thought it was terrible that the downtowns were being gutted."

Putting a Serras restaurant in the project was a good idea. Putting the project in Toledo was not. "The thing with Jim was he thought he could save every downtown," says Serras. "He thought he could go open these festival marketplaces in cities of 400,000, instead of Boston and St. Louis. It was really proven wrong. The problem was the concept was really developed as a tourist attraction, and when you do one in Flint or Toledo, those aren't tourist communities. They didn't have a long-term appeal."

Nonetheless, Serras says, "We spent five real successful years in Toledo with Real Seafood and Portside. That gave us a huge amount of visibility. We were getting at least five phone calls a week from everywhere in the country, from people wanting us to do restaurants. We actually went to Richmond originally to do another festival marketplace. Again, it wasn't successful long-term, but our restaurant still exists down there."

And so does the Tidewater Grill in Charleston, West Virginia, which occupies a special niche in the Serras saga. "We always try to identify what we think isn't in the market," he says, "so when we went down to Charleston, we introduced a real seafood restaurant, no pun intended, with the same product that we used at Real Seafood, coming right out of Boston and the Great Lakes. We set the standard. Across the street, they opened a Red Lobster. Now this was in what you would typically think of as a Red Lobster market, a blue-collar, working-class town. But the Red Lobster failed, and the reason it failed is we set the standard."

Serras believes his and his partners' meticulous research—of cuisines, concepts, and markets—has been a sufficiently significant factor in their success to qualify as a competitive edge.

"We do a lot of it," he says. "We find places that resemble ideas that we have. With the Mexican concept, for example, we traveled to Texas, to several cities in California, to Mexico, and ultimately to Chicago. When we went to Mexico, we took the designer with us. The colors really exist down there. You see blue doors, trucks painted yellow and red. We brought a lot of that back here. And what we found out about Mexican food was that, just like in Italy, there are regional cuisines, so we started to identify the different regions and the different flavors, some of which were tremendous. That's what we really brought here. But even though we wanted the purity of the concept, we still felt we had to service the market that's going to visit this place. If you look at the menu, it isn't what I call 'order five things and they all look alike.'"

The stop in Chicago was to work "with someone who is considered to be one of the best in the business in Mexican dining," says Serras. "From there, food-wise, we really let our executive chef loose. If he doesn't understand something—say with the Mexican again, all the different types of peppers used in the sauces—he does the research required to get it right. I don't want to say we create an illusion when we do a restaurant, but we create a design that makes you think this is what's in Mexico."

In addition to the usual investigative journeys, the research for one of his current projects, a clubby, old-fashioned steak house on South Main Street, included studying old menus from luxury liners. "That's what you really had on those 12-13 day trips to Europe, a top-of-the-line steak house," he says. "My two partners smoke cigars, so they're leading the attack on the cigar room, which will be very small, in the basement, a place where you can get 15-18 people to eat steak, drink single malt scotches, smoke cigars, and drink sherry. There's a market for that in this city."

Serras is aware that he's never going to match the numbers of the chains, but that's not what he's about. "We like downtowns, and we like downtown restaurants," he says. "Each has certain qualities that are peculiar to itself. It doesn't put you on a real fast track for growth. To a certain degree, it limits your growth. But they're more exciting to operate. It's just more fun."

One thing Serras doesn't do is grow too fond of any particular restaurant. The Mexican research alluded to above preceded the transformation of Maude's, his second restaurant and one that was still among Ann Arbor's most popular, into Arriba early in 1998.

"I changed a restaurant that was probably doing more business than 85 percent of the restaurants in this city," he says. "I shut it down and changed it. There aren't many people that would do that, but I thought Maude's had lived its life cycle. I really believed just remodeling it wouldn't have given me another 15 years, especially with the competition that exists in this town now. I had Maude's all redesigned, it was all planned, and we canned it. I felt that redeveloping into a totally new concept gave it a new life cycle.

"Unlike other retail businesses," he adds, "where typically your third year is your best, in the restaurant business, I can tell you in three months if a place will be a success. The test is have we developed something that will appeal to the market that we've developed it for, a little younger market than Real Seafood and Maude's."

The market gives you a report card in a hurry, and there's no room for sentiment if the grades don't measure up. Serras says he would even reinvent Real Seafood, if it came to that.

"I think Seafood's great, I really love it in concept, but if the need ever arose that something really different had to be done with it, such as a concept change or a name change, I wouldn't hesitate," he says. "I used to say 17 years was the life cycle of a good restaurant. Because of the proliferation of good restaurants, I think it's a lot shorter now. If you can squeeze nine years out of a concept, you're doing well. I see Seafood for at least the next nine or 10 years. There's such a thing as an institution, but institutions die, too."

Just as Serras once worked for Chuck Muer to "steal expertise," so he now finds some of his own staffers emulating his entrepreneurship. "A couple of our folks left in the last year who actually opened their own places," Serras says. "One thing I'm pretty proud of is our people. Until those folks left, our average general manager had been with us over 11 years, which is really unusual in this business. We tend to keep our management. I think we do as good, if not better, than most companies in our business."

It's also another arena in which the breadth and, as he says, "purity" of the concepts provides a competitive edge, especially at a time when the restaurant industry is suffering more than most from a regional labor shortage.

"We have real interesting places," says Serras. "We offer environments that are special, and I think people being managers and saying they work in these restaurants gives them a certain amount of recognition. I know we treat people fairly. I don't know that we are the highest payers in the industry; I know we're not the lowest. I think we're real competitive in what we pay people. We try to give them the feeling that they're part of an organization, so they've got some stability. We also give them, in the same breath, the feeling that they have some say-so in their operation, that they can make a decision, they can make a difference. The fact that we keep people suggests that we do that.

"I know they feel they can learn something; that's a big part of it," he adds. "Sometimes we're fair to a fault; we'll stick with people too long, but we try to make it work for them. We really feel we get paid back; sometimes we don't, but in the long run, I'd rather do business that way."

One institution to which his allegiance is keen is family, and the one formed by his and Ellie's daughters, Alisha and Maria Nicole (known as Niki), and their parents is as close as the one in which he grew up.

The summer of 1998 was the first in 10 years that they didn't spend at least four weeks in Greece together. Alisha was on the threshold of her senior year at Huron High School, where Niki was a sophomore, and visits to prospective colleges made it impossible to put together sufficient time.

"We travel a lot together," says Serras. "We're really family-oriented, very private. Because of my business I'm in the public eye all the time, and our home life is really entirely different. Most of our meals are shared in our home. We have the traditional Sunday dinner with my mother-in-law and her friend Will, and Uncle Jimmy. It's been the same group for years. That Sunday sit-down dinner is real important, which we always did when I was a kid."

One bonus of the administrative turn his work took as Serras' company's roster of restaurants grew, was a more conventional work schedule. "When our children were born, I worked until 10 at night," he says. "Now I go to work early and go home fairly early and I'm there most nights. If you were to ask my kids what they remember, they'd say their dad was home most evenings. That really isn't typical if you own and operate a single dinner-house style restaurant."

The Serrases are also on guard for any adverse effects their affluence might have on their children. "It's hard to say you fly your own airplane and live a simple life," Dennis laughs. "When Niki was four or five, somebody said what does your daddy do, and she said, 'Oh, he's a pilot.' My kids assumed that when you went somewhere, your dad flew you and that was how everybody did it. But I think if you met my children, they would never come across as snobby rich kids. They're really down to earth. They look at their friends as who they are and not how they live or where they live. My children have been able to fit right in. I don't know whether it's the chemistry between Ellie and me that we've brought up our kids with, but we just have a very close-knit family.

"Our kids shared the same room for nine years," he

says. "We didn't let one tattle tale on the other. If one did something, they both took the rap. To this day, they're still exceptionally close, even though they have their own group of friends. When we take trips, they're just inseparable. If I take the little one shopping, she'll always say, 'I want to buy my sister something.'"

Perhaps, too, the children have learned from their parents' attitude. "I used to be a little bit embarrassed at having what I have," says Dennis. "I'm a lot more comfortable today with it. I know I'm pretty well off, but I also know I'm probably lucky, in so many ways. I'm lucky in my success in business. I'm lucky in my pick of a mate who's been a tremendous influence in my life, and my daughters, my family in general."

Meanwhile, Mainstreet Ventures continues to grow, although Serras maintains size alone is not among his goals. "This year (1998), we've got three places going, which is a lot: two together on the river in Toledo and the steak house in Ann Arbor," Serras says. "My ambition is some steady growth, but no mountain climbing anymore. There's no reward for me personally to see how many restaurants I can open in the next five years. I want to open enough restaurants to keep the good people that we have interested in a growing company, but I don't want cookie-cutter restaurants. I like doing what we do. I hope we still create."

He's also at a point in life where his definitions of creativity and success are somewhat larger than formerly. "One daughter's graduated from high school. The other's in 11th grade. Our lives are going to change," he says. "I don't know if it will increase or decrease my desire to work. Right now, I've just got a nice balance. I'm 52, and I see enjoying life as much as I can and more than I have."

The prospect does not include a successor to his one "real" job in the '70s. "I don't say you have to have done well financially because I know people who are happy who have nowhere near what we have," he says. "But I have a personality now where I wouldn't want to work for anybody else. It's just not in me. In the society we live in, in a capitalist world, a person has to do something to earn the things he wants. For me, those things are not condos in Acapulco, or seeing how many toys I can gather or how many trips I can take. It's just a good, solid life, being able to buy fresh fruits and fresh vegetables, and going out when you want to go out."

Speaking of fruits and vegetables, what do the Serrases eat at these family dinners?

"We grill out a lot," he says. "We have Weber kettles and use real hardwood charcoal. We grill a lot of fish, chicken, Italian sausage. We eat a lot of pastas, a lot of vegetables, some done simply, others done Greek style with string beans, tomatoes, olive oil. We use a lot of garlic. There isn't a can in our house, period. Well, maybe there's a can of cocoa."

"We're trying to create a culture and an environment where people can thrive and feel proud."

Ned Thomson

Ned Thomson believes doing business entails not just making money but making a society. "We're on a little bit more than the typical crusade," says the co-founder and recently retired president of Thomson-Shore in Dexter, Michigan. "We're trying to do more than just print books. We're trying to create a culture and an environment where people can thrive and feel proud."

In fact, he doesn't even think profit should be one of a company's goals.

"We don't set out to make a profit," says Thomson. "We set out to do everything we do as well as we can. If you're in a decent business, and you do enough things right, profit is going to be the inevitable result. But it shouldn't be a goal. Be as honest as you can be. Do the best you possibly can. If I do my best, and I can inspire my people to do their best, hell, we can't fail, unless lightning strikes or something."

In a little over 20 years, the relentless implementation of its founders' philosophy helped the company grow from those two people—Thomson and his partner, Harry Shore—to a business with 300 employees working three shifts to print, bind and ship so-called "short run" books, i.e. those for academic, religious and other specialty publishers who require no more than about 6,000 units.

The primary tenet of their creed has been to erase the traditional line between labor and management. At Thomson-Shore, to a large extent, everyone is both. All major corporate decisions are made as democratically as possible. Anyone can "stop the line" if he or she spots a defect or problem. Anyone could go into Thomson's or Shore's office and speak his or her piece with impunity. No one has a reserved parking space, or wears a tie. There is no sales department.

"We're the only company in the country in this business that doesn't have a sales force," says Thomson. "That's what makes this business go—that we can attract customers with the quality of our work. Harry and I met with every new hire. There's no one that can't affect what the customer thinks about us, and what the customer thinks about us is what gets the business in the door. If customers get pissed off at us, it's our fault, not the fault of some salesman who promised something we couldn't deliver.

"Everybody takes so much pride in the fact that we don't have sales people—this is a big deal in this company. But that puts the onus on every one of us. It creates a quality level that's probably higher than it needs to be. You can almost say it's a greedy way to run a business."

But when it came time to sell it, Thomson and Shore were anything but greedy. Profit's not the goal, remember? "We sold the business to the employees at below book value," Thomson says. "We could have put this up for sale and sold it to some entrepreneur or venture capitalist for half again as much money. But 11 years ago, we said when Harry and I are ready to leave, we want to leave the company under the ownership of the employees."

Those employees will pick the next CEO, or perhaps not even to have one. After all, Thomson himself was asked, politely but firmly, to leave one of the last committees he served on before retiring.

"Most of the committees aren't run by supervisors," he explains. "There may be supervisors on them, but they're run by hourly workers. A recent one I was on was to set up a customer satisfaction survey. Since I had the most customer contact, they said I should be on the committee. There were five or six people on the committee and I was the only one who had had any customer contact, which is why they said I should be on it. I had a fair amount of input because I was the guy who had the most experience. They would bring up a subject and sort of turn to me for the answer. That was fine with me.

"But about halfway through the meetings—these are ad hoc committees and we set a time limit—the guy who was the facilitator, he runs a case-maker, came to my office and said, 'I think you should drop off the committee.' It didn't bother me, but I asked, 'Why is that?' He said, 'We all look to you to make the decisions. You're the guy who knows the most about it, so we just accept it. We'll get better input from the rest of the people if you don't go to the meetings.'"

Such scenes are at least as satisfying to Thomson as any commercial successes. "I was pleased that that happened," he says, "that he had the nerve to walk up here and sit down in the office of the president of the company and say, 'We don't need you on the committee anymore, you're doing more harm than good.' Once he explained his position, I said, 'You're probably right. If I were in your shoes, I'd feel the same way.'"

He also remembers an employee who spotted a defect that Thomson's own eyes couldn't detect, even though the remedy the worker implemented didn't exactly "go through channels."

"This happened with a job for the University of Pennsylvania many years ago," Thomson says. "An hourly worker doing shrink wrap rejected a book. I picked up the book, and he said, 'Look on page 11.' I still couldn't see it. When he finally pointed it out, I said, 'It's incidental. But how would it be if I go in and call up Carl Gross, the guy in charge of the job at Penn, and we'll send it to him today, and if this isn't acceptable, we'll rerun the job for him.'

"I did that, and Carl, as it turned out, was not in. About three days later, I went back out to the plant and said, 'I finally heard from Carl and, by the way, where are the books?' He said, 'We threw them out. We decided we weren't going to ship that.' They never hesitated. They knew what I was doing but their judgment was such that they didn't need to wait for me. I thought that was pretty positive, that they didn't wait for me. Their attitude was, 'What does Ned know about that? We don't want people out there thinking this is the kind of work we do.' Our people will have arguments about what's good enough and what isn't. We tend to go with the highest common denominator."

Although members of both of their families have been Thomson-Shore employees, the principals never conceived of the enterprise as one that would be perpetuated on a genetic basis.

"That was one thing I consciously did when we started the business," says Thomson. "All of our kids worked for us when they were in high school, but I let them know that as far as I was concerned, we weren't going to run this like a family business. I didn't think that was the way a business should be run. I let them know that and I let our people know that. Whoever is going to be the next president is going to be the next president because they've been a long-term employee and deserve the position, not because they inherited it."

But democracy can be unpredictable. The committee on succession, so to speak, "decided they wanted to see this business run by a committee rather than a single CEO," says Thomson. Imagine.

"We had told them we were going to leave this business under whatever circumstances they wanted to see: our retirement, our resignation, our withdrawal from management, as well as the disposal of the stock we have in the company," he adds. "They met for six months. Anyone could come to the meetings and participate. Among other people, they interviewed my wife Mary Jane. When we were done, they ended up with a book, and it said that was how they thought it should work. We just accepted it verbatim."

There were two experiences in Thomson's life that were crucial in shaping his ideas on how a business should be run. One, which might be called the negative reinforcement, was working for a boss who viewed labor-management relations as, to say the least, adversarial. The other, more positive, was an executive training workshop on the merits of group decision-making.

In 1967, a company called Shaw-Barton, a maker of novelty advertising and calendars, bought Braun-Brumfield, an Ann Arbor book printing business. Shaw-Barton was probably the largest business in Coshocton, Ohio, where Thomson grew up. As his father did, he had worked for them. He had since moved on to General Electric, but now Shaw-Barton wanted to hire him back to, as Thomson puts it, "understudy Carl Braun, the president, and sort of be their spy" in the newly purchased operation. "Carl turned out to be a very good friend," says Thomson, "and I turned out to be much more on his side than on the parent company's side."

A month and a half after Thomson's arrival in Ann Arbor, Braun suffered a heart attack. Thomson found himself, in effect, running the company. "Hell, I didn't know what a book was," he says. "We had no sales operation. I went to New York probably once a month and called on customers because we needed work. I just got a list of addresses of publishers out of the yellow pages and started going to see them."

One day, the parent company's president came to town for a confab. "He asked me for a recommendation on what to do about salaries," Thomson recalls. "We were doing well, growing like crazy, making exorbitant profits. I came up with a recommendation, a percentage. He said, 'I can see you've got a lot to learn. In business, there's two sides—manager and worker. And if you don't take advantage of them, they'll take advantage of you. This is way too big an increase.' I realized then we were never going to get along."

On the other hand, he had learned a lesson well. "I have him to thank for the feeling we developed about the way to treat people," Thomson says. "The guy who's responsible for our philosophy, and for me feeling so strongly about it, was the president of the parent company."

Between stints at Shaw-Barton, Thomson worked in market research for GE, which sent him to a retreat in Pine Mountain, Georgia, that was, he says, "one of the single most meaningful business experiences I ever had."

The participants had all answered in advance a series of questions about personnel issues and other managerial matters. Now they were divided into groups of eight, each sitting around a table in a windowless room, to see what kind of answers they would come up with collectively.

"We didn't know another soul in the room," says Thomson. "We were all from different divisions. The object of this was to get you to work well as a group. You had to sit around and listen to each other. We had one guy who withdrew. He wouldn't share his answers. He'd say, 'I know the right answer; I don't need you other guys.' After the first day, he broke his chair, left the room and flew home."

It may have cleared the air, however. "Our group started functioning very well together," says Thomson, "and every group that functioned well ended up answering those questions better than any single individual in the group could answer them. That had a big impact on how I developed my philosophy. You've got to listen. You never know where the right answer is going to come from. The guy running the press on the third shift may have the answer, and we've got to create an environment where that person can sound off and be listened to and we've got to be willing to accept it.

"There, in a nutshell, is our philosophy. If you realize

that everyone has something to offer, you're going to be respectful of them and allow them to participate. You don't ever want to squelch a person, no matter how wild the comment they make. They arrived at that opinion for a reason."

The path by which Thomson arrived at his opinions about running a business was a bit more straightforward than the one by which he arrived at actually running one.

He was born in Coshocton in 1931, the second and last child of Ed (Ned is actually Edward Jr.) and Helen Thomson. His parents were both alumni of the University of Michigan, as was his sister Barbara, six years his senior. "All my life, I thought I would go to Michigan," he says. "My folks assumed I would go to Michigan because they had gone there."

When his senior year in high school rolled around, he obtained an application from U-M. "It had a couple of pages that were blank on it for something called a philosophy of life," he remembers. "I said, 'God only knows what it is, and I'm not going to make one up, so the hell with it,' and I didn't apply."

In the town of Granville, 35 miles east of Coshocton, there was a college (now a university) called Denison. "I went there," says Thomson. "They had a much easier application."

He started out majoring in physics, but "by the end of my sophomore year, I was probably going to flunk out," he says. "I ended up majoring in business, or economics, one or the other. I never paid much attention to college. I always figured what I learned there wouldn't have a whole lot of impact on what I would eventually do."

There was apparently at least a bit of an entrepreneurial streak in his gene pool. His father had been a distributor for Pennzoil until World War II, when rationing effectively put the kibosh on that business. "He ended up starting a small defense plant that treated webbing for parachutes," says Thomson. "Someone from an ordnance base knew of him because he had access to chemicals that prevented mildewing, so they asked him if he could treat this stuff. They had five or six companies around the country doing it."

They also had fairly complicated instructions for how it was to be done, which the senior Thomson ignored. "He already had chemicals and a building," says Ned. "He said, 'I bet we could take that roll of material, dip it into a 50-gallon drum of the chemicals, stick a broomstick through there, let it drip a couple of days until it's dry, then send it to 'em.'"

It worked so well that "they called him up and said, 'You're getting such good penetration; we want to know how you're doing it.' And he wouldn't tell them."

It was also a great place for the 12-year-old Ned to hang out. "Working there, all you had to do was dip a roll, let it sit in the tank an hour, then pull it out and sit around the rest of the day," he says. "I'd go play cards with the workers after school.

"My dad was, I think, a nice guy to work with," adds his son. "He was very easy-going, very understanding. I never thought about him as an influence on my life but if he was, it was a good one. I had a lot of respect for my father, other than the fact that he was a mediocre golfer, and a lousy eater. He never got drunk, never swore, never beat his wife. He was a good, successful small-town business-man. He probably needed a strong leader he could work for, I suspect. I've never been in that position. Whether or not I've ever needed one, I never had one."

His dad went to work as the treasurer of Shaw-Barton after the war ended, and Ned went to work for Warner-Swasey, an industrial machine manufacturer in Cleveland, after his graduation from Denison. He and his wife were living in an apartment that they rented at a discount in return for helping the owner with maintenance. When the person the owner sold the building to refused to continue the arrangement, the young family, recently enlarged by the addition of son Bruce, quit Cleveland in a huff.

Says Thomson: "I called up my dad and said, 'Do you think I can get a job at Shaw-Barton? I went down that weekend, applied, and got a job in the office doing not much of anything. I worked there four or five years."

Then he got a job in market research, "which was sort of fun," through a tennis-playing friend who was GE's manager of market development for laminated plastics. Four or five years later, Shaw-Barton bought Braun-Brumfield, and Thomson was rehired to "go up to Ann Arbor and keep an eye on things."

That was where he hooked up with kindred spirit Harry Shore, who managed several areas at Braun-Brumfield prior to Thomson's arrival. By the time they were sitting together on an airplane, bound for Denver and some sort of business meeting, the two were pretty much in charge of the company.

"He and I were sort of running the company then," says Thomson. "Carl Braun was back at work from his heart attack, but he didn't like running the company. It wasn't his style. Harry and I started talking and decided that, if we were really going to be happy in this business, we wouldn't be doing it for the guy (the Shaw-Barton president) we were doing it for. And then we started talking about how we would do it differently."

And so it was that in June of 1972, at the age of 41, with his son about to enroll at Colby College in Maine, and with two daughters, ages 15 and 7, still at home, Ned Thomson, and his friend Harry Shore, started a business.

"We started the thing on no money at all," Thomson says, noting that Bruce's tuition at Colby took about 40 percent of his pay that year. "There were times when we would have to go over and borrow money from the bank in order to meet the payroll. The business was doing okay but we never had any money in the bank; it was all in receivables and inventory. Bruce Benner, who was president of Ann Arbor Bank, lived across the street from me and was a good friend. The bank had a lot of patience with us. I had everything pledged as collateral for loans except my wife and kids."

Thomson says he and Shore didn't take a single day off for the first year they were in business. It wasn't so bad for the first few months: they both worked one shift of 10 hours or so. But then they hired someone to work the second shift, running a press.

"You couldn't leave one guy by himself to run the press because if he got hurt, there would be no one there," says Thomson, "so Harry and I had to split up the second shift. There were times when the alarm would go off at three in the morning and I wouldn't know if I was supposed to be getting up or going to sleep."

But they were having fun, and doing it their way. For example, one item in their complete suite of used equipment and furniture was a file cabinet Thomson had found in a Detroit warehouse. "I spent a whole day cleaning it and painting it metallic gold," he says. "I was really proud of that. We had the only gold file cabinet, I suspect, in all of Washtenaw County. It just glistened. Those were what we describe as the good old days. There were some nerve-wracking times there, but we never gave a moment's thought to the possibility it could fail, and we always had more business than we could handle. And it was such a relief to be in a situation where everyone wanted to participate and wanted to help out. Even our customers got turned on by our operation. We've had very loyal customers. Probably the majority of the first ones are still with us."

While Thomson-Shore's flattened hierarchies were drawing attention long before the concept became almost fashionable, in the beginning there were no hierarchies to flatten.

"Harry was manufacturing, his wife laid out negatives, I was marketing, my wife was the accountant, and she had never kept anything but her checkbook," says Thomson. "My son made deliveries. Our oldest daughter was our janitor. For the first six months, I was the janitor. Harry refused to clean the rest rooms, so I wound up being the janitor. All three of Harry's kids worked in the plant in those days."

Sometimes this modest cadre's operations bordered on the desperate. "For almost a year, we didn't make any

FICA payments," Thomson recalls. "We kept track of 'em. We knew what we owed. And we knew we would have to make them."

The company had about a dozen employees at the end of its first year. Luckily, one of them was Homer Ruegger, the former treasurer at University Microfilms (now UMI). "He kept us honest and we caught up in FICA by the end of that first year," says Thomson.

The hardest part of starting Thomson-Shore might have been breaking the news to his parents. By now, Thomson's dad was not only Shaw-Barton's treasurer but also on its board, and a good friend of Mr. Shaw's.

"I went down to see Mr. Shaw to resign, and tell him I was going to start a company that would be in competition with him," Thomson remembers. "He was not pleased."

But it got worse. "I went home that evening to stay at my parents' house," he says. "When I told them, they just about hit the ceiling. My mother cried. My dad said, 'You don't know what the hell you're doing. You're going to bring disgrace on the family. You're undoubtedly going to go bankrupt and how are we going to support you?' Mr. Shaw thought my dad was financing the operation, and my dad didn't even want me to do it. He didn't have a cent in it. Whenever I would go back to Coshocton, a county seat of 12,000 people at the time where everybody knew each other and said hello, my dad wouldn't even let people know I was in town. He was so embarrassed and so insulted that I would leave the company he was involved with and go into competition."

Eventually, the fences were mended, and Thomson's parents spent the last few years of their lives in Ann Arbor. "By the time my folks passed away in the late '80s, any strained situation they still had in Coshocton had long since gone," he says. "I don't know if they would have said they were proud of me, but they accepted the fact that I hadn't screwed up and disgraced the family."

When Thomson refers to his father as a "lousy eater," he has evidence to back up his claim. His dad's health habits influenced him as powerfully as Mr. Shaw's management theories, and as antithetically.

"My father had an absolutely terrible lifestyle," he says. "He never exercised, would not eat a vegetable to save himself, didn't like fruit, and had M&Ms and Hershey bars beside him all the time. He smoked for 70 years, starting at 14 and keeping it up until the day he died; Camel cigarettes, no filters. My mother only smoked 50 years; she didn't start until she was 35."

Under the circumstances, their longevity was amazing. One wonders how long their son, their polar opposite in the fitness department, will last.

"It seems to me I've exercised every day of my life," he says. "I was on the track team in college, I've always played golf and tennis, and I'm always on some sort of program for staying in shape. I did the Royal Canadian Air Force exercises 30 to 40 years ago, then jogging came into fashion, and I jogged for about 15 years. Then they started doing aerobics. We used to do aerobics at work. Now they do yoga. I go home for lunch and have every fruit and vegetable in the refrigerator. And I've had a peanut butter and jelly sandwich every day for lunch for probably 60 years. Peanut butter and jelly is just beautiful."

In his view, "much to my wife's dismay," so is the salad bar at Wendy's. "I have forever been frugal," he says. "I've never spent a lot of money. I absolutely cannot tolerate going to expensive restaurants. I don't like 'em. I always feel they're phony."

But, then, this is a man who makes his own cereal, as well as most of his and his children's furniture. He probably made the jelly in his sandwich, too. Other than the furniture-making, the only hobbies he admits to are reading books from the local library, and the stock market.

His activities therein are remarkably high-tech for someone who did his purchase orders, invoices, quotes—and all his other customer correspondence—in longhand for the first six years he ran a business. "We had some typewriters," he says. "I just never liked to use them."

Now, he tracks the 90 or so companies in which he

owns stock via computer. It's just frugal. "I used to buy four or five shares of stock and get killed on broker's fees," he says. "Now I invest over the Internet; no matter what I buy, the flat fee is 12 bucks. I have the portfolio on computer, and I can call up the financial statement of almost any company in the country."

He says he has generally "done quite a bit better than the market. This year, I've lost 25, maybe 30 percent. But it doesn't bother me. I don't have to have the money, so I just ignore it. If it goes up, I look at everything. If it goes down, I just don't look. I really don't care that much because I'm not about to sell anything. My wife says, 'Don't you want to know how you're doing?' and I say, 'If it's bad news, why look it up?' Most of the things I buy are things you never heard of."

This activity, too, can be traced back to Coshocton. "I think the first stock I ever bought was Universal Cyclops, which made steel, when it built a plant in Coshocton. This was when I was probably 25 years old and I remember investing something like $100 in two shares of their stock. I just went into the bank and said, 'How do you buy stock?'."

Years later, he saw to it that Thomson-Shore employees would know the answers to such questions. If their participation in the enterprise were to be well informed, knowledge of the business was essential.

"We work three shifts, and I'm sure some of the people on the third shift may not have seen me since they were hired," he says, "but we do have quarterly meetings where we go over the financial statement and company plans with every employee, from five or six in the morning until late afternoon. If we're going to borrow money, change insurance coverage, buy a new press, we talk about it. They're all entitled to understand what the company is going to do. The meeting may last for an hour, then we spend 15 minutes on basic finances: what depreciation is, where profits go, where we pay bonuses, why we made a bonus or didn't make a bonus. If they understand all that, hopefully they can all think they're working on a cathedral."

That's a reference to the classic story of three men working at a construction site, each of whom is asked what he's doing. The first says, "I'm laying bricks." The second says, "I'm making $20 an hour." The third says, "I'm helping to build a cathedral."

Classes in finance, and a plant that has five rooms and an auditorium for meetings, are some of the visible evidence of the philosophy of reciprocity in action.

"The company owes the employee its dedication," says Thomson. "We've got to provide our people with a steady income, good working conditions, a business where you feel part of it and part of a family and enjoy what you're doing. The employee also has an obligation—to do his or her best, be a team member, work well with his or her neighbor, realize that the company is only going to do as well as he or she does.

"If you're going to spend 40 hours a week there, or 48 or 50, you sure should have a job that you enjoy. If you feel you're being screwed or taken advantage of, you're not going to enjoy it. It's going to be a pain in the ass to go to work, and life shouldn't be that way. If you're going to be affected by a decision the company makes, you should have a say in that decision. We've been able to do that pretty successfully. This is not a philosophy we adopted in 1980. This is a philosophy we adopted the day we started this business."

And he suspects it's not quite as rare as the publicity given to the "Chainsaw Al" types would lead people to believe. "The world should know that everyone doesn't do that," says Thomson. "All business isn't cutthroat. There are companies in the world that will treat people with respect and devotion. But the ones you read about are the ones where the bosses gave themselves a 200 percent raise while cutting everyone else's pay. I would like to think that there are people who have a more Christian attitude about their fellow man. I guess people who run businesses tend to be egotistical and greedy, but I think you can run a business for the benefit of the employees and the benefit of the customers and not be greedy about it, and still run it the way we run it. Given this philosophy, we get a superior effort from just about everyone. We rarely have people quit."

And there are benefits for the president, too: "It's so much more satisfying to walk through the plant and have people talk to you and smile at you and ask if you're still driving the same car. I'd hate to think I'm a powerful figure at Thomson-Shore. I have influence. But power, I don't know what it means—that I don't have to mess around with the common man? There are people at Thomson-Shore who have gotten as much satisfaction out of working here as I have, maybe more. Maybe telling our story in a book will help people realize that businesses can and sometimes do have respect for all their employees."

His retirement turned out to be a severe test of his principles. He is not a sit-by-the-fire type (unless he's reading), and he dreaded the end of his Thomson-Shore career. On the other hand, he felt the manner of his going had to be a validation of his philosophy. "I was committed to retiring from Thomson-Shore," he says. "The people needed to know what was going to happen. Otherwise, whatever we've created here would have been down the tube."

And yet, and yet. "I'm afraid I'm going to have trouble in retirement," he says. "I was out in Arizona for four months last winter, riding a bike, climbing mountains, playing tennis, doing aerobics. And I thought, 'God, there's got to be something better you can get out of life. I'm not contributing anything. I'm just existing. Am I at a point in my life where I no longer have anything to contribute?' I keep thinking I should start another business. I don't know if I'll have the guts to do it, but I don't like the idea of not producing anything."

A few items do remain on his agenda. For one thing, he says, "It's always ticked me off that we haven't done better than we have. We have more dedicated employees, we're nicer guys, we treat our customers as well as our employees fairly. I think we have the right attitude and the right idea, and by and large we've done very well, but one way or another we've never pulled it off as success-fully as we should have. We should have been three times as successful. The opportunity is always there to do things better. That's what keeps business forever enter-taining."

For another, the more companies such as his, the bet-ter. "I'd like to think if you ran enough businesses this way," he says, "you'd end up with a pretty good country."

"If you had to limit it to one word, it would be honest, first on the list."

Nub Turner

What's ironic, says Nub Turner (and anyone with a degree in English from the University of Michigan ought to recognize irony), is that losing his left arm was "not a big deal, really. The hit in the head was the big deal. I was smart and good-looking before that."

It was January 1969, and the 30-year-old Turner, already prosperous enough to be taking a skiing vacation in Switzerland, was sitting atop his gear on a platform in the Lausanne railway station. He never saw the train coming from the other direction.

"One of those grab bars that come out from the engine caught me on the head, threw me on the tracks and ran over my arm," Turner says. "So I'm told. I don't remember any of this. I was out like a light for weeks."

After a month's hospitalization in Switzerland, he was strong enough to return to the United States for the rest of the repairs. "It crushed in the right side of my head," he says, pointing to the area. "This is all plastic and whatever else they throw in there. It lowered my IQ about 50 points. The arm was fairly immaterial. You can live through that with ease."

Given such an attitude, it's easier to understand that when it came time to wade into battle with Chrysler Corp., 13 years later, Turner never blinked. After all, they were going to close his company, so he was just trying to save his job...by buying it. Which he did. And 16 years after that, he and his partners in what became GT Products—and their employees—cashed out handsomely.

Things had been perking along pretty steadily for Turner up until the accident—student council president at Ann Arbor High School, a solid U-M career, two years in the Army, good jobs with General Foods and Detroit Diesel, a return to his home town in the sales department at King-Seeley Corporation, and his engagement to Janeth McKay of Midland. It was Janeth who brought him back from Switzerland, and they were married four months after the accident.

It was one of the first and strongest signs that Turner was not only going to live through this with ease, but also that he wasn't going to miss a beat. He loved to drive sports cars, ski, play tennis, sell stuff, write, and work in the auto industry, and he saw no reason to give up any of it.

"It doesn't affect your life dramatically, quite honestly," he says of losing an arm and almost his life. "You tend to forget about it. One thing I can say for sure is it's the kind of thing where other people see it as a much bigger deal than the person involved. A lot of people are running around with extra arms that they don't seem to know how to use.

"It doesn't affect skiing, the sport that I basically did the most at the time," he says. "Everybody thinks it affects your balance, but you compensate. The only way it ever affected my activities was I got kicked out of a Porsche time trial in Waterford because the local club there didn't like the idea of a one-armed driver. So I went up with another group of guys who rented the track for a day, and had the second fastest time."

The older, by 16 months, of the two children of Amherst Hale and Signe Carlson Turner, Amherst Hale Turner Jr. got his lifelong nickname prenatally. The family story, he says, is that "My dad would pat her tummy when my mother was pregnant and say, 'There's your little Nubby.'"

Little Nubby grew up in an environment that combined creativity and entrepreneurship with academics. His dad, a native of Cincinnati, had moved to California as a youth, where he spent several years as a singer, pianist and arranger for his own pop combos. He was vacationing with a fellow musician in St. Ignace when he met Signe, the daughter of a Swedish family from the Upper Peninsula. She was also on vacation, from her job as a home economics teacher in the Detroit public schools.

By the time of the Nub's arrival in 1939, the couple was living in Ann Arbor, where his father owned and operated a grocery store at State and Dewey, across the street from Ferry Field. "Even after he came here, when I was a kid, he'd have little bands that he'd take around and play in," says Turner. "Then he finally decided to get a day job. Once he got married and had kids, that changed his lifestyle."

The day job was sales manager at radio station WPAG. "Dad had an office in Ypsilanti," Turner recalls, "and he was marshal of the Fourth of July parade there the year the Tucker was the parade car. I rode in it, and there was a picture of it in *The Ann Arbor News.*"

Not long after, Turner's father started a radio station in Clearwater, Florida, while maintaining his links with his family. "He never sold his house up here," Turner says. "I actually lived in Clearwater for a year in the ninth grade."

His dad returned to Ann Arbor after selling the station, and started yet another career at age 50, investing in commercial real estate, mostly student apartments, for about 10 years before retiring.

"There's probably some strain of salesmanship along the way that makes sense," Turner says. "My dad was certainly a good salesman, and I think one of the most important things anyone will ever learn in life is you have to sell yourself and your ideas."

Despite the music that surrounded him as a youngster, Turner found the siren song of business more seductive. "I always had a business orientation, for whatever reason," he says, "but I probably thought of big business, as you tend to do as a kid."

Not that his artistic side ever shut down completely. Some time in the 1970s, he doesn't remember exactly when, he self-published a book of his poetry, and he and Ann Arbor musician Chris Benjey have collaborated on a score or so of country and western and swing tunes.

Unlike himself, Benjey is "a musician in real life," Turner says. "He writes commercials for General Motors. He writes the music and I write the lyrics. Billy Ray Cyrus recorded a promo on one of our songs, 'Daddy Ran Shine,' and we helped Cyrus' people with a song that I think we got credit on, but I haven't seen it yet. We're thinking of coming out with our own CD, just for fun; a vanity CD with about a dozen songs. We might break through and get a song published here one of these days."

Turner's first song was based on "Samantha," one of the poems in his book, which he says he wrote "because I felt like doing it."

A friend who died young asked that a poem Turner wrote about him be read at his funeral. "A lot of the people who went to the funeral said, 'You ought to publish your poetry sometime.' One thing led to another. I think Borders sold 10 copies."

Couldn't the ace sales guy prevail upon them to display it next to the register? "They did," he laughs. "It still sold 10 copies. Even my mother didn't ask for a second copy."

At least one of the poems arose from his experiences in Korea, where he spent 13 months of his two-year Army hitch. "I was a lieutenant," he says, "and ended up running the supply and maintenance platoon for an infantry battle group up by the DMZ."

Back stateside, he was sent to Ft. Benning, Georgia, then became the property book officer at Homestead Air Force Base in Florida, from where the ill-fated Bay of Pigs operation was launched. "They were going to paratroop in guys out of there," he remembers. "They should have, but they didn't. We could have taken Cuba easily at that time, but Kennedy backed down and dropped the ball completely. We didn't give 'em air cover. I ended up partying with some of those guys, and it would bring tears to your eyes to hear how we let them down."

Turner's bloodlines evidenced themselves early. His first full-time civilian job was in sales for General Foods in southeast Detroit. "Cereal, Gainesburgers, dog food, what else did I sell?" he chuckles.

Well, he considered Corvettes. "I always thought advertising would be fun, and I was always a car nut," he says. "A fraternity brother of mine worked for Campbell-Ewald Advertising, they had the Corvette account, and it sounded like a natural to me. I drove a Corvette at the time, and I figured maybe I could sell a few for them."

But by the time the renowned agency offered him a job, he had already accepted one in the sales training department of Detroit Diesel, a division of General Motors. "I was actually a writer type," he says. "We were responsible for putting on programs for our dealers and distributors."

Turner was happily combining two of his vocations, and he had "a great boss named Jim Albrecht. But one day, the King-Seeley sales guy that handled the Detroit Diesel account came in and asked if they could talk to me about a job," Turner says. "A chance to come back to my own home town was the last thing in the world I ever thought of as a possibility. You didn't think of Ann Arbor back then as having that much in the way of business opportunities."

But here was one, and back he came. Two years later, in 1968, Chrysler bought King-Seeley's plants in the city of Ann Arbor and Scio Township and renamed them its Introl Division. The auto maker was primarily interested in King-Seeley's gauges and electronics products. The downtown plant manufactured only one product, a diesel engine governor, for one customer, Detroit Diesel Allison Division.

By 1978, Turner had risen to head of sales for Introl, but Chrysler itself was not doing that well. In fact, it was about to be rescued from the brink of bankruptcy by a U.S. government bailout. One of the requirements thereof was the disclosure of detailed corporate financial information to the Chrysler Loan Guaranty Board. "They did a complete asset-based appraisal on everything they owned," Turner recalls. "It was in a green book. We happened to see that when it came through, and we saw what they appraised the assets for out here, and we knew this was a product that had nothing to do with Chrysler's future. We were making governors for General Motors, in effect. It was only logical that at some point they would get rid of the plant at First and William."

That point came in October 1981, when Chrysler announced it would close both plants the following summer. By then, Turner had been negotiating to buy the Ann Arbor operation for a year or more.

"We were pretty much ignored at first," says Turner. "I think we pre-empted their ability to get their act in gear to find out what they wanted to sell when. When they saw it made sense, they started to look at us, and then when they saw we had the capability to buy it, they started to look seriously at our proposal."

The idea of buying his own business had occurred to him before. "I think, in all fairness, that I was always looking around for something to do on my own," he says. "Bob Gustine (who was to become the 'G' in GT Products), whom I had worked with since the King-Seeley days, and I would talk about it. We actually looked at the Porsche dealership in town, but Howard Cooper sort of had the inside track on that, and a lot more money than we did."

Money wasn't going to stop him this time. He and three friends pooled their resources, then secured a $7.5 million line of credit from Barclays American/Business Credit. "That's what made the whole deal work," says Turner. "You borrow on your assets and your receivables. It's typical asset lending, a leveraged buyout, the classic LBO of the '80s. It's become a pejorative now, for some reason, but we couldn't have done it otherwise. It was clearly highly leveraged."

This all happened while Turner was commuting between offices in Ann Arbor and Highland Park; Chrysler had made him sales manager at several plants, including Huntsville, Alabama, a forging plant in Indiana, and several facilities in Europe. If they were trying to wear him out, it didn't work.

While some observers expressed surprise that a partnership absent a "financial guy" could pull off what they achieved, Turner believes it would have been superfluous. "We didn't have any financial guys as such; we all came out of the sales department," he says. "There wasn't necessarily a need. We had a pretty good grasp on what we could make the part for, what we could buy the company for and make a return. This isn't rocket science; it's manufacturing."

There may also have been a tactical advantage in their perceived disadvantage. "We probably weren't as naive as we let people think we were," Turner smiles.

Another edge that first appeared in the guise of a problem was when the plant's employees twice failed to ratify the contract negotiated between GT Products, Turner's company, and the leadership of UAW Local 630. While the proposed contract did call for fairly dramatic cuts in wages and benefits, a key part of Turner's ability to get credit, GT had no legal obligation to deal with the union at all. The UAW's contract was with Chrysler, and it ended when Chrysler sold the plant.

Only those employees whose applications had been accepted by GT were eligible to vote, and both votes were close—35 to 27 on February 18, 1982, and 35 to 34, on a slightly revised proposal, six days later. Turner had less than three weeks to replace more than half of his workforce.

"The good news was we didn't have a union (to deal with)," he says. "Although unfortunately we had to hire off the street, which was pretty shaky, we were able to keep the best of the Chrysler employees, and that helped a lot."

So did the 16 percent unemployment rate in Michigan at the time. Despite offering $5 an hour for jobs that had fetched $11 just over a year before, GT received a thousand applications for about 50 openings.

"There isn't really a need for unions in today's marketplace," says Turner. "In days gone by, certainly, the workers had no voice, but as the free market becomes global and as the free market becomes freer, anyone with any skills can basically get a job anywhere he wants. A union can only guarantee good wages for a short period of time. A free market guarantees good wages indefinitely and rewards people for their ability."

An anti-union position is not necessarily anti-labor, he believes. "The unions are just like a private company taking advantage of its employees," he says. "The only ones who make out are the union leadership. When plants close, it doesn't change the UAW leadership. The only ones losing their jobs are the people in the plants."

GT Products went on not only to create jobs—its workforce quintupled between 1982 and 1998, when it was sold to Eaton Corporation—but also to reward the people who did them, as well as the company's owners.

"The media, in my opinion, way overemphasizes the ability of a CEO to somehow single-handedly change a company or make a company successful," Turner says. "Like a football team, it's only as good as the makeup of the components. Sure, the quarterback is important, but if the wide receiver doesn't catch the ball, what do you have?

"The bottom line is that the biggest challenge in business is people. You have to have a team effort. You have to inspire people to do the best they can. If you can accomplish that, you can have a successful business."

Turner saw this even more keenly than most, thanks to the circumstances under which GT Products was launched. "Once the union was voted down, we realized we had to live up to what we said we were going to do, because if we didn't, the employees would lose confidence in our integrity and we would lose their support," he says. "The only way to run a business is completely honestly and above-board. I think we were pretty successful in running a company where anyone could say what they believe, be treated in an honest manner, and have confidence that everyone would do what they said they would do. It's the key to business success in my book. If you had to limit it to one word, it would be 'honest,' first on the list."

In terms of inspiring a workforce, "rewards" and "respect" would also rank fairly high. "One thing we were real proud of is we were able to give a lot of people not only a chance to work but a chance to move up according to their ability," says Turner. "We had people who started on the floor move up to department heads. That's as high as you can go; department heads report to Jay Hartford. He's the president and chief operating officer of GT, and also a partner.

"We paid for college courses, too. I was proud of that, that we had so many success stories along the line. When you look over the ranks of GT Products, from top management on down, you don't find any Harvard MBAs, just basically guys who showed they could do the job and worked their way to the top. It becomes an example. We point out to people that you don't need overstated degrees to make it around here. Show you can do the job, and we'll give you a chance."

And when the partners sold GT to Eaton Corporation, they also gave a million dollars of the purchase price to their workers, distributed according to length of service. "That was a way of saying, 'Thank you for taking the ride with us,'" Turner says. "We treated them as shareholders as well, because in effect we always considered them as once-removed shareholders. We had a lot of people who stuck with us in the bad times as well as the good times, and they deserved every cent of it. Along the way, employees would ask if they could buy stock in the company, and it's not practical in a closely held business. But we hope this sort of made up for that."

The respect was manifested in the implementation of employee suggestions, most notably for a work week of four 10-hour days. "Once a month, I'd take three employees who wanted to go out to lunch. As a result of that, several good suggestions came up and one of them was the four-day work week. The only downside risk is what will your customers say, but we figured we could cover that in the obvious manner, still have people available and around, just not run a full shift on Friday unless we had to. We could also run an overtime shift on Friday and still have the weekend off. We gave it a try and it worked beautifully. We've done it ever since."

All of this is, of course, predicated on staying in business, and Turner knew from the first that the diesel governor that was his only product would soon be obsolete.

"We knew when we started that we probably had a 10-year window before things really went sour," says Turner, "meaning that mechanical governors would be nothing but service. They would no longer be a manufactured item."

It actually took 16 years before Detroit Diesel finally stopped making the two-cycle engines that used the governors, but sales had already started to dip alarmingly by the mid-1980s.

"We had to find a new product fast," says Turner. "That's when we started with valves. That was Rudy."

And Rudy was Rudy Bergsma, who spent 31 years with King-Seeley and then Introl, eventually rising to chief engineer before retiring in 1982 rather than accept a transfer to Alabama. Four years later, Turner prevailed upon the then 63-year-old Bergsma to return to work as a consultant, although he wound up coming to work every day anyway.

"Rudy and I would sit together and try to figure out what we could do," says Turner. "We looked at the PCV valve first, and then we hit the rollover business at a great time because Ford was having the famous van fires, and for that matter everybody was having problems."

The problem was a phenomenon known as "corking," which would happen when the gasket in a valve that vented fumes from a car's gas line would get stuck, bottling up the emissions. The results were potentially disastrous, both from the pressure in the tank itself and the flammability of the concentrated gases.

Bergsma had learned from former colleagues that neither Ford nor General Motors was at work on a new valve. This was after he had proposed redesigning the valve to Chrysler. The troubled auto maker shied away from the investment; Turner didn't.

"We knew our competitor's valve was corking, so simply by producing a non-corking valve we became a hot item pretty much out of the chute," says Turner. "Hot" as in running the factory around the clock for a year to fill the first batch of orders from Ford, which was itself hot to get the valves once its own engineers got a look at them.

"Rudy can design more on a napkin over lunch than most guys in their lifetime," Turner enthuses. Turner kept him in napkins, so to speak, and Bergsma responded with designs. Since he joined the company, an astonishing 80 percent of the products designed by its engineering staff (which grew from one to more than several dozen by the time the company was sold) have been commercially successful. One of them, in particular, became even more lucrative than the non-corking valve.

Called the ORVR (onboard refueling vapor recovery) valve, it channels gas tank fumes back to the engine, which reduces emissions. This is not only noble and desirable but also increasingly mandatory. U.S. Environmental Protection Agency regulations required 40 percent of all 1998 passenger cars to have such a valve, and they will be compulsory equipment on all cars in the 2000 model year. GT's ORVR valves are currently installed on all GM cars, 80 percent of Ford's, and 50 percent of Chrysler's.

"Everything keeps notching up," says Turner. "Some lines, they've been running pretty much around the clock. Where we can't get enough product out on time, we're running a lot of overtime, a lot of Fridays and Saturdays." Sales passed the $50 million mark in 1997 and exceeded $80 million in 1998, when the company was sold to Eaton.

"A growth pattern like we've been on, where you go from 30-some million dollars to 80-some million in a couple of years, really puts pressure on everyone," he says. "For us, finding the business was no challenge at all. Assuming you have sales, the biggest challenge to me is the quality and timeliness of your effort to get your product out, and that depends on people."

Thus, Turner's focus on the company's relationship with the workforce. Thus, too, that workforce's response with both the quantity and quality of its products. Every single valve that is built is tested before it is shipped. GT made millions of valves for six years for Ford before the company had its first warranty claim due to a GT part. Such reliability holds down warranty costs (Detroit Diesel's fell 85 percent due to GT's improvements in its fuel pump), and that keeps the customers happy.

GT's success had attracted many suitors before Eaton. "We kissed a lot of frogs before we found a prince," says Turner, "or a princess in this case. Eaton was the perfect candidate in that they are in the fuel systems business, and they have a lot of parts in the front of the car, and of course we monopolize the fuel tank at the rear of the car and we also make fuel senders. It gives them perfect synergy for the fuel system front and back."

Turner continues to think of GT as "we," even though he has actually been retired since he and his partners sold out to Eaton. When he's not in Colorado skiing or in Europe or Japan watching his son, Matthew, race sports cars, Turner divides his time between Michigan and Florida, where he maintains his legal residence. Matthew is Eaton's European sales representative; selling apparently keeps company with fast and classy cars in the gene pool's affections.

"I've always been a car nut," says the senior Turner. "For years, I played around with sports cars. I used to compete in Sports Car Club of America races and, after I had one arm, I won a hill climb in Ohio with a '57 Ferrari. In fact, Fred Leydorf, who was one of our four original partners and investors in GT Products, was president of the Ferrari Club. That's how I met him. We used to race together and play around with cars together."

He now owns "maybe a dozen" autos. "To call it a collection is way too pompous," he says, "but basically they're collector cars: Ferraris, Porsches, hot rods. My son just raced a Viper at the 24 Hours of LeMans. They took fifth in their class, 19th overall."

Both Matthew and his younger sister, Laura, a 1998 graduate of Dartmouth, have followed their father's tracks, if not all of his footsteps. Laura was captain of the ski team at Dartmouth, a Division One school in the sport, for three years, and Matthew captained the club team at the University of Michigan. Laura was also an English major, and has started a career in advertising, one of the fields that tempted her father early on.

"I'm a big believer in the individual in society and in the free marketplace," he says, "and certainly I feel I'm an example of the benefits of living in the only country in the world that offers any type of entrepreneur the advantages that have been afforded me. That's why everybody looks to us as an example of how a free marketplace should be run. I will always be a proponent of anything along that line. Unfortunately, even though we probably still have the best system in the world, it's extremely disappointing in many aspects. We all agree that Jefferson was a genius and started out correctly, and it went downhill from then on. It's too bad. Congress seems to get in the way, such as with the tax code. I don't mind paying taxes, but why does the code have to be that thick? I'm not a total dunce. But I can't read my return even after it's been prepared for me. That's our Congress at work."

Not that Turner admits to possessing any rare expertise. He thinks the singularity of entrepreneurial ability has been as exaggerated as the role of the CEO in a company's success. It's the will, not the skill, that's hard to find.

"People don't realize there has to be at least a thousand middle managers out there in the Big Three who could leave tomorrow and be successful in running their own company if that's what they desire to do," he says. "Anybody with good basic skills and good basic people skills, if they choose to run their own company, should take a try at it. I think the media somehow tends to over-state the ability that it takes. The only thing an entrepre-neur really does differently than anyone else is he's will-ing to take a risk. Other than that, an entrepreneur could be any good manager anywhere. Of course, you have to have the will to do it. You have to want to."

And, he adds, "You have to have a wife who supports the idea. I remember discussing it, buying Introl, with Jan, and she said, 'If you don't try it, you'll regret it the rest of your life. You'd better get it out of your system.' Without her support, I wouldn't have been able to do it. It needs to be a team effort."

Despite his air of nonchalance—a word *The Ann Arbor Observer* used three times in the first four paragraphs of a 1982 profile—Turner's will has never been in question, certainly not by him. His relationship to God's will, how-ever, has been a persistent challenge.

"I've always had what I consider a strong belief in a supreme being," he says, "and I would say that the most difficult thought process during my life has been trying to define man's position with his own God. I've certainly always felt, and some of this may be because of the high-risk lifestyle and the accidents, that in some little way I may be fulfilling some purpose somewhere. I may be doing something right, balanced by doing a lot of things wrong. I'm certainly not saying that I've come to any con-clusions that are meaningful."

Jan's father was a Methodist minister and president of Garrett Theological Seminary at Northwestern University when Jan met Turner, and they have actively supported Calvary Methodist Church in Ann Arbor and the Campus Crusade for Christ. However, Turner is far from certain that institutionalized religion is the most effective medium for exploring fundamental theosophical questions.

"Unfortunately, religion is sometimes like Congress," he says. "They seem to get in the way, they harm more than they help. The institution becomes predominant; you have other men making decisions for you, which is probably the worst position you can be in in life."

Turner likes the positions he's in now—on the slopes, at the races, and en route. He sits on a few boards, but his dual residency limits much of that activity, and "other than that, I really have no intentions right now," he says. "I'm not actively looking for anything. However, if something came along that we could invest in or of a charitable nature, that would somehow light my fire, I might get interested."

Maybe it will be the Amherst and Janeth Turner Foundation, which was funded and began operation in 1999 with Janeth as president. Or maybe not.

"My approach to life is that, at some point, you have to realize you're on the downhill side of your performance curve," he says. "Although I certainly may still be able to do a couple of things correctly, I wouldn't oversell that position. I could help somebody out doing something. And who knows? I've always believed in some sort of divine direction in life. Maybe there's something out there that needs to be done before it's all over.

"If not, I'll sit and look at the water. That would be okay with me."

"You've got to give it everything on every single play."

Monty Vincent

Like the kid who drives his high school guidance counselor nuts because he just can't decide on a career, Monty Vincent still doesn't see himself in terms of categories. By his own reckoning, Vincent led at least seven lives when he was an undergraduate at Lewis and Clark College in Portland, Oregon, and that was after he had already realized one boyhood ambition—serving in the Navy like his father, uncle, brother and cousins before him. That experience unexpectedly got him into electronics, much as going to Lewis and Clark on a football scholarship unexpectedly got him into biology.

It started in a conversation with his older (by three years) brother Larry, just out of military service himself and always setting the bar pretty high for his only sibling. "He said there was a new field opening up, and the base course was 54 weeks and it covered not only what he was trained on but also computers, which were then being put into the fleet," says Vincent. "It was the longest school that the Navy offered and seemed to be the most advanced technology they offered, so I took the test and was selected to be one of those people. They would train us and then put us on a ship when they installed the equipment on a ship. So that's how I got into electronics.

"When I was in the Navy, I really studied. You were either in class or studying 10 hours a day because if you didn't pass the exam each Monday morning, you took the week over. And if you didn't pass two weeks in a row, you went to sea and chipped paint and washed dishes. That's really where I learned to study. I rose through the ranks by passing every exam and taking correspondence courses. So I came out as an E-5 in three years, which is steaming through."

He says the plan was "when I got out of the Navy that I would continue to pursue that avenue, and I was going to live with my brother in Corvallis and become an electrical engineer."

His brother did, in fact, fashion a distinguished career as an engineer. For Monty, however, it would not be that clear-cut.

The first complication was football. Vincent had been all-conference at Tigard High School in suburban Portland and continued to play for the Navy team in San Diego. When he came back, his stepsister and her husband were living with the family while the latter finished his degree. "He was a great athlete," says Vincent, "and he convinced me that I should take a crack at college football. Between him and my high school coach, who by then was assistant at Oregon State, they got me a scholarship to a small school, because I wasn't big enough, mean enough or fast enough to play in the Pac-8."

The school was Lewis and Clark College, which "had a fetish for football in those days," says Vincent. "They had won the national small-college championship in 1950 and thought they had a shot at another. So I took the scholarship and went on to Lewis and Clark, which is probably the best decision I ever made in my life."

Ironically, the fact that he played football at all had

nothing to do with any decisions on his part. After his schoolteacher mother died of cancer when he was nine, Vincent's father sent his two sons to St. Mary's Home for Boys, just outside of Beaverton, where they lived for two years.

"In the '40s, there weren't support services available for single parents," he says. "I got a good taste of religion, working within the rules, and sports, and learned to be independent at ten years of age. If you didn't take care of yourself, no one else did. The true orphans were actually looked after better by the nuns than students like myself who were boarded there. Not that it was necessarily bad, but at ten, you were really taught to be independent. You did what you were supposed to do."

That included going out for football. "One of the first days I was there, the coach said, 'You're the new Vincent kid, aren't you? Well, I want you out for football.' So I went out, got suited up, and started playing football. A couple of weeks later, he came to me and said, 'You're not Larry Vincent. I'm looking for the eighth grader Larry Vincent. You're only in the fifth grade; fifth graders can't play football.' My brother had never had any inkling. He was tall and thin and very bright. I was short and squat and found that I loved to play football."

That love persisted through high school, where his agenda was "play football, chase skirts, and, almost as a dream, go to the University of Oregon and play for the Ducks and become an architect. Norm Van Brocklin had been at Oregon and Oregon was big-time football. That's why Oregon was a dream. I don't know why architecture. But neither one was a serious possibility."

The scholarship offer, however, was not only serious but also essential. "Lewis and Clark was about four or five times more expensive than Oregon State, so the only way I could afford to go there was to get an athletic scholarship," Vincent says. "The original thought was, hell, I can play football for a couple of years, get a scholarship, just have a ball, and then when I get through my sophomore year, transfer down to Oregon State and get into engineering school."

Instead, he found himself seduced by Lewis and Clark just as he was seduced by football. "Lewis and Clark was a significantly different kind of school than major universities," he says. "We had a PhD for about every 12 students. We had no teaching assistants. The school was not films and computer-driven; it was the hands-on, eyeball-to-eyeball kind of teaching. And it was international in scope, in that when we studied anything, they took a much more worldwide approach than most academic institutions that I'm familiar with. They had a very heavy base program that every student had to go through, civilization and humanities, an integrated program that was team-taught, so that when you studied, say, Greece, you would have lectures in the architecture by architects, and when you wrote papers for English, they would be on Greece, so they totally integrated. If we studied medieval history, professors of art would teach the art. It was just incredible; it integrated everything, instead of taking bits and pieces and trying to put them together."

The Pioneers never did win that second national championship—"We ended up being an average team," Vincent says—but his football experience inadvertently led him to another love, biology. "In addition to the high demands of that core curriculum, plus practice hours, in the fall of my freshman year I had to fit in some hours of non-core classes, and the only one that made any sense whatsoever was a course in biology."

This was before the days when a faculty member's job description included making students feel comfortable. "The first day that we met," Vincent recalls, "the professor asked, 'How many football players are there in this course? Raise your hands.' Being freshmen and proud of our athletic ability, we all raised our hands. Then he looked at us and said, 'I'll guarantee none of you can make it through this class. There are a lot easier courses for you guys to be in. It's a waste of your time and mine for you to be here.' Some of the guys took his hint and left. Another young fellow, who went on to become a dentist, and I stuck it out. As I recall, we both four-pointed the course. I was in that course because it was the only course given at the time of day that I had for it, but he challenged us, so I swore I was gonna stick it out and prove him wrong."

Vincent far exceeded merely proving the professor wrong. Only three years later, he had earned his degree in biology, capped by one of those Lewis and Clark requirements, a senior project that, as he says, "really taught you what biological research was.

"It was on the possibility of a commensal relationship between a type of rotifer—a cute little guy, he really is—and an asellus, a fresh-water invertebrate," Vincent recalls. "The rotifers have little hairs that rotate, and there are hundreds of different kinds. The asellus lived in rotted leaves in swamps, so you're wading out into swamps and picking through leaves. First you had to find the bloody things and identify the specific one that you were working with. One was a giant and the other was like a flea. Once you found the asellus, you had to wash it off, take the water from around where you found it, and see if you could find the specific rotifer in the effluent. Then you had to concentrate them and stain them to identify the species, and you had to make your own tools to work with these things, such as a little shovel that was actually a matchstick with one flattened, sharpened toothbrush bristle at the end to move the rotifers, and do all this work under dissecting binoculars."

He earned his degree early by going to school year-round, but his life was hardly one-dimensional. In addition to playing football and majoring in one of a demanding college's most demanding disciplines, he also found time to get married, father his first child, hold down a part-time job in real estate, belong to a fraternity and two clubs, and be sports editor of the Lewis and Clark yearbook.

"When I was with the science and biology geeks, I did things that science geeks do," he says. "When I was showing real estate, I had to be in real estate. And at the same time I was with the fraternity and hazing and doing all the crazy things you do. I look back on it and say it was a very involved time. But I think I've always tried to keep multiple things going in my life."

His chances for success in that department soared when he and Julie Aikman, his high school sweetheart, got married over Christmas break of his freshman year. They had already planned a spring wedding, but the holidays seemed to occasion a heightened sense of urgency.

"I really missed having a family," says Vincent, "and I'd been in love with her since I was 15 and she was 13. And my parents' home was going to be vacant until spring; my father was out of the area working, and my stepmother was in California visiting her sisters and was going to stay there through the winter. Julie worked, I had the GI Bill and the athletic scholarship, so with the free room and the other factors, we could survive. We got married in three days—had to break a lot of rules, go in front of judges, get the team physician to draw our blood, but we got it all done."

The news was not received placidly. "My mother-in-law about had a stroke," he says. "My father-in-law looked at me and said, 'How in the hell can you support a wife?' But we calculated out that we could do it."

And then there was the clincher—"I just wanted Julie to be my wife."

Eleven months later, daughter Kim was born. Moreover, "I'd fallen in love with biology," says Vincent. "I took all the classes to become a high school football coach and a biology teacher."

Meanwhile, on the domestic front, his stepmother not so cordially invited him and his young family to move out of his father's house. They were now living in a tiny apartment, and Vincent took a part-time job showing model homes in order to procure both some income and a place to study.

"Working for a builder worked well for me because, with the rainy season in Oregon, no one likes to build from October through April; everything's so damn wet," he says. Hardly anyone looks at model homes, either, but they still had to be open for the few who did. Finding himself with what he deemed "extra hours on my hands" after the football season ended in December, he "manned the models" in the late afternoons and early evenings.

"I could go to a model house, put a pot of coffee on, stick a frozen meal in the oven, and study," he says, "so I volunteered to take all of those hours that, if you were just a regular salesman sitting there, you would die of boredom. If a day went by and nobody showed up, it didn't bother me a bit. I was really there studying. I ended up being the number-one salesman in the company, doing it part-time."

About midway through his junior year, he began to think seriously about going to medical school. "Some of my professors were pushing me more toward research, however," he remembers. Then he learned that he had enough credit hours to finish school in three years, an academic achievement that eluded even his brother.

After 40 years of "me being jealous of my brother being the great student," Vincent was to learn that Larry, whom he had tried so hard to emulate, was secretly envious of his kid brother's ability to get good grades—although not the equal of Larry's—with so little apparent effort. "And the final blow was when I got my degree in three years," he says.

At the time, however, it only added to a list of options that already seemed too long, one that was complicated by the impending arrival of another little Vincent.

"The decision was one of the toughest I ever had to make in my life," he says. "Medical school, graduate school, coaching and teaching, and one I haven't mentioned yet...business. And that one came in kind of haphazardly."

That late starter eventually lapped the field, but not without overcoming Vincent's skepticism about it, which persisted for years. One factor was academic fatigue; he had spent 54 straight weeks in school in the Navy, followed by three full years at Lewis and Clark, and was ready to at least try something different. Another factor was two job offers in business.

Says Vincent: "I met a pharmaceutical representative when I was sitting in a waiting room while my wife was at the gynecologist's. We talked about his job, and then it was out of my mind. Then I saw an ad, about a year before graduating, from a pharmaceutical company. I called the guy and said I was still in school, my major at that time was pretty strongly oriented to pre-med, but I had one child and a second one on its way, and I wasn't so sure that I could stand going to medical school and I would just like to talk to him about the job. When I was graduating, he called and said they had an opening and he'd like to talk to me again."

Nor had the real estate company forgotten him; the sales manager there called and offered him the job of sales manager for half of the company, the west side of Portland. "That was the first time I really thought of business as a career," he says, "and it all kind of just happened."

The real estate job was the first to be dismissed. "I had no interest in it," he says. "I didn't like the culture of that kind of business, but it got me started thinking about business. Then when this major international company that was doing great things in the pharmaceutical field came after me and told me about their home office in New York, six weeks of training there, getting a new car, getting a salary that was 25 percent more than any teaching jobs I was offered, I figured, what the hell, let's give this a try. If I don't like it, I can save enough money to go to medical school, it'll be a nice break, and working for a pharmaceutical company I could learn some things about the medical field."

The company was Pfizer, Inc., and Vincent would spend the next 11 years of his life rising rapidly through its ranks. That sentence makes it sound simple enough, but it required a certain boldness on Vincent's part to set the chain of events in motion.

"I had never thought in my life of working for a major

international company," he says. "In those days, in Portland, Oregon, you didn't think of that. You were in agriculture or timber-based industries, or you were in a service industry—teaching, police, government, civil service. There were no major international businesses located in the area, and I had never known anyone who had worked in that kind of company. It was a little scary. Big companies were a different world from the one I was raised in. My father was really an entrepreneur; he had owned businesses or run them most of his life. But those were local businesses."

They included various trucking enterprises, and running a restaurant and bar. "A very unsuccessful restaurant and bar," says Vincent. "He worked long hours for very little profit, and that was kind of my idea of what business was about."

His father's first name was Esmond, though he went by "Vince," and he gave his sons conventional names. When Vince was about eight years old, his father was killed in a logging accident. He worked on farms for a while to help support his mother and two siblings, then got a job driving a truck for the Portland Fish Company when he was 15. At the time he applied for the job, he had never driven any vehicle, much less a truck, in his life. He eventually started his own trucking company. When it was wiped out in the Depression, he went back to driving, this time for a beer distributor, and wound up managing the company.

On the one hand, there were Vincent's dreams of being a doctor or teacher or coach, and an inherent wariness of "business." On the other, there were "financial security, a new car, a trip to New York...and I knew there were a dozen things I could do if it didn't pan out."

First, he had to sell Julie on his becoming a salesman. As he had assessed his career choices in his last year at Lewis and Clark, she had told him "You can be anything you want when you graduate—doctor, coach, teacher—anything except a salesman." Fortunately, he made the sale.

At first, he was a student, attending Pfizer training

classes in Brooklyn and living in Manhattan. The role of student was one he undertook regularly, preferably as part of his compensation, and New York was a venue he came to revisit.

But in the summer of 1960, he was back in Portland, selling pharmaceuticals to doctors and hospitals. And in 1961, he was Pfizer's top sales representative in the region and number 17 of 600 nationally. "I was totally honest with myself and my customers," he says, "and I worked damn hard. I used to work at being efficient in covering my territory. Although the Pfizer structure tried to force that on you, any smart guy that wanted to take off and play golf could always beat the system. But I didn't. I went with the system and I followed it."

All the way to its limits, where what was allowable included "a lot of entrepreneurial kinds of things."

One of them was the vaccine gun. "Flu vaccine had become a commodity in the mid-'50s," says Vincent, "and big hunks of business were mass inoculations like the teachers association, lumber mills, the firemen, etc."

Unfortunately, it had also become a volatile commodity, on both the supply and demand ends. The manufacturers had to guess right about both the strain to prepare and the public's perception of its need. "There might be a big scare one year so everyone would get vaccinations, and the next year there'd be no big scare so no one would get vaccinations," says Vincent. That led to pharmacists, who bought from the sales reps and supplied the physicians, hedging their bets by ordering from multiple companies.

"Whoever came through first, they took, and canceled the rest of the orders," says Vincent. "It was a real bad situation."

Then he heard about a mass inoculation instrument that the military was using, "where they would actually shoot the vaccine into your arm rather than inject it with a needle. Immediately, I understood the value of this."

He bought one of the injection guns and formed a partnership with a pharmacist friend who had an autoclave— the device had to be disassembled and sterilized between uses—and contacts.

"I sold the vaccine to him, and we went out and sold it to large inoculation programs with the idea that if they used my vaccine, they could also use my gun," Vincent says. "I charged the same fee for my gun as they would pay for syringes and needles. Every time they pulled the trigger on my gun, I picked up like 20 cents, which covered the cost of buying the gun and maintaining it, plus a little profit, plus we locked up all the mass inoculation programs in the Pacific Northwest almost instantly. I sold more vaccine in the good years and the bad years than all the other representatives of my company on the West Coast combined, and more than any of our competitors. These little kinds of entrepreneurial things paid off. I was promoted."

Repeatedly, as a matter of fact. By 1965, he was based in San Francisco as western regional manager of the company's new diagnostic division, which he helped launch. "I moved out of the pharmaceutical side," he says. "The diagnostic division supplied chemicals and immunological reagents and biological materials to laboratories. We acquired about four companies to start out. Because of my background in biological science, this worked out really well for me. I was really at home."

He was also equally successful. The diagnostics division repeatedly offered him jobs in New York City and he repeatedly turned them down. Such a move represented a statement he wasn't yet prepared to make. Says Vincent: "Leaving the West Coast and going to Manhattan to work and to live really meant a commitment to this career vs. 'Hey, if this doesn't work out, I can always go back and coach,' so I resisted a number of opportunities in both the pharmaceutical business and the diagnostic business."

But eventually, he says, he had nowhere else to go: "I was in charge of the western third of the United States, and if I was going to do anything further, I had to move."

Besides, the job they wanted him for—Product and Special Projects Manager of Pfizer Diagnostics—would make him part of a team looking at companies and product lines for acquisition and "that sounded really interesting." He extracted a condition, however: If he were going to pledge himself to this business, and the business of business, he expected reciprocity.

The condition was this: "Fellas, my background is not business, my education is not business. If I come back, I'm making a commitment to be in business and your commitment to me is that I'm going to have to get educated. You've got to send me to, and pay for, any courses that will help me. And since the acquisition business isn't a nine-to-five job anyway, I think that could work out."

From the Wharton School of Finance to the New York Advertising Club, from the American Management Association to Dartmouth College, "wherever there was a course, I took it. If I was going to be in business, I had to know what I was doing."

One of Vincent's greatest gifts has been his ability to find room for his entrepreneurialism within the allowable limits of what companies wanted and needed. Thus, in fewer than eight years, the reluctant businessman started a division, moved to San Francisco to run it, then transferred to world headquarters, where he found himself commuting from Darien, Connecticut, to Manhattan every day (except when he was on the road evaluating potential acquisitions or going to school or meeting at the new plant and research center in Groton, Connecticut), and being groomed, he was told, for a division presidency.

Instead, he got a vice presidency, and it was in Ann Arbor, not New York. The promised position at Pfizer became vacant after his promotion to director of marketing, but an officer from another corporate division was hired to fill it. About six months later, he says, "We found out that he was only being temporarily parked there, and there was going to be another person brought in, also from outside our division. For the first time in the 12 years I worked at Pfizer, I felt depressed," he says. "At 35, it appeared I would have to put in another 15 years to reach top management there."

One of the potential acquisitions he had looked at was a place called Gelman Instruments. "We saw they really wouldn't fit into the Pfizer mode," says Vincent, "but they had some products that would fill out one of our lines, so Chuck Gelman and I continued a conversation about him building those products for us, but I could never sell that program internally. Pfizer's management had a great fear of instrumentation."

Right about the time Vincent got the bad news about his prospects at Pfizer, Gelman called and said he wanted to resume their discussions. "I told him frankly that I couldn't get the powers that be to accept handling instruments," Vincent recalls. "He said, 'Well, I'm down in the lobby of your building at 42nd and Second. Could I come up and talk to you anyway?' I said sure. When he got to my office, he said the phone call was a ruse, that what he really came to do was see if he could convince me to work for him."

Timing may not be everything, but it's way ahead of whatever is in second place. In the Vincents' case, that was location. "Since it was one-third of the way back toward the West Coast, Julie and I flew out, looked around the town and loved the Ann Arbor area, so I accepted the job, and we've been in Ann Arbor ever since," he says. "We never made it all the way back to the West Coast."

There were, of course, other factors relating to the company and the job itself. He would be vice president of sales and marketing, stock options would enhance his remuneration, and there would be opportunities for personal growth, always a powerful incentive for Vincent.

"While the pay was good at Pfizer, the living expenses basically used it up," he says. "At 35, with three kids and a wife and living close to Manhattan, I wouldn't see for many years ever getting significantly ahead financially. I would be on the treadmill. But with going to Gelman, the potential was there for much greater financial remuneration. I would also have full charge of all sales and marketing. So if I wanted something, it wasn't a big long negotiation. I would be a member of a small team of people running a full business, rather than a group of people in a division of a huge corporation, where it would take six months to even get a chance in front of the board of directors to make a presentation to acquire a company. At Chuck's size, and since he was the founder and major entrepreneur, if we wanted to make a decision, it could be done in days or hours rather than months and months. It was a fresh new challenge, I was a big fish in a little pond rather than a little fish in a big pond. And if it didn't work out, I was one-third closer to Oregon."

The move paid off handsomely, in every sense of the phrase, for both Vincent and the company. In his six years at the helm of Gelman's marketing program, from January 1972 to December 1977, the company's annual sales more than quadrupled, from $5 million to $22 million. Hitherto, the Gelman Instrument Company had focused on designing and manufacturing instruments and accessories, filters among them, for laboratories and industry, but a significant part of its growth in the 1970s (when the company also changed its name to Gelman Sciences, Inc.) was in the fairly new area of medical filtration devices.

On the wall above the desk in Vincent's home office, directly in his line of vision when he turns to the window, he has affixed a framed yellowed clipping that says, "The business of business is to address the major unmet needs of society." He says he "tore that out of something, it must be 30 years ago, and I kept it to remind me on a daily basis."

It's been in every office he's had since. "It's good socially, but it's awful damn good practical marketing, too," he says. The medical device business is a case in point.

"The opportunity was there," says Vincent. These devices could solve problems, say in intravenous applications, where the only option was bulky stainless steel hardware that required repeated disassembly, cleaning and sterilization, and whose connections were for industrial use, not IV tubing.

"What we were doing at Gelman, and what Millipore, another major manufacturer, was starting to do, was design and develop lightweight plastic housings that could be made in large quantities at relatively low cost," he says. "They could be sterilized, packaged and disposed of after a single use. So we took a laboratory or industrial material and by vertically upgrading that material into a medical device, we made it useful in a whole new field."

Gelman and Vincent evolved a harmonious professional relationship, lubricated by booming sales. "It worked out wonderfully, the whole time," says Vincent. "Chuck really gave me both the responsibility and the authority."

By the end of 1976, Vincent saw what seemed to him a fairly gaping need that could only be corrected, or at least addressed, with bold strokes. The process began at a routine business luncheon.

"I was complaining to their face about production not making the quantity of product I needed, engineering not developing the new products I needed, quality control not doing its job," he recalls. "I was really lambasting, I think, every department in the business, and either at that luncheon, or shortly thereafter, Chuck says, 'If you think you can do it better, why don't you do it yourself?' I stopped at his office afterward and said, 'Do you mean that?'"

A few minutes later, they had come up with the basic foundation of a new Medical Device Division, with Vincent as its president. The division had become necessary, says Vincent, "because it really had some requirements that were significantly different than the requirements for their standard products, and it was a different mode of business than we had with our standard products. And Chuck supported that effort and it became one of the more successful parts of the company."

The division's annual growth and profits compounded at nearly 40 percent in the seven years Vincent ran it. Along the way, he also oversaw the planning and construction of a new, 40,000-square-foot facility to house the division.

And he began to see unmet needs and untapped markets that would be better served outside the Gelman context. "We had really been a pioneer in a new field," says Vincent, "taking the laboratory/industrial filter out of its raw form and transforming it into filter devices for a variety of applications. It was an area that had explosive opportunities in growth."

What he was beginning to envision was a company that would draw on the complementary skills and experience of several colleagues and himself to meet the needs—not only unmet but, in many cases, unimagined—of a different population than the one Gelman serviced. Arbor Technologies, as he had named the new enterprise, "would be more of a medical company and do more medical kinds of applications," he says, "where within the Gelman corporate structure, the major part of the business was more laboratory and industrial. At Arbor tech [the dba of Arbor Technologies] we transposed the concept of a filter company who made some medical filters to a medical company who specialized in filters. We changed the paradigm."

The shift began in the fall of 1984. Attila Vadney, who had been vice president of operations for Gelman's Medical Device Division, had retired. Shortly thereafter, Vincent also left Gelman and contacted his former colleague, but Vadney's contract prohibited him from working for a competitor for a few months more.

Meanwhile, "I started pulling together the business plan and doing all the things you need to do to start a company," says Vincent. And he was doing it in his home. "I shut our dining room off, moved in file cabinets, stapled a green felt cloth over my wife's dining room table, and got a bookcase, calculator, a few of the basics," he says.

He added Mary Boomus, his successor as president of Gelman's Medical Device Division, to the new company. "Mary let me know that she would like to join the new organization," says Vincent. "I agreed, so she then resigned from Gelman and became my first employee and partner. I was the founder of the Medical Device Division and had the biomedical knowledge to understand the medical applications, Attila could design and build the equipment to make this stuff and had been the production head, and Mary was an industrial engineer who had specialized in plastics. She was the engineering person actually developing the products in the MDD's early days. Almost everything it was doing had originated from one of the three of us—in products, applications, markets, etc. So the three of us started addressing areas that we knew had not been tackled previously. It was the birth of a new industry, if you will."

The team was rich in resources but, because of its provenance, its members felt obliged to tread carefully. "Very specifically, we stayed away from those things we had done a lot of at Gelman," says Vincent, "so for the first few years, there wasn't a lot of direct competition. If we'd used a material in the past, we'd use a different material at Arbor tech. If we'd used a technology in the past, we would use a new technology in the future. We did not want to be just a new, small Gelman Medical Device Division, and we didn't want anyone to say we walked out using the same technologies.

"For one thing, we wanted to try some new technologies in production, and we wanted to look at some new markets in the marketing side," he adds. "For another, we didn't want to be thought of as just a knockoff of what we had previously done. Third, and not least, is we didn't want Chuck suing us for walking out with his technology."

The company was incorporated on New Year's Day, 1985, but didn't really begin operations until the following April 1, when they went around and picked up checks from their initial investors. "We kind of picked that date purposely," says Vincent. He worked at his dining room table, Vadney worked in his basement machine shop, and Boomus worked in her family's den.

By August, they were out of basements, dining rooms and dens, and into a facility in Airport Plaza, an industrial park across I-94 from Briarwood Mall. "They had what I fondly call rent-a-slots, buildings cut up into five different units, each being 40 feet wide and 80 feet long," says Vincent. "Since we really expected to grow, we had in our lease agreement the right of first refusal on the next two slots at all times, and the owners, Jake Haas and Don Butcher, were very cooperative in not putting anyone into adjacent slots who would invest a lot in any internal structures. We kept expanding with them until we built our own facility down State Street and moved in the spring of '95."

When they initially moved to Airport Plaza, they hired their first employee, John Costello, Jr., "who is still with the company and is now in charge of manufacturing," says Vincent. "We, all four of us, ran the molding machines, swept the floors, cleaned the toilets, and ran to answer the phone. Our first products started going into the market in the winter of '86, and we hired our first actual production people that spring."

Early in the following year, a major potential customer expressed interest in the fledgling concern. Whatman PLC, a centuries-old British company and the world leader in making filter papers for chemical analysis, wanted to expand into membrane filtration. "They were interested in jumping into the new technology of filter devices," says Vincent. "They came to us and wanted a broad line of scientific laboratory filter devices. To fund the operation, we sold them 10 percent of the company, with those funds to be invested to allow us to bring out the product line, and we signed a mutual exclusive distribution agreement for laboratory filters worldwide."

Laboratory filters were not exactly what they had originally had in mind, but the deal meant too much to the company for them to pass it up. As it turned out, the relationship not only enhanced Arbor tech's product portfolio, but also forced it to diversify its customer base.

"We took some innovative new steps in design, development and manufacturing, which in turn proved to be very successful in the marketplace, and our relationship with Whatman continued to grow over the years," says Vincent. "It was also a stimulus to us to push hard in the medical field because we did not want to become just a supplier to Whatman. We set a goal that we never wanted more than 25 percent of our business to be with any one customer, so we had to run to keep up our sales of other products. At times, it was difficult, because the Whatman product line became so successful."

The company finally got into the black in 1991. "There was a time when our burn rate was $3,000 a day," says Vincent, "so it took a lot of gumption to continue to spend the money and continue to invest in product development, people development, systems development, company development. With hindsight, I wonder why some days I didn't just get up and take 3,000 one-dollar bills and sit in front of my fireplace and roll them into balls and chuck them into the flames. But those were thoughts that never even crossed my mind at the time. We had a plan, we had confidence, and I had the support of my board, my staff and in the good and bad days, we just kept choppin' away, gettin' the job done."

And done well. Arbor tech developed more than 100 commercially successful filtration devices in its first eight years in operation, was listed as one of the fastest-growing private companies in Michigan annually from 1990, the year it won the state's Leading Edge Technologies Award, through 1993, and maintained a yearly growth rate of 40 percent.

Attila Vadney retired from the new company in 1987 and was replaced by Leonard Knoedler, a senior manufacturing officer from Sarns 3M who was recommended by Dick Sarns, one of Arbor tech's original investors. "Leonard bought Attila's stock," Vincent recalls. "He had put in 26 years of manufacturing of medical products at Sarns, so this really benefited us in getting our manufacturing into a medical high-volume mode. The three of us basically ran the company through the spring of '95, when we moved into our new facility, and at that time, I created a new management group of people and transferred the authority and responsibility from the three of us, who had been owner-managers, to this larger group which included the head of engineering, the head of research, the production supervisor, the head of quality assurance, the head of finance, and formed a real team approach to managing the company. That was a major shift from three people running the company and making all the major decisions."

The new facility was also a major shift, a 30,000-square-foot factory and headquarters on State Road south of the Ann Arbor Municipal Airport that cost $2.5 million to build.

"That period of growth was not exactly straight line," says Vincent. "We hit situations where markets exploded on us because of new technologies and new applications, and we were running three shifts seven days a week to keep up with shipments, but the field became more and more competitive. We pioneered, we grew fantastically, things were rosy, and then the competitors' troops stormed in and battered us."

Just nine months after the company moved into its new digs, Whatman came calling again, this time as a suitor. Whatman's original agreement with Arbor tech included the option to negotiate the purchase of more stock, but the price was never established and the option had, in fact, expired by early 1995, when the firm indicated its renewed interest.

"During this period of time (the early '90s), Pall Corporation and a number of other lesser players in the world had come to us," says Vincent. "How many were serious, I don't know, but I probably got an average of a letter every three weeks wanting to discuss acquisition, merger, investment, etc., and I had ignored them all, basically, until Whatman made a serious re-entry into that discussion. And then I had to take Pall's interest seriously because they are the dominant filter company in the world."

There were several reasons for negotiating with Whatman. "When we started Arbor tech, we had a master plan, and in the spring of '95, we had reached most of the major goals that we had set for ourselves: We had about

100 employees, an incredibly great new factory, a good management staff, and we had gone into and pioneered a number of markets that we wanted to address, so we were now looking at what we were going to do in kind of the second phase of Arbor tech. Also, Leonard and I were looking at hitting our 60s, and you have to start thinking about what's going to happen to you and what's going to happen to the company on your retirement. The other thing was looking at the marketplace and seeing the consolidation that was taking place in the industry. The route to market for a large share of our business was tied to Whatman, and we realized that if we didn't join with Whatman, they were going to continue to acquire companies, and it was not guaranteed that we would continue to be their premier supplier of filter devices."

The fate of those 100 employees was a major consideration, Vincent says: "When Pall came to me, they wanted a ballpark valuation put on my company, and I jacked up what I was looking toward possibly obtaining from Whatman by 25 percent and chucked it at Pall, because I could not envision that Arbor tech as it was, in the location that it was, would survive a merger with a Pall."

Vincent was convinced that a sale to Whatman would produce a different story. "We made the decision to put our company in the hands of Whatman. That was the best for Arbor tech, its people, and its customers," he says. "They find this a very good location to do what we do, they've transferred manufacturing here from other locations, and they dramatically increased their research budget, so they're funding a significant expansion of work at the University of Michigan."

The outcome is even more gratifying given that this is also the site that Vincent and his family eventually chose to call home.

All of the Vincents' offspring have attended college in Michigan, they all married Michiganders, and two of them still live in the state. And, as he did in college, Monty has participated in numerous "extra-curricular activities" in the community, running the gamut from president of the

Pioneer High School Booster Club to co-founder and chairman of the board of the Michigan Technology Council to vice president of the board of Peace Neighborhood Center.

The Michigan Technology Council got started when "the University of Michigan pulled together a group of six or seven of us from the major technical companies in Ann Arbor," says Vincent. "There were perceived to be glass partitions between industry, academia and government. The example I gave was one Sunday I sat reading an article in the newspaper about a professor at the University of Michigan who was a consultant to the Brazilian government on the quality of potable water. In the same paper, there was also an article about the problems they were having in the Ann Arbor water supply system. And at the same time, I was working at Gelman, where we made the equipment and supplies for a number of the laboratory tests used to control the quality of potable water. And it just became laughable to me that here are the three parts of the triangle—the end user, the world-class expert and the manufacturer of the equipment used—and that probably not any of us had ever talked to the other person."

Vincent says one of his "secret weapons" for assembling a quality workforce in a tight labor market was a willingness to hire women for key positions before, and not because, it was fashionable. "I had long ago found a gold mine in the marketplace, and that was that women were underutilized and underappreciated by industry in general, and I took advantage of that, because I had so much experience with really great people who happened to be female," he says. "Our management team (at Arbor tech) was basically half-female: the head of finance, the head of quality assurance, and the head of marketing were all women. And down through the ranks, by not having biases for gender or race or anything, it just expanded my opportunities to get good people."

Just as he doesn't consign other people to categories, he declines to identify himself that way. Rather, he sees himself in terms of setting out on quests, having adventures, tackling projects and mastering them—like turning education into enterprise, and vice versa; seeing a problem and solving it; seeing a need and meeting it; starting a business with a burn rate of three grand a day, or going to Kenya with his wife and two friends to spend their days among the Samburu tribe, or just erecting the 40-foot flagpole that his kids gave him for Christmas...by himself.

"You won't accomplish anything unless you try it," he says. "The scarier it sounds, maybe the better the opportunity to stretch yourself. I learned from my background in sports that if you really put out everything you've got every time you get a chance, somehow you'll always come out a winner. You can't just say you're going to hold something back for the next play or the next negotiation. You've got to give it everything on every single play."

And despite his retirement from Arbor tech at the end of 1997, he's still looking to get into the game.

"I'm open," he says, "for one more good challenge."

"I didn't want to believe other people's truths."

Iva Wilson

Glass ceilings can be broken. Obstacles can be overcome. Even iron curtains can be parted. After coping as a child with World War II and its aftermath in her native Croatia, Iva Wilson didn't find mere attitudes all that daunting.

When she was a little girl, living with her mother in Zagreb after her father was killed in action, she saw bodies floating down the Sava River. When her mother remarried, she saw the repressive Tito regime expropriate the company her stepfather had spent his life building. She also saw her great uncle return from America, only to be betrayed by the government he thought intended to build a comparable democracy in his native land. When she finally negotiated the labyrinth of red tape required to get a visa for graduate study in Germany, the UDBA, the Yugoslav secret police, had her under surveillance.

This was all before she got to America, and that was long before she became not only the first woman executive in the history of N.V. Philips (now Royal Dutch Philips) but also the first woman president of Philips Display Components.

"My mother was not only in charge of me but also everything else," says Wilson. "She was essentially my role model, so when people ask me how did a woman of your age get into your position, to me this question is totally out of place. In my world, I was supposed to do something, I was supposed to learn, I was supposed to become something so I could be independent and achieve my dreams."

Her mother was an attorney, in itself an uncommon career for a woman in that time and place, and her skills came in handy for Wilson more than once, especially when she was jousting with the UDBA.

Although hopes rose for a time after the end of the war, it soon became clear to the little girl that, in this new Yugoslavia, "the freedom everybody was talking about didn't seem like it was coming. We became a Communist country."

Her first experience with what that meant was when the man who became her stepfather was arrested and jailed. "He owned a factory that he built himself, making soap, sort of like Procter and Gamble," she says. "He did all this with his own hands; he was an entrepreneur. The government had to accuse him of something and convict him so they could take away his belongings, which they did."

At about the same time, her great uncle, the brother of her maternal grandfather, returned from America, where he had lived for more than 30 years. "He wanted to be in his home," says Wilson. "He believed that the Communists were bringing freedom for the working class, which is what he was. He wanted to be part of the new world that was promised to him, and so he returned. He came with his savings and his car, which was too big to fit on our street.

"This was 1948. I remember him lying on the couch in our living room and me sitting next to him and him telling me about America, and how he went there and why he went there and why he came back. I thought, well, this is really great, he thought he was going to find his world on the other side of the Atlantic but he realized his world was back here and he's going to be with us. I was very happy. Everyone who returned to Yugoslavia after the war had six months to decide whether to stay or go. After six months, he decided he's going to stay, he loves it here. Another brother was a Communist, a very prominent intellectual, and so everybody was happy. But then some interesting things happened."

First, he had to turn in his car; as a private citizen, he didn't have the right to own one. Then, he had to exchange all his American funds for the local currency...at the official rate of 50 dinars per dollar, compared to the 300 that each would have fetched on the black market. Overnight, his wealth was a sixth of what it had been.

"There was one thing after another," Wilson recalls. "Then one day I heard that he had gotten ill. He had lung cancer. Three months later, he died. Then I heard in the family the discussions about what had happened, how it happened that he didn't want to fight for his life. He didn't want to see a doctor; he wasn't interested at all. His dream was shattered, his dream of coming to his home country and having it become what America was not, a place where working-class people would have the same power as the capitalists had in America.

"This was when I started for the first time questioning the right from the wrong. Who's telling the proverbial truth, and what is truth all about? Today, I know more than ever, there's not only one truth. There are many truths. And the only truth I can go by is my own truth. From that point on, the only thing I was always looking for was what is it that I need to do and learn so I can be free like my great uncle wanted to be. I didn't want to believe other people's truths."

She did, however, want to please her mother. "Her dream was to be a doctor," says Wilson, "so she, like many parents, wanted to actualize her dreams through her child. And since I was the only child, there were not many choices."

Besides, it seemed to meet Iva's requirements for her life's work. "I was an excellent student in everything I did, straight A's," she says. "I could have chosen to do anything I wanted, and my choice was to have a career specifically designed so I could leave where I was and have a profession that would carry me any place in the world."

From that perspective, being a physician seemed to be "a reasonable choice; human bodies are the same wherever you go in the world. If I learn about medicine here, it's the same medicine in the rest of the world. Little did I know how lucky I was that I did not become a doctor, because what I thought was true wasn't. If you wanted to practice medicine in America, anything you learn in any medical school that isn't accredited by the American Medical Association is null and void. You either have to go back to medical school or take very difficult exams that, in my judgment, are designed to let as few doctors into this country as possible to limit competition."

But it wasn't calculations like those that erased her medical aspirations. "When I was a senior in high school, I went to medical school to attend an anatomy session," she recalls. "Friends who were older than me were telling me, 'You better check whether your stomach goes through that easily or not.' Having seen cadavers float down the river, and having felt the war in its ugliness as a child, I guess I was very uncomfortable with dead bodies, but I said I'm going to try. I went in there and tried to be attentive and not smell the formaldehyde and not think about this brown stuff as being a human being. The next thing I knew, someone was putting salt under my nose trying to wake me up. That was the end of medical school. That's how I decided to study engineering.

"When I revealed this to my mother, I thought she was going to die. 'You're going to go to engineering school?' she said. 'There isn't a woman any place who does that.'"

Actually, there were 12 other young women, out of a total of 350 students, in her freshman engineering class at the University of Zagreb. This was partly because young women at that time recognized that getting skills and a vocation were very important in order to have a prosperous life, and partly because the Communist regime strongly supported gender equality.

But there was a more pervasive kind of prejudice—against anyone who was not a member of the Communist party. It cost her a student teaching position that she had earned as recognition for her academic excellence.

"I went to talk to my professor who was my mentor and he said there is nobody who's as good as you, and I choose the best people," Wilson recalls. But when a student with poorer grades and no experience was given her job, the professor, who was a party member, told her, "My allegiance to my party goes beyond any other allegiance, so I had to agree to select the other student."

She worked at a company called Rade Koncar in Zagreb through her last year in college, graduated summa cum laude in electrical engineering, then went to work for the company full-time. "But the idea of trying to get out of there was still strong," she says. "I managed to travel a little bit to the West on company business, and I was making my mark. I was hopeful that I would be able to go back to teaching if I published, which I did, and make a name, which I did."

It seemed to her that the most promising route was to go abroad for graduate study, but this plan introduced her to a whole new world of obstacles. "In order to obtain an American scholarship given by American foundations, such as Fulbright or Ford, I had to apply through a central office in Yugoslavia," she says. The major foundations had an arrangement with the Tito regime under which the government made the initial selection of candidates and the foundations made their final selections from that list.

Fortunately, she learned of a German foundation that operated differently. "I could apply directly to Bonn through the embassy in the United States, because they did not have such an agreement with the Yugoslav government," Wilson says. "They extended scholarships based only on merit." She got one, and was soon on her way to the University of Stuttgart to continue the research in which she had become immersed.

First, however, there were to be more complications. Wilson had two passports: one for business travel, obtained through Rade Konca, and one for personal use. She applied for an exit visa, required of every Yugoslav every time he or she left the country, on the business passport, which would have allowed her to return with her status and seniority intact, and was denied.

"So now I had a choice of getting out—which I could— on my personal passport, but potentially losing everything and maybe not even being able to come home," Wilson says. "My mother was very uneasy about that. Being a lawyer, she was even more attuned to the difficulties I could run into."

She turned to her boss at Rade Konca for help. He said he would see what he could do and, several weeks later, called her into his office and gave her a name, an address, and an appointment. "I have, I think, solved the potential misunderstanding that might have been there," he said, "and he will give you the exit visa."

"So I came home all happy, told my mother about it, and she informed me that the address was that of the UDBA, and that the man I would be meeting with was the head of that organization. I think I had diarrhea for a week before I went there. I was absolutely, terribly frightened. I knew what happened in those places. The doors close behind you and you never come out."

That day, the door closed behind a beautiful, paneled office. The cordial man behind the desk chatted amiably, disarming Wilson somewhat. Then he pulled her passport out of a drawer and said he was ambivalent about giving it to her. Although happy that she would be able to continue her research, he was concerned that, well, she might fall in with the wrong sort in Germany.

"If you meet people, and you should meet people, you should get to know the people in the country you're in," he said, "and if they start talking to you about Yugoslavia and their thoughts about Yugoslavia, then you ought to find out why they're asking that and let us know who those people are so we can help you in dealing with them."

Suddenly, the light dawned. "I still pretended as if I didn't know what he was talking about," she says, "so finally, he said, 'We would like you to help us—to help your country—prevent those elements from doing anything against our country, and be in contact with us while you are abroad. Will you do that?' At that moment, I made the decision to lie. I said, 'Sure, if I ever hear from anybody, I'll let you know.' He gave me the passport. We shook hands. I left."

She told her mother that, of course, she had no intention of aiding the secret police, and how she didn't know what would happen after she crossed into Germany.

"Mother said, 'Don't worry about it, they're not that tough. If you don't have anything to say, they can't force you to say anything,'" Wilson recalls. "She tried to calm me down. And she did. I went to Germany, but I was very uneasy about the whole story."

Three years later, she became the first woman ever to receive a PhD in electrical engineering from the University of Stuttgart.

The situation back home had relaxed. The secret police had left her alone for a while. "But I knew this was not going to work for me," says Wilson. "I also knew that I didn't want to stay in Germany, because Germany was not a place that accepted people with different origins. So I decided to give myself a graduation present. I got a ticket to fly to America, because I had a college friend from Yugoslavia in Chicago who wanted me to come and visit her. She tried to convince me to stay, tried to help me find a position, but I wasn't interested. I had just spent three years in Germany, and I wanted to spend some time at home."

But the two stayed in touch, and one day in 1968 her friend's former boss at Zenith Radio Corporation called Wilson and invited her to Chicago for an interview, which took place during that year's turbulent Democratic National Convention.

"I didn't really know what was going on," she says, "but one day I got a phone call from my mother, who was in a panic because she had seen what was going on in Chicago on television. I said this is not where I am.'"

Zenith offered her a job at their laboratories in Niles, Illinois, as a research engineer. She accepted, then returned home to get the necessary papers and visit with her mother. The two were enjoying breakfast one morning while vacationing at the seaside when they heard a radio report that the Soviets had invaded Czechoslovakia.

"We were very close to the Italian border, maybe an hour's drive or less," Wilson says, "and my mother said to me, 'If things get worse, you hop in a car, go to Italy, and wait there to get your papers. I'm afraid what will happen to you here.' Fortunately, nothing really happened. The Yugoslavs stayed neutral to all this, and the Russians didn't go any further than Prague."

But now her immigration application was delayed by the crisis. "All the open slots were reserved for people from Czechoslovakia who might seek political asylum," says Wilson. "Since the Slavs were grouped together, I realized this was going to be a problem for me."

Luckily, Zenith agreed to sponsor her, which put her to a different category. On November 18, 1968, she sailed from Bremerhaven, Germany, for America "with two big trunks, $500 that I borrowed in a pocket, and that was it."

She landed in New York a week later, the Monday before Thanksgiving. "Sailing into the New York Harbor and seeing the Statue of Liberty, there is nothing like it, nothing like it," she says.

What seemed curious to her, if not downright amazing, was that Zenith "hired me because of my experience in using computers for design. I would have never thought such use of computers would be exotic in America," she says, "but it seemed to be very exotic at Zenith. Computers were used mostly by the financial organization to crunch data, not by the design people. So I came to bring computers into the design of electron devices."

It may sound simple, but it wasn't. After she inherited her predecessor's files, "I wasn't surprised he quit," she says. "This was an impossible job for one person to do. I was to develop a computer program that would make the trajectory calculations for electrons that travel from a cathode to an anode in various electron devices, like vacuum tubes, television tubes. It required a very complex set of differential equations with a lot of non-linearity, and multiple initial conditions. All in all, it didn't seem like this was a job that I could complete on my own."

She found help in the person of a Dr. Hermannsfeld, who headed a group that had created such a program at the Stanford Linear Accelerator Center in Palo Alto, California. "A few weeks later, I was on a plane to California," she says. "Because the program was developed under a NASA contract, it was public property. The only thing I had to do was adapt it for the application I was to use it in, but when all was said and done and I had something we could use for a design, the other engineers at Zenith were not interested in using it. They didn't trust it. They had their methods, and what could this crazy woman from Yugoslavia with a German accent bring that they didn't already know?"

While the program languished, she busied herself with other projects, one of which brought her into contact with another young engineer, Tom Wilson. His reputation was that of a "tough cookie," Iva Wilson says, "but one day, he came to my office and said, 'Look, I have a problem with an experiment I have done, and I can't figure out what it is. Can you and your computer maybe help with that?'

"Several things happened. My computer and I solved the problem. Tom Wilson got the confidence that maybe Iva can do something that will help his work. He told this to others and suddenly I had more customers and I was starting to get a name."

Romance also bloomed. "I suddenly also learned that Tom Wilson is not such a grouch as I thought, and pretty soon I was in love with Tom Wilson, and a little bit later, we were married."

But not before a conversation that was illuminating to her, although not particularly romantic or even pleasant. "During the time that we were dating, I learned from Tom

that he was making about 50 percent more than I was,"
she says, "and I had a PhD, and most of the people who
had PhDs were making more money than he was."

When she asked about this, the personnel director told
her she was the highest paid woman in this laboratory.

"I replied that that would not be a surprise to me,
because I'm the only professional woman in this laboratory," she recalls. "Then he said I was going to get married
eventually and have a husband who makes a lot of money
and you'll make a lot of money together. I said I didn't
think that what I was doing for Zenith was contingent on
my getting married."

But she didn't get the raise until Tom went to see his
own boss, who "stepped up to the plate," says Iva Wilson.
"Now why did his boss do that? It's very simple. There
were a whole bunch of us on a project who were all bach-
elors. No obligations. He was very concerned that any of
us could leave at any time and he didn't want to have
that. Especially, he did not want me to leave."

She was supervising a department by then, starting to
look for other opportunities, and had an offer to teach in
Argentina. "Tom suggested that I make that known," she
says, "and I got a raise."

She also got an unemployed husband. "The day we were
going to get our marriage license in Chicago was the day
that he found out that his entire department was laid off,"
she remembers. "We've always joked how it wasn't just
love, it was also fortuitous for him to get a license to
marry a woman who had a job."

Soon, she was pregnant. "So we had a pregnant wife
who had a job and an unemployed husband," Wilson
laughs. "A great match. He realized that maybe he should
start seriously looking for something else, and he got
rehired into Zenith, into another division, at 75 percent of
his previous salary. Sounds familiar? And so he took the
job. There was at that time no maternity leave, nothing."

She found it wasn't just her fellow engineers who looked
askance at her chosen path. "I will never forget standing
with a glass of champagne with two other women at a New

Year's Day brunch at a neighbor's, and one of them asking me, 'You're working, right?' I said, 'Yes.' 'So what are you planning to do with the child when it's born?' And I had the urge to tell her, 'I'll throw it in a garbage can. Would that make you happy?' I was so offended by that question, as if I were worth less as a mother because I was going to work. Obviously, I didn't make a lot of friends in that neighborhood, but I didn't care to make friends with people who had that kind of view."

When their daughter, Ann, was born, "I started following in the footsteps of my mother, pretty much," says Wilson. "My mother worked, I had a nanny, but my mother gave me, always, her best times. So I looked for the same for my daughter. And that's a whole 'nother story about finding appropriate care that will insure that which I wish my daughter to have. We were fortunate that we were two engineers with sufficient income to afford live-in help, but finding somebody who would be acceptable was very, very frightening to me."

Rightfully so, as it turned out. Several nannies proved unacceptable, but then Chris, "this wonderful young woman from Belize," came into their lives. "She had been a teacher in Belize, was separated from her husband, and came to America to earn a few dollars so she could build a better life for her son, who she had to leave behind. I always say if it weren't for Chris, I would have never become what I am and what I was. She was with us for about seven years, and eventually became a second mother to Ann. She was the woman at home when the mother was the woman in business. I was able to build my career, and be also a responsible and loving mother to my daughter."

By the time Ann was eight years old, it was time for Chris to move on, and Wilson was beginning to feel the same way about her career. "I decided to go to business school," she says. "Most of my training was in technical areas, but I had no training in the business arena, and especially since I grew up under Communism, my understanding of the more important details of the capitalist system as it impacts business decisions was lacking."

Zenith agreed to send her to the executive program at the University of Chicago, where she spent two years as a full-time student, in addition to her full-time-job.

It was perhaps more educational than she or Zenith could have foreseen. "It became obvious to me that the future of Zenith was in great question, and my future at Zenith, therefore, as well," she says. "The president of the division I was in quit and left to go to Philips. We got a new boss, and my chances of moving upward were, in my mind, very remote, since my boss didn't get promoted into the president's job. I did try to see whether there was an opportunity in Zenith for me outside of the picture tube division. I got a lot of answers that weren't answers, and that answered my question very clearly."

At the time, Tom was director of development for a company that had spun off from Zenith. Ironically, it had developed to the point where its founders were no longer able to manage or support its growth. He and Iva decided that whoever got a job first, that's where they would go, and the other spouse would look for work in the same community.

In August 1983, the family was vacationing in Holland, Michigan. "One morning, I was preparing something we would have for dinner on the barbecue, before joining Tom and Ann on the boat, when the phone rang," she recalls.

It was John Torre, her former boss at Zenith who was now president of Philips Display Components. "He made it very quick, very brief," she says. "'My chief engineer just resigned. He's going to RCA. I need a chief engineer. Are you interested?' I stood there with my jaw in my hand. First of all, I realized he did not call my boss, who was the chief engineer; he called me. He made it very clear that he would never consider my boss for the job because he thought always that I was better. Well, this was the beginning of trying to figure out what to do."

For one thing, the job was in Seneca Falls, New York, about halfway between Syracuse and Rochester. When they broached the possibility of moving to Ann, she burst into tears. And Tom thought maybe things were improving at his company; besides, he wasn't sure he wanted to move, either. "It took us about six months to go through the process and decide that I will take the job as vice president of engineering at Philips and he will quit and look for something else in that area," she says.

They also decided that, at first, there would be no nannies. "We decided to live by ourselves, find someone to take care of the house for us, and we would cook and take care of Ann," she says. "This is how Tom became an excellent cook."

And, as it turned out, he became a full-time, live-in parent. Although he explored numerous possibilities, including starting his own business and franchising, he was never employed—with the big exception of parenting—again.

She was excited about going to New York, "the town in which the women's movement at the beginning of the century started," but Seneca Falls was a long way from the Apple, and not just in miles. "This was a very male-dominated, I would say backwards, kind of a company," she says. "They treated women the way people at that time thought women should be treated, like mushrooms: keep them in the dark and feed them horse manure. And there I was, the head of engineering, as a woman."

She was also a woman whose husband, as she says, "was the proverbial spouse who gave up the career for the other spouse, only in this case the spouse was not of the expected gender." This did not sit well in some quarters.

"Women didn't accept me because I was different, and men didn't accept me because they didn't know how to deal with me," Wilson says. "Most men in my generation have had relationships with women only as mothers, because everyone has a mother, and maybe sisters, wives, lovers, mistresses, but not colleagues. And many of the women were jealous because, for them, the only relationship they had had with men was that of being a wife, mistress, sister, not a peer and equal partner in building something together. So they had no other explanation for me being there but that which would fall into their individual experiences in relationships with men."

At least, she would be working with John Torre. "He was my mentor," she says. "He was president of the picture tube division of Zenith, and he was the one who hired me from research into engineering."

While she was in research, she had led the effort to develop a better focused electron beam, resulting in an improvement in the performance of the television picture tube. "When the time came for Zenith to introduce that for production, what happened is what usually happens," she says. "Everyone in the factory thought this was just a pile of b.s....who needs to make these kind of changes... things are running fine—the stories we hear in big corporations all the time. John was very clear on the potential importance of this device, and he decided that he would transfer the project into engineering."

Torre had appointed a project manager and Wilson was his assistant, but six months into the project, when it became clear the task was beyond his capabilities, she succeeded him. "I was asked to take over this project and its implementation in the factory, something I had never done in my life," she says. "I was a researcher. But I learned a lot about what kind of manufacturing issues there could be and how those could be addressed. Fortunately for all of us, it worked. We made it happen."

Unfortunately for Zenith, the device was integrated into a more complex change of the picture tube "that was a bomb that eventually failed," says Wilson, "but our device continued. Even today, it's being produced, with further modifications. The thinking behind the design of this device, the novelties that we brought into it, changed the whole picture tube industry in the world. Every manufacturer started to do similar things, trying to avoid Zenith's patent as best they could, but essentially moving the industry in a different direction."

Her professional goals were also on the move. "I discovered how much I enjoyed implementing my ideas in production, seeing the stuff that I held in my head become real and make a difference. In the process, I also learned how to work with people of diverse backgrounds, friends and foes, and bring together something that we were all proud of. I did not want to go back to research."

Nor did she. Her charge at Philips was to infuse that company's renowned technological prowess into the Sylvania division it had recently acquired from General Telephone. "What Philips wasn't known for was the ability to take its technology to the marketplace so as to capitalize on it," says Wilson. She soon began to understand why.

"One of the main reasons I chose to stay in the electronics industry instead of looking for opportunities elsewhere was because I had a strong conviction that Philips, unlike Zenith and so many other American companies, had the resources necessary to be globally competitive," she says. "Little did I know, at that time, that those in the acquired company who were responsible for developing and using technology in the product we produced, resisted greatly the infiltration of Philips technology. The 'not-invented-here' syndrome was alive and well, like in most other places."

Alas, the mistrust was mutual. "Those that were responsible for technology development on the other side of the pond were not ready and willing to transfer that technology," she says. "Not only were they were not sure as to the competence of the receiving party, but they were also very concerned that the technology would leak to the competition, especially the Japanese, whom they greatly feared. So the dance of the tug-of-war started. Those who were to provide the technology looked for ways of preventing that from happening, while continuously speaking in the tongue of encouragement. Those who were to receive it, indeed, lacked the competence necessary to take what's best and integrate it into what we already had. I felt most of the time as if I were on a teeter-totter."

Even as she restructured her department, the company's financial fortunes sagged, and Torre, her mentor, began to prepare for his retirement. "When John hired me, he made it very clear to me that I would never have a chance to get his job," she says. "Number one, I was too new in the company. Number two, I was a woman."

Initially, this was of no consequence. She was happy with her job and had no desire to change. But as she learned more about Torre's potential successors, "it became clear to me that if any of these individuals became president of the company, I would quite likely sooner or later look for another job. I would probably not be able to respect any of them in the way I respected John."

So she put her name in the hat and, in October 1985, she was informed that she would be taking over the business, effective the following February 1. "Around that time," she says, "I also found out that the managing director of the display components business group in Europe, who I also knew very well, was going to retire and be replaced by Ton Vervoort."

Vervoort was scheduled to begin his new duties a month later. "I knew he was coming," Wilson adds, "but I didn't know how he would be." She soon learned.

Philips Display Components was a division of North American Philips. Although it operated as an independent company, 52 percent of its stock was owned by Royal Dutch Philips. This meant Wilson had bosses in both New York and Europe. The fact that they were also often at loggerheads turned reporting to her superiors into a harrowing and delicate task.

"My profit-and-loss responsibility was to Ton Vervoort," she says, "but my boss in New York was in charge of unions, employment, compensation, those local matters that are different in every country. The judgment of my boss from Europe on these issues would usually carry less weight in the total picture than the judgment of the boss in New York. This exacerbated things because I had to be in a continuous juggling act. My relationship with Ton Vervoort eventually allowed me to perform that in a way that made possible what we created in Ann Arbor."

That relationship, quite simply and refreshingly, was one of trust. "Even today, he's one of my best friends," she

says. "The important point here is that there is no way
you can build a business relationship without having a
relationship of two human beings who understand,
appreciate and respect each other. Everything in business
is relationships; we all know that. The only thing is a lot
of relationships in business are manipulative."

Theirs was not. "That was the basis for the relationship—I was doing exactly what he thought somebody
would do who wants to cooperate," she says, "instead of
having this nagging thought in his mind that I'm trying to
manipulate myself into some position. I had the same feeling about him."

After she got the job, she found her evaluation in the
personnel files she inherited from Torre. "In every
attribute category, I was rated higher than any of the
other candidates," she says, "while in the comment category, it stated 'but she is a woman.'"

It soon became clear to her that she was a woman
whose first budget as president "would not be achievable.
There was nothing I could to prevent the red ink from
flowing."

Her report was not happily received at New York headquarters. "Here I was, the first woman division president
in history, coming to volunteer bad news," she says. "I still
vividly remember that meeting in the board room, with
the executive committee, the CEO, and my boss, and their
amazement when I reported on the status of the company, projected the losses. This was not necessarily considered a heroic step, but a downright unacceptable level of
honesty not previously experienced in that boardroom. It
was much more acceptable to hold on to the old forecast
in the hope that a miracle will happen, until such time
that there was no exit but telling the truth, and then do
everything possible to blame it on somebody else. That's
what respectable executives do every day."

The choice was to radically restructure the business or
close it. Wilson opted for the former course, closing a factory as well as the Seneca Falls headquarters. One of the
largest remaining plants was—and still is—in Ottawa,

Ohio, so she started looking for a Midwest location to consolidate operations.

In the middle of 1988, a year and a half of deliberations and consultations led them to choose Ann Arbor. In the meantime, Royal Dutch Philips had bought up the remaining shares of North American Philips at the end of 1987. Thus, that company ceased to exist as a separate entity, and Vervoort became Wilson's boss.

"At our first meeting after that," she says, "he made it clear to me that the resources would be made available to bring the company up to speed, starting with the move to Ann Arbor. He was instrumental in helping us here in the United States come to a decision that would, in my judgment, benefit the company. After he took over, it seemed like everything changed."

The move and consolidation "meant that there was an opportunity to streamline the technology integration and the business integration into a global entity," Wilson says. "Although everybody spoke about it, the actions taken on both sides of the ocean did not always align with the proclaimed objectives. Fortunately for me, Ton Vervoort was an exceptional individual. He was instrumental in creating the space I needed to do what I was capable of, and providing support for me to accomplish the goals I set for the company."

Now came the hard part: actually doing it. "Moving the company headquarters meant not only moving the equipment and assets we needed to run the company, but also moving 70 families, dislocating them from their origins, plopping them into a new environment, and doing all of this without skipping a beat," says Wilson. "As a matter of fact, the year 1989, in which we accomplished that task, was the first year we made a profit."

Now she wanted to make a new kind of workplace, a dream that had persisted since her first visits to Japan in the early 1970s introduced her to "their capability of integrating processes and equipment into a whole system of manufacturing color picture tubes. I wanted to do the same while I was at Zenith. Unfortunately, Zenith did not have the capital resources for such a vision to ever be actualized. Philips did. And here I was, at the threshold of that vision becoming a reality."

Philips had approved $100 million for a state-of-the-art manufacturing facility in Saline, Michigan, to produce color CRTs for the U.S. market. In addition to top-flight equipment and processes, says Wilson, "The plant would also contain a social/technical environment in which people, processes, and machines would be integrated into a common whole, such that that which requires human skills will attract and nurture a different kind of workplace for those who work there."

She had evolved from the thrill of seeing her ideas for products become reality to the even headier possibility that her ideas about human systems would follow suit.

"It was 1990," she says. "I turned 52 that year and was looking forward to the last phase of my career in taking that vision into reality. But as is often the case, things that we do not anticipate do happen. Philips got into serious financial difficulties and our project got postponed, and, by late 1991, permanently cancelled. A great disappointment. A letdown. In my mind, not a terminal blow, because I never give up."

Soon, though, the temptation must have been as strong as it ever could have been. "Early in 1992, my husband was diagnosed with esophageal cancer, one of the most deadly forms, with only a 20 percent chance of survival," she says. "Only people who have been there know what that is and how it feels for the spouse. There is no sharing that would make it possible for others to understand. Fortunately, he's a cancer survivor for seven years now. That had a major impact on my thinking about life, the world, business, everything."

Another quantum leap was in store for her thinking. She had been intellectually acquainted with Peter Senge; her vice president of manufacturing gave her a copy of his *The Fifth Discipline: the Art and Practice of the Learning Organization* as a Christmas present in 1990 and she had spent most of a so-called golfing vacation the following

summer reading it. Now she was about to become per-
sonally and professionally acquainted with him through
C.K. Prahalad, a renowned professor at the University of
Michigan School of Business Administration.

"This was not an easy task," she says. "Peter happened
to call me the day before Christmas Eve 1991. I was bak-
ing cookies. And after two hours on the phone with him, I
discovered that he and I had very similar professional
backgrounds. He studied systems and I studied systems.
As a matter of fact, this was my professional direction
before I came to the United States, as well as my doctorate. I switched from systems into electronic devices, and
Peter switched from technical systems to business systems and systems in general."

She eventually flew to Cambridge, Massachusetts, to
meet him at the Massachusetts Institute of Technology,
where his Organizational Learning Center was based.
"That connection started another phase in my professional career," she says. "I suddenly realized that there is
another way, a better way, to create a new strategy for
Philips Display Components. We needed to rethink our
entire strategy by building a shared vision with the larger
community of employees, and by developing new tools of
engagement between various departments, parts of the
company, and individuals. Our company became one of
the members of the Organizational Learning Center at
MIT and we started the journey of building a learning
organization.

"I also knew that to build a learning organization, I
would have to be a different kind of leader, who would
enable the building of an environment in which people
would be able to create what they truly desire. We started
slowly making progress."

Too slowly for some. A suddenly soaring demand for
Phillips' products sorely taxed the plant's capacity. "The
only thing we were able to do was to drive our workforce
harder, get them to work more hours, and though they
made more money, the morale and the satisfaction in our
factory were dwindling," says Wilson. "The pressures were

unbelievable, but we had no other choice, or at least we did not know how to look for other choices."

In 1994, the union rejected a negotiated contract by 51 votes out of a thousand, and the plant went on strike. "Another blow for me," she says. "It came like a cold shower."

It was also a test of her commitment to empowering the workforce. "If I would now come down with repercussions and punishments, I will destroy everything I've built so far," she says. "Instead, nobody got fired. We gathered the top 60 people from headquarters and the factory to start strategizing by first understanding why the strike had to happen. The strike lasted only five days. Everything I learned by doing the work with the Organizational Learning Center told me that if I continued using the same tools and methods that I started implementing in the company as part of that journey, then we will find a way out. And sure enough, by spring of 1995, we reopened the contract negotiations which we previously thought would have never happened. But at the same time, I was at the end of my strength."

To make matters worse, Vervoort had been succeeded by a former colleague of Wilson's who was less than enthusiastic about her methods. "The strike did not help that relationship, and that was just the beginning of the end," she says. "Finally, in a pretty heated argument with him, I turned in my badge. The argument was substantive in nature because he wanted me to do something in the United States that I wasn't willing to do. We agreed to disagree, and I resigned."

Her focus now is on disseminating and implementing Senge's ideas far beyond the confines of one company. She led the team that spun off his center from MIT as an independent entity, the Society for Organizational Learning, a not-for-profit membership organization consisting of corporate, research, and consulting members, which she served as its first president until January 1998.

"I decided to stop commuting, traveling, and running around, and focus on what I really want to do when I grow up," she smiles. "I'm either going to coach other leaders to create working environments that are kinder to people, or I'm going to be a leader coach in an organization in which that would be practiced."

Her own family life has been a study in thinking "out of the box," as the new cliché has it. "My husband was a man who left his job for his wife's career, who was a parent at home," she says. "Without him, I would have never built my career. He is as responsible for me becoming the woman that broke the glass ceiling as I was, or as Chris, our nanny, was. They get as much credit as I do. And my daughter, who was raised by a nanny and a father, with a mother who was not always at home, became a wonderful young woman who any parent would be proud of."

Also, according to Wilson, her daughter became her teacher. "We had our differences when she was a teen, which is very normal between mothers and daughters," Wilson says, "but we are today the best of friends, also the best of partners, and she is my teacher, and I am her role model. I am happy to say that I am her role model in a different way than my mother was my role model; I'm the kind of role model that learns from her child. Without my daughter's help in those difficult years of going through my husband's cancer, losing my dream, and eventually having to quit my career and move on at age 57 to start thinking what I'm going to do with the rest of my life, I wouldn't be where I am today. Her maturity, her understanding of the world that I did not have when I was her age, has made her a learning partner for me.

"My message is that we cannot pass judgment about what the family needs to look like and what is better, what is worse, what's traditional and what isn't traditional," she says. "We really have to be open to the opportunities around us to create that which we desire together, in a family, in an institution, in a country, in a world, and that is the reason I have chosen the path I am on right now, to create a better world for our children. It really doesn't matter to me any more whether others approve of me, or like what I do or dislike what I do. It is as important for me to be as to do."

Wherever her interests lead her from here, her espousal of Senge's ideas achieves a pleasing symmetry in her career. "Originally, my doctorate was in control systems, all in technical domains," she says. "I never connected that to human systems until I read Peter's book. What attracted me was the possibility of explaining a lot of things that were going on in a way that would be understandable to both technical and non-technical people. Business organizations are also systems. Unfortunately, we have looked at the world, in the West, very much based on reductionist thinking and scientific method, which are attempts to solve problems by dividing them into smaller parts, looking for solutions in the smaller parts, putting them all together, and hoping this will be the answer."

But, she says, it is not, certainly not in business. "Corporations are organized, governed, and managed based on the philosophy that if you divide an organization into a hierarchical structure and you control the individual elements of the structure and disperse power through the structure, you will achieve optimum results," she says. "Unfortunately, this is not so. Without looking at corporations and institutions as systems and revising that thinking, we run the risk of not achieving that which is possible."

A specific example, she says, is that "in our reductionist way of thinking, we look at, for the most part, only shareholder value, thinking if we satisfy the shareholder, everything else is going to fall into place. And it's not that simple. As long as a corporation is viewed as a mechanical system instead of as a living system, all these things will not change. A much better view is to satisfy human needs, because shareholders are human also, customers are human, suppliers are human, employees are human, and that focus on people is much more conducive to creating more wealth and better economic conditions.

"It's much harder because humans are systems themselves, but it is the right path. If Galileo had believed what the church wanted him to believe, we would still be in the Dark Ages. I'm happy to have finally learned something important from Galileo: without questioning our belief system, there is no hope for new ideas."